JOSIAH
WEDGWOOD

JOSIAH WEDGWOOD

Entrepreneur to the Enlightenment

BRIAN DOLAN

HarperCollins*Publishers*

HarperCollins*Publishers*
77–85 Fulham Palace Road,
Hammersmith, London W6 8JB

www.harpercollins.co.uk

First published by HarperCollins*Publishers* 2004

1 3 5 7 9 8 6 4 2

A catalogue record for this book
is available from the British Library

ISBN 0-00-713901-2

Typeset in PostScript Linotype Adobe Caslon
with Spectrum display by
Rowland Phototypesetting Ltd,
Bury St Edmunds, Suffolk

Printed and bound in Great Britain
by Clays Ltd, St Ives plc

For Professor Robert A. Hatch
and
M. Ismael Boulliau

CONTENTS

ILLUSTRATIONS

All photographs courtesy of the Wedgwood Museum Trust Limited, Barlaston, Staffordshire, England, unless otherwise credited.

Portrait of Josiah Wedgwood approaching his fiftieth birthday by George Stubbs.

Collection of early Staffordshire wares, saltglazed stoneware, typical of production *c.* 1750s.

The Churchyard Works. From a nineteenth-century engraving.

Plan of the town of Burslem, *c.* 1750.

Portrait of Thomas Whieldon.

Cauliflower teapot, *c.* 1763.

A page from Josiah's guarded 'Experiment Book' (begun in 1759).

The Ivy House Works, Josiah's first independent potworks.

Thomas Bentley. Attributed to Joseph Wright.

Joseph Priestley, radical chemist and dissenting philosopher.
   Attributed to Ozias Humphrey (British, 1742–1810), oil on canvas, 30¼" x 35⅛", Chemists Club Collection, Chemical Heritage Foundation, Philadelphia, PA, USA, photo by Will Brown. Courtesy of the Chemical Heritage Foundation Image Archives.

The Brick House Works.

Dr. Erasmus Darwin, great-grandfather of Charles, and close family friend and physician to the Wedgwoods.

Sarah (Sally) Wedgwood, in a portrait by Sir Joshua Reynolds in 1782.

Selection of 'Queen's Ware' – creamware – pieces.

A 'Queen's Ware' teapot manufactured by Josiah *c.* 1770.

A portrait medallion of Josiah's patroness Queen Charlotte.

The *virtuosi* – aficionados of the antique – shopping for ancient vases in Naples, Italy. *Unattributed.*

Lady Jane Cathcart. *Sir Joshua Reynolds © Manchester Art Gallery.*

One of six 'First Day Vases' Josiah threw to mark the official opening of the Etruria Factory, near Burslem in Staffordshire, on 13 June 1769.

Etching of Etruria Factory.

Etching of a throwing room in Etruria.

Matthew Boulton, the Birmingham 'buckle maker'. *By Lemuel Francis Abbott, Birmingham Museums & Art Gallery.*

The Portland Vase.

A wood engraving depicting a one-legged Josiah as conceived by a Japanese artist, *c.* 1880.

Portrait of the Wedgwood Family on the grounds of Etruria Hall by George Stubbs, 1780.

Josiah's final words in one of over a thousand letters to Bentley.

ACKNOWLEDGEMENTS

While researching this book I have amassed a debt of gratitude to many friends and archivists, librarians, and museum curators who helped me along the way. Helen Burton at the Keele University Special Collections was tireless in her assistance and skilful in helping me navigate my way through the Wedgwood archive; I am grateful to the Trustees of the Wedgwood Museum Trust, Barlaston, for permission to consult and quote from the Wedgwood Archival Collection, and to Gaye Blake Roberts and Lynn Miller for their kind assistance during my research at the Wedgwood Museum in Barlaston. I offer a special thank you to Lynn Miller for taking the time to read the manuscript and for offering excellent suggestions both on the text and on illustrations, most of which the Wedgwood Museum has also kindly provided. Hilary Young at the Victoria & Albert Museum; Hugh Torrens at Keele University; Michael Greenslade at the William Salt Library in Stafford; the staffs at the Staffordshire Record Office, the Stoke-on-Trent City Archives at Hanley Library, Cambridge University Library, the British Library, the John Rylands Library in Manchester, and the London Library all deserve special thanks for their repeated help during my visits.

For providing manuscript material from which, in instances, I have and was permitted to quote from, I wish to thank R. J. Chamberlaine-Brothers at Warwickshire County Council Record Office; Rachel Watson at Northamptonshire County Council Record Office; S. Williams at Hertfordshire County Council Archives; Wiltshire County Council Record Office; Claire Sawyer at Bedfordshire County Council Record Office; Christopher Whittick at East Sussex Record Office; David Reeve at Dorset County Council archives; Dr Mike Rogers of Lincolnshire County Council archives; and Richard Childs at West Sussex Record Office.

Friends and colleagues have provided invaluable input: at the Department of History and Philosophy of Science at Cambridge University I would like to thank Jim Secord and Simon Schaffer, for their dedication to and passion for exploring the history of Enlightenment science and society, Henry Atmore (whose own interest in Etruria catapulted me into the project with stimulating discussions at the start), Dave Abramson, Shelley Adler, Will Ashworth, Paul Blanc (with special thanks for access to his rare books on the history of occupational health), Robin Boast, Jeff Brautigam, Mike Bravo, John Brewer, Roger Cooter, Janet Dolan, Nancy Ernst, Sandra Evans, Bob Hatch, Dan Hayes, Gale Hennelly, Stephen Jacyna, Kathy Keenan, Nick King, Nat Marshall, Jim Moore, Iwan Morus, Carole Paul, Joad Raymond, Janet Todd, Sue Woolsey, and those who I am no doubt forgetting have all helped me along one way or another, especially by reading drafts and talking biography. Additionally, the scholarship of certain individuals deserves special recognition. Dr Neil McKendrick's pioneering articles from the 1960s onwards and Robin Reilly's magnum opus, the two-volume collector's edition of *Wedgwood*, a history that covers the period up to 1986 and which has an incredible wealth of illustrations, are both invaluable sources for anyone researching the history of the Wedgwood business. More recently Gaye Blake Roberts of the Wedgwood Museum has uncovered various hidden nuggets of Wedgwood history, and her articles on these can be found in *Etruria*, the magazine of the Wedgwood International Society and *Ars Ceramica*, published by the Wedgwood Society of New York.

I would also like to thank my new colleagues at the University of California, San Francisco for being so welcoming and for helping my wife and me settle in so comfortably.

I am grateful to Peter Robinson and Kathy Anderson for their continued encouragement, and to Michael Fishwick and Kate Johnson at HarperCollins for their interest and expertise.

Finally, two special acknowledgements. First, to my mother, Janet, who provided invaluable assistance in organising materials, proofreading during the last few months of writing and, not least, in braving January winds to revisit many of the original sites in Staffordshire. Second, to Dorothy Porter, for her unfailing support and desire to understand and cheer the efforts of the youngest member of a large family.

ONE

A Place for Thomas

A MONTH BEFORE his ninth birthday, Josiah Wedgwood stood against brisk winds in the graveyard of Burslem church at his father's funeral. It had become a familiar ritual to the Wedgwood family: Josiah's mother had already lost two young daughters and two sons. Now Mary and her eight children, the youngest being Josiah – or plain 'Jos' as he preferred – were forced once again to mouth sombre hymns and thank the preacher for his avuncular comforts. Thomas had been fifty-two when he died, an average lifespan in 1739 for those fortunate enough to outlive adolescence. But Thomas Wedgwood would have considered himself to have been above average in many other respects. After all he came from a family that owned much of the land in the area of Burslem, where generations of Wedgwoods, some more privileged than others, had been born and laid to rest.

The 1730s had begun in peace and promise. Benjamin Franklin wrote the first of his guides, *Poor Richard's Almanack*, in Philadelphia in 1732; John Kay patented his 'flying shuttle', a landmark in textile mass-production, leading some to dream of building large mills; Voltaire wrote *Lettres sur les Anglais*, championing democratic government, and David Hume developed his empiricist philosophy in his *Treatise on Human Nature*. But the end of the decade brought turbulence as England declared war on Spain, one of many wars that would haunt the rest of the century.

Events such as these would have seemed far removed to the

inhabitants of Burslem, though future developments would show this belief to be misplaced. The village was tucked away off a well-worn road that cut through the West Midlands carrying travellers from the capital to the bustling Liverpool port and mercantile centre of Manchester. The countryside here, in the north part of Staffordshire, ripples with hills and valleys, often windswept and scraped by heavy, steely clouds.

This is where a group of medieval Benedictine monks once began taming the uncultivated meadowland, building an isolated monastery and clearing modest stretches of granges and crofts to cultivate wheat. The place name 'Burslem' was ancient, derived from 'Barcardeslim' as recorded in the Domesday Book. By the sixteenth century Burslem had become a parish, implying a certain level of administrative importance and autonomy.

In the hundred year period spanning the 1400s and 1500s, one man acquired much of the sloping ground of Burslem, and to declare his presence he adopted the place name, calling himself Thomas of Burslem.[1] Thomas Burslem had enough wealth, esteem, and land to guarantee that future sons would possess the honourable status of 'gentleman' and 'esquire'. Eventually this privilege, benefiting directly from the expansive Burslem family properties, would be possessed by Josiah Wedgwood's own family. This was due in part to the luck and shrewdness of Josiah Wedgwood's great-great-grand-father, Gilbert.

All Josiah's family knew how much Gilbert's life had changed their fortunes. Some listened to the stories of his endeavours appreciatively, while others quietly harboured feelings of envy and resentment. Gilbert had been born in 1588, the youngest son of six, just a few miles north of Burslem.[2] His father was a church administrator; his brothers were local husbandmen, and they lived in a single, small farmhouse. But Gilbert had ambition, energy, talent and charm, and the self-confidence to make the most of the kind of life he was given, and that life revolved around pottery.

Gilbert knew, from long walks through the undulating countryside, or around the lanes of Burslem, that most work in the area was agrarian – rearing and shearing sheep, cultivating wheat, cattle-keeping and tanning. But a few locals had begun working with clay, which they dug and, when the sun was out, they dried in 'sun pans'; this they would then form, with their hands, into coarse vessels for butter and beer – useful things for the farmers – and finish in a round, blackened oven, about as tall as a man, made of earth clod and fuelled by coal dug from local pits.[3] Gilbert learnt from these workers that the process involved exploring dense woods and rocky ridges to seek out the clay, prodding the 'gouty, moorish, peaty black land'. It also required imagination to see and feel finished forms emerge from clumps of cold, wet earth, and strength of both head and hand. Gilbert watched closely and repeated the practice. He was diligent and learned quickly. In the early 1600s you could walk for a day in any direction and only meet a handful of potters – no more than about a hundred were working up and down the slopes of the region. In time Gilbert became one of the best – he was the first Wedgwood to be called a 'Master Potter', though there were never any guilds to enforce the status, the term simply meaning that he had learned all aspects of the craft, from collecting clay to firing it. Gilbert's descendants would marvel at the crudeness of pottery and the fact that all it took back in his days was a shovel to dig the clay, coal and a simple oven. Yet there was also something romantic in the image of creating something from nothing, a way of life that had already been lost by the eighteenth century.

One event which perhaps chimed louder than anything else in the stories Josiah and his siblings heard about their great-great-grandfather was his marriage. This had been to Margaret Burslem, the daughter of the wealthy Thomas Burslem, a descendant of the first Thomas of Burslem, and the new principal landowner in the area, owning two large manor houses and hundreds of acres of meadowland, woods and fields, with an income from farmer tenants and the family's new interests in coal mining.[4] Margaret and Gilbert's first child, a son, was named Burslem Wedgwood. In time, the couple would inherit Overhouse estate, and over a hundred acres of land at the heart of Burslem would pass into Wedgwood hands.[5]

In a world that had barely moved beyond feudalism, and where an extreme minority owned the majority of the land, the right of primogeniture was often ruthless in its execution, but occasionally the weight of tradition shifted good fortune onto the shoulders of the unsuspecting. Burslem Wedgwood died young, and his inheritance passed to his younger brother, Thomas, Josiah's great-grandfather. Suddenly, at fifty-two years of age, Thomas became the largest landowner in Burslem. A gentleman by title, he moved into Overhouse, the prestigious manor house on the north hill overlooking Burslem and the vales of north Staffordshire.[6] Apart from the roomy timber-framed house, the estate comprised 'barns, stables, outhouses, cowhouses, yards, folds, orchards, and gardens', and even a 'fish-pond and fish' out front.[7]

With the eldest son enjoying sole inheritance, tradition necessitated that the second son would be trained up in the family craft and prepared to make a living for himself. The other children, parents hoped, would either be married off, or at least would find labouring jobs to keep them. Before his unexpected inheritance, Thomas's place had therefore been in his father's business, his damp and dusty 'pot-works'. Gilbert trained Thomas to work the clay as he had taught himself – to feel it, to form it and fire it. In time, Thomas, as dedicated and conscientious as his father, went on to become a Master Potter, taking on apprentices and journeymen, and improving his craft. Gilbert also taught his son the need to expand a business – to always look to acquire another acre, or an additional plot on which to build another workman's shed. The more ground one had the more opportunity was at one's feet, and the greater the scope for future development.[8] Thomas followed his father's instructions and by his fortieth birthday had become, by the standards of seventeenth-century Burslem, reasonably successful. He owned two small potteries, one formerly belonging to his father, each with one mud-clod hovel and one grey stone 'pot-oven'. He added a third pottery later.[9]

Before moving into Overhouse estate, Thomas had lived with his wife and father-in-law in Churchyard House, a thatched cottage at the bottom of a field on the south side of Burslem, a stone's throw between St John's church toward the village and the Crown and Mitre alehouse further down the hill.[10] This was the oldest part of Burslem, the spot where monks had settled long ago, and where Thomas bought some uncultivated land adjacent to his house on which to build himself some new 'workhouses and pot ovens' with a 'horse mill with the buildings thereto'.[11] This would always be Thomas's main place of work as a Master Potter. Following tradition, Overhouse estate would go to his eldest son, John, and the new pottery prepared as the inheritance for his second son who would be trained here in the craft as another Master Potter.

Therefore, when Thomas died, in 1717, Churchyard House and its pot-works were left to the eldest son, another Thomas – Josiah Wedgwood's father. The detached pot-work in the southern fields of Burslem had become, over sixty years and two generations, a busy pot-works comprising mud and stone sheds with thatched roofs. It was now known as the Churchyard Works.

The potters worked here in dark clammy hovels, old barns built alongside Church Lane, the winding dirt trail used by packing horses heading out from the village centre and cows changing pastures. The grey walls of the 'workhouses' constantly dripped with pungent condensation. Here mounds of unctuous rust-coloured local clay, dug from a coal pit by a hired-hand, were dumped into large square 'slip-kilns', tin trays about ten inches deep, which were then gently heated to steam off any water soaked within to give the clay the right feel before it was 'beaten' and 'turned'. The other sheds Josiah's father called 'shops' and these were lined with 'plank boards & shelves . . . & all other implements at the said workhouse, belonging to the art or trade of pottery'. Thomas spent most of his waking hours here, stocking wooden planks and shelves with simple pots.

The pieces were crooked and crude, child-like to a later perspective. Although Thomas was a fourth-generation Master Potter he was not thought to be a particularly gifted one.

Indeed later in life Josiah criticised his father's and his grand-father's output. Both men showed a profound lack of financial acuity, Josiah thought, and wasted too much of their menial profits on unnecessarily high weekly expenses. They were uninspired and artis-tically lethargic. His father was satisfied with producing common black and mottled ware – simple in substance (the clay was not specially prepared) and design: baking dishes, jugs, porringers, and the like. The pieces were cheap and cheerful: 'he was apparently content to carry on the old-fashioned peasant pottery', in the judg-ment of a later Wedgwood.[12]

In the few years that Josiah's father and grandfather's trade over-lapped – in the 1710s, before grandfather Thomas's death in 1717 – each mustered an annual trade worth a mere £36, from which every-day living expenses needed to be drawn. Looking back over the Churchyard Works' accounts, Josiah did some calculations of his own, casting a critical eye on those early days. He headed a piece of paper: 'Men necessary to make an Oven of Black and Motled, per week, and other expenses.' He added up what they paid for the clay, coals, couriers, packing straw, and labour. It totalled £4 5s per oven load. The problem was that a crate of final goods was some-times only worth £4, and often they could not get much more than one crate's worth into their one oven. Josiah calculated that the best any pot-work in Burslem could do was to turn a profit of a mere 16 shillings per week, and Josiah's father made even less.[13] Regardless of the organisation of the pot-work and the lack of innovation at the time, Josiah still thought that a few minor adjustments by his father or grandfather could have yielded a little more profit, maybe even another 5 or 6 shillings a week – enough for one man's weekly wages. 'The Wear and Tear,' for instance, 'and some other things, are rated too high', Josiah wrote. The expenses could have been tightened up, '4*l* per Oven-full is thought to be sufficient, or more than sufficient, for the Black and Motled works of the largest kind'.[14] This was, in Josiah's eyes, hardly the model of a successful business, or the figures that would allow one to be thought of as a gentleman. His father's income approximated to the annual interest accrued from a landed gentleman's average annual income of £2,000 (the equivalent of £140,000 today), and even fell short of a country squire's salary of around £300 (£21,000) a year.[15]

But day after day Josiah's father returned to his workshops, where Josiah's brothers and sisters also spent long, laborious hours. The boys pulled leather straps to turn lathes for forming the contours of the clay and the girls dipped the pieces in glaze and fitted handles onto mugs.[16] The centrepieces to one shed were Thomas's throwing wheel and the rough, water-stained oak modelling tables, coated with a fine film of dark dried clay, like blood stains, as were the handles of the carving tools used to put the finishing decorations on wares.

The work that required the most muscle was performed just outside the sheds, across the mud yard, by horses turning a wooden 'pug mill'. Every other day, Josiah's brothers were required to carry loads of clay from the slip-kiln in the workshop to the mouth of the pug, an insatiable maw that swallowed up each shovel-full, while fierce metal blades attached to a revolving shaft turned by the horses gnawed away at the clay, removing any air bubbles, and forcing it through a tube where the clay emerged as a condensed log, ready to be taken to the thrower's wheel.[17] In the other corner of the yard, adjacent to the buildings and the coal fold, largely blocking any southern view of neighbouring pastures, were the large, brick ovens, the icons of the cottage industry whose output kept Josiah's family fed and clothed.

From these sheds a path wound through a wooden gate embedded in the furze hedges on the north side of Churchyard Works and led on to Burslem church. Here, in the shadow of the church's Elizabethan stone tower, were the graves of grandfather Thomas and great-grandfather Thomas Wedgwood, Master Potters who had spent their lives at the pot-works next door. And by the stormy June of 1739 Josiah and his brothers and sisters were standing over the freshly dug grave of their father Thomas.

Josiah was too young to have started work in the Churchyard Works – now the largest pottery in Burslem. But none of its buildings was ever bound to be his, for this was now a place for his eldest brother, Thomas.[18]

TWO

A Will and a Prayer

T HE WINTER that drifted into Burslem in 1739 was fierce; nobody had ever seen anything like it. According to the weather logs the freezing temperatures across England plummeted to depths never previously reached (–24°c in some parts by January 1740), setting a record that would not be surpassed for another two hundred years.[1] As R. D. Blackmore wrote of that winter in *Lorna Doone*, 'it was impossible to milk a cow for icicles, or for a man to shave some of his beard . . . without blunting his razor on hard gray ice. No man could "keep yatt" even though he abandoned his work altogether, and thumped himself, all on the chest and the front, till his frozen hands would have been bleeding except for the cold that kept still all his veins.' Across the Continent thousands suffered in a European-wide famine triggered by the exceptional and protracted winter.

The livelihoods of Burslem craftsmen and merchants would be threatened in other ways too. A couple of months earlier in the New World, a war of commercial rivalry had been declared by England on Spain after accusations that the English were smuggling goods and slaves, violating a twenty-year-old trade agreement, and posing threats to trade routes – one of many wars to impact on Burslem's potters.[2]

Josiah and his family were forced to sit out the winter beneath the frosty thatched roof of Churchyard House, the Wedgwood family home since great-grandfather Thomas received it, along with fifty acres of meadow and pasture deemed to be 'of great yearly value', as part of his wife's dowry in 1653.[3] The timber-and-mortar framed house was simple, unassuming, and 'convenient'. 'Comfortable' was not a word that ever applied to common country cottages like this.[4]

Since the days soon after great-grandfather Thomas moved in with his wife and father-in-law, Churchyard House had thronged with children. Josiah's older brothers and sisters were born here while their aunts and uncles – their father's youngest siblings – were still living at the house. When Josiah was born here in 1730, six, if not all seven, of his three sisters and four brothers were still living together. When their father died nine years later, Mary and six of her children were still living in the house, including Thomas, Josiah's eldest brother, who was twenty-three.[5]

At night, Mary and her daughters would slide bed warmers under the blankets of the featherbeds in both bedchambers – one for themselves, the other for the four boys. Still, the family woke stiff and wheezing from the 'intolerable smoke and stink' that lingered in the rooms when the night candles snuffed themselves out.[6]

Downstairs, the largest room in the house was the kitchen.[7] Here six wooden chairs circled a large oak table, a walnut chest of drawers sat against the wall; cleavers and hammers hung on hooks, and 'china'[8] cups, saucers, and ale glasses were stacked on open shelves. The kitchen was where sitting, talking, and eating took place. All cooking was done in the 'backhouse', a small earth shed housing 'iron boylers' beyond the back door.[9]

For many evenings after their father's death, Josiah's brother Thomas would sit in the leather armchair in the kitchen in silence, contemplating the weight of his new responsibilities as head of the household and owner of the pot-work, while Josiah and his fourteen-year-old brother Richard traipsed back and forth between coal fold and kitchen, making twice as many trips as usual to feed the fire. The crunch of each shovel must have rung like coins in young Thomas's ears. Each delivery of coal cost about 10 shillings. Normally this would be split between the workhouses and the home hearth, but not at the moment: working life had numbed to a halt in Burslem and all the family could do was sit in the deep inglenook that dominated one wall of the kitchen, and wait for the thaw.

Thomas would not have been a man to curse the frozen ground, not when it yielded the raw materials for his family's own survival, but with the turn of season and circumstances it would have been remarkable if he had not questioned God's benevolence. Since the time when Gilbert first started the family on its endeavours as potters, Staffordshire had become a county as notable for its unique geology as for the common earthenware that it increasingly produced. Beneath Burslem lay 'the vein of that clay for which this country is so famous', remarked a visitor in 1750. Famous may have been an exaggeration, but it was true that bricks, tiles, teapots, snuff-boxes and butter cups were made in Burslem and delivered all around the country. 'They bake 'em in kilns built in the shape of a cone which makes a very pretty appearance, there being a great number of them' in the area, the visitor thought.[10] What the old miners called 'coal measure', which formed a subterranean seam contiguous to the clay, fuelled the kilns and ovens. Both these natural resources were essential to the potter's craft.

But coal was expensive, almost twice the price of clay. Each pannier cost about threepence on delivery (£2 today), and that would be used just for cooking the day's meals. Heating the house for any length of time and providing the fuel for one burning of a kiln could cost up to £1 (£70), more than the families of the men who dug the coal and clay from the ground had to live on a week.

But the earth was frozen solid and it was impossible to shift the clay and the well next to the churchyard along with the natural spring that supplied it would not flow again for months.[11] Thomas pored over the family account books and pieced together a history of evaporating finances.[12] The death of his father and the abominable weather weighed on his mind, but more worrying for the long term was the realisation that the pot-works had yielded poor returns while under his father's management.

Burslem was not a crowded place in the early eighteenth century, just a few hundred people living in cottages clustered along the lanes surrounding the maypole which rose from the centre of the village. About forty babies a year were baptised here, although many would not survive infancy. The stream of people coming from the fields looking for work would, however, help the village grow into what would be considered a town before too long.[13] There were four smithies, two butcher's shops, a joiner's, a cobbler's, a barber's and a 'bakehouse'.[14] Most conspicuous was the smoke billowing from the twenty-three family pot-works scattered about the main hill and the mammoth 'shord piles' where broken pieces of imperfect pottery were dumped.

In the village centre, about a mile up Church Lane, the only signs of life emanating during the winter of 1739/40 came from the alehouses. Burslem had nineteen public houses, some just one or two rooms in someone's home, often packed to the gills with itinerant labourers – men who had migrated from agricultural work to assist in the potteries or squatters in search of butts of arable land who would scrape together a living by digging for supplies of clay and working nearby mines.

When conditions were so not impossibly arctic men could often be seen digging holes all around Burslem. Sometimes they went to the meadows or wasteland, but more often they found it easier to edge away at a lane, since the ground was already worn and broken (hence the origin of the term 'pot-hole'). People were liberally granted a right to do this, on very easy terms – a small rent charge or 'fine' – which invited them to dig for clay, coal, and ironstone in such a manner.[15] It created a curious sight, but some travellers who cursed the treacherous paths could also see the benefits that could be derived from this practice. Robert Plot, naturalist and keeper of Oxford's Ashmolean museum, visited the area while researching his book, *The Natural History of Staffordshire*, in the 1680s, and observed: 'the greatest pottery they have in this county is carried on in Burslem, where for making their several sorts of pots they have as many different sorts of clay which they dig round about the town all within half a mile's distance'.[16]

Digging was a menial job requiring little skill, just a shovel and a pannier for carrying the clay to the potter who would pay 3–4 shillings per load. The diggers who dug and hauled the clay were the poorest paid in the hierarchy of pottery workers. Hired hands who worked within the pottery could command a better wage since they required a degree of training. Labour costs were the Master Potter's biggest expense. For about 7 shillings a week peasants would grind flint, stock the kilns and shovel coal.[17] Artisans performed more skilled aspects of the craft, monitoring kiln temperatures, mixing chemicals in the clay, and operating lathes; the throwers who worked the wheel earned up to 12 shillings a week, as did the modellers, mould makers, and other apprenticed positions.[18] 'Packers' – often the potter's wife or daughter – loaded the goods into oak boxes which were then passed to a constant queue of men for delivery. To Plot's amazement, he learned that these 'poor *Cratemen*' would then strap on a pair of loaded pistols and carry the boxes 'on their *backs* all over the *Countrey*, to whome they reckon them by the piece', earning perhaps 5 or 6 shillings each week of their absence.

Josiah would later muse on the days when his father was in his prime, raising the family and running his pot-work. He tried to imagine the primitive conditions in which the workers toiled. He talked to older potters to create a vivid picture of the pottery industry's earliest days, jotting down notes as they spoke. There was 'only one horse and one mule kept' in the village, he discovered. 'No Carts scarcely in the Country', although the roads would have been too rough, pitted and mired for them to be able to be of use anyway. 'Coals carried upon Men's Backs,' he continued. It was the only way then.[19] Josiah would have agreed with the observation of one local historian who later concluded that the conditions in which the labourers worked were 'mean and poor'.[20]

By the time of his father's death there were more beasts of burden around, Josiah found, more labourers camped in lumpy tenements, and more hollows scored into the earth. When dusk crept into the valley telling everyone it was time to leave work, tired workers piled into one of Burslem's pubs, the Jolly Potters, the Turk's Head or the Red Lyon – where, a thirsty Robert Plot noted, 'they make an excellent quick sort of drink', discouragingly named 'Dredge Malt' – a brew of oats and barley.[21] 'Meety noice and verry strung' was the drink, written the way the Burslem accent was spoken ('mighty nice and very strong'). Towards the end of the evening, as pennies dwindled, songs, usually ending with the slurred cheer 'Up the Potter!', would get louder, and drunken brawls would break out.[22] John Ward, the historian who characterised the labourers' living conditions as 'mean and poor', thought no more highly of their behaviour, declaring that 'the manners of the inhabitants were not superior to their habitations; and their pleasures and amusements at their wakes and holidays were gross and brutal'.[23] During the rowdy seasonal festivals, the Burslem wakes, Ward noted that the workers were entertained by mountebanks, and 'bull and bear-baiting, as well as cock-throwing, were in high favour'.[24]

John Tellwright and Ralphy Leigh were two local potters who grew up with Josiah. Much later in life the two met up at the Turk's Head with a historian who asked them to reminisce about their youth. They downed a few jars of gin 'whoile we tawken oud matters o'er', said John, in his strong Burslem accent. 'Coom, sup it Rafy. Ere's to thee'. The account of their conversation is worth quoting at length:

> 'If you remember Ralph, those old potters couldn't find two ha'pennies to rub together to make a start in their trades', said Tellwright.
>
> 'Yes, that's very true', remembered Ralph. 'Although they

pretended they were the best and could make the best, the result was that in the end they achieved nothing. And even before they could begin they were beaten by their bad habits.'

'The old master potter was a companionable man,' Tellwright added. 'Very much one of the boys and part of the crew – men who liked a good time.'

'They were that, Mr Tellwright. Just as soon as they had placed the ware in the ovens, off they'd go and make straight for ye alehouse on Swan Bank. And there they'd drink n' drink 'til the ware would be ready to be taken out, or so they thought, relying on guesswork and the state of intoxication they found themselves in. The master potters always took their labourers with them to the alehouse, and when they were all half drunk, many a row and fight would break out, each man taking his turn in the arena, arguing over whose turn it was to pay. And when they eventually returned to their oven with sore heads, all their pots would be spoiled.'[25]

Although Josiah's father was not terribly adept at managing his small family business, he would never have tolerated a full kiln's yield being wasted due to drunken irresponsibility. He believed in strict codes of conduct and the prominent puritanical values that he was raised on, which he and Mary in turn passed on to their children. Josiah too found the stench of ale reeking from steamy pubs, the gambling scrums and the idleness of workers infuriating. For many difficult years when Josiah was trying to enter the trade he would hang his head and lament of how he was 'teazed of my life with dilatory, drunken, Idle, worthless workmen'.[26]

It was acknowledged that there was a difference between respectable craftsmen and unprincipled hired hands. Skilled craftsmen – those who created the wares rather than merely dug for the raw material – were taught to take pride in their responsibilities. Boys hoping to enter the trade would sign an elaborate and formidably formal parchment agreement that laid down the rules of their apprenticeship, spelling out that they were committed to 'behave and demean himself toward his said master' and that 'at Cards, Dice, or any other unlawfull Games he shall not Play; Taverns or Ale Houses he shall not haunt or frequent; Fornication he shall not Commit, Matrimony he shall not Contract . . .'.[27]

Josiah's father was especially concerned that his children grew up to have an air of respectability and to know and have the manners of the gentrified classes. He, of course, was no gentleman, nor was Josiah's brother – the material wealth having passed over them – but Josiah's grandfather *had* been a gentleman, as well as churchwarden, responsible for supplying bread and wine for midsummer parties, for buying new Bibles and for the general upkeep of the pulpit.[28] This mattered to Josiah's father. It affected the way he saw himself in Burslem; he did not wish to be seen as a struggling Master Potter. The Wedgwoods at the top of the hill in Overhouse estate were distinguished by wealth from the Wedgwoods at the bottom of the hill. He even devised his own display of *noblesse oblige*, laying out an extraordinary £7 to purchase a seat in the front pew of the parish church so that his neighbours and kinsmen sitting behind him would consider him 'one of the gentry of the village'.[29]

Besides being imbued with puritan probity, Josiah also saw for himself that the people he passed every day in the streets inhabited a very different world from his own and from his relatives up the hill on the opposite side of town in Overhouse estate. Indeed criticism from above on the condition and behaviour of Burslem's poor was louder and more acute than had ever been heard before. And it was not just businessmen, concerned for falling profits and the impact of a slothful workforce, who were complaining about the deleterious habits of the 'lads' in the alehouses. After the winter and shortages of 1739/40 the town as a whole began to feel vulnerable to being crippled by the burden. Throughout January and February 1740 no one had been able to move in or out of Burslem – the roads had been impassable – and no one worked.[30] It did not take long before all the 'dilatory, drunken' men ran out of money and fell weak and emaciated. The village had in the past relieved its poor through its own parish vestry, distributing up to 1 shilling a week per pauper for food from a fund raised by charitable donations and levies on land.[31] About one or two dozen people had been registered to receive help in this way at any given time over the last few decades, but when Burslem thawed out in April the destitute that survived emerged in unprecedented numbers – more than could be looked after with traditional poor relief. As trade began to creep forward again, the churchwarden and overseers devised a new system that would at once deter people from descending into bad habits and introduce discipline to that element of the community. That year they built their first parish 'poorhouse' for paupers, and it opened a year later.[32] This 'foul ward' for the haggard and indifferent proved a grim addition to a hill already crammed full of weary and distressed pot-works.

The poor harvests of 1740 kept the potters of the parish praying for divine intervention, and kept Josiah's brother Thomas at the empty kitchen table pondering the accounts. The fifty acres of land said to be 'of great yearly value' that came with the Churchyard House and Works were not yielding the amount needed for the family's survival. That plot of land, 'a croft or two of hay, one or more of oats and barley, and a cow, or a few sheep, grazing on the adjacent waste', usually offered a few extra bushels of food they could sell, along with a bit of beef and some moorland mutton for a few extra shillings. But in the tough seasons of 1739 and 1740 they were able to get very little for their produce: a bushel of wheat was going for 4 shillings, a calf for about 8 shillings, and a pound of beef for a mere twopence.[33] Even though their small-scale farming was supplemented by a minor income from renting an adjacent field and a tenement – something a few other Master Potters managed to do as well, which was another mark of difference between the growing 'employing class' and the hired hands – it did not add up to much.[34]

Worst yet, the debt father Thomas left behind was growing and young Thomas was struggling to think of ways to improve business and pay it off. Securing a reliable cash flow was hard. In 1740 the arrangement between a potter and the crateman who carried the wares to the customer meant that the cratemen took no invoice of goods with them, and upon returning 'they rendered no account of sales effected, or of the expenses of their journeys, but merely emptied their pockets of what money was left'.[35] 'Money' was often in the form of trade tokens representing the value of halfpennies and farthings – small change was scarce – but more often exchanges were made on trust, the potter paying the courier their wages of 5 or 6 shillings a week after their journey and reported sales, and this would be collected once the account was large enough.[36] Josiah realised that this was a poor way to conduct business and he could see the implications of such practices on his brother's trade.

However, what was clear to Thomas was that pieces of pottery were not enough to pay off his father's debt and provide for his family's future in the manner that would meet his father's wishes. His father's last will and testament stated that the property he inherited was to be used:

> in the bringing up of my younger children, and in raising the sum of £120, which I hereby charge my Real Estate with. And my will is that the said sum be equally divided amongst my six younger children, viz., Margaret, John, Aaron, Richard, Katherine, and Josiah; and that in paying the said sums, the elder shall still be preferred to the younger.[37]

For Josiah and his brothers and sisters, £20 would have been ideal. The problem was that Thomas was unable to raise the money to pay the legacies. He did not even know how he was going to afford to 'bring up the younger children' without laying aside their inheritance. His father had already bound himself for the sum of £50 to his aunt Margaret in order to raise money to pay off previous debts in 1727, and the interest on that was still being collected. The will said that the executors had the power to mortgage the estate to raise money, but it was already mortgaged to the hilt.[38] Ten-year-old Josiah would have known times were tough, but he could not have known the extent of it.

THREE

'Creators of Fortune and Fame'

BOTH JOSIAH'S great-grandfather and great-grandmother, formerly of Overhouse estate, had tried their best to enrich the lives of the next generation by setting aside legacies earning 'interest therein determined and my said children educated'. This firm and explicit provision for the education of the children in the family distinguished their wills from any other in Burslem at that time.[1] It was also a clear expression of the Protestant sentiments of duty, discipline, and determined improvement that would be passed down to Josiah's day, even though the financial legacies would grow too thin to support the weight of such pledges.

Indeed, Josiah's parents had tried hard, through bonds and mortgages, to provide for their children's education. Mary, the daughter of a Unitarian minister from Newcastle, knew it would be hard for Josiah to establish himself in a world where everyone was 'preferred to the younger', and she helped him learn to read and write, as she had done with her other children, looking over his shoulder while he diligently practised his script, repeating his signature to perfection. Josiah learned well, and at seven he followed in the footsteps of his elder siblings and one or two cousins and attended lessons at the school in Newcastle-under-Lyme, a three-and-a-half-mile walk along the treacherous towpath along Fowlea Brook and through the meadows of Wolstanton.[2] (Burslem would not have its own 'English Charity Schoole' until 1749, and even then 'two parts of the children out of three are put to work without any learning'.[3])

According to his teacher, Thomas Blunt, Josiah proved to be 'a fair arithmetician & master of Capital hand'.[4] But however committed either young Josiah or his widowed mother were to his education, it was not long before he was abruptly moved from the classroom to the workshop, for his brother Thomas needed his labour.

Josiah's muscles were now forced to develop faster than his mind – following the normal path taken by boys and girls born to labouring families. Early each morning Josiah started his routine, taking a thin brass wire and slicing off chunks of leathery clay from the weathering mound and carrying them on his shoulder into the workhouse. He lifted lumps the size of his head up high and whacked it down as hard as he could on to the bench. 'Blunging' the clay in this way softened it, preparing it to be dried and sifted to remove clumps of dirt and pebbles. Next he brought it to a 'beating board' where he 'beat it till it be well mixed', then 'brought to the waging board' where he 'wage it, i.e., knead or mould it like bread'.[5] 'Waging', or 'wedging' the clay, removed air pockets, helping to improve its texture and malleability.

It was arduous physical work, strengthening shoulder and back muscles while toughening the skin on hands that were soon stained dirty red from working the iron-rich local clay. In the evenings Josiah and his brother Richard, who was learning the first stages of forming the prepared clay, would emerge from the gritty workhouse hungry and exhausted, having worked a twelve-hour day (six days a week in the summer).[6] Rising food prices meant less real sustenance and yet demanded more intense work in order to survive: it was a vicious circle in which Josiah's whole family struggled to reach subsistence level.[7]

Josiah's father would have been devastated to witness the family's struggles. Now even the court magistrates were keeping a watchful eye on the family. Josiah's mother, Mary, had been asked to travel to Litchfield and stand before their bench to receive instructions about how to administer her late husband's ailing estate in light of the burden of debt. She was to 'administer all the goods, chattels, credits of the said deceased', they said. 'And we require you to make a true inventory of all and singular the personal estate of the said deceased and a true account of your said administration and to exhibit the same into the registry.'[8]

Probate inventories of all the deceased's possessions were not unusual, but this was to be prepared with a view to carving up and selling items off to service debts owed. The gravity of the situation was made clear when two of father Thomas's appointed executors, Mary's brother Samuel and her nephew John Wedgwood, went before the magistrates and 'judiciously renounced their right to the probate of the said will'.[9] They did not want to be involved with a bankrupt estate, especially one they knew could not 'pay the legacies'.[10]

Neither meant offence by renouncing their executorships – it was, indeed, 'judicial' and prudent, on their behalf. Mary's brother was a physician in Newcastle-under-Lyme, with his own career obligations to worry about; John Wedgwood, meanwhile, was preoccupied with his own pottery business. But of the two, it was John Wedgwood's decision to renounce his executorship that pained Josiah's brother Thomas the most.

Josiah's cousin John – or 'Long John' as he was called on account of his lanky, gaunt stature – could be easily spotted walking through Burslem towering above the leather-capped heads of the workers. He was thirty-five years old, about ten years Thomas's senior, and a potter. Long John and his elder brother, another Thomas, were inseparable. They lived together, worked together, ate together, and planned their future together – which for most of their lives excluded all ideas of marriage or the courtship of women. The brothers focused purely on refining their skills as potters, and on further improving on the performance of their potter father Aaron. He, unlike Josiah's father, his cousin, had been a potter of some quality. He had set high standards for the craft and trained his two youngest sons well, determined not to see them left behind in a world that favoured the eldest son.

Brothers Long John and Thomas came from the side of the Wedgwood family that, stretching back to the time of Gilbert, had been bypassed by inheritances of either Burslem land or wealth. The cousins might have briefly looked up the hill to Overhouse estate envious of the family fortune that passed to the other side of the Wedgwood family, but they soon walked around town with the kind of prestige that eluded Josiah's father and brother, for they excelled in their trade and in business. This made Long John's decision not to become involved with his uncle Thomas's estate all the more delicate. Josiah's brother knew how much the town admired his cousins' enterprise and how much pride they took in their self-made accomplishments. They 'left their father's service, to commence business for themselves in Burslem', the local historian Stebbing Shaw was told, relaying a sense of the respect they mar- shalled in town. 'As there was not then an instance of any Master Potter, who did not most diligently apply himself to some branch of the business, usually throwing or firing, their well-known industry, experience, and ingenuity warranted the expectation of a portion of Success.'[11] This was a modest appraisal. Their 'portion of Success' in Burslem was the lion's share, and Josiah's family was all too aware of it.

It may have been that Thomas could have worked with his cousins and tackled the problem of debt and the troubled trade through a family arrangement – it was the sort of solution commonly struck within families across England. But although the two branches of the family lived within a mile of each other, their relationship was formal. There had been two instances of marriage between cousins from each side – two of Josiah's aunts from his father's side had married two of Aaron Wedgwood's boys, the most educated and accomplished ones, Dr Thomas junior and Richard, a Master Potter who died young. But relations had cooled since then. Besides, Josiah's brother had inherited his father's stubbornness and pride and preferred to find his own solution to their financial problems. Long John and his brother may not even have given the matter of their cousins' plight much thought that year, 1740, for despite the unfavourable conditions, *their* business was booming. They had just taken possession of new premises, bought from an aunt of theirs for £280 (£19,600 today), and with a crisp new account book looked forward to an increasingly profitable future.[12]

Josiah would later reflect on the success of Long John and Thomas and talk to older potters to find out more about his cousins' craft from the days before he was born. He learned that they were associated with a new 'white glazed ware' that was made at the pottery next to the Red Lyon in the middle of town and at the pottery attached to Overhouse estate, which, through an aunt's short-lived marriage to her cousin, was briefly linked to that side of the family. The production of this ware had created a great sensation in Burslem at the turn of the eighteenth century, when their grandfather was starting out as a potter. 'There was no ware made in these parts that was glazed' in the manner of this new 'white ware', Josiah wrote in his notebook, 'before the Dutchmen used it with white ware.'[13]

'The Dutchmen' were John Philip Elers and his brother David, brothers from Amsterdam. Josiah had heard of them before, but he now discovered from the potters' reminiscences that his cousins' success could be traced back to the activities of the pair. The story recounted to him revealed much about the role of chance luck, deception, and innovation in creating a successful business, and it would prove a valuable lesson to Josiah.

John Philip and David Elers arrived in London in the 1680s as entrepreneurs. They had family connections with the city: an uncle who was a merchant involved with the China importing trade and their father who sold decorated glass and 'East Indian rareities'.[14] Enticed by the example of their father and uncle, John Philip and David moved to London and by 1688 were managing their own silversmiths shop.

The brothers would have felt a vague sense of familiarity with late-seventeenth-century London in many other ways too: England had a new monarch, the former Stadholder of the Dutch Republic, William of Orange, and although the English capital was three times the size of Amsterdam it too was a fast growing, innovative city with promising commercial prospects. The brothers were relieved also to find that Londoners had developed a passion for coffee houses, long established in Amsterdam. Whether it was Miles' in Westminster or The Turk's Head down the road in the Strand, coffee houses had become the place where all the wits and literati, from Pepys to Pope, would drink and debate. A new topic of conversation had emerged amongst the usual arguments over natural philosophy, constitutional principles and the future of the monarchy: it was whether or not this new drink called 'tay, alias tee' was a good thing for the British people.[15]

It seemed that no one was quite sure what to do with tea: some people would boil the leaves in water for a period before laying them on a wooden plate, buttering them, and eating them with knife and fork. To his surprise, Pepys had once left The Turk's Head for 'Home – and there find my wife drinking of tee, a drink which Mr. Pelling, the Potticary, tells her is good for her cold and defluxions'.[16]

Whether or not it had medicinal qualities was partly the issue. Sceptics thought that, at up to £10 per pound, it was more likely that such ideas were promoted by greedy nostrummongers. They could point to a circular distributed by the London merchant Thomas Galway that seemed to promise just too much: 'The drink is declared to be most wholesome, preserving in perfect health until extreme old age,' Galway announced. 'The particular virtues are these':

It maketh the body active and lusty.
It helpeth the headache, giddiness and heaviness thereof.
It removeth the obstructions of the spleen.
It is very good against the stone and gravel, cleaning the

kidneys and ureters, being drank with virgin's honey, instead
of sugar.

It taketh away the difficulty of breathing, opening obstructions.

It is good against tiptude, distillations, and cleareth the sight.

It removeth lassitude, and cleanseth and purifieth acrid
humours, and a hot liver.

It is good against crudities, strengthening the weakness of the
ventricle, or stomach, causing good appetite and digestion,
and particularly for men of corpulent body, and such as are
great eaters of flesh.

It vanquisheth heavy dreams, easeth the frame, and
strengtheneth the memory.

It overcometh superfluous sleep, and prevents sleepiness in
general; a draught of the infusion being taken, so that
without trouble, whole nights may be spent in study,
without hurt to the body, in that it moderately healeth and
bindeth the mouth of the stomach.

It prevents and cures agues, surfets, and fevers, by infusing a
fit quantity of the leaf, thereby provoking a most gentle
vomit and breathing of the pores, and hath been given with
wonderful success.

It (being prepaired and drank with milk and water)
strengtheneth the inward parts, and prevents consumption;
and powerfully assuageth the pains of the bowels, or griping
of the guts, and looseness.

It is good for colds, dropsys, and scurvys, if properly infused,
purging the body by sweat and urine, and expelleth
infection.

It driveth away all pains of the collick proceeding from wind,
and purgeth safely the gall.[17]

Some nations, he added, known for their 'knowledge and wisdom,
do frequently sell it among themselves for twice its weight in silver',
but his customers were encouraged to visit his place in Exchange
Alley where they could get it for a bargain, by comparison. This
was the sort of entrepreneurial spirit the Elers brothers would have

applauded, but public scepticism still had to be quelled. Even in about 1680 the London market for tea was glutted when the East India Company delivered nearly 5,000 pounds of the leaf.[18]

But by the end of the decade, just as the Elers brothers were settling in to their home above their silversmiths shop, tea was finally beginning to catch on. The brothers may have wondered what all the fuss was about, since their compatriots had introduced Europe to tea drinking in the first place and the Dutchman Cornelis Bontekoe was even encouraging people to drink up to two hundred cups of tea a day 'for health'.[19] Indeed it would not be long before members of London's elite were reportedly guzzling up to fifty cups of tea a day, supplied by Tom Twining's new tea warehouse in the Strand.[20]

But the brothers had spotted something intriguing in the behaviour of tea drinkers themselves – who were mainly wealthy women, who found the new tea shops a refreshing alternative to the men's coffee houses and the 'base, black, thick, nasty, bitter, stinking, nauseous Puddle Water'.[21] They watched these women, in their silk camlets and satin laces, sipping eager amounts of the 'China Drink', while stroking with admiration the fine rose-coloured 'tee pots' – also a new import from the East India Company. They were elegant: delicate, yet tough, with a smooth, unglazed satin finish. The Elers brothers were amused by the site of such fixed admiration for the Chinese pot. In Holland, tea drinking was more common and a number of manufactories had been established for decades to produce their own imitations of the teapot.[22]

The English market lagged behind in all areas of the production of fine pottery. London dealers frequently complained about their inability to supply a growing market, especially in what they called 'Dutch jugs', 'stone bottles', and 'China ware'. 'The potters made dishes and painted wares', explained one retailer in ceramic tiles to a 1673 committee for 'encouraging manufactures in England', 'but not the sixth part of what the shopkeepers vend'. What the English potters did produce 'was not so good as what came from Holland',

and worse still, it was 'double the price of what the Dutch made'.[23] There were even stories circulating of merchants going to Holland 'to bring a person well skilled in that art' back to England for work. This is what had brought Uncle John Elers to London years earlier.[24]

The Elers brothers first set their sights on improving on the rough, brown earthenware mugs commonly used to serve ale or coffee. To achieve this, however, they needed some practical information about raw materials and available pot-works. They also needed to speak to people who were pioneering new pottery techniques. No one suited their needs more than John Dwight and his philosophically minded friends who were involved with the recently established Royal Society, a 'society of Experimenters in a Romantick Model'.[25]

John Dwight was an Oxford-educated lawyer who acquired a passion for experimental chemistry from his tutor Robert Boyle, a regular attendee of the meetings at the Royal Society where small groups of gentlemen met to discuss the findings of their private philosophical investigations. Dwight's own experimental findings had recently attracted considerable attention, for he boastfully announced that he had discovered 'the misterie of the stone ware' that was generating so much interest in London tea shops, and he was able to manufacture 'an opacous redd and darke coloured Porcellane' in imitation of the Chinese pots.[26] Thinking that this was going to make him a fortune, he took out two patents to protect his innovations.

For a couple of experimentally minded Dutch entrepreneurs (rumour had spread that they once trained with the eminent chemist Johann Becher, who spent some years in the Netherlands working on a scheme to recover gold from silver by means of sea sand), Dwight was exactly the person they needed to meet, or at least, steal his ideas.[27] They considered themselves fortunate, therefore, when they had the chance to quietly listen to Dwight discuss his chemical experiments as guests at a private meeting of the Royal Society. Having absorbed information about different kinds of clay found locally around Britain, and about his technique for rendering it 'opacous', the brothers suddenly and mysteriously disappeared. But by the time anyone noticed their absence they were already en route for north Staffordshire.

Few Staffordshire potters had any conception that their area contained such rare deposits of clay, they just made pots where their fathers had made them before. Informed travellers, however, were aware it was a special spot of earth, even if they cared not to theorise about the reasons why. Later, 'natural historians' (historians of nature) would explain that the site of the potteries was prepared by nature for the staple they produced. God had provided the ground for their way of life. Geologists then told of how epochs of land submergence and elevation had worn down the grit and limestone rocks to form clay, while the coal and ironstone seams that appeared in strata in hillsides mixed with the presence of different ores and minerals (particularly iron oxide) to render a unique composition and colour to the clays. The red clays so striking within the Staffordshire landscape came from a geological formation (now called the 'Etruria Formation') lying immediately above the coal measures – a formation and clay unique to the English Midlands.[28]

In about 1698 the Elers brothers moved into Dimsdale Hall near Burslem and rented a pot-work a mile away at Bradwell Wood which sat on a seam of rich, red clay. The brothers' presence immediately became a great source of rumour and speculation among the local potters. Both Dimsdale and Bradwell Wood were tucked away in secluded situations, well off any regularly used road, and just within squinting distance of Burslem's hilltop. Day after day curious eyes caught glimpses of the strangers' busy activities: new kilns had been erected; the Dutchmen would spend hours digging the land for clay and would then disappear into their workshop. Brazen visitors to Bradwell hoping to look at their hideaway were politely encouraged to leave.

It was 'their extreme precaution to keep secret their processes', wrote Stebbing Shaw, recording what people had said about their new rivals, 'and jealousy lest they might be accidentally witnessed by any purchaser of their wares'.[29] The ale-fuelled gossip about the Elers brothers' 'precautions' grew extravagant. They had manufactured clay pipes which they ran underground from Dimsdale to the workhouses in Bradwell 'to intimate the approach of persons supposed to be intruders', it was said. And for procuring hired hands as extra labour they resorted to 'employing an idiot to turn the thrower's wheel, and the most ignorant and stupid workmen to perform laborious operations, and by locking up these persons while at work, and strictly examining each prior to quitting the manufactory at night'.[30] But soon their isolation was broken.

One day Burslem awoke to discover a soaring, dirty stain on the horizon. The sky above Bradwell Wood was thick with voluminous smoke. 'The people of Burslem were then very much surprised with the smoke', Josiah was told by one of the eye-witnesses, 'and ran in great numbers to see what was the matter.'[31] As they approached, they observed that it was caused by the kilns, erupting like Vesuvius, exhaling billows of black, sooty, noxious fumes. The Elers brothers were on ladders, pouring buckets of salt from mounds into 'feeding holes' built high into the sides of the tall bottleneck ovens, which quickly vitrified in the red-hot interior, coating the wares with what they called a 'salt-glaze'. The like had never been seen before.

The wares that emerged from the slowly cooling kiln were striking. The Elers brothers had produced high-quality, finely-shaped white pitchers and dinner plates. From another kiln emerged something even more outstanding. They had successfully manufactured smooth, unglazed, matt-red coloured teapots, remarkably similar to the imported Yi-Hsing teapots so popular in London, where their new products were shipped to be sold in their new store in Poultney. Unbeknown to anyone around Burslem other than the Elers brothers, the red wares were also remarkably similar to John Dwight's 'opacous red and darke coloured Porcellane'.

Dwight became outraged when a correspondent wrote in to the Royal Society to report on some 'new' pottery he had just come across, made from a 'soft oar like Clay'. 'I have this to add,' he wrote:

> [the clay] is as good, if not better, than that which is brought from the East Indies. Witness the Tea-Pots now to be sold at the Potters in the Poultney in Cheapside, which not only for Art, but for beautiful colour, too are far beyond any we have from China. These are made of the English red clay in Staffordshire, as I take it, by two Dutch-men incomparable Artists.[32]

Worse, the Dutchmen were shortly to be celebrated in the pages of a journal published by the very Society that Dwight had announced *his* discovery as a rival to the Chinese teapots. Dwight immediately suspected that the Elers brothers had acquired an invitation to one of the Royal Society meetings he had spoken at or that they had prized information from the members. He even suspected that they had bribed his workman, John Chandler, for secrets of the process.

Dwight filed a lawsuit against the Dutchmen, seeking 'to hinder and restrayne them from making, practicing, imitateing, counterfeiting, and vending of the severall wares and Manufactures in the plaintiffs bill.'[33] But it was too late. It appears that the 'idiot' employed by the Elers brothers in their covert workshop in Staffordshire had in turn betrayed his employers, and had each night set to work imitating their methods.[34] Soon similar wares were being produced by other Burslem potters, most prominently Aaron Wedgwood.

Josiah found much that was instructive in the potters' tale. He saw how a potter could benefit most from learning skills beyond those traditionally associated with the craft. The 'art and mystery' of experimental chemistry, for instance, could produce remarkable results: trying to understand the secrets of nature could reveal how melting salt under certain conditions could form a special glaze, or how grinding particular minerals could affect the colour of the finished piece. He learned that new techniques had been introduced to Burslem through the Dutchmen because they had been anxious to harness a burgeoning London market. He also saw how through espionage rivalling that of the Elers brothers', his Wedgwood cousins had profited from the stealing of secrets. Indeed, a few months after his original lawsuit, John Dwight added the names of Aaron Wedgwood and his two sons to the suit, citing their 'unjust and injurious practises', claiming that they had also 'insinuated themselves into the acquaintance of the said John Chandler and enticed him to instruct them and to enter into partnership together . . .'.[35] While Dwight was able to reach an agreement with the Elers brothers, his own patents were soon to expire, and the courts favoured commercial competition over private monopoly, thus ending his hopes of recouping any damages.

John Philip and David Elers continued their work at Bradwell Wood for almost a decade, using all the accessible rusty clay on their plot of land. Finally, the increased competition from the Burslem potters, particularly the Wedgwoods, drove them out of business, allegedly declaring: 'The Fulhamites can come and go, but Wedgwoods will go on forever' (an allusion to John Dwight, who was from Fulham, and his Staffordshire rivals[36]). By the time Aaron Wedgwood died, in 1701, the Elers brothers had already disappeared as mysteriously as they arrived. 'Where they went he knoweth not', wrote Josiah, after posing the same question to the old potters of Burslem.[37]

At the time that Long John and Thomas were entering the family trade in the 1720s, their father Aaron was expanding it at a pace, moving to new premises, building new kilns, and boldly seeking out that lucrative London market. He worked non-stop imitating and trying to improve on the 'Red China Ware' developed by the Elers brothers, concealing pieces he thought successful in the garret of his house.[38] The sons followed suit, working secretively and in a close dedicated partnership, hoping to ape the success of the Elers brothers. They determined that there were two areas of the potter's craft that mattered more than any others: 'throwing' or forming the clay at the wheel, and 'firing', controlling the heat and timing of the kiln.

Operating the potter's wheel while forming a lump of clay with wet hands was one of the most skilled, and difficult, techniques of the craft. There were two ways to spin the disc on the wheel: by anchoring one foot for purchase and using the other foot to push a pedal on the 'kick-wheel', or by rigging a rope around a shaft and having an assistant (Elers' 'idiot', but more commonly a child) drive the wheel by hand. The kick-wheel allowed the thrower to work autonomously, a cheaper and more efficient method. Most potters preferred this, including the Wedgwoods on both sides of the family. Cousin Thomas focused his efforts on becoming the best thrower in Burslem, while Long John concentrated his energy on becoming the best 'fireman' in the trade.

Many potters knew that unless they left their wares in the kiln for exactly the right amount of time at precisely the right temperature they would lose the entire kiln load. The transformation of earth to art that took place in the oven was a hidden process, the 'mysterie' of the craft which apprentices would learn could only be acquired through years of experience, the tacit knowledge of the 'fireman'. Human error was costly: a week's worth of wares, a mound of coal, clay, work and profits wasted. But the right experiment, using new mixtures of clay, firing times, and temperatures (producing a recipe that could be patented, or stolen), meant gaining a margin of superiority over the competition and more profit.

The new process of fine-salt glazing relied on knowing when the kiln reached very high temperatures, whereas producing non-glazed wares, such as the red teapots or cream-coloured 'earthenwares', required lower temperatures. No thermometer had been invented which could be attached to the kiln for reading internal temperatures (though in 1740 Long John would invent what he called 'pyrometrical beads', clay pellets placed in the oven to help gauge the temperature by monitoring the change in their appearance).[39] Next to the bricked-over entry, where people entered the kiln to stack the wares along the interior, were holes where firemen shovelled in coal. Only experience and constant attention to the heat that blasted from these small apertures provided information about the internal condition of the kiln.

Long John and cousin Thomas became local celebrities who set the standard for other ambitious potters in the area. Visitors and early historians of Burslem regularly referred to Cousin Thomas and Long John as 'the one an excellent thrower, the other a most skilful fireman'.[40] Their reputations spread beyond the local area. Their trade grew, and more than anyone else in Burslem their accounts were enriched with an 'export' market, not only to London, but to many other areas of England. In Simeon Shaw's estimation, the brothers provided:

> a most pertinent illustration, that every man is the maker or marrer of his own fortune; that, he who depends upon incessant industry and integrity, depends on patrons the most noble, the most exalted, and who never desert, but are the founders of families, the creators of fortune and fame, controuling all human dealings, and converting even unfavourable vicissitudes into beneficial results.[41]

On 21 April 1743, Aaron, their father, died. The next day, their mother Mary died. Both were buried in the graveyard of St John's, Burslem, in a prominent place closest to the front door of the chapel (the graves are there to this day). Their estates, lands and pot-works were distributed amongst their three sons, thereby edging Long John and cousin Thomas's status another step forward. Their brother, Richard, took his inheritance and pursued a new business venture as a cheese factor in the leafy, peaceful village of Spen Green, about twenty miles north towards Manchester. Josiah was twelve when he attended the funeral, and before long he would be starting his formal apprenticeship under his brother (or so he imagined). Long

John and cousin Thomas had no children, they were still too busy with business, but their brother Richard did. Sarah was nine, and she, along with her only brother, was set to benefit from her family's industrious success. For the side of the Wedgwood family that had once looked up the hill with envy to those who inherited much of Burslem's wealth, things were moving ahead at a pace. But for Josiah and his family the chances of improving their prospects remained slim.

FOUR

Acts of Toleration

I T WAS WITH GREAT PRIDE that on 11 November 1744, Josiah took a pen in hand and approached the large vellum parchment spread out on the table as his mother and brother looked on. Signing an apprenticeship indenture was a moment that changed the lives of many fourteen-year-old boys in and around Burslem. They were often the privileged ones since other poverty-stricken families sent their children as young as nine to the workshops. It was a sign of prosperity to wait that long to begin a formal apprenticeship, a symbol of the success of the trade, and Josiah's family, however dispirited, would not break with a proud tradition.[1]

The indenture Josiah signed spelled out the responsibilities assigned to him and his 'Master', brother Thomas. He was bound 'to Learn his Art, Mistery, Occupation, or Imployment of Throwing and Handleing, which he, the said Thomas Wedgwood now useth, and with him as an Apprentice to Dwell, Continue, and Serve from the day of the Date hereof, unto the full end and term of five years.' He was formally required to protect the business of his Master, 'his secrets keep, his Lawfull Commands Every will gladly do; Hurt to his said Master he shall not do, nor wilfully suffer to be done by others . . . the goods of his said Master he shall not imbezil or waste, nor them Lend, without his Consent to any.' As was customary, he was forbidden from swearing, drinking, gaming, and marrying, but will 'Demean and behave himself'. For his part, Thomas 'shall and will Teach and Instruct after the best way and manner he can', and will provide 'Meat, Drink, Washing and Lodging, and Apparell of all kinds, both Linen and Woolen, and all other Necessaries, both in Sickness and in Health.'[2] And so, it announced, 'by the grace of God, King of great Brittain, and so forth,' Josiah became an apprentice.

In a craft where trade secrets clearly meant so much, this formal document represented a bond of trust between master and apprentice. A new relationship between the two brothers was created, one enshrined in a legal and technical tradition. When Josiah watched his mother sign her name below his, and then his brother next to that, it meant that they were agreeing to see him through this rite of passage. For Josiah it brought some comfort, a sense of stability in his life, prospects of future employment, and, above all, the pride and prestige that came with receiving skilled training in the craft.

To Thomas, it meant doing what he could to give Josiah the training he needed, but more importantly for him it meant he had a boy that was bound 'well and faithfully to serve'. Thomas needed all the help he could muster. Josiah's other brother Richard had just completed his apprenticeship with Thomas and decided instead to join the King's army and become a soldier. His decision to join was timely. France had declared war on Britain in a fight over colonial possessions in the New World, while, more urgently for the Staffordshire community, the Young Pretender, Charles Edward Stuart, had in 1745 advanced his Jacobite army, aiming to overthrow the Hanoverian monarchy, all the way to nearby Derby. It is said that Richard hid in the hills and watched the army march toward London, listening to them sing their Jacobin songs, and witnessed their retreat to Scotland as the invasion of England was deemed a failure.[3]

Richard's departure for the army freed up urgently needed space at Churchyard House: Thomas's new wife Isabel had just given birth to their first child, baby Thomas. The new family circumstances presented Josiah's brother with another concern. He could give Josiah a start at the trade, teach him on the wheel that he was taught on, just like his father before him, but he could not guarantee Josiah's professional future.

Indeed trade at the Churchyard Works had never adequately recovered from the difficult times following their father's death and the harsh winter. In 1742 Thomas had assumed the added burden of working at Overhouse estate, on the northern ridge of Burslem hill, leaving Richard, still then his apprentice, to see through the day's work. Each day Thomas would walk up Church Lane, up the steep Shoe Lane to the russet-tinged fields called the 'Brownhills', to where the Overhouse pot-works were perched.

The house and estate were owned by his Aunt Katherine, the only child of John Wedgwood, who had inherited it when Josiah's grandfather, being the younger brother, inherited the Churchyard House and pot-works. Katherine was an eccentric, but also an admirably strong-willed woman. She was fifty-nine-years old and had lived an unusual life. At twenty-five she had married her forty-year-old cousin, Richard, from the 'Aaron' side of the family (who had benefited from the Elers' brothers débâcle) and who was running one of the most profitable potteries in Burslem after that of Long John and Cousin Thomas.[4] They had their first child the year they married, but exactly ten years later, Richard suddenly died, followed tragically the next year by their eleven-year-old son from smallpox. The next year Katherine married another, more distant, cousin, Thomas Bourne, and they had a daughter, Sarah, who did not survive infancy. Katherine's second husband died seven years later. She then married for a third time, to a gentleman named Rowland Egerton; there were no children.

Aunt Katherine certainly did not need to levy any rent from Josiah's brother for using the once profitable pot-works that her first husband had built. She already leased much of the near 200 acres of land that comprised her estates, land that occupied views from all directions of Overhouse – the Oldfields to the northeast, the rugged expanses of Oxley Croft and Meadow Hill on the northern hilltop behind her, even dark and damp Dale Hall Crofts – all of which brought her a rent-related income of about £100 per annum.[5] It was an income that allowed her to be charitable as well as a touch extravagant.

Katherine was the only 'gentlewoman' in Burslem, and became something of a local celebrity. She should have been able to look down upon everyone else in Burslem from up at breezy Overhouse, but she was often incommoded by the 'vast volumes of smoke and vapours' billowing from the salt-glaze ovens down below, an irony she found amusing. She employed two 'servant maids', Sarah Marsh and Mary Lowe, and a 'serving man', Peter Yarwood, to make her comfortable at Overhouse. She commissioned expensive furniture, and would ride through town in her private chaise, a rarity in these parts.[6] But beyond all the pomp and ceremony, she was deeply committed to helping her family – all extended branches of it – as well as the community in any way she could. She was admired for her charitable gifts to the poor and the parish. And she had no reservations in helping out her struggling nephew, Thomas, for whom she seemed to have special, if during her lifetime, silent regard.

Thomas worked each day in the converted barns next to the stables. Each week the kiln from each of his two pot-works produced another batch of plain butter pots and the cloudy, 'mottled', black speckled saucers and mugs. Profits were thin, no more than 10 shillings a week, not enough to hire any additional help. Thomas relied on his young brothers – and when Richard was gone it was left to Josiah, still learning the trade, to oversee the Churchyard Works.

Despite all the customary duties between Master and apprentice formally assigned within the indenture, the agreement between Thomas and Josiah was unusual in one respect: Josiah was not to receive any pay at all. In return for his 'training', the 'Meat, Drink, Washing and Lodging, and Apparell' were all Josiah would receive. Unlike other indentures, this one did not provide for any 'earnest money', a lump sum paid up front.[7] These were added expenses saved by Thomas – who was so short of money that he was preparing to borrow £100 from a Thomas Adams (who may have supplied the Wedgwoods with coal) – but more significantly it deprived Josiah the opportunity to put aside for his own future ventures.[8]

Finding ways to endure life's trials was a topic frequently addressed by Josiah's Unitarian minister grandfather, Reverend Stringer. It epitomised the rational approach to life that he so often preached. The Stringers, like the Wedgwoods, were a pious family, but religion to them was more about reading than praying. Unitarians were different from followers of the Church of England: they rejected the doctrine of original sin, and did not believe in the Holy Trinity; instead they believed there was only a divine 'unity'.[9] It was irrational to believe otherwise, they argued. Even the recently deceased national hero Sir Isaac Newton believed that the doctrine of the Trinity was based on 'two corruptions of Scripture' and should no longer be relied upon.[10]

Mary was taught that rational ethics – knowledge based upon reason, experience, and experiment – was preferable to dogma. She and her family believed in free enquiry, free worship, and voluntary prayers rather than thoughtless allegiance to a church. 'God that made the World', wrote the prominent Quaker clothier John Bellers (a dissenter with Unitarian sympathies), 'dwelleth not in Temples made with Hands', but within everyone, everything, everywhere.[11] To study nature was to seek the truth. To cleanse the body was to care for God's 'temple'.

Reverend Stringer talked much about the Unitarian philosophy, and, because it encouraged individual resourcefulness, it gave Mary a strong sense of ability and prudence. Even though Parliament had passed the Act of Toleration in 1689, allowing those with views that dissented from the established canon to preach in public, Unitarians still received short shrift from the authorities. They spread 'damnable heresies', Anglican clerics cried. Josiah's grandfather remembered well the antiquated laws that quashed attempts at rational inquiry into how *literally* liturgies should be taken and how learned, scientific men were eliminated with their investigations. He would have shuddered to think of the story of the eighteen-year-old medical student at Edinburgh who was overheard repeating some statements from a shallow infidel tract he had read, and was promptly arrested. Denied counsel, he admitted the charges made, but, despite his repentance and pleas for mercy, he was hanged. His was the last execution for heresy in Britain and it happened when Mary was nine.[12]

It would have been difficult for Reverend Stringer to spot much by way of progress a half century later. Unitarians of his generation still spoke quietly and cautiously, if firmly, about their views. Since no Unitarian church was to be established until 1774, the most effective preaching was that which occurred among one's own family and neighbours. It would prove to be even longer before Unitarians' beliefs were granted full 'toleration' but Josiah, like his mother, was already converted.[13]

Josiah had grown up with what was deemed by metropolitan lawmakers as unorthodox, even dangerous, beliefs about God and his creation. Grandfather Stringer's guarded discussions might have celebrated rational principles of education for his daughter and her children, but because they were dissenting ideas they also promoted a sense of segregation, making 'the Potteries' feel all the more isolated, something that any Wedgwood wanting to break beyond provincial prejudices and join the commercial world would need to overcome.

In 1744 Mary's faith in reason and rational care was fully tested when Josiah contracted smallpox. Josiah, feverish and nauseous, was placed in what was once the 'priest's chamber' for the parish chaplain, a fetid, airless room. Mary had already lost five of her children to the disease, but Josiah would have been too ill to register his mother's fear that he as well might die.

Smallpox was the scourge of all England that no generation

escaped, a disease that tormented villagers as they watched church-yards fill with corpses and friends fall ill with the familiar symptoms. Josiah had entered the 'febrile state', following a pattern spelled out in a recently published and immensely popular bedside book, *A Treatise on the Small Pox*. Beginning 'with a coldness, shiverings, and shakings', Josiah then developed a fever and suffered aches in his back and joints, sending torrents of pain throughout his sweating, emaciated body as it heaved to vomit.[14] Entering the 'eruptive' state, his skin became itchy and burned as the spreading rash on his skin raised and filled with pus, which after rupturing left pockmarks on his skin, a sign that would forever tell those who looked at him or his truthful portraits that his life was only just spared. His arms, hands and fingers swelled and his bowels stopped evacuating.

That year's cattle plague, whence 'we dare not eat milk, butter, beef nor anything from that species', had made things worse since it had left Josiah poorly nourished and less able to resist the onset of the disease.[15] If he survived it was likely that he would live with one of its effects, besides the pock scars, for the rest of his life. 'It turns many into frightful spectacles', wrote one dissenting preacher, who outspokenly supported 'experiments' to cure the small pox, 'and is attended with the most dismal Consequences, Loss of Sight, Lameness, long Confinement, a broken Constitution, Countenances so altered that their nearest Relations hardly know them.'[16]

But if Josiah survived, the outlook appeared dismal in many other ways. He had no inheritance and with the family business failing he might well face such poverty that he would be sent to the new workhouse, to a life of disease, destitution, and early death. Distant politicians flattered themselves into believing that young men would learn discipline and piety in such institutions. In truth such a con-signment was atrocious. In some poorhouses the death rate was 100 per cent, affirming one philanthropist's damning comment that parish officers who send children to the poorhouse 'never intend that they should live'.[17]

For weeks Josiah lay still in bed, fading into delirium, 'as the small-pox in him took a confluent form, covering him from head to foot, and leaving him, when absolute danger was past, in a state of deplorable weakness'.[18] The notes on observing the symptoms and attempting remedies offered in the popular medical handbook on the pox would have proved useful to Mary in attending her son:

> If with a quick, and strong pulse and great heat of the Body, bad symptoms occur, you must conclude that the pulse is too quick, too strong, and the Heat of the Body too great; and therefore, you must endeavour to abate them. For this purpose, give the Sick plentifully of diluting Liquors, acidulated with the Juice of Lemons, or Oranges, or with a few drops of the Spirit of Vitriol . . .

Alternatively, if the pulse was weak and the 'vital heat' not much different than in times of health, but yet 'bad symptoms occur',

> you must conclude that the pulse is too weak, and the vital heat too little, and therefore you must endeavour to raise them. For this end you give the sick Mountain or Sack Whey, with a little Nutmeg, Panada's, Gruels, Caudles, &c made with Wine, and water sweetened with sugar, and warmed . . . but wine and spice must be used more or less, as the weakness of the pulse.

Finally, the fever broke. Josiah's pustules began to form seed-like crusts on his skin, and he began to move. Though he had gained enough strength to emerge from his bed, he found it difficult to walk. He had survived 'a season of severe bodily affliction, owing to a humour that had settled in his leg after the small pox, and which on every slight accident became painful and sore', recalled a later relative and long-term friend. But Josiah seemed well enough to resume his apprenticeship, and he limped back into the workshops on a crutch, and 'for some half the time of his apprenticeship he sat at his work with his leg upon a stool before him'.[19]

However ill the practice of the trade may agree with the health, the ability, or the inclination of an apprentice: whether his mind is directed to prefer the study of another, by a riper understanding, which would render him more competent to excel in it; or whether, by the loss of a limb he is disabled from pursuing the first to which he is placed; by *that and that alone* he must abide: he is, in the one case, as irretrievably fixed in that trade, as if he belonged to one of the Castes of India; in the other he has no alternative; he *must starve!*[20]

It was a sentiment years in the making – the 'laws' of apprenticeship were harsh. They were prohibitive of pleasure, exclusive and isolating, and, because the positions were competitive, favoured only the fittest. Josiah, however, was determined not to let his weak leg jeopardise his duties, as impossible as he now found them.

The 'art and mistery' of throwing – seeing a final form in one's mind as the carefully prepared wet clay spins beneath one's hands – was central to learning the Master Potter's craft. The problem was that the only way practised at the Churchyard Works required the use of both legs: one foot to anchor the body, the other (usually the right) to operate the kick-wheel. There was an alternative but this would have meant acquiring a different kind of hand-spun wheel and hiring a labourer to work it.

But there were other techniques of making wares that saved Josiah the struggle of independently working at the wheel; his disability led to versatility. New ways of preparing clay and forming pieces were beginning to appear which attracted his attention, not least since the diversity of pottery enriched the trade and might prove a valuable addition to the stock of family skills. By 1745, potters not only in Burslem but all around Staffordshire had now adapted to the production of salt-glazed wares and the newer invention of 'cream-coloured earthenware', or creamware, which produced a richer, more varied and polished glaze on the pieces. The better quality of these demanded more work, however. For a start, creamware required two firings, whereas other types of pottery needed only one. During the first the freshly formed piece was transformed into a hard, plain, porous 'biscuit' state. At this point the worker who specialised in glazing would apply newly ground, powdered lead to each piece. These were then fired again at a lower temperature to produce the finished, smooth and glossy product. Not only was it more labour intensive, but potters soon linked the lead-glazing process to the failing health of their workers.

This was a problem that was tackled by a creative potter in Tunstall, just north of Burslem. Enoch Booth was well known for manufacturing creamware, and just as Josiah was beginning his apprenticeship, Booth had been experimenting with a new method of lead glazing which was applied in a liquid state, helping to alleviate the problems linked to making and using a toxic powder.[21]

The use of powdered white flint stones which were shipped to Staffordshire from the English coasts via the River Weaver for the first time when Josiah was young created another hazard.[22] When dried and mixed with the clay it added strength to the pieces so they could be made more thinly and fired at the crucial higher temperatures. But like the lead, grinding flints caused alarming health problems. 'Any person ever so healthful or strong working in this business,' announced one concerned engineer named Thomas Benson, 'cannot possibly survive above two years, occasioned by the dust sucked into his body.'[23] But Benson had a solution, and a decade before Josiah began his apprenticeship had patented his improved mill for grinding flints under water, drowning loose dust, and saving some from onset of 'potter's rot' – lung disease.[24]

This innovation, coupled with the new use of liquid lead glazes, entered the manufacture of pottery just as Josiah entered his apprenticeship in the 1740s. The community of potters devoted much thought to improving their craft and producing higher quality wares whilst also protecting the health of their workers. It was a delicate line of enquiry: experiments were expensive, and often potters could not afford errors in the trials.

However, Josiah's brother chose to stick to his father's tried-and-tested, if rather unimaginative, methods. Others risked it. Long John and cousin Thomas never stopped investing in expansion and building the latest mechanical devices to advance their trade. In 1744 they rented land owned by a gentleman in the nearby parish of Norton 'To take, farme, & Rent ye old furnace at Lawton & convert it into a flint Mill at the price of Twenty Guineas a year for the Terme of Seven years certain' – making them one of the earliest known Burslem potters to construct a flint mill. They knew the venture had risks, however, adding in their agreement that they would honour their obligations 'in all advantages that shall accrue and also ALL Disappointments or Disadvantages yt shall ensue'.[25]

The newly erected mills and special rooms for the added stages of production were visible proof that the craft and business was moving forward in Burslem. There was even an emerging sense of camaraderie in the community. Rivalry judiciously gave way to rallying in support of a new technique or tool which would draw more widespread attention to the kind of quality wares that could be produced in the town. The stakes were raised after 1744 when new English porcelain manufacturers were established in Chelsea, Bow, Derby, and, nearer to Burslem, in Pomona and Longton Hall. Fortunately for the Staffordshire potters, their newly improved durable wares were still cheaper to produce than the delicate soft-paste body of English porcelain.[26] There were still concerns, however, over whether their customers would favour pottery or porcelain.

Compared to their competitors in Burslem, the Churchyard Works was lagging behind the times. Some of the wares that Josiah worked on from dawn to dusk were made of clay that was mixed with water to a semi-liquid, creamy state called 'slip'. This could be poured into plaster moulds to produce decorated teapots and tureens (after a thin layer of the slip dried inside the mould the rest of the liquid clay was poured out to keep the piece hollow), but it could also be used to make 'mottled' or marbled ware, something his family had done for many years. Different coloured slip – orange, white, and red, sometimes altered when ingredients such as iron-ore (called 'magnus') were added – was poured over the surface of the ware and 'combed' or blended to imitate a veined hard stone, such as agate, with bands of colour.[27] It was simple but creative, producing pieces bursting with vibrancy that made the pottery look like jewellery.

Josiah enjoyed working on those pieces; it enabled him to develop the art of the craft, allowing him to concentrate less on the physical aspects of pottery and more on the creative. By 1749, five years after signing his indenture, Josiah's apprenticeship came to an end. He had managed successfully to demonstrate that he had learned 'the art, mistery, and occupation' of the potter; he had come a long way from the days of working in the potting sheds with his brother Richard, 'seated at two corners of a small room', throwing and shaping balls of clay in the wake of their father's death.[28] Staying on to work for his brother in the Churchyard Works, he was now able to earn his own wages and assume his role of responsibility in paying for food and clothes.

For three years following his apprenticeship he worked with Thomas, contemplating ways to improve the potter's art, hoping to gain wider acceptance as an equal in the family business. It would have been natural for two brothers working together to form a partnership, to divide their skills and mutually invest in their trade. If Josiah needed a model example of the potential effectiveness of such a working arrangement he had, of course, only to look at Long John and cousin Thomas, who in 1750, the year after Josiah finished his apprenticeship, were noisily celebrating the completion of their new residence and works in Burslem. The townspeople were awe-struck by their imposing house that now dominated the town centre, on the corner plot next to the Red Lyon: three storeys high, it was double-fronted in rustic red brick with a pedimented porch supported on Doric columns. It also had a tiled roof, making it the first non-thatched home in Burslem, which, according to one townsman, 'was considered a ridiculous expense' until it was finished, then it 'astonished the natives'.[29] The brothers brazenly named it 'Big House', declaring that theirs was a business not to be over-looked.

But Josiah and his brother never formed the kind of close relation-ship that their cousins enjoyed. Thomas, perhaps thinking that Josiah was too daring and indulgent in 'endless illusive projects', was not willing to enter into a partnership with his younger brother;[30] Josiah for his part was dissatisfied with what he considered Thomas's unimaginative approach to the art of pottery.

That year, Thomas's wife Isabel gave birth to their fifth child. Mary would be only the fourth of their children to survive infancy, as they had already suffered the loss of their second son only months after he was born. But this had been a difficult birth: there was nothing the midwife could do, and Isabel died. As if the frailties of life had not tormented Thomas enough, in suppurating sorrow he watched his two-year-old daughter fall feverish and pass away soon after.[31] In July 1752, Thomas married again, to Jane Richards. At Churchyard House eight-year-old Thomas performed the menial duties that had previously fallen to Josiah when his father died, feeding the large fireplace in the kitchen and assisting in the pot-works across the muddy yard. Josiah's mother continued to look after the girls of the house, her granddaughters: three-year-old Sarah and two-year-old Mary.

Josiah had just turned twenty-two and he wanted to move on from the family home. It was never going to be easy. 'No single handed man can live,' a contemporary tradesman had written, reflecting on the importance of relationships, 'he must have a whole family at work, because a single-handed man is so badly paid he can scarce provide the necessaries of life.'[32] But Josiah was stubborn. That summer he collected his few belongings and left, determined to move on, by himself.

FIVE

Discipline & Dissent

J OSIAH HAD LEFT HOME, but he was not going far, just down
the gentle hills from Burslem and into the next town of Stoke,
about three miles south. He had found a new place to live as a
lodger in the home of Daniel Mayer, a successful tradesman who
shared the Dissenting religious views of Josiah's own family.

Daniel Mayer ran a busy business as a 'Tailor, Draper, and Man's
Mercer', earning enough to build a house in the middle of town
which was roomy enough not only to house a lodger, but also to
accommodate his shop in the front rooms along the street.[1] Unlike
the home of even Josiah's wealthiest cousins, where the mess of raw
materials from the pot-works was deliberately separated from the
'dwelling house', here the working areas were integrated into
the larger home. Passing customers entered the front rooms of the
house, the workshop rooms, where the tailor was surrounded with
cloth from orders in progress. Everything was custom made in trades
such as these, with all supply on demand and with close interaction
between the merchant and customer. Josiah took a room at the back
of the house, near the rest of the 'family apartments'.[2]

Mayer's house was on the main street running through Stoke,
which not only served his business well, but was convenient enough
for Josiah to get to the Cliff Bank pot-works where he had found
new employment. The man he principally worked with was Thomas
Alders, a potter who manufactured the usual lead and salt-glazed
tea sets, mugs, and 'blue ware' items. These were then decorated

by women 'flowerers' who scratched patterns into the pieces vaguely resembling flora or Chinese pagodas and then dusted them with powdered smalt, a blue pigment derived from zaffre.[3] Alders's business had received an infusion of cash from a Newcastle-under-Lyme merchant named John Harrison, and they took on Josiah to improve their production of hand-pressed or moulded wares.

Here Josiah continued working on the colourful marbled agate ware that he specialised in at the Churchyard Works. He also began trying his hand at decorating creamware pieces with new kinds of glazes in imitation of some of the goods appearing from his cousins' Big House manufactory. There was a niche fashion at the time for moulded round teapots made to look like fruits and vegetables, with a surface emulating a head of cauliflower or a pineapple, for instance. A modeller or artist would carve the original specimen with the desired decorative motif and produce a mould of it for future casts using the creamy 'slip' clay. When the clay crust had dried and the item was ready, Josiah would mix different kinds of ground metals – copper, manganese, iron, cobalt, and so on – and dust or sponge them onto the piece before applying a clear lead glaze after which it would be sent to be fired.

The effects were sometimes dramatic. A potter down the road on the opposite side of Stoke named Thomas Whieldon had been developing what was known as Tortoiseshell ware, named after the mingling of brownish-purple and deep, smoky greens on the final finish. Customers across the country adored it, and their eagerness to buy it spurred on Whieldon's business, allowing him to recruit new apprentices and labourers. The more heads and hands driving the creative process the more likely something new and eye-catching would appear.

Creative potters were always eager to peer into the cooled saggars being unloaded from the kilns in which the new batches of wares were placed for firing. No one knew what they might discover. It was no longer just a process of digging for different kinds of clays and altering firing temperatures and times. Fifty years after the Elers brothers first showed the Burslem potters what effect pouring salt into kilns could have on the products, it seemed sensible to some to grind up other sorts of elements and chemicals to see what effect they might have on the pottery.

The crude equation that coal and clay were enough to provide a meagre living became as outmoded as the feudal dogma that peasants were bound to their subservient rank in life by divine ordinance. The outward signs of this social advancement were quite conspicuous. Families could move from thatched hovels to big brick houses because they believed that nature hid treasures accessible to anyone who was willing to work hard enough – to dig deep enough – to find the reward.

Not everyone shared this progressive view, but Josiah did. Unlike the swathe of migrant labourers whose principal concern was to find enough food and drink to carry them through the next day, Josiah's ambitions were informed by the religious and political principles preached by his Unitarian minister grandfather. He was taught to believe that there were resources within nature that could benefit those educated to identify and use them. This line of thought was an extension of the 'dissenting' emphasis on 'natural' rather than 'revealed' religion – that God's handiwork was best understood through rational enquiry rather than the high churchmen's ecclesiastical tradition that relied on biblical exegesis.

It was the fear of the subversion of that tradition of conformity that caused people like grandfather Stringer to be alienated from gentrified, conservative, Tory society. It was a national debate; it was what kept similarly minded men from earning degrees at England's ancient institutions or holding public office.[4] Critics decried the alchemical commitment of radical natural philosophers who searched for the philosopher's stone that would turn dirt into gold. Burslem potters such as Josiah, whose workshop tubs stank of chemicals and mixed, wet metal oxides, might not be attracting the same kind of attention as the natural philosophers of the Royal Society, but their experimental practices would prove to have a profound effect on life in the most disparate areas.

Even if in the 1750s Staffordshire was not seen as much of a threat to the establishment politically or religiously, there was certainly a reforming zeal amongst dissenters, and prominently so in Josiah's family.[5] They were taught to support the reforming Whig political party – those politicians who were suspicious about the residual political influence of the Church on the government – and the men accordingly cast their votes in the elections.[6] But there were other ways to effect change.

While Josiah's mother had once relied on her beliefs in the powers of nature and the rationalisation of disease for strength during her son's illness, others in the family looked to nature to provide a source of power to improve their family position. None of the Wedgwoods pursued their business with a desire to accumulate money for its own sake. They certainly took pride in their success, and they enjoyed the attention earned by their rising eminence, but they set an example of entrepreneurial paternalism that would be followed by others. As George Courtauld, a later Unitarian industrialist, would declare: 'the aim of business is to provide for the wants and comforts in the world'.[7] That aim could be accomplished – improvements in standards of living and moral worth achieved – through the pursuit of 'free enquiry', a belief that bound the thoughts of so many dissenting early industrialists.[8] From a business point of view, any effort to improve the kinds of wares produced by experimenting with nature's ingredients offered a chance to reinvest some wealth in the community.

Josiah's cousin, Long John, had elaborated on the importance of pursuing lines of experimental enquiry to improve the trade. In his 'Essay on Pottery', written in 1743, he explained that 'Potmaking chiefly depends on a knowledge of ye nature of Earth, Air, Fire, Water, Clays, Marls, & Stones, & some Minerals', all of the natural elements that had long been the focus of experimental natural philosophers, and that pottery should be no different. 'Earth,' he wrote, as it relates to the 'potters Art, is to be considered in the light of the Chymist's principles because it undergoes ye operation of fire', adding that a range of other raw materials such as 'Oyls, Salts, Sulpher & Water' also have material effects on potters' products.[9] Owing to the diversity of natural resources, it was essential that the potter become a researcher.

'Clays are of various sorts,' he continued, 'same partaking more of ye earthy nature, others more of ye Marley nature, the fatter & better ye Clay for fine pots ye nearer to a Marly nature for course pots of a poorer sandy or Earthy quality.' There were potentially endless varieties of colours and consistencies, 'some proper for one kind of ware & some for others, some are of a very soft tough nature others very brittle & hard so as to come near stone, some burn very white in the fire others not so white,' and the attempt to regulate these results required a record of analytical trials, 'which may be considered how great an improvement might be made in the potter if ye nature of all sorts of Marls were more fully known'. The potter's success rested on his knowledge of nature and his ability to manipulate it. 'In short,' Long John concluded, 'to try which proportion of each sort will work kindly together, Limestone, Alabaster &c ye natures of them may be tryd by several Experiments in mixing with others, Chalks, red Earth, & other Coloured Earth fullers may be considered.'

Long John's essay was a masterclass in the importance of natural philosophy, experimental enquiry, and record keeping in order for a potter to advance his craft. The success he and his brother enjoyed was proof of the merits of his formula. But Long John also made it clear that the Christian mission of practical service to society, aiming to benefit its economic as well as moral interests in equal measure, should be encouraged amongst the community. This trans-lated into direct support for the dissenting cause. In a will drafted in 1755, Long John devised that Josiah's brother, Thomas, would be responsible for 'one Clear Annuity or yearly rent Charge of forty Shillings a year so long as there shall remain a Congregation of

Dissenters and shall be preached to at the Dissenting Meeting House at Newcastle under Lyme in the said County of Stafford whereof I am now a Member'. The money was to be given in yearly or 'equal half yearly payments unto the Minister for the time being of the said Meeting house'. His gift would keep alive the congregation where Josiah's grandfather once preached and where the Reverend William Willets now preached.[10]

Reverend Willets thought very much along the same lines as Long John, promoting the view that social improvement and 'truths' about God's creation were revealed through experimental practices. He also practised what he preached, attempting to answer a call from the late 'illustrious Sir Isaac Newton' for an improved design of a telescope. Calling himself a man of 'good will to Philosophy', he wrote a letter to the Secretary of the Royal Society 'to lay before them a Project of his' for improved methods of grinding glass for better telescopic lenses.[11] It was a confident move for which he begged the Fellows of the Royal Society forgiveness for the 'Presumption of a Stranger' to write to them, and even when they replied stating their opinion of the shortcomings of his design, he was undeterred. He wrote back boldly asking if their objections 'are assured by experiment (to which all conjectures must yield)' and that he had faith that 'our ingenious mechanicks' could produce what he planned. He clearly lived by his adage: 'Invention without Experiment signifys very little.'[12]

This was a philosophy that twenty-four-year-old Josiah was beginning to learn very well, due in no small part to the example set by his successful cousins and by Reverend Willets himself (who in 1754 married Catherine, Josiah's sister). While Josiah thought of himself as standing 'on the lowest rung of the ladder' in his trade, he gained much support for his experiments from Willets, that 'truly good man', as Josiah called him.[13] Josiah's own 'service to Philosophy' was developing at the same time that the local community was beginning to witness widespread benefits of such work. Realising the 'great philosophic fact' that 'the sources of truth and knowledge are limitless', Josiah began to borrow books on chemistry from his brother-in-law Willets and copy passages into his note-book.[14] Josiah was beginning to see that there were many facets to business life that were far more stimulating that anything he had encountered at the Churchyard Works.

What Willets or cousin Long John had not written about was how to find the right partner with whom to develop a successful business. And whether it was because Harrison and Alders frowned upon the expense of Josiah's trials or because Josiah preferred the kind of activities he discovered were going on in other pot-works, he did not stay in their employment for very long. In fact, it was the experimentally minded potter on the other side of Stoke, Thomas Whieldon, that Josiah became most interested in. In 1754 Josiah went into partnership with the 'Tortoiseshell man', who for his part was interested in the 'secrets' that he knew Josiah alone possessed.[15]

Just a few minutes' walk along the road heading south from Stoke lay Whieldon's cluster of 'Pot ovens, houses, Buildings, Ware houses, Work houses, Throwing houses', and strips of mown lawn.[16] They were well organised and well managed – Whieldon had only been in his new works a few years, having outgrown his other pot-work which he still controlled, about a mile away across wild meadowland. His new premises outstripped all the previous pot-works Josiah had worked at, not only in terms of the number of buildings used for the business but in the number and quality of people who worked for Whieldon. He organised his workers into teams responsible for various tasks, loading bricks for the ovens, stacking wares, and clearing away heaps of oven waste and dumping the rejected, smashed up pieces into the 'shawd tips' where they were buried (thus preventing snoops from sneaking off with a fragment of the latest experimental innovation to copy, to say nothing of the skilled labourers in the workhouses).[17]

Whieldon was thirty-five years old when Josiah joined him, and he already had an impressive command of his business. In the estimation of one historian:

> He was shrewd enough to guard his trade secrets carefully, even going to the extent of burying shards to prevent them being imitated by competitors. He had excellent trade connections, especially with the Birmingham metal mounters and silver-smiths, whom he supplied with considerable quantities of snuff and other boxes, buttons, and vanity items which when mounted found a popular market.[18]

He was skilled at delegating tasks to people responsible for main-taining the premises, looking after the affairs of the second pottery, and supervising the daily work of his teams, 'from whom he exacted scrupulous obedience, respectful behaviour, and strict punctuality'.[19] It clearly paid off. Where he had leased his pot-works in the 1740s he now bought them outright, and he had just purchased Fenton Hall, closer to Stoke, which he rented out (either in part or the whole of the roomy home) as a £106 annual supplement to his income.[20] He lived with his wife, Sarah, about a mile away in Penkhull, but had also just bought land and was building a new grand house which he called 'The Grove', from where he could oversee the activities of the pot-works.[21]

The teams of workers at Whieldon's manufactory found their employer's rigour and discipline trying at times, amounting to a judgment that he was 'not a very likeable character'.[22] He needed to be stern and imposing with his standards – London aristocrats who were now receiving crates of his wares were discerning cus-tomers. Josiah admired the way Whieldon marshalled respect from his workers by paying them well on an incentive scale, with their pay proportionate to their productivity. Knowing the importance of having skilled firemen monitoring the kilns and skilled throwers working the wheel, he paid each of his own an above-market price of 8 shillings a week.[23] He was also generous with his apprentices, and, above all, he took care of their housing needs: he bought

'6 tenements or dwghouses' and 'two other Cottages or Tenements' within walking distance of the pot-works which he let to his workers; he was probably the first person ever to do this.[24]

Housing his workers was Whieldon's solution to a problem that had been a matter of national debate, and local concern, since that controversial Act of Toleration was passed fifty years earlier, in 1698. While the Act allowed Josiah's family to pursue their liberal, dissenting brand of faith that in turn encouraged innovation, it also created apathy amongst the provincial poor. Parochial clergy were alarmed to report in their 'Visitation returns' that church attendances had plummeted, and commentators charged that the Church had lost its authority over the moral and religious behaviour of parishioners.[25] Many believed that those boozing, brawling punters who wasted their last pennies in local alehouses were the result of a new breed of 'toleration'.

Some had argued that this was the result of a waning coherency of the dissenters, who had 'lost that good character for strictness in religion, which had gained them their credit' back in the days when Josiah's grandfather was preaching. Now, there was such ill-discipline in the community that 'from a delicacy of taste', gentlemen and rich patrons 'were ashamed to continue amongst so unpolish'd a people'. This damaging allegation about the conduct of free-thinkers was challenged by one outspoken dissenter, Philip Dodd-ridge. 'I think an honest mechanick, or day-labourer, who attends the Meeting from a religious principle . . . is a much more honour-able and generous creature than such a gentleman' as may turn his back on these people 'destitute of the ornaments of education, or splendid circumstances in life'.[26]

This was the sentiment shared by Josiah's cousin Long John, and an important rationale behind his patronage of the local dissenting congregations. 'I can imagine nothing more imprudent,' Doddridge declared, 'than a neglect of the populace (by which I mean all plain people of low education and vulgar taste, who are strangers to the refinements of learning and politeness)', and here he was describing those who *did* attend the congregation meetings. More work to improve the condition of an uneducated poor was clearly needed, but not through the abstract or 'haughty reasonings' of the high Church, but by 'speaking *plainly* to them' and showing them how useful, and morally valuable, their education can be.

It was bad for business that the 'day-labourers' were shunning education − religious education was the only kind they would ever receive − not only because the consequent lack of 'polish' alienated the dissenting community from their custom, the gentlemen and gentlewomen who were beginning to buy expensive pottery, but because the labourers made for difficult employees in manufactories that relied on their work. It was an economic concern expressed by the politician Sir Francis Brewster, who at the beginning of the century wrote of a looming national disaster. 'The neglect of the Poor seems the greatest mistake in our government,' he appealed, 'to have so many Thousand Poor, who might by their Labours Earn, and so eat our Provisions, and instead of sending them out, as export Manufactures.' The poor, he claimed, were a 'secret weapon' in the battle for improved trade.[27]

This gripped the attention of Sir Humphrey Mackworth, a conservative Member of Parliament, who devised a radical plan to instil discipline and harness untapped labour for commercial reward. The able-bodied poor should not merely earn their own maintenance, as the Elizabethan legislators of the Poor Law had suggested, but they should be put to work in state-owned 'parish manufactories' when they could turn a profit for the state. In 1704 he read out a bill to the House of Commons explaining that Overseers could 'raise a convenient stock' of raw materials 'for the Imploying or setting to Work the poor who are able to Work'. It would be lawful, he said, for the Overseers to take one or more house or houses, with their Appurtenances, for the more convenient imploying and setting the Poor to Work; and also one or more Ware house or Ware houses, for the safe keeping of such Goods and Merchandizes to be Manufactured as aforesaid, until the same can be sold to the advantage.

Children, boys and girls, would be given appropriate apprenticeships, supported from 'a perpetual fund or stock, for the binding out poor Children Apprentices to Trades and Manual Occupations, whereby much advantage may accrue to the Common-Wealth'.[28]

Not everyone thought this was a good idea. The ever politically-active Daniel Defoe attacked the idea of turning 'Parishes into Ware-houses'. Naturally, he admitted, 'Multitudes of People make Trade, Trade makes Wealth, Wealth builds Cities, Cities Enrich the Land round them, Land Enrich'd rises in Value, and the Value of Lands Enriches the Government,' but the proposed system was one of 'Oppression and Tyranny of the Poor', and this quashes the freedom of market forces, especially in determining the value of labour. 'Trade, like all Nature,' he concluded – in a spirit of rationalism that would chime in the ears of later industrialists – 'most obsequiously obeys the great Law of Cause and Consequence', and 'even all the greatest Articles of Trade follow, and as it were pay Homage to this seemingly Minute and Inconsiderable Thing: *The poor Man's Labour*.'[29]

Sir Mackworth's bill was not passed, but Defoe's optimism in the natural laws of trade was no more immediately successful. The 'crowd of clamouring, unimploy'd, unprovided for Poor People, who make the Nation uneasie, burthen the Rich, clog our Parishes, and make themselves worthy of Laws, and peculiar Management' were still there.

But just after Josiah began working with Whieldon, Admiral Edward Vernon – a national hero following his victory over the Spanish at Portobello, Panama, in 1740 – had successfully lobbied for the establishment of a local governing body to set up a 'House of Industry' in south Suffolk. Its mission was 'to administer proper comfort and assistance to the sick, infirm and aged, introduce sobriety and virtue among them, and in an especial manner to render their children useful to society by acquainting them with their duty towards God and man'. In 1758 Vernon lent £1000 (charging 3.5 per cent interest) to build the institution, and when it was finished, it was declared that now 'many children are rendered useful who otherwise would have figured nowhere but in a landscape of Gainsborough's, the spawn of gipsies, lying upon a sunny bank half naked, with their bundles of stolen wood by their sides'.[30]

Whieldon and Josiah already had a certain intimate knowledge of Admiral Vernon. They had been busy examining his body and face for blemishes in their slip-casts of him that were produced to celebrate the Portobello Victory. And while they were also familiar with his accomplishments in expanding the British Empire, it is less likely that they knew of the experimental House of Industry he spearheaded in Suffolk. Instead, entrepreneurial potters such as Josiah's cousins Long John and Thomas, or his new partner Whieldon, were discussing their own solutions to the problem of a flagging workforce that hindered the growth of their businesses. Whieldon's small-scale scheme to provide nearby housing for his workers was the most innovative in Staffordshire. Just as experiments with nature presented new kinds of wares for the trade, Whieldon's experiment with social organisation yielded a new form of loyalty and commitment from his workers; both forms of experimentation proved successful.

When 'Siah', as Whieldon called Josiah, joined the team, Whieldon spotted the traits of ambition and creativity that had already been a boon to his trade. He also realised that Josiah would complement others on the team well, some of whom had trained with Whieldon as apprentices. One of those former apprentices whose creative energies had earned Whieldon's respect was twenty-one-year-old Josiah Spode, now a journeyman whose weekly pay of 7 shillings and sixpence matched 'the highest wages then given' in the region for someone just coming out of an apprenticeship.[31] Trained to be just like his Master, Spode was 'a Man of Energy, Promptitude, Decision and great Aptitude for Business', traits that were beginning to shine through in Josiah.[32]

Compared to Josiah, Spode (three years his junior) came from an extremely poor family – his father was buried in a pauper's grave when Spode was six – but he and Josiah shared an ambition to prove to others that they were capable of producing the most admired and innovative pieces of pottery. Right now both young men wanted to impress Whieldon – this was natural for a maturing apprentice and a new partner who wanted to show rewards for the faith Whieldon had showed in them. But both Spode and Josiah struggled with a deeper desire to prove their worth to the man who was not only sedulously devoted to improving his business, but bestowed new levels of responsibility on them at a time in each of their lives when they needed a leg up to the next 'rung of the ladder', as Josiah would phrase it. As Whieldon passed through the workshops on routine supervision, Josiah was desperate that he would leave feeling proud of him. Josiah had never had this kind of paternal respect. Neither had Spode. They worked twice as hard because of it, making sure each piece of pottery they produced would gain the admiration of an authority they both lacked as children.

This suited Whieldon. From his perspective, he demanded consistency in the high standards he set for each piece of pottery and he needed new, creative ideas. He agreed a partnership with Josiah precisely because he needed fresh hands and an experimentally inclined mind to liven up his trade. He thought the kind of work Josiah was doing across town at Harrison and Alders' had shown real promise, and Josiah was grateful for the encouragement. 'I had already made an imitation of Agat which was esteem'd very beautiful, and a considerable improvement,' Josiah recalled, reflecting on his early days with Whieldon when he was finally able to pursue a wider range of possibilities for creating new kinds of pottery.[33]

'At this time, our Manufacture was in a very unimprov'd state, & the demand for it decreasing, so that the trade was universally complain'd of as being bad, & in a declining condition,' Josiah wrote;

> White stoneware was the staple Article of our Manufacture, but this had been made a long time, & the prices were now so low that the Potters could not afford to make it as good in any respect, or finish it so high as the ware would otherwise admit of, & with respect to elegance of form, that was a subject very little attended to.

Josiah then noted something that would have disturbed Whieldon personally, which was that even 'the next staple Article in the pottery' that had once gained Whieldon such a prominent reputation, 'an imitation of Tortis-shell', was also failing to sell. It was no mystery as to why: 'as there had been no improvement in this branch for several years past, the Country was grown very weary of it, & though the price was lower'd from time to time, in order to increase the sales, the expedient did not succeed & something new was wanted to give a little spirit to the business'.

Whieldon hoped that Josiah would provide that 'little spirit', and right away Josiah thought of improving colours and glazes. He recognised that 'the Country had been surfeited with variegated colours as a sort of blue & green had already been mixed with the Tortis-shell, & this induced me to try for self colour'd Glaze'. This was also something that Spode was interested in (eventually he would become as famous for perfecting blue underglaze printing on bone china for which Spode is still known today), but he and Josiah did not work together for very long.

Not long after Josiah joined Whieldon, Spode decided that it was time to start up his own business as an 'Earth Potter' (with some financial help from his new wife, Ellen, eight years his senior), but that there were other creative hands who could help. This included an eighteen-year-old modeller, or 'block-maker', named

William Greatbatch, whom Josiah and Whieldon paid around
2 shillings and sixpence a week to make and trim the moulds that
were used in slip-casting for the mass production of elaborately
shaped items, whether figurines or teapots (shaped like fruits or
anything else).[34] Greatbatch was a highly-skilled modeller and was
thought of as an 'ingenious young man' even to those who harboured
jealousy toward him. He was clearly someone for whom Josiah
had much respect, as their enduring professional relationship would
show.[35] The friendly acknowledgement of Greatbatch's talents
served the boy's confidence well, which was important, since he was
filling the place of one of the Wood brothers, who were widely
acknowledged to be the best modellers in the area. Aaron Wood
had left Whieldon's employment a few years before Josiah arrived,
and his brother Ralph was employed by Long John and cousin
Thomas. It was therefore a relief to Whieldon's competitive spirit
that Greatbatch turned out to be an adept replacement.

Greatbatch was challenged to come up with new shapes and
designs for the wares, and 'he seems to have given birth', thought
one of Josiah's relatives, later on, to the 'STILE ornament to the
art of modelling'. This struck Josiah as exactly the kind of approach
that could prove beneficial to the business, including 'new green
earthenware in forms of leaves, plates, molded fruits, agate snuff
boxes, &c'.[36]

Over the next five years the team at Josiah and Whieldon's manufactory was busy. Each week the ovens rendered another batch of
'redware', salt-glaze, 'solid-agate', and black ware, and a wide range
of particular items were packed into crates and shipped out. A large
strip of land out the back of the pottery became the graveyard for
imperfect and experimental pieces:

> 'solid-agate' teapot lids, a fragment of a massive redware punch
> pot with applied grape and vine-leaf decoration, green glazed
> wares, toys (both redware and tortoiseshell), press-moulded 'bis-
> cuit' plates with raised fruit decoration, cauliflower lids,
> creamwares ('biscuit' and glost) a black glazed teapot on tripod

feet, tortoiseshell plates, a 'solid-agate' mustard pot and a cauliflower cream-jug, two varieties of tureen-cover in the typical
green, yellow and brown colouring, much kiln-furniture (earthenware and stoneware) a grape 'block' mould, rabbit finials for
teapot lids, a tortoiseshell button, 'solid-agate' taws and a cube.[37]

It was frantic work, but over time Josiah noticed that Whieldon
was gradually relaxing his attitude toward the business. In 1758,
following the death of Sarah, his first wife, Whieldon remarried.
He was thirty-nine years old and The Grove, his elaborate home,
was becoming more attractive a draw than the pot-works which he
could see from his drawing-room window. His contentment struck
twenty-eight-year-old Josiah as odd. He feared that it would not
be long before 'the Country' would once again grow weary of their
latest moulded and salt-glazed productions, pineapple mugs and
cauliflower teapots. 'The age,' Samuel Johnson declared, 'is running
mad after innovation,' and without it business itself was doomed.[38]

This was no time to take a break. At Chelsea and Bow, the first
English porcelain figures were entering the market; in Liverpool,
manufacturers of English 'Delft' ware were producing 200 printed
wall tiles an hour using a newly invented process of transfer printing.
In 1757, the Dean of Gloucester, Josiah Tucker, observed with
bemusement while travelling around England how prominent
mechanical, labour-saving devices were becoming. 'Few countries
are equal, perhaps none excel, the English in the number of contriv-
ances of their Machines to abridge labour,' he wrote.

> Yet all these, curious as they may seem, are little more than
> Preparations or Introductions for further Operations. There-
> fore, when we still consider that at Birmingham, Wolverhamp-
> ton, Sheffield and other manufacturing Places, almost every
> Master Manufacturer hath a new Invention of his own, and is
> daily improving on those of others; we may aver with some
> confidence that those parts of England in which these things
> are seen exhibit a specimen of practical mechanics scarce to be
> paralleled in any part of the world.[39]

Gradually the force of these inventions which would become the tools of the industrial revolution disturbed this same commentator, who later bemoaned the unsettling, Republican tendencies of those behind 'practical mechanics' who were united, he would agree, by 'dissent, that religion of trade and manufacturers, the cradle of Philistinism'.[40]

But as Whieldon eased into a life of retired complacency, Josiah's efforts crystallised with confidence. He had just moved into some comfortable rooms at Fenton Hall, Whieldon's estate up the road nearer the centre of Stoke, and was spending his evenings jotting down lists of possibilities 'for the improvement of our manufacture of earthenware'. 'These considerations induced me to try for some more solid improvements as well in the Body as the Glazes, the Colours, and the Forms of that article of our manufacture,' Josiah wrote.[41] Glaze provided both a functional and decorative finish to the ware. All articles made from natural clay remained porous in their 'biscuit' (once-fired) state, and needed a coat of glaze to make them impervious for culinary or domestic uses. Simple glaze was added by dusting the piece with powdered lead ore contained in a parcel of coarse muslin; during the second firing of the piece, the powdered lead would then be gradually roasted to lead oxide, which, in its turn, melted and dissolved the outer skin of the clay vessel. But Josiah was interested in applying more complex glazes, which used a mixture of different chemicals – soda and boracic acid, for instance – to alter the colour and texture of the wares.

So he converted his kitchen into a small laboratory and turned to a fresh page in his notebook, 'Experiment Notebook I'. 'This suite of experiments was begun at Fenton Hall in the parish of Stoke-on-Trent,' he wrote. Page one: 'Feb 13 – 1759 – Experiment No. 1'. Josiah began mixing different proportions of chemicals and applying the resulting glaze to small sample pieces of plain biscuit earthenware (swatch-like samples), carefully taking notes on each one. He was systematic, altering slightly the quantity and kind of his ingredients. Each week he eagerly laid out each new piece from that oven's batch of his experiments, hoping to identify the one colour that surpassed anything else he had seen. It was a time-consuming process because it was impossible to tell what the applied glaze would look like until it emerged from the kiln, during which time the heat would have caused a chemical reaction altering the composition, and therefore appearance, of the glaze. Like all processes involved with firing, this was part of the hidden 'mystery' of the potter's craft. Josiah, however, was becoming a master at it.

'23 March 1759. Experiment No. 7.' Josiah was very excited. He jotted in the margin of his notebook, next to the recipe, 'A green glaze, to be laid upon Common white (or cream colour) Biscuit ware. This moment, this feeling, is what he was hoping for. 'This is the result of many experiments, which I made in order to introduce a new species of colour'd ware to be fired along with the Tortisshell and Agat ware in our common Gloss Ovens to be of an even self-colour, & laid upon the ware in the form of a colour'd glaze.'

The next day he went to the workshop and placed a cream-coloured earthenware tea canister in front of him, and began to apply his new brilliant translucent green glaze to it, which 'should completely cover the piece as evenly as possible', he noted to himself. He then turned it upside down and on an unwitting impulse inscribed 'JW' on its base.[42] That proud, if simple, act of labelling would prove to be one of the most important of his career.

When the piece came out of the oven, he sighed with euphoric relief. It was an elegant green glaze that surpassed all others that anyone had ever done, even Long John and cousin Thomas, whose family had long worked on their own version of green glaze, to little effect.

Josiah had made his first innovation and had produced a distinctive, unique look to the wares produced at their manufactory. Rather frustratingly, Whieldon seemed less than captivated by his partner's progress. Josiah wondered whether or not Whieldon's apathy would impact on their business. If he himself continued to work at improving it, perhaps it would not matter. But in that case, why split the profits?

Josiah felt more confident in his work than ever. He was now sure he could do better for himself if he had total control over the kinds of wares he wanted to produce. He tucked his experimental notebook into the saddle bag on his new horse Willy (his first big purchase, the horse would be with him for the next twenty years) and rode past the workers' cottages and headed up to Burslem.[43] He had a meeting with Long John and cousin Thomas scheduled and a proposition for them that he had rehearsed in his head over and over again. Once more, Josiah wanted to go at it alone.

SIX

Dues & Demands

Donning a new jacket and light brown wig (accounts and portraits reveal that he could be meticulous about his appearance), Josiah approached Long John and cousin Thomas's Big House without a hint of trepidation. He would have walked with long, strong strides had his right leg not continued to trouble him. Fourteen years after his sickness he was still bothered by numbness in his knee and fatigue in the muscles he used to compensate when walking, causing him sometimes to grimace unhappily.

Josiah was long past the point of being daunted by his cousins' elaborate home which fronted their extensive pot-works (they now had five large bottleneck ovens adjacent to the Red Lyon Inn turning out a steady range of wares every week), but he nonetheless admired the elegance of the new architectural design. In the 'house place', or the front hall, was a grand oak staircase with three turned balusters to each step and walls of fine panelling. As Josiah was taken through to a large reception room off the vestibule he was struck by the number of mirrors. Very few people could afford to have mirrors in every room. Josiah, like the people of 'quality' who owned so many mirrors, could not resist glancing into them as he passed by, showing him what he looked like in such elaborate surroundings.[1]

The timing of the visit could have made for an awkward atmosphere. Only recently, on a Friday morning, Long John's wife, Mary – whom the long-standing bachelor had married the previous summer, in 1758 – had given birth to a stillborn baby girl.[2] It would have been their first child. But fifty-four-year-old Long John was too fixed in his business ways to miss a meeting, and he greeted Josiah cordially, happy to see his young cousin, 'Thomas's boy', whom he knew to be doing so well for himself.

Josiah was delighted to have gained the respect of one of the two most highly regarded potters in Burslem, and he knew that the other, his cousin Thomas (who still spent all his time in the pot-works, while Long John took care of the accounts), felt the same about him. Josiah could not imagine cousin Thomas and Long John disagreeing about anything, being as close as they were. Even though Long John was married the two brothers still lived in the same house together, while Thomas had begun courting a cousin, hoping for his own marriage one day.

The last time Josiah had the chance to present himself to Long John had been three years earlier, at the funeral of his rich, eccentric aunt Katherine. Even though she stipulated in her will that 'there may not be above Sixty persons invited to my funeral', it turned out to be a lavish and crowded affair. Together with the Wedgwood clan who lived in and around Burslem had come Long John and cousin Thomas's brother Richard – the now wealthy cheese factor from Spen Green, twenty miles away. But it was not the arrival of his successful elder cousin that had distracted Josiah's eye, but that of Richard's daughter, Sarah. He had not seen her since her grand-father's funeral thirteen years earlier. She had deep, dark, radiant eyes, fine, fair hair and creamy white skin. As cousins they shared some physical traits – they both had thin lips and a curved nose, but 'Sally', as she preferred to be called, had high cheekbones and a narrow chin, unlike Josiah's round face and fleshy jowls. From that point on Josiah was besotted.

Even the poor had peered through the brown furze bushes to see Katherine's friends and family gathered around the churchyard, all dressed to her specification ('the women to have gloves and the men hatbands and gloves', she instructed).[3] The poor were amongst the many beneficiaries of her will – after the funeral £3 was to be divided up and distributed amongst them as part of a total of £1,000 in cash legacies she bequeathed to the town, servants, and family. Hers had been a life of 'genteel competence'. She had possessed an extraordinary ability to manage her extensive properties, bankroll charitable societies, and generally conduct herself in what were then considered gentlemen's skills, setting an example that far outperformed the landed aristocrat whose talents lay 'with gambling, duelling, sporting and sexual prowess'.[4]

Her death changed many people's lives, but no one more so than Josiah's brother Thomas. He inherited a substantial share of Aunt Katherine's property, nearly 200 acres in total, including the prestigious house at Overhouse estate and its pot-works, where he had laboured for the past twelve years. The estate which had passed out of Josiah's side of the family two generations ago, bypassing his father, was now once again in the hands of a Thomas Wedgwood. After almost two decades of struggling to keep his small trade going, Josiah's brother now had the privilege to call himself a gentleman.

Not that this brought instant wealth, for Thomas had fallen into massive debt. Josiah and his other brothers and sisters were still waiting for the £20 inheritance their father had wanted to leave them, and they would now have to wait even longer for it. But Katherine remembered everyone – every cousin and kinswoman from distant labouring bricklayers to the Big House brothers – in some way, in her will. Josiah's cousin, Sally, was left £5; Josiah himself was left £10. (Katherine's long-serving maid, and friend, Sarah Marsh, received £60.)

A few years on, Josiah had still not touched a penny of that £10, and he even managed to save a bit more since he and Whieldon had been doing respectable business. He needed Long John to know this, as they sat and talked in the Big House. It was a point he wanted to stress since it was testimony not only to his industry, but to his attitude toward financial responsibility. It may have appeared strange that he was approaching Long John rather than his gentleman brother Thomas about this matter. Josiah preferred not to talk about his relationship with Thomas, but it was no secret that he had been offered no helping hand in life from his brother, who seemed only concerned about his own son, Thomas, now an apprenticed potter.

Josiah came to the point. His goal was to start up a business by himself. He knew he had the talent and energy, and he saw what fruits could be had if he dedicated himself the way Whieldon had done when he was Josiah's age. He had been out of his apprentice-ship for ten years; he had gained experience working with two different manufacturers and had overseen the labour of people rang-ing from prominent modellers to children who were hired to 'tread the wheel' (Whieldon's throwing wheels were not self-powered, allowing Josiah to work them occasionally without using his sore leg).[5] He had also learned how to manage a sizeable pot-work, how to keep accounts, and where to look to employ suppliers of goods – he could order flint from the same supplier that Whieldon used, for instance.[6]

He also, of course, had the skill to help ensure his batches of pottery would not go to waste and cost him an ounce of profit – and he certainly would never be found whittling away hours at the alehouse. He knew that if the clay he moulded was too damp, it would immediately crack when fired. He could estimate what temperature his wares needed to be heated to for appropriate hard-ening, though he was not as precise as Long John, he humbly added. He knew how to judge the change of colours while firing and that the resultant hue depended on chemical compositions, and that if air is introduced to a clay containing iron oxide it will turn the wares red, but if air is excluded by heating it in glowing charcoal, it will turn the pieces blackish-grey. The way to go, he believed, was to present 'all the appearances of a most extensive Laboratory and the machinery of an Experimentalist'.[7] Above all, Josiah had proof of his endeavours. He had the new green-glazed ware to show his cousin, and promised that in his private notebook there were more promising trials he was pursuing.

What Josiah lacked was an opportunity to break out on his own. He did not have enough capital to buy his own pot-works and all the equipment it would need, and, with no bank to turn to (and even if there was, he would fall into that class of workers that even a century later was condemned to be 'manifestly ineligible' to borrow), he could only look to the family for support.[8] He had £10 to put toward his start, and the confidence that he could turn a profit and pay his debt.

Long John no doubt recognised something of himself in young Josiah, the youngest, without family privileges who resolutely persists where so many others would not bother. He also had to acknowledge that Josiah possessed something that few others in his family had – actual talent at the family craft. Long John had just the thing in mind for Josiah.

One of the properties Long John and cousin Thomas had bought as an investment over the years was a pot-work around the corner from the Big House, towards Burslem's centre square, on Shoe Lane. It was a modest size with two ovens (one for lead-glazed wares, the other for 'red wares'); it had well-built, tile-covered worksheds and rooms, and a small ivy-clad dwelling cottage facing the road. This, Long John proposed, was Josiah's to rent, if he wished.

Long John's decision to offer the 'Ivy House Works' to Josiah for rent demonstrated a considerable confidence in his young cousin, especially since this was not long after the spectacular failure of their brother-in-law's attempt to succeed in the trade.

Long John and cousin Thomas's older sister Sara had fallen in love with the yeoman son of a local baker named Jonah Malkin.[9] They married in 1740, just as her brothers were first branching out to operate a pot-work independent of their father, and just as Jonah was looking to enter a new trade. He did not have much money to begin with, he had been trying to raise money for at least a year, borrowing up to £5 from local Burslem potters who accepted on trust his IOUs. This was not initially a concern to Sara's family – after all, they had run their history of risks in order to settle themselves in the trade. But after his marriage to Sara, Jonah raised the stakes, attempting to secure enough capital to establish his own pot-work and entering into a series of bonds for larger amounts – £40, £50, even £60 plus interest – with a number of people, including local potters. These bonds, which were a common way to raise capital for small-scale business endeavours, soon exceeded the debts through mortgages and bonds that Josiah's brother needed to enter to make ends meet during the same period. Having built up this base on debt, Jonah proved to be an inept potter. Soon he was working with the hope simply of paying off the interest on his loans, for which he turned to his new family for support. 'His father lent him £40, his wife £40, the Reverend Jonah Malkin of Wirksworth £25, his sister Margaret £40, his mother's annuity of £70 came his way, his brother-in-law Richard Wedgwood loaned him £111, and John Wedgwood £32.'[10] It was a staggering amount, accumulated by hiding existing debts, sliding new loans toward old ones, and rapidly, but humbly, asking for help. He was never going to recover and his efforts to manage his debts soon surpassed any attempt to turn a profit in his small pottery.

In 1749, just at the time when his brothers-in-law Long John and Thomas were drawing up plans to build the Big House, Jonah and Sara were forced to sell their household effects in a desperate attempt to mollify their creditors. When the sale was over, they managed to raise a paltry £36, not enough to cover but one of the bonds. Next went the farming stock. On his way back from paying off one debt with the money raised he had a bill worth £13 in change. It went straight to Long John, who scribbled on the back of it 'J.W. has taken to his Account'.[11]

That was four days before Christmas. By 24 January a warrant was issued for Jonah's arrest, including a writ declaring that he had gone into hiding. After £4 of Crown expenses, including a 10 shilling fee for the 'Bailiffs for endeavour to arrest Defendant' and a 16 shilling journey to the Newcastle gaol, Jonah was behind bars.

Long John agreed to offer what assistance he could because he wanted to support his sister. He instruct his Newcastle-under-Lyme attorney Samuel Boyer to meet with Jonah to determine the depth of the debt. 'It is more money considerably than I imagin'd it would amount to,' Boyer delicately wrote to Long John a month later.[12] The list of creditors was more than probably anyone could have imagined. Boyer tried his best to represent Jonah in a kind light, since 'I really believe,' he said to Long John, 'he has taken the time to think of every body': but his findings revealed that Jonah owed upwards of £1,000, with £80 in growing interest alone. A plea in *Aris's Birmingham Gazette*, showed the gravity of the situation:

> April 8, 1751. To be sold. A messuage with a set of potworks at the Hammill near Burslem, in the County of Stafford, late in the possession of Jonah Malkin, and also several fields of pasture land and meadow ground thereto belonging, being freehold, wherein are five several mines of coals and a great quantity of clay for the potters use. For further particulars enquire of the said Jonah Malkin at Burslem aforesaid or of Mr Boyer at Newcastle-under-Line, Staffordshire.

The failed business was to be sold off, along with the remaining pieces of land he owned on the eastern slope of Burslem, with 'ALL and Singular my Goods Cattle, Chattells, and personall Estate whatsoever or of what nature or kind Soever the same does consist (the Wearing Apparrell of myself & wife only excepted and foreprized)'.

Indeed, a few months later all they had left were the clothes on their backs. On the eve of Jonah being sent off to the debtors prison, Long John opened a letter from Boyer advising that the sale of the buildings and lands had been unsuccessful, and Long John once again stepped in. He offered £950 cash 'for his Estate at the Hammell with everything within & without Doors whatsoever with all Mines' with which Jonah was required 'to Pay all Dues & Demands'. The price was not generous: the estates could have secured a higher price under less trying circumstances and Jonah was still left with residual debt and borrowed again from his sister. Long John did not want or need the land he bought from Jonah (part of which Jonah had originally bought with Sara's dowry) so he allowed the existing tenant to remain. Jonah was put to work on the land, ploughing Long John's fields on a labourer's wages.

Jonah's sad fate was a sharp reminder of the perils of venturing into business. But Josiah was eager to take the risk. When he told Whieldon that he was ready to move on, excited about the new glaze he developed, he allegedly declared: 'I saw the field was spacious, and the soil so good, as to promise an ample recompense to any who should labour diligently in its cultivation.'[13] With Jonah's recent débâcle a warning, Josiah now realised how difficult it might be to bring one's ambitions to fruition.

SEVEN

'A Good White Glaze!'

T HE IVY HOUSE was not especially large, but Josiah rattled around in it as if it were a mansion. Ivy on the front of the century-old house framed five sets of thin, iron mullioned windows – two on the ground floor, next to the wooden front door, and three upstairs. The house had two small fireplaces, one each side of the house and a steep wooden staircase through the middle which acted as a partition between the two living rooms downstairs and the two chambers above.

Out the back across a small, hard earth courtyard were the split-level workshops and ovens, with their rounded, hollow bases and tall brick necks, on either side. The workshops too were small, but efficiently designed – a miniature of what Josiah had found at Whieldon's, and nothing at all like the Churchyard Works. It was busier and noisier than any place Josiah had previously worked, being in the centre of a town: sounds of grunting sows gave way to masters' shouts and smashing shards. His yard was contiguous with his neighbours': the potter Ralph Wood behind him, the Turk's Head alehouse to the left, and Ruffley's, another pot-works to the right.[1]

Ivy House itself was separated from Shoe Lane by a small front garden enclosed by a waist-high brick wall that kept the convoy of horses and carts at bay by little more than two paces. The road had become much busier than when Josiah last lived in Burslem, partly due to the creeping growth in population but also to the works in the town centre where a market square was being constructed. The maypole had been taken down and the hazardous pot-holes were finally being filled in after years of people digging for clay. Work had also started on building Burslem's first town hall, next to which an open-air meat and vegetable market was soon to be held every Monday and Saturday.[2]

Long John had made clear to Josiah that theirs was a formal business arrangement and that he was not prepared to grant his cousin any special favours. Consequently the Ivy House Works did not come cheap: the annual rent for the house and workhouses was set at £15, beginning May Day 1759. In addition, Josiah had to purchase the wheel from his cousins at £1 8s and other materials for just under another £1, making his first year's bill £17 6s.[3] Josiah was to pay quarterly, and the only concession he eventually received from his cousins was a £2 reduction after he argued that some of the workhouses needed building work.

Josiah had other expenses of course, the largest being the wages of his journeyman whom he had just employed, another cousin named Thomas Wedgwood (the sixth son of uncle Aaron). He was four years younger than Josiah, and, after serving his apprenticeship, had worked as a journeyman at a manufacturer's in Worcester where he learned how to make a form of porcelain recently pioneered by his master. For a 'potter ambitious to improve and refine creamware', as Josiah certainly was, his new employee would prove most useful.[4] So much so, in fact, that Josiah came to dub him 'Useful Tom', a sobriquet that stuck.

However, Useful Tom came at a high price, £22 a year, above the average for a skilled artisan, but akin to the respectable wages Whieldon had paid his prized employee, Spode. Amongst the lessons Josiah learned from Whieldon was that good labour was worth paying for; he recognised too that by offering rewards he could earn the respect of his more highly trained workers. For the less skilled – the many who were hired to do routine, manual tasks – the way forward was less clear, and Josiah continued to lament the problem of undisciplined labour. Whieldon's scheme of housing his workers close to the manufactory was extraordinary, and far beyond Josiah's means, at least at the moment. For now, he needed to suffer the 'idle, slovenly, irregular habits' of the itinerant men who still needed to be 'enlightened', whose souls were sought by the men of religion.[5]

In the eyes of some, Burslem was in the most desperate need of God's word. A year after Josiah settled in at the Ivy House Works, the town's new market square received a visit by the Methodist John Wesley.

For some twenty years Wesley had been on his mission to proselytise the Western world, particularly America and England, in Methodism, his new brand of dissenting belief. He travelled thousands of miles every year, making his way from village to village, preaching in the open air to curious congregations about how important it was for their souls to feel and acknowledge their sins, to see and love God every moment, and to pray, rejoice, and give thanks evermore. In early March 1760 Wesley came to Burslem.

Upon arriving in what he described as 'a scattered town on the top of a hill, inhabited almost entirely by potters', Wesley found a central spot, put down his soap box and began preaching to 'a multitude'.[6] 'Deep attention sat on every face, though as yet accompanied with deep ignorance', he recorded in his journal. 'But if the heart be toward God, He will, in due time, enlighten the understanding.'

He soon had an inkling that it was going to take some considerable time. The next evening, Sunday, he returned to his spot at five o'clock, hoping for a good gathering on the day of rest. As he preached, there were disturbances from the back, 'five or six were laughing and talking till I had near done', at which point one of the lads lobbed a clod of clay 'which struck me on the side of the head', but he managed to maintain his composure.

It was not the first time Wesley had been abused by the first

thing a local 'prophet of evil' (one of Wesley's more forgiving charac-
terisations) could find to hurl at him. Farmers had been known to
throw turnips at him, and his brother Charles, who worked in
tandem with John, had his own notable experiences when visiting
the area. Some years earlier when he was preaching in south Staffordshire, he described how the street became 'full of fierce Ephesian
beasts (the principal men setting them on), who roared and shouted,
and threw stones incessantly'. Breathlessly concluding his sermon
and hoping he had weathered the worst of the brutality, 'a stream
of ruffians was suffered to beat me down from the steps, I rose,
and having given the blessing, was beat down again, and so a third
time'.[7]

This was not the normal reception townsfolk gave to visiting
preachers. But Wesley's Methodism had triggered great scepticism
among the majority, people believing that he was trying to dupe
them into giving up money under threat that their souls would be
condemned to hell. Only recently angry crowds in a nearby town
proclaimed that they had identified a devious pattern to the Wesley
brothers' visits. First Charles Wesley arrived and, 'preaching publicly
in the streets and fields', announced that he was going to 'reform
the colliers, and other illiterate and ignorant Persons', and inti-
mations were given that 'a Charity School was designed to be built
and endow'd' to teach children Christian principles at no cost to
the community, and as he left Charles gave a gift of a guinea to
the poor for bread.[8] His brother John soon followed, proposing a
subscription among 200 people for implementing the plan of their
charity school – requiring a small donation per head, whatever
they could afford. Finally a third preacher arrived, a disciple of the
Wesleys, who preached about the shortcomings of other faiths,
referring to the Church of England clergy as 'dumb Dogs' who,
when offering Holy Orders, 'pretended to be moved by the Holy
Ghost, but was all a mere farce', and then he talked of 'eternal
damnation' and accused any who rejected his word 'of being enemies
of his Majesty'.

The increasing number of men who preferred to attend the ale-house and indulge in rituals that required singing pub songs rather than hymns were not without opinions and prejudices. They were not prepared to stand around and tolerate threats from travelling preachers peddling new brands of faith. From then on whenever the Wesleys came near the town, they were attacked by people 'flinging Stones and Dirt at them', and smashing the windows of anyone who put up the preachers for the night. By the time John Wesley rode into Burslem for his first visit, his reputation had preceded him, and he found himself assaulted by 'the beasts of the people' and praying that God, who held 'the bridle from above', would restrain them. Wesley was ultimately forced to concede defeat, and that March 1760, fifty-seven-year-old Wesley rode off 'over the mountains, through furious wind and rain, which was ready to overthrow both man and beast', leaving his work to be finished at another time.

The reactions of a certain element in the town to the preacher's visit epitomised the problem Josiah and other employers faced: unruly men who dismissed authority and laughed while doing so.

Josiah did not personally care for Wesley's form of Protestantism: he thought the preacher's gospel about original sin and the super-natural – Wesley's belief in witchcraft and Satan – was simply ludicrous, but he did admire the old man's perseverance. Despite the disruption of clods of clay being bounced off his forehead, Wesley managed to get through to at least a few people each visit, and it was clear that his brand of religion was gaining a substantial following throughout the country. He made sure his visits were not ephemeral. He left behind small gifts, free pamphlets of his prayers, and prodigiously produced cheap abridgements of classics such as *Paradise Lost*, 'Milton for the masses', as well as grammar books and the immensely popular *Primitive Physick* (1747), a self-help *materia medica* for the poor.[9] Despite the preacher's wayward beliefs, some of his writings would have appealed to Josiah's own taste for 'useful' literature, such as the tract Wesley had just finished writing: 'Electricity made plain and useful', which was a summary of Benjamin Franklin's achievements.[10]

Wesley had discovered that the marketplace was an excellent medium to spread his word. He was a travelling salesman – and his advertising ploys did not escape Josiah's notice.

Josiah's strategy to 'convert' his workers into a more disciplined life involved working as closely as possible with them. Each morning he summoned his employees to work by blowing a horn, as did most other Master Potters, just as the postman did to announce his arrival in the town square. This sometimes led to confusion, or so it was claimed, since the workers did not know who was calling whom, something that Josiah would later improve on. Josiah would sit on the workbenches beside his men, demonstrating exactly what he required them to do, forming models of items he wanted them to imitate. He looked after all the apparatus in his workshops, the 'lathes, whirlers, punches, gravers, models, moulds, drying-pans', and other tools, sharing the jobs of working the ones that required the experienced 'knack' with Useful Tom.[11] At night in the kitchen of the Ivy House, Josiah returned to his chemicals, potions, dyes and swatches, continuing to record hundreds upon hundreds of experiments in his treasured leather notebook.

During the day Josiah wasted no time getting to work on producing the tried and tested and easily marketable products such as the familiar agate ware, knife hafts and handles for other sorts of utensils, tiles, tortoiseshell and marble plates finished in a lead glaze – the sort of items he had produced with Whieldon. He also made the stock-in-trade 'greengrocery' wares, the teapots and accoutrements shaped like cabbages, cauliflowers, melons and vegetables, but covered with his new trademark 'grass green' glaze.[12] It was easy to manufacture such items since they allowed a small degree of error in their production – blemishes and 'irregularities' did not matter so much when they were intended to look like oddly-shaped fruit and vegetables. And true to his own expectations he had just developed another unique glaze, this time a yellow-orange one. He thought it would be perfect for a new moulded pineapple-shaped teapot, incorporating 'grass green' leaves that sprouted from the base of the item.[13] The West Indian fruit was popular with the rich, who found the matching teapot amusing.

His unique glazes were what, at this time, distinguished Josiah's wares from anything else in the marketplace. There was nothing distinctively 'Josiah Wedgwood' about the forms of the pieces themselves. In fact, the decorative bodies of the teapots, canisters, sauce bowls, and the like that were produced by pouring slip into a mould were identical to that which was being issued from Whieldon's and many others' factories. In this respect, Josiah still 'had other difficulties to encounter arising from the novelty of his works', as a relative of his explained:

> Workmanship of the pottery was at this period in a very low state as to its style – The whole country and those in the habit of forming common vessels made in white stone ware enjoyed only three professed modellers – one of these was brought up under Mr Whieldon [during Josiah's] partnership.[14]

The gifted modeller was William Greatbatch, whom Josiah came to know so well while working with Whieldon, and who exclusively designed and crafted the models for Whieldon. It was necessary for Josiah to strike an agreement with his old partner to buy plain 'biscuit ware only – for the new work in Burslem where it was sent to be coloured and glazed'.[15]

This helped Josiah enormously since hiring an artist or modeller – especially with the talent of Greatbatch, or any of the Wood brothers – was expensive and the cost of casting master moulds or an original block-cutting was, for Josiah's budget, prohibitive.[16] Where Josiah was able to bring subtle distinction to his wares was in their hand-finishing: Josiah, like most skilled craftsmen, had a particular touch when forming the knob on a lid, or of rolling on a handle, or shaping the spout or feet of an item.

Other local potters had begun to engage in collateral trade with Josiah, including Long John and cousin Thomas, as well as others around Burslem, such as the Meir family, potters from Lane Delph, where Josiah had regular dealings with Sarah Muir, the daughter of the Master Potter who handled the accounts (and in 1762 became proprietor of the pottery) and haggled over prices with Josiah for the sale of biscuit wares which he would glaze.[17] The arrangement worked well for all. Whieldon for one was happy to supply his young protégé with plain wares to help him along in business, and Greatbatch was looking to build a portfolio of regular accounts since, partly urged on by Josiah's example, he was thinking of going into business by himself. He was even looking at a property to rent in Lower Lane, off the newly improved road leading in to Stoke. Josiah's business relationship with Greatbatch was getting closer. It appears that Greatbatch had travelled down to London where he was in part acting as Josiah's agent, 'dealing with customers, orders, and shipments of pottery, such as that left at the Cross Keys', a coaching inn near the major trading centre of Cheapside, where the Elers brothers had once sold their pottery.[18]

There were two main cities on Josiah's mind as he worked his long days at the Ivy House Works producing all the wares he could. One was London, where his products were distributed to local customers and markets, the other was Liverpool, from where much of his merchandise was exported. Liverpool was also where 'new sorts of decorations' were applied to some of Josiah's wares. This involved a process of transfer printing developed by John Sadler in 1756, and specialised by the Liverpool printing firm Sadler & Green. It involved applying a special metallic-oxide ink to an image engraved on a copper plate which was transferred to paper and then, while the pigment was still wet, pressed onto the ware, transferring the refined picture. It was an immediate triumph. Only weeks after Sadler had devised the technique (independently of an Irish engraver named John Brooks, a little earlier), he and his partner signed a sworn affidavit for a patent application stating that, 'without the aid or assistance' of anyone they did, 'within the space of six hours . . . print upwards of twelve hundred earthenware tiles of different patterns', which were 'more in number and better and neater, than one hundred skilled pot painters could have painted'.[19] It was this feat that had so impressed commentators on England's 'mechanical' ingenuity. In ways similar to modelling and block moulding, it was simply cheaper at this stage to send out the wares and have them decorated than to commission one's own copperplate engravings.

But printing could not be done on just any piece of pottery – the surface of typical salt-glazed stonewares was too dimpled for the detail of the printed picture. Happily for Josiah, his diligence and perseverance in his experimental trials had again served him well.

He had recorded over 400 experiments, filling 169 pages of his notebook, and was in hot pursuit of a pristine white glaze which would substantially improve cream-coloured earthenware, which for all manufacturers still tended towards a dirty-cream or yellowish tinge. Back at experiment number 68, he had stumbled upon a recipe that stirred him, the proportions of ingredients scribbled as: 'India porcelain 5 ½ / 8, London crown glass 7/7, Flint glass 16/6. White enamel 4/67, and White lead 32 1/8/3'.[20] But 338 experiments later, writing much more cryptically in a code that only he knew how to read, he was on the verge of victory. He recorded the formulae in the left column, quantities above coded ingredients, and the results of the trials:[21]

Expt No:

406 *1/16 = 4 grs.*

362 *3*

This seems to separate, part is run thin like water, and is a good colour.

407 *1/16 = 4 grs.*

362 *4*

Much the same but less the watery part.

408 *1/16 = 4 grs.*

362 *5*

Much the same but less still of the exuded watery part.

409 *1/16 = 4 grs.*

362 *26*

Rather better.

410 *1/16 = 4 grs.*

Fired *362–4* –

Worse colour but not separated like the above Nos, is more of an uniform Glass but not clear, is what we call *Scummy* on the surface.

411 *1/16 = 4 grs.*

336 *3*

A GOOD Wt. GLAZE!

The best of all these trials — uniform — Transparent and nearly colourless.

The 'good white glaze' Josiah was thrilled to document produced a uniformly smooth, sugary, ivory cream-coloured ware, unrivalled in its consistency and perfect for transfer printing. By the end of 1761, he was ready to send batches of his new creamware to Sadler & Green in Liverpool for decorating – '5 doz 18*s* & 24*s* Teapots at £1.5.0' and the final firing.[22]

Josiah's timing was perfect. The detailed pictures and words trans-ferred onto wares were creating a sensation amongst consumers. Pictures of 'Pipe and Punch Parties' were printed on punch bowls, fashionably-clad women were depicted sipping tea on teapots and canisters. Popular satirical prints were reprinted onto mugs. Josiah had Sadler reproduce onto a mug 'The Triple Plea', a sardonic print from 1725 satirising the three professions, with verse that comple-mented Josiah's dry sense of humour:

> Law, Physick, and Divinity;
> Contend which shall superior be,
> The Lawyer pleads He is your Friend,
> And will your Rights and Cause defend,
> The Doctor swears deny't who will,
> That Life and Health are in his Pill,
> The grave Divine with Look demure,
> To Patients will Heaven assure.
> But mark these Friends of ours & see,
> Where ends their great Civility,
> Without a Fee, the Lawyers Dumb;
> Without a Fee the Doctor – Mum;
> His Rev'rence says without his Dues,
> You must the joys of Heaven lose,
> Then be advis'd: In none confide,
> But take sound Reason for your Guide.[23]

There was no end to possibilities of what one could do with printing on pottery. Now the piece was virtually incidental to the message or illustration on it, a strange but nonetheless exciting new way to think about his wares. Josiah contemplated what the public were interested in. They liked humour, but that had been done. They liked rustic scenes from literature – that too was now available on items such as punch bowls. It had become very fashionable to own depictions of famous people, of national heroes, that was why figurines sold so well. 'Plates & Drawings! I believe you have not considered this', suggested Sadler.[24] People on plates; the idea was appealing: much simpler to make than cast figurines.

Following the coronation of George III in 1760, Britain and the Colonies were being acquainted with their new king through pictures of him in popular engravings and portraits, since few subjects would ever get the chance to see or hear their king (and if they had, few would probably have understood his heavy German accent). These depictions were often derisory, portraying the monarch as 'a blind simpleton'. 'The bulk of the people in every city, town, and village,' noted a somewhat bemused John Wesley, 'heartily despise his Majesty, and hate him with a perfect hatred.'[25]

Whilst Josiah did not hate the new monarch, his Whiggish and dissenting views led him to be sceptical about the monarchy generally. Indeed he felt similarly about most of the aristocracy: he refused to manufacture 'armorial ware', arguing that such personalised trinkets were difficult to work with ('very bad things for us to meddle with'; and Crests were 'as useless', he said, 'as Crest wearers are'.[26] The new king did not quite fit the bill as 'national hero', but there were plenty of other candidates, people whom Josiah genuinely admired or had an interest in – certain politicians and admirals for example. And by 1761 such individuals seemed even more relevant to Josiah's future.

Since 1756 Britain had been embroiled in a complex war which escalated from competing French and British interests in North America and the 'newly discovered' West Indies. In part it revolved around British westward expansion on the North American continent. With a population thirty-three times the size of the French's, Colonial governors felt it was time to expand over the Appalachians, which infringed on vast French territories starting in the Ohio valley. But the conflict grew into an international affair, and the fighting soon spread to the West Indies, India, and Europe. What became known as the Seven Years War in part concerned who would control vast territories of land, but it was also crucially about who controlled thriving trade routes.

London merchants had for some years been anxious about developments in the New World. In 1742, just before the last war with France, they had petitioned Parliament for information about the number of ships deployed to protect and escort merchant convoys conducting trade with the New World. The Admiralty's reply was calm:

> The trade of the West Indies has been so well protected by Vice Admiral Vernon, and the ships stationed at the islands, that we hear of no losses in those parts; and even in North America, where it is alleged that ships have been lately taken, the same is not imputed in the petition to a want of cruisers but of proper care in some of your Majesty's commanders stationed in those parts.[27]

Admiral Vernon not only captured territories, but secured trade routes – becoming a hero for the merchants of England. Almost twenty years after Vernon's early triumphs, Josiah still monitored the latest developments in this story, since his wares were amongst the nation's stock involved in West Indies and North American trade.

While working at the Ivy House Works Josiah's mind was often filled with images of the New World: pineapples, the sun sparkling off the sea, large ships sailing in to ports and then leaving laden with exotic goods. Many people thought of the New World in this way, especially British America and the West Indies, and many English people found these images refreshing since they reminded them of the lucrative trade and potential riches that were to be had. America was already a land of opportunity. As the growing population of colonials created new wealth, more luxuries were being demanded from the manufacturers in the mother country.

The colonial gentry did not want their remoteness to deny them the amenities enjoyed by their European kin, and they sought the same goods for themselves. Pre-revolutionary Americans, it was said, 'were more English than they had been in the past since the first years of the Colonies'.[28] The new gentility required the amenities of polite life, as the young Benjamin Franklin discovered one morning when his wife presented his breakfast without the usual 'two penny earthen porringer with a pewter spoon'. Instead, 'I found it in a china bowl, with a spoon of silver. They had been bought without my knowledge by my wife, and had cost her the enormous sum of twenty-three shillings, for which she had no other excuse or apology to make but that she thought *her* husband deserved a silver spoon and china bowl as well as any of his neighbours.' Over the next ten years, 'as our wealth increased', so too did the appearance of improved china and pottery.[29]

The young entrepreneur Franklin was not alone in indulging in what some colonials thought were improvident expenditures. The appetite of colonial Americans for such wares was becoming insatiable. 'Our importation of dry goods from England is so vastly great,' commented one New York journalist, 'that we are obliged to betake ourselves to all possible arts to make remittances to the British merchants.'

Josiah's first years at the Ivy House Works coincided with America's first consumer revolution. Josiah knew he had to get as many crates as possible to Liverpool and on to fast ships bound for the New World if he was to take full advantage of the boom (much of Josiah's produce at this time crossed the Atlantic on a vessel owned by the Liverpool trader, William Reid, appropriately named the *Racehorse*). Once the crates from the English manufacturers had been unloaded, the vessels would be restocked with 'cotton from St Thomas's and Surinam; lime-juice and Nicaragua wood from Curacoa; and logwood from the bay' – all part of the transatlantic trade, 'and yet', the journalist exclaimed, the cost of imports 'drains us of all the silver and gold we can collect'.[30]

Thankfully for Josiah, the colonials' new Englishness embraced a love of tea and the recent fashion for eating off fine 'china'

(English-manufactured pottery). 'Our people, both in town and country,' continued the New York journalist, 'are shamefully gone into the habit of tea-drinking', and where tea drinking abounded, so did accoutrements. So much so that a gentleman travelling through the American countryside reported that even in a simple cottage, a family had stocked up with 'superfluous things which showed an inclination to finery', including pewter spoons, a mirror, and 'a set of stone tea dishes, and a tea pot'.[31] In the New World, Puritan entrepreneurs and independent farmers alike 'sought English manufactured goods and in other ways acted as agents of capitalism', especially as their opportunities to manufacture their own wares were not yet available.[32] Not until after the Revolution would potters in America be able to manufacture teapots and cups capable of holding such hot liquid, let alone match the aesthetic quality pioneered in Josiah's home town, not least by him.[33] In the years leading up to the Revolution, 'colonists set their tables with steadily finer dinnerware. Among the poor, pottery replaced handmade wooden plates. Among the better-off colonists, crude pottery was replaced by finer pottery, much of which was imported.'[34]

During the 1760s, the colonial American and West Indies market for English goods exploded. 'Already,' observed one European traveller in the early 1750s, 'it is really possible to obtain all the things one can get in Europe in Pennsylvania, since so many merchant ships arrive there every year.'[35] As each wave of merchant ships arrived, a flurry of advertisements appeared in the local press advertising what the captivated and eager consumers could expect next. As early as 1754 the *Boston Gazette* was advertising 'new fashioned Turtle-shell tereens', 'Tortoise Shell Teapots' and other coloured glazed wares that Wedgwood had been busy making since his days with Whieldon.[36] Following this, the *Boston News Letter* excitedly announced shipments of the 'new Cream colour printed, printed & gilt, & plain enamelled, double & single Rose' wares, but still advertised 'Agate, Tortoise, Mellon, Colly flower, and Pine-apple wares'.[37]

The year Josiah set up business for himself, all eyes were on the English Secretary of State, William Pitt the elder, who was working with the largest budget hitherto approved by Parliament – £13 million for the year – to fund the latest war with France over new territories.[38] Josiah, 'no politician' as he acerbically confessed, had faith in him. And while the London literati debated the finer points of Pitt's character (an 'absolute master' of the House, thought Horace Walpole), Josiah worked to complete another order bound for British America on the *Racehorse*. This time, he decided to travel with his goods, as far as Liverpool, to see the great port for himself.

EIGHT

By the Docks

B Y THE EIGHTEENTH CENTURY Liverpool had established
itself as the main port for America and a thriving trade centre,
having grown steadily throughout the past hundred years. It was
the most convenient port for the Lancashire textile industry and
attracted the greatest number of ships from the New World, with
a surplus of ships ready to return to America offering freight
transport at competitive rates.[1]

Josiah was impressed by the town, one of the 'cleanest and best-
built', according to the indefatigable traveller John Wesley. Josiah
was taken with its size, its damp, salty smell, and even the colour
of its bricks which he was unused to. He thoroughly enjoyed indulging in the local cuisine, particularly the oysters, not least since 'for
10 pence, a man dines elegantly at an ordinary consisting of a dozen
dishes', and even sipped the extraordinary 'West Indies rum punch'
– a local specialty.[2] It was certainly very different from what he
humbly referred to as the 'rugged Pot-making spot of earth', otherwise known as Burslem.

Liverpool housed about 30,000 people, and was growing fast:
thousands of large, well-built stone and brick houses lined a grid
of flat, cobblestone streets:

> The dwelling house was frequently elevated with the first
> storey elevated considerably above the level of the street, with
> high flights of steps, in order to obtain large vaults for the
> storage of merchandise. In the back part of the house there

were often offices under the same roof, and a warehouse erected in the yard.[3]

As trade developed with the Americas and the West Indies, the city became the second most important port in Britain. Merchandise – whether Cheshire salt, Lancashire coal and textiles, Birmingham metal goods, or Staffordshire pottery, passed out of the port, while sugar, spices, molasses and plantain crops were brought in. New docks were built: the 'Old Dock' at the beginning of the century and recently Salthouse Dock (1753), which together with the well-used dry dock and the new pier pushed the shipbuilding and repair businesses industry further up river.[4]

All the shipping activity, the stacking of crates and general quay-side bustle, filled Josiah with immense excitement about the future. He visited the artists at Sadler & Green whom he had contracted to work on his wares, and personally checked the quality of the transfer-printed pieces as they came out after the final firing before being crated up for despatch to America. He also took the opportunity to check that the company was not breaking its agreement to print images exclusively on his new 'cream ware'. It was essential that work associates remained loyal in such a competitive market, since any new look could give a competitor a slight edge. 'You may rest assured,' Sadler told Josiah, 'that we never printed a Piece for any Person but yourself.'[5]

'I have had a good deal of talk with Mr Sadler,' Josiah later wrote, and as always 'find him very willing to do anything to improve his patterns.' Sadler and Josiah always discussed potential new designs – on this occasion Sadler tried to push some of his newly etched copperplate engravings – but the final decision on whether they were tasteful or marketable enough was always Josiah's. 'He has just completed a sett of Landskips for the inside of dishes &c with childish, scrawling sprigs of flowers for the rims, all of which he thinks very clever, but they will not do for us.' Josiah was never shy to express his judgment. 'I am afraid of trusting too much to their taste, but they have promis'd to offtrace & copy any prints I shall send them without attempting to *mend* or alter them.'[6]

After his meetings Josiah went down to the docks to watch the ships sail out. Fortifications along the banks of the river – hastily erected in response to the approach of a French naval expedition the previous year – stood as a reminder of the perils of war, a particularly acute concern to such an important trading town. Only a few minutes' walk away from the river were the coffee houses where merchants and traders from a broad range of industries met, talked business and made deals, and it was here that Josiah had come to have talks with a local trader named William Reid.

Besides the trade for which Liverpool was famous it also boasted 'two glass factories, salt, iron, and copper works, eight sugar houses, thirty-six breweries, twenty-seven windmills, fifteen roperies, and a stocking manufactory'. But above all, 'Earthen ware manufacture is more extensively carried on [here] than in any other Town of the Kingdom', a statement that referred not only to the hundred or so potters that made wares in mid-century, but a whole range of families, merchants, and artists 'all of whom were connected to the potteries'.[7] To Josiah's mind, Liverpool's potters had all the advantages: most of their raw materials came in by sea – 700 tons of clay, for instance, was brought in from Ireland annually, and while some was bound for potters in Bristol most of it remained in Liverpool; neither had the worry of inland transport difficulties.[8] They also were part of a business community which allowed them to develop their businesses. Josiah knew he needed connections to help his own business along, and he was anxious to find out what exactly this community of traders and merchants – his competition – was up to. This is partly what had led him to arrange a meeting with Reid.

William Reid was originally a house painter by trade. The son of a local merchant, he was energetic, clever, ambitious and confident, and he had discovered that if he talked to enough people, especially the kind that flooded into Liverpool looking to do business, he would find someone with shared interests with whom to set up a business venture. In the mid-1750s Reid had found partners who were willing to invest in a Liverpool China Manufactory, which would 'sell all kind of blue and white china ware, not inferior to any make in England, both wholesale and retail'.[9] The resulting outfit, Reid & Co., opened their warehouse in Liverpool's Castle Street, just off Dale Street, on the way to the market. They also rented about a third of an acre of land off Brownlow Hill – out of town, in the fields on the east side – and built a pot-work.

Reid was not interested in the technical aspects of the potter's craft: at most he would oversee some of the pot painting carried out in-house. His main concern was to produce pottery in bulk to be sold to foreign markets, where, he realised, the real money lay. He hired potters to form basic cups and saucers and others to enamel them, and he placed a few notices in the *Liverpool Advertiser*, calling for 'any young persons with capacities for drawing and painting' to decorate the wares as close to the current style as possible.[10] Before long Reid and some business associates, were able to buy their own ship which they named the *Racehorse*, and Reid began acting as an agent for other potters keen to get their goods to the New World markets. It was this aspect that particularly interested Josiah.

When Josiah saw Reid at the coffee house he was in full flow, haggling with a group of men – the investors in his Liverpool China Manufactory – over insurance rates on cargo he was planning to ship to America (business of this sort was always done in the coffee house – Lloyds of London was once Lloyds Coffee House). Reid owed the men money stemming from their original investment in his business, and had devised a scheme to repay them by giving them each, as underwriters of the insurance policies, a merchant's cost to cover their individual cargo (usually about 2 or 3 per cent of the value of the goods, rising to anywhere between 6 to 10 per cent during wartime).[11] They knew there was potential to make attractive profits in these deals. Insurers offered a range of coverage:

All perils of the seas, men of war, fire, enemies, pirates, rovers, thieves, jettisons, letters of mart and counter mart, surprisals, takings at sea, arrests, restraints and detainments of all Kings, Princes, and people, of what nation, condition or quality soever; barratry of the master and mariners, and all other perils, losses and misfortunes, that have or shall come to the hurt, detriment, or damage of the said goods and merchandises, and ship, or any part thereof.[12]

Despite the obvious risks, underwriting was big business, especially in Liverpool. The premiums in part corresponded to the known 'skill, ability, and knowledge' of the captain, but the currently high wartime premiums attracted many to the market. Anyone could be an insurer, 'however unable he might be, from poverty, to make up the losses insured against, provided the merchant was weak enough to trust to such a security'.[13] In a market that could yield huge profits to insurers, Reid did not have trouble getting his investors to agree, but only after he conceded his cut as 'broker'.[14]

After closing these negotiations, Reid turned his attention to Josiah, and explained what he could offer. For a transportation fee and the cost of insurance, Josiah could have his wares put on board the *Racehorse* of which Reid was part owner; Reid, as 'husband', or manager, of the ship was obliged to 'provide a vessel tight and staunch, and furnished with all tackle and apparel necessary for the intended voyage', and to proceed according to schedule and 'without delay'.[15]

Josiah would have agreed with one traveller's passing comment that Liverpool merchants 'are hospitable, nay friendly, to strangers'.[16] Reid was both friendly and persuasive; he was well connected and appeared to have the perfect credentials to introduce a potter, such as Josiah, to the foreign export market. Josiah did not need much persuading, though. He looked around and saw haggling and trading everywhere; he saw crate after crate of pottery being loaded up and shipped off to the New World. He wanted to see his there as well.

Reid and Josiah struck a deal immediately. Within days all hands

were set to work at the Ivy House Works on the first export shipment. Within weeks the *Racehorse* and crates of Josiah's wares were
somewhere in the middle of the Atlantic Ocean, bound for the
colonists who, spending well over £3 per capita annually on imported goods, seemed to have an insatiable appetite.[17] Josiah's
business in Liverpool was over for now; he would have to wait until
his next trip to find more merchants like Reid to take away his
wares. His new export trade promised to bring in lots of money.
But as he returned to Burslem his visions of success dissolved as he
stared at the words in a letter before him. The *Racehorse* had been
captured by French privateers and its cargo had been seized as
booty.

England's commercial prosperity in the eighteenth century made
numerous French commentators irritable. 'The territory of Great
Britain is only about a third of France and her lands do not compare
with ours in goodness,' protested François Chaumont in 1760. So
how could it be that 'she has a very rich agriculture, more than
twice our trade, and immense shipping'?[18] It was a concern that
grew decade to decade, and was highlighted in times of war, when
French speculators were convinced that England aimed at mono-
polising world trade and, especially, at destroying the trade of
France. 'France would become dependent on England,' French
foreign secretaries had been warning for years, 'in this case, our
manufactures and our navigation will die out and England will
become formidable.'[19]

Ever since Voltaire made the observation that foreign 'trade,
which has made richer the citizens of England, has helped to make
them free', French critics had kept a close eye on what they saw as
the double threat to their own security, freedom and prosperity:
England's manufacturing ingenuity and the rigour with which they
traded throughout the world. People like Josiah – or any of the
other English manufacturers who concentrated on making export

part of their business – personified this threat. 'Everything is speculation, enterprise, or manufacture,' a worried Marquis de Biencourt
reported. 'The Englishmen are sensible enough to manufacture for
the people much more than for the rich,' allowing them 'to sell a
great deal regularly'. Another French official summed it up: in England 'everybody is seaman or mechanic'.[20]

When England went to war with France in 1756, maritime trade
became dangerous and insurance costs for vessels soared. In a war
which was in part over the control of New World territories, merchant ships bringing back valuable cargoes of raw materials naturally
became the focus of attacks. In such a climate French merchants
saw their economic prospects dwindle further, and instead *armateurs*
began financing privateers, hoping to benefit from war booty – the
best chance there now was of making money. When war was
declared the Bayonne Chamber of Commerce enthusiastically
declared that the southern French port would be the first to send
privateers to sea: indeed hundreds of ships and thousands of armed
men sailed from the port and on to Dunkirk in search of British
merchantmen. Heading out empty with more hands to tend rigging
and sail than the sparsely manned merchant ships, privateers could
often outmanoeuvre and catch British vessels, or at least retrieve
cargoes dumped by an escaping ship. Few merchant captains chose
to resist, and if they did, 'the prize was usually taken by fierce
hand-to-hand combat'.[21]

Despite the advantages of manoeuvrability, it remained the case
that most (just over half) of the French privateers who went out
in search of a prize returned empty-handed. The British admiralty
had responded to merchants' concerns by providing what they could
by way of protection, travelling in convoys and sailing to more
accurate timetables to coordinate with ships for extra protection,
but with a war to fight and vast oceans to cover, merchants and
their insurers realised that they traded at their own risk. William
Reid knew this when he set sail with the *Racehorse*, but he would
also have known that most ships sailing out of Liverpool avoided

capture.[22] The *Racehorse* had been unlucky. When confronted, Reid, the husband of the ship, along with the captain, opted to surrender, thereby saving their own lives and those of the crew.

Josiah lost a few hundred pounds in weight in pottery (in crates containing about a thousand items of substantial value) when the *Racehorse* was captured, part of the cargo which Reid had insured for £3,050. But Reid himself lost much more. His own pot-works barely turned a profit and he relied heavily on the income made from his shipping endeavours. With the *Racehorse* and its cargo lost, Reid had no other way to raise money to keep bills and creditors at bay. When he was allowed to return from France in 1761, he went straight to the Liverpool magistrates and declared himself bankrupt.

Reid's underwriters had originally agreed to insure the vessel's cargo, confidently (if riskily) expecting to pocket £250 they had received in premiums. Much of this was in lieu of a portion of a debt Reid already owed them. Now, with the cargo lost, they were responsible for paying out an additional £2,800. With Reid 'bankrupt' they had no way to recoup their additional losses. Feeling cheated, they devised a scheme.

They reasoned that since Reid owed them money to begin with, and that he was now bankrupt, they would withhold money from all the *Racehorse* insurance policies under his name and claim it as compensation from his estate, telling the magistrate, they 'refuse to pay their said subscriptions alleging that the said William Reid the Bankrupt was indebted on his own private and separate account to them'.[23] The money they owed in the policies taken out under Reid's name 'was sufficient fully to pay their respective portions' of the debt he owed them. Unfortunately for Josiah, his own merchandise was insured under Reid's name. And because 'Reid the Bankrupt' owed the six underwriters money (ranging from £100 to £300 each), Josiah would not be compensated for his lost cargo.

Josiah was not the only one whose livelihood was threatened by this affair: the Liverpool merchant John Dobson was another. He and Josiah submitted a lawsuit in an attempt to recover their losses. Not everyone had lost money in the debacle, however. The insurers had paid out £1,800 to Reid's business partners, who were neither indebted to them or bankrupt. The insurers argued that they had a right to retain Reid's share of the ship, £1,000 toward 'settling off mutual debts', the sum covered in policies taken out 'in the name of God amen Mr William Reid' – Josiah Wedgwood or John Dobson were not mentioned in any insurance policy. It was a technicality. When deals are done in coffee houses, with few legal guidelines, problems are bound to arise.

However, the court also learned that: 'It is the usual custom amongst merchants when any of the partners live out of the town of Liverpool, for someone resident there to transact all the business which Reid the Bankrupt did.' Josiah's lawyers argued that it could not 'be pretended that the policies of insurance are made in the sole name of Reid', and that they 'plainly declare that such policies were made for the two other persons besides Reid'. There was '£1,000 owing from owners of the Ship *Racehorse* to different tradesmen for the cargo and outfit . . . and such tradesmen demand their respective debts.' Fortunately for Josiah and Dobson, the other petitioner, the Lord High Chancellor of Great Britain, agreed that 'an order be had for the Creditors of the *Racehorse* be immediately paid their Debts'.[24]

Settlement still proved difficult. The underwriters, themselves merchants in Liverpool, appeared unable to come up with the £1,000 for Josiah and Dobson, although they had taken possession of much of 'Reid the Bankrupt's' property and were raising money by selling off tea ware and other remaining stock. But following the petition to the court, the creditors decided to assign ownership of Reid's premises to Josiah and John Dobson, who promptly placed an advertisement in a Liverpool newspaper. It read:

To be sold by public auction on the 5th January next [1762] at 6 o'clock. All these new erected buildings now used as a China

Manufactory, with the Colour mill and premises appurtenant thereto, situated on Brownlow Hill, near Liverpool and lately occupied by Reid & Co. of Liverpool, held by lease under the Corporation of Liverpool. Any person desirous to view the premises may apply to Mr Wedgwood at Burslem in Stafford-shire, or to Mr John Dobson in Liverpool.[25]

It was the Jonah Malkin story all over again – a hopeful entrepreneur gone bust, his property and premises laid bare for public scrutiny.

But the auction saved Josiah. He was able to recoup enough losses from the capture of the *Racehorse* to rescue his own business. But the whole episode had cost Josiah valuable income. He was unable to pay his rent to Long John and cousin Thomas for some time and was only able to stay afloat after the brothers agreed to take his wares in lieu of cash payment.[26] This did not make things any easier for Josiah. It was akin to borrowing money to pay existing debts – he was spending his time producing goods that would not return any money.

Between 1761–2 Josiah redoubled his efforts, sending crate after crate to a well-known dealer in London named James Maidmont, whilst petitioning his old friend William Greatbatch to set himself up in Lower Lane near Stoke to provide moulded wares. Just after the auction of Reid's property, Greatbatch wrote back to Josiah with the news he wished to hear:

> Having considered what you and I were talking about . . . I am come to the Resolution to proceed and have hired men, taken a place . . . and am preparing things in readiness. I intend to come over to Burslem as soon as opportunity offers. In the interim shou'd be glad to have your proposals what you can afford to give per dozen for Round Teapots all sizes together, Likewise oval, &c.[27]

Greatbatch now had an exclusive supply of modelled wares which Josiah could fire, send to his decorators in Liverpool and then export. 'I have four men pressing constantly,' Greatbatch wrote to Josiah again, 'and will push forwards as fast as possible. There will be I expect 60 Doz in about a fortnight time ready and 120 Doz. more in 3 weeks after that, in the meantime shall be glad to have your advice in the form of plates if you have an opportunity.'[28] Josiah also explored ideas to expand his business in new directions, ordering an 'apparatus for Tile' from Sadler to begin making tiles worth about £6 a crate.

There were also signs that Josiah was willing to use sharp practice in order to edge up profits: he sternly complained that his suppliers, including Greatbatch, were earning more profit per piece than he was, although this was unlikely (for instance Josiah was buying biscuit teapots from Greatbatch for 3½d each and selling them to be glazed at Sadlers for 5d; a potter's dozen – 6 pots and 6 lids – amounted to a profit of about 1 shilling and sixpence, giving Josiah a profit of around £1 per shipment[29]). He also worked out arrangements whereby he could pay Sadler & Green for their services with wares, which soon added up to £30 worth a month. Josiah supplied Sadler with all the wares he wanted for resale so long as Sadler not only prioritised Josiah's printing orders but also printed exclusive images for his creamware. But the wares that Josiah sent as payment for Sadler's services sometimes broke in transit, and Sadler & Green had to absorb these losses themselves. This provoked a complaint from John Sadler: 'Consider the discount we allow you – and the Carriage we pay, the Expence of [engraving] Plates, fire, wages, & the Loss we have by the crack'd and second[-quality] ware you send us, not with your Knowledge I believe, but thro' haste in sorting!'[30]

Such problems could be discussed in a few days time when Josiah intended to ride for Liverpool again.

NINE

Paradise Street

IT WAS IRONIC that during an era when buildings were becoming more durable, owners began to furnish them with items that were easily destructible. Unlike wood, brass, or pewter objects, pottery and glassware were often broken even before they arrived at the home to be used for the first time. This was a problem that Josiah, along with all the other provincial manufactures, had to confront. At the Ivy House Works the cratemen would line the oak boxes with as much hay and straw as they could to cushion delicate items such as tea sets and snuff boxes. But the long journey to America was often treacherous, and no amount of attention to packing would prevent pieces from breaking as crates toppled off carriages or were smashed when rough handled by wharfmen and stevedores loading them onto the ship.

Occasionally Sadler & Green would receive a crate of Josiah's wares – usually containing about 130 items, such as 'large oblong dishes, 9 inch plates, fluted tea pots, mosaic teapots', adding up to 250 lbs in weight with a value of between £7-£8 – only to find that the pieces were cracked or, more often, soaking wet.[1] The latter affected the printing process since 'the ware getting wet', Sadler explained to Josiah, resulted in 'some of the Tea pots flying all to shivers in firing'. Wet wares at this stage of firing was detrimental. Josiah then had to explain this to his workers, imploring them to be careful, pointing out that 'our common Bisket ware by long exposure to damp Air acquires a certain quality which will not permit it to Glaze kindly'.[2]

Given the state of the roads around Burslem it was amazing that any of the potters' goods survived more than the first few miles of the adventure. The roads were so notoriously bad that many travellers were lost for words. 'I know not, in the whole range of language, terms sufficiently expressive to describe this infernal road,' complained a twenty-seven-year-old Arthur Young, conducting a tour of England to inspect the 'condition' of the country. 'To look over a map, and perceive that it is a principal one, not only to some towns, but even whole counties, one would naturally conclude it to be at least decent.' But the roads were far from decent. They were narrow, twisted and uneven, often muddy, and worst of all, gashed with ruts worn from the wheels of farm carts. Then there were the holes pitted along the sides, dug to collect clay, causing horses to trip and carriages to jolt.[3]

While travelling through the country compiling statistics about the development of agriculture and manufactures, Arthur Young's carriage tilted to the side and ground to a halt just outside Burslem. As he climbed out his leather boots sank deep into the mud and he saw a group of men contemplating 'a cart of goods overthrown and almost buried'. He bent down and slid a stick into the rut; it was four-feet deep. 'I actually passed three carts broken down in these [last] eighteen miles' on his way from Liverpool and Burslem, he noted. This time, though, the lane was too narrow for his cart to manoeuvre around another toppled cart in front of them. 'I was forced to hire two men at one place to support my chaise from overthrowing', while they forced it up the bank and around, jolting the carriage 'in the most intolerable manner'. Indeed the national survey of roads for the times, *The Traveller's Guide* of 1711, concluded that Burslem remained the most difficult town to get to in England. It was a geographical oddity that Burslem, 'this rugged Pot-making spot of earth' as Josiah would refer to it, was the centre of production of pottery yet remained thoroughly inaccessible for lack of decent roads.[4]

The local manufacturers were acutely aware of this problem. Long

John and cousin Thomas were already supporting plans to improve the turnpikes – following the example of the improved road that lead south out of Stoke – and investing in schemes to build canals for navigation from the River Trent to the Mersey. Since 1755 preparatory surveys had been conducted to consider how canals might create a network between these rivers and the Thames and the Severn, and three years later an ingenious engineer named James Brindley began work on detailed surveys of the actual route.[5]

Brindley was well known around Burslem. He was a cheerful looking man with large round cheeks and wide eyes who loved to stop and talk to all the manufacturers about his ideas to improve their daily routines. In 1756 he became the first person anyone from Burslem knew to build a Newcomen steam engine, which he did for a colliery at Fenton Vivian, near Whieldon's works. The steaming, grunting machine stimulated much discussion between Whieldon and Josiah. Two years later Long John and cousin Thomas commissioned Brindley to build them a large windmill for grinding flints on land on the top of Burslem hill, where it stood as a proud monument to Brindley's industry for many years to come.

But engineering a canal of the sort that would improve trade by carrying goods on calm water from Burslem to Liverpool or London was a major challenge. Cutting across valleys required a range of complicated features, such as tunnels, embankments, and aqueducts. It would take time before any ground would be cut – if at all. Not only were engineering skills an issue, but so too were the financial cost and the political negotiations involved – it could mean cutting through many a landed gentry's property for instance, and patronage from the right people was necessary before any of the manufacturers would stand to benefit.

'Here let me pause,' Arthur Young calmly wrote, attempting to conclude his previous diatribe. 'I must in general advise all who travel on any business but absolute necessity, to avoid any journey further north than Newcastle-under-Lyme,' indeed, 'to avoid it as they would the devil.' If travellers did not head his warnings, 'a thousand to one but they break their necks or their limbs by over-throws or breakdowns'.[6]

Josiah certainly was not comfortable with travelling to Liverpool, a five-hour horse ride, but it was for business and therefore an 'absolute necessity'. He was going to be busy in Liverpool: besides meeting with Sadler and Green he needed to meet with other merchants and those with whom he arranged to have his wares exported. Liverpool was growing to be an increasingly important place to Josiah: correspondence to and from the city occupied much of his time, and his business connections there were multiplying.

As Josiah approached the outskirts of the city on the road near Warrington (a 'most infamously bad' road), it seemed that Young's prophecy was proving true. Josiah was forced to grip hard on to the reins of his horse as it shuffled along the side of the path while carts edged narrowly by, but Willy, his horse, stumbled on a rut and fell beneath him. Josiah crashed to the ground, landing on his weak leg.[7]

Josiah continued the journey in anguish. His leg throbbed and each mile closer to his destination it grew more inflamed. As Liverpool's familiar horizon came into view Josiah noticed that the sky was blacker than usual, with a red glow just above the buildings. People passed him, fleeing frantically with children and sacks of belongings. A quarter of the town was ablaze. But he was relieved to find that the 'great conflagration' was being contained, and it did not appear to have affected the side of town Josiah was heading for.

When he finally reached his lodgings at the Golden Lion in Dale Street, Josiah was assisted up the stairs and collapsed into bed.[8]

Matthew Turner was the local surgeon anxiously called by the landlady of the inn to treat Josiah. Turner, like Josiah, was in his thirties, a Dissenter (he would eventually openly declared his atheism) and a staunch Whig in politics. He was also 'a good surgeon, a skilful anatomist, a practised chemist, a draughtsman, a classical scholar, and a ready wit'. 'Very clever indeed', was the judgment of those who knew him.[9]

He spoke little as he examined Josiah's leg, concentrating on making a diagnosis. It was hard to tell; it was likely that there was a slight fracture of the shinbone, but the general weakness of the leg worried him. Josiah told Turner about the infection he suffered as a child, that it had always given him problems and that he was increasingly relying on a cane. Josiah had always known there was something to worry about, he knew that the bad humours in the leg could spread. This was exactly Turner's concern: the only option would be to amputate, and until there were significant signs that the leg was causing more widespread problems he preferred to wait to see whether the leg would improve.

Turner asked Josiah where the accident happened. He knew the location that Josiah described well, explaining that he was about to start teaching 'anatomy and the theory of forms', as well as chemistry very near the treacherous spot, at the recently founded Warrington Academy, which had been set up for the education of Dissenters and 'young laymen of the like persuasion'.[10]

This fascinated Josiah. Suddenly discussion of the leg was dispensed with and Josiah quizzed his new acquaintance about the Academy's scientific experiments. He discovered that Turner's research interests were manifold and that they embraced all aspects of chemistry – medicinal, culinary and artistic. Turner experimented with 'varnishes, fumigations, bronze powders, and other chemical appliances' which Josiah took particular note of, and Turner explained that he always emphasised the importance of 'some of the principal Experiments in the Elements of Chemistry' when teaching his students.[11] Clearly impressed, Josiah asked Turner about the scope of the course he was to present to the students. 'As near as I can guess,' Turner opined, 'it may be finished in twenty Lectures.'[12]

Josiah thought back to all the discussions he had with Whieldon about establishing a programme for educating the lads of Burslem, and his own family's support for the local Dissenting congregations.

What Turner described sounded like a model institution for people who shared their beliefs in promoting 'useful', practical education. Turner explained that the Academy had been set up five years earlier by a committee who made 'arrangements for obtaining suitable accommodations for the several tutors, and a public hall, library and class room, with a view to the commencement of the first session, early in the autumn' of 1757. 'Accordingly,' as one student later recalled, 'a range of buildings at the north-west end of the bridge [over the River Mersey] was engaged, to which was attached a considerable extent of garden ground, and a handsome terrace-walk, on the banks of the Mersey; possessing, altogether, a respectable collegiate appearance.'[13] Instructors were at that time moving into the new buildings, where 'a room was properly fitted up, and useful apparatus provided for the cultivation of this most valuable branch of natural knowledge'.[14] The patrons of the Academy invested handsomely in it – the scientific instruments alone costing £100.

Josiah could not have made a more appropriate contact, even if it was by chance. In the words of the trustees of the Warrington Academy, Matthew Turner was 'a gentleman deservedly esteemed for his abilities as a Chemist', and a skilled lecturer in 'practical and commercial Chemistry' – a teacher 'very much to the satisfaction of all who attended him'. Turner was equally absorbed by Josiah's description of his own chemical investigations and ideas about the improvement of pottery. Josiah described his pot-works in Burslem and his own interests in promoting the education of the local men, along the same lines of rational dissent that the Warrington Academy had been established. To their amazement they also discovered that they had mutual acquaintances – Turner knew, at least by name, Dr Harwood, the Dissenting minister at Congleton, and the Reverend William Willets, Josiah's brother-in-law at Newcastle-under-Lyme. There were people in Liverpool that Turner was sure Josiah would enjoy meeting, and vice versa. There would be plenty of opportunity for that, Turner assured his patient, since convalescence was going to take a few weeks, at least.

However this was not news to cause Josiah any delight. He had a business to run, workers to supervise, orders to fill, crates to pack, money to make, and a stack of bills to pay. In the weeks that followed he was forced to rely entirely on his cousin, Useful Tom, at a time when he hoped to be able to expand and develop his business. His only comfort was that he could correspond regularly with Tom, and that his cousin was always prompt in replying to his anxious queries.

Josiah wrote to his mother too from Liverpool, trying to put her at ease about his condition. But there was one other person who was relieved, even elated, to hear from Josiah. They had been keeping in touch since meeting again at Aunt Katherine's funeral in 1756, six years earlier, nervously revealing more about their feelings toward each other in every letter: his cousin Sarah, or as Josiah referred to her, 'dear girl', his 'loving Sally'.[15] She was the only one other than his mother who still called him 'Joss'.

Josiah was not left to recover in isolation for any long stretch of time. On one of Turner's follow-up visits, a friend whom he desired to introduce to Josiah accompanied him. His name was Thomas Bentley.

Bentley was a man of weighty presence: 'courtly' was the preferred description of his friends.[16] He was heavily set with strong, but friendly, features. His head seemed unusually large, even though he was bald, save the wrap of brown hair at the base of his skull, from ear to ear.

He was just a few months older than Josiah (he was born in Scropton, Derbyshire, on New Year's Day, 1730), but he came from a far more privileged background. His father was a minor country gentleman, a successful farmer who owned lands in Dovedale, on the borders of Staffordshire and Derbyshire. His parents were Dissenters, and they sent their only son to the nearby Presbyterian Collegiate Academy where Bentley had the luxury of studying for six years.[17] He had the benefit of a broad-based education: he studied the classics in Greek and Latin, he learned French and Italian, and he practised composition and mathematics. It was the kind of well-rounded education he later, as a financier of Warrington Academy, helped to ensure that other youths would receive.

Bentley had a well-trained mind for trade and commerce. When he finished school at sixteen his father indentured him to a wool and cotton manufacturer in Manchester, where he served a seven-year apprenticeship and 'underwent a training in accounts and acquired an insight into the ways of business'. Completing that, as well as a Grand Tour through France and Italy when he was twenty-three, Bentley moved to Liverpool and rented an office on King Street where he worked as a shipping agent for cotton manufacturers and shortly after opened up a woollen warehouse in partnership with James Boardman, a like-minded gentleman who was interested in promoting plans 'for a charity school among Protestant Dissenters in Liverpool', something that had begun back in 1739.[18]

Bentley had a magnetic personality, and, as Turner had anticipated, he and Josiah hit it off from the start. He became a frequent visitor to Josiah's room overlooking Dale Street, he would pull up a chair and they would discuss ships, pottery, literature, education, religion and politics. Bentley, Josiah discovered, was eminently liberal in his views, and struggled with the fact that some of his merchant business was linked to the nefarious slave trade. They pondered the principles that governed the sometimes beastly nature of business, which had the force to strip humanity of its dignity and shackle unwilling people to a violent life in a strange new world. Josiah learned that Bentley had tried to 'persuade the merchants and masters of vessels trading to Africa to promote a trade in ivory, palm oil, woods, and other produce of the country', but it was to no avail. 'Sinews bought and sold' afforded better profit, 'and the bells of Saint Nicolas's Church rang their merry peals on the periodical returns of the ships from their diabolical voyages'.[19] It left each in a period of silent reflection.

But they also hoped that a rational analysis of how to enhance education and opportunity for people would lead to a better society. Josiah admired Bentley's passion for 'improvement'. He learned about Bentley's ambitious plans for Liverpool, and how he used London's cultural institutions as a model of development. Within the last decade the much-celebrated British Museum had been established, as well as the Society for the Encouragement of Arts, Manufactures and Commerce; the Society of Antiquaries in London's Chancery Lane had just received its royal charter. It was all currently centred on the capital, but Bentley wanted to see these things happen in Liverpool. Thankfully his friends, such as Matthew Turner, were happy to offer him all the support and encouragement he needed.

Everyone had faith in Bentley's endeavours, especially since he had already succeeded in doing so much. He was one of the most energetic founders of the new Liverpool Public Library and he had orchestrated the founding of an Octagon Chapel in Temple Court in the town centre for independent services which was in the process of being built. His latest ideas involved establishing a Liverpool Society of Arts.

It dawned on Bentley that he had seen Josiah's name before – he recalled the advertisement in the local press about the auction of Reid & Co.'s manufactory. Suddenly Josiah's trip to Liverpool became all the more worthwhile, despite the inconvenience of being incapacitated. Bentley volunteered to offer some assistance – after all, he was rather more successful than Reid at organising foreign trade, and he knew a host of people in Liverpool that Josiah should meet. The tutors and learned gentlemen connected to Warrington Academy often gathered at his spacious home on Paradise Street, in the fashionable part of town, and as soon as Josiah was back on his feet, albeit gingerly, he was added to the guest list.

The house was handsome – elegantly furnished and well looked after by Elizabeth Oates, Bentley's sister-in-law. His wife, Hannah, had died three years earlier in childbirth and Elizabeth, Hannah's elder, unmarried sister, agreed to move from her home in Chesterfield 'to take charge of his household'. Josiah liked her immediately; she was 'bright, clever, amiable, and interesting', just as her sister was.[20]

Soon they were joined by a chattering crowd, and Josiah was introduced to a number of people who would fast become friends: the young lecturer in languages and *belles lettres* Joseph Priestley, who was on his way to becoming one of the most famous chemists in history, the tutor in divinity John Aikin, the chief minister of Warrington Academy John Seddon, and some of Bentley's other friends including his neighbour, the skilled 'mechanist' and watch-maker John Wyke (the first watch manufacturer in Liverpool).[21]

Josiah was honoured to be invited to such an event. He felt it was more than a polite gesture to a wounded stranger marooned in town. He could see that this was a close group of friends. 'The tutors at Warrington have sufficient society amongst themselves,' explained Priestley, that 'we had not much acquaintance out of the Academy.' He, like the others, knew where to go for entertainment in the evenings. 'I was always received by Mr Bentley,' said Priestley. It was a relief to Josiah to be so readily accepted in their 'society'.[22]

Everyone shared a common interest in what Priestley declared was 'the serious pursuit of truth', and the discussions that emerged from their lectures at Warrington, which 'often had the air of friendly conversations', spilled over to their evening soirées. Every-one was encouraged 'to make whatever remarks we pleased, and we did it with the greatest, but without any offensive, freedom'.[23]

Josiah found it enthralling. Every remark seemed intimately related to his everyday concerns, but he was not surprised: after all, he was surrounded by people who had devised a five-year plan of study on all subjects 'intended for a life of Business and Com-merce'.[24] They were subjects designed to appeal to people like Josiah. The Academy trained people like Hugh Mulligan, 'an engraver for the potters, as well as a painter of porcelain' – maybe Josiah will hire him, his new friends added, jovially. Josiah would not forget the suggestion.[25]

Amidst all the exciting conversations about art, politics, and the future of Liverpool, Josiah and Priestley settled in a corner and talked science. Priestley, a Unitarian and political liberal like the others, was three years younger than Josiah, but taller and thinner. He was a man who was curious about everything but who had given deep thought to all his beliefs, and who would contemplate philosophical problems at great length. He had a mature intellect and was demonstrably erudite – it was said that at the age of four he could repeat all 107 questions and answers of the Shorter Westminster Catechism 'without missing a word'.[26] He had grown up in a strict, Dissenting Calvinist community and studied Hebrew, Latin and Greek under the direction of a local minister.

Yet despite all his abilities he sometimes appeared to lack confidence. He spoke with a stammer which, when combined with his growing reputation as a 'furious freethinker', prejudiced potential employers' faith in his ability to lecture. Frustrated, he had even announced his intention to open his own school, 'but', observed a biographer, 'not a single pupil came to him'.[27] His friends at Warrington, however, had great faith in him. On the contrary, 'I greatly admire Mr. Priestley,' said Turner, 'and am certain that any school must flourish that has such teachers in it.'[28]

Priestley returned the compliment, and, sharing Josiah's keen interest in philosophical experiments, praised those conducted by Matthew Turner, whom he called 'a considerable artist this way'. 'I attended a course of chemical lectures' by the 'ingenious' Turner, said Priestley. 'I was one who assisted' him, thus whetting his appetite for the science that he had decided to dedicate so much of his life to. Those lectures at Warrington Academy proved to be the beginning not only of an intense passion for science and philosophy, but of new discussions – often debates – about social inequality, money, education, and religion.

The discussions at Bentley's went on late into the night, and Josiah was sorry when it all had come to an end. Besides being a great host, Bentley was, as Priestley said, 'a man of great taste, improved understanding, and good disposition'. Josiah agreed, and as he travelled back to Burslem – almost a month after his accident – he sensed that this might be the beginning of a powerful and profitable relationship.

TEN

'Improveable Subjects'

As soon as Josiah returned to Burslem he eagerly penned a letter to his new 'much esteemed Friend', hoping Bentley 'will not think the address too free', but declaring that 'I shall not care how Quakerish or otherwise antique it may sound, as it perfectly corresponds with the sentiments I have & wish to continue towards you'.[1] Josiah was profoundly touched by the 'many kind offices I receiv'd in my confinement at your hospitable town. My good Doctor & you in particular have my warmest gratitude for the share you *both* had in promoting my recovery.'

It was the first of what would be thousands of letters of a profitable correspondence. What began as a fortuitous introduction evolved into a friendship intent on promoting each other's self-improvement (Josiah jokingly referred to himself and his friends as 'his Majesty's improveable subjects', conscious that Dissenters were often condemned for their 'inferior', and often threatening, beliefs about 'divine rights' of rule). While not as stimulated by natural philosophy as Josiah, Bentley nevertheless appreciated the values of experimental science as a route to increasing knowledge of Nature, and was eager to discuss various ways that they might offer mutual support for their business ventures.

In fact, Josiah had grown so restless in his sickbed 'confinement' and so inspired by the conversations he had with the Warrington Academy circle that he already 'found time to make an experiment or two upon the Aether', mentioning to Bentley that he had also written to Matthew Turner seeking his input on other experiments on 'crucible making' as well as 'the nature of clays'.[2] He had new ideas about improving glazes, colours, and materials which now involved applying more technical chemical principles to the processes. For this, he welcomed help.

According to Priestley, scientific discussions were 'likely to provide the principal basis of friendship'. Such enlightened intercourse was encouraging, engaging, philosophical and productive. As he told Josiah, he valued having acquaintances to whom he could voice his opinions and elaborate his ideas; it made sense to listen to each other, he thought, 'for the pleasure of communicating our discoveries is one great means of engaging us to enter upon and pursue such laborious investigations'.

Josiah agreed. 'I have told you what a troublesome correspondent you may have of me,' he playfully warned Bentley soon after returning to Burslem; 'you may think more for your ease to drop than continue the correspondence.' Like Priestley, Josiah relished the thought of having a sounding board for his ideas, someone he could call on for advice: 'at other times I may call upon you for assistance to settle an opinion – or to help me form a probable conjecture of things beyond our ken and sometimes I may want that valuable and most difficult office of friendship, reproof'.[3] Rarely would he finish a letter to one of his new acquaintances without relaying some information about his scientific research. This was true even in letters to old family friends whom Josiah encouraged to conduct research for their own benefit.

Besides beginning a new stream of correspondence with Bentley, Josiah started to spend more time engaged in thoughtful discussions about literature with two people close to him for whom he had much respect: his sister Catherine and her husband, the learned Reverend William Willets. When Josiah returned from Liverpool he formed a small reading group with them, taking recommendations on what books to read from trusted friends, with Bentley now being a heavy influence, or from reviews in journals such as the popular *Gentleman's Magazine* (which began monthly publication in 1731), the *Monthly Review* (1749) or the *Critical Review* (1756). Unimpressed with that week's recommended read – Gessner's *The Death of Abel* (Collyer's English translation was just published) – Josiah volunteered an alternative read to a family friend. 'I have lately purchased some chymicall books,' he put in a letter he co-wrote with his sister Catherine, 'which, amongst a variety of other things, treat a good deal about metals, their affinities, mixtures, &c and the result of their various combinations. If you think these would be of any use to you,' Josiah offered, 'I will with pleasure lend them to you.'[4]

Josiah's reading group exchanged ideas and impressions of a wide range of literature in ways typical amongst literate, 'improving', men and women. 'Critical and curious' minds contrasted and collected 'data' (a word Josiah used, referring to any 'given fact' derived through research) with such fervent ambition that a demand even emerged for the compilation of encyclopaedias – new publishing ventures at this time (the first volume of the *Encyclopédie* was published in 1751; the *Encyclopaedia Britannica* was still six years away) – to impose some order on the torrent of new knowledge, *scientia*.[5] Monthly magazines moved from one page to the next discussing new books that overlapped the subjects of science, politics, history, travel, literature and religion just as swiftly as Josiah turned from his sister's comments on Gessner's popular epic poem to tracts on chemical affinity. Dipping in and out of genres provided hours of evening entertainment and stimulation. While some pious readers preferred the Bible – always the bestseller – with its deep-seated truths about the world, others, like Josiah and his circle of friends and family, were enthralled by what secrets may be unveiled within the thousands of pages sailing through printing presses every day.

'Secrets', or informed whispers, about the government were high on Josiah's list of worthy revelations. A surfeit of anti-ministerial pamphlets published at this time were promising sources, and an irritating phenomenon to government spokesmen. Writers of political pamphlets attacking the government were 'more numerous' than ever before, complained a contributor to the Tory-loving *Critical Review*, 'as well as more indecent, more shallow, and more incorrect because', he claimed, 'the bulk of them write only for the profit of their publications' rather than on matters of principle.[6]

Josiah would have disagreed. Bentley, for instance, was well educated, well travelled, and well read; he opened Josiah's mind to critical perspectives on a whole range of social issues, from current affairs to historical conditions of governmental rule. From their start in 1762 the letters between Josiah and Bentley cautiously examined and elaborated their views on what they considered legitimate reasons to criticise the government. Urged to explore social commentary expressed in newspapers and periodicals, Josiah quickly found his voice. One fiery issue that attracted his attention was that of the young King George III's determination to exercise in full his constitutional prerogatives. He had particularly alarmed Whig politicians and their constituency (with the Wedgwoods and Bentleys among their number), when he used royal patronage to break up the political regimes of Sir Robert Walpole and the Pelhams, a powerful force until 1760. Worse, the costly war over territory in the New World had now entered its sixth year, with Spain recently declaring itself an ally with France to challenge Britain for a colonial empire, prompting British attacks on Havana, Dominica and Martinique, and causing further disruption to trade in the West Indies.

Amongst all the political events that occupied the popular press and stimulated discussion amongst Josiah's circle, the war, unsurprisingly, was often the leading topic, since it directly affected trade. This was why Josiah laid aside discussion of German literature and volunteered the donation of his 'chymicall books' to their friends, two brothers who lived in Walsall, near Birmingham, who confessed to Josiah that their 'business is so much affected by our war with Spain'. Praising their 'joynt industry, and you must not think I flatter if I add ingenuity too', Josiah was quick to serve up science as a possible remedy for their ailing business. This was fast becoming

Josiah's golden rule of business: reading chemistry served mercantile interests since it had the potential to provide creative impetus to productivity, especially in trying times.

However high-ranking science was in Josiah's view of worthwhile literature, he needed to confront the challenges others waged against the concept of self-improvement by developing an appetite for reading. While to some the events of the 1760s invited reflection and informed commentary, other self-promoting 'guardians of culture' opined that the decade was becoming one of publishing decadence. The commercialisation of reading – driven in part by profit-seeking booksellers, 'those pimps of literature' according to another conservative critic in the *Critical Review* – was reducing a respectable intellectual exercise into a hedonistic and indiscriminate pursuit.[7] 'Novel *manufactories*' were peddling romance rather than religion; learning to read, Anglican academics argued, no longer equated with learning how to behave properly. Curiously, even the enlightened programme of extending education to the poorer of His Majesty's subjects by founding charity schools – something Josiah's sister was directly involved with – was blamed for the corruption of conduct.

It came down to a prejudice reinforcing the hierarchy of education within society. Charity schools were too concerned with enhancing reading skills rather than encouraging manual 'labour and industry' amongst the poor. What good was it to improve one's head when it was only through the use of one's hands that a livelihood would be earned? Josiah, along with friends and family linked to his reading group, were developing their own response to such a question.

Encouraged by Bentley, Josiah spent long evenings thinking about the values of learning to read and write, and the importance of articulating points of view clearly and effectively. He also thought about the opportunities available for exchanging ideas. Pamphleteering gave a voice, a presence, to Dissenters and marginalised groups who had long suffered from political subjugation. Of course, as Josiah had experienced at Bentley's house in Liverpool, likeminded individuals had the chance to exchange views on any subject in the privacy of their homes and to a lesser, more guarded, degree through their correspondence. But the soaring phenomenon of cheap, mass printing provided a persuasive force for propagating views, whether discontented or prescriptive.

'Publish!' was Josiah's advice to Bentley, whom Josiah spared 'a tedious acct of acids, alcalies, precipitation, saturation, etc' to instead encourage Bentley to make public his 'excellent piece upon *female education*'. Josiah was not the first to receive Bentley's attention and guidance in developing a 'life of the mind'. Bentley believed in promoting education for all, stressing the importance of education amongst children, and of establishing non-denominational chapels to cater for these needs. One of Bentley's current philanthropic endeavours was the founding of an independent and self-governing chapel at Temple Court in Liverpool, named the Octagon. Similar to the Octagon Chapel built by Unitarians in Norwich in 1756, the shape of the building symbolised the congregation's responsibility to recognise diversity in worship.[8] As part of what Josiah called Bentley's 'instinctive goodness', and his commitment to promote 'the finest feelings of the improved human mind', Bentley had sketched out a plan for extending greater education to women, a manuscript which Josiah read while laid up in Liverpool. While Josiah among others commended the piece, Bentley continued to mull over it.[9]

'Why will not the benevolent author be prevail'd upon to publish a thing which would benefit thousands without hurting one!' Josiah demanded to know, somewhat surprised about Bentley's reservations when he was otherwise so encouraging of open conversation. 'It is not perfect,' replied Bentley, revealing a modesty and caution, rather than arrogance, that would come to irk the more impulsive Josiah. 'It is perfect enough to do a great deal of good,' retorted Josiah, 'therefore on behalf of myself & many others ... male [as well] as female, who are daily lamenting the want of a proper education, & would gladly make use of such a help as you have prepared, I say in behalf of myself and 10,000 fellow sufferers, I do now call upon you to publish the above mentioned book.' Forget what 'a few hypercriticks (for such only, I think, you have to fear)' will say, advised Josiah, and reflect on 'how soon our young folks nowadays grow up to be men & women & enter into the busy world; I cannot help regretting that unless you get the better of your scruples soon, one generation at least must lose the benefit they might otherwise receive from your generous labours.'[10]

For five months Josiah had been encouraging Bentley to put 'the finishing hand to his valuable MS' and send it to the printers, but for five months Bentley remained 'a *talent buried*' in his study. During the same period Josiah and the Willets continued their reading group, expanding their reading list, perusing polemical and theoretical tracts which provoked more thoughtful discussion than Josiah had ever experienced.

'I am about to furnish a shelf or two of a book-case,' a newly intellectualised Josiah told Bentley, 'if you would assist me with your advice in the furniture, I should esteem it a particular favour.' Apropos recent discussions and just translated into English was Rousseau's *Emile, or, On Education* (1762), which, if Bentley gave the nod, Josiah was ready to devour.[11]

Through all the literature Josiah was consuming with Bentley's advice, whether in the area of politics, science, history, or philosophy, he was beginning to question whether the capacity for moral and mental improvement was determined by 'instinct' or a product of 'charity'. He pondered whether self-improvement, especially in the 'younger part of our species', was attainable as a result of human determination and instruction, or whether those ranked ignorant and poor as distinguished from the educated and privileged were destined ever to remain so.[12]

Josiah started to think broadly about the concepts of equality and inequality in society, and about what improvement could mean to the children of artisan labourers, such as himself. While some literati proclaimed that 'Mr Locke's excellent Treatise of Education is known to every Body' – a presumptuous if almost forgivable comment seeing as it had gone through twenty-five English editions since its publication in 1693 – Josiah was just beginning to discover Enlightenment philosophy.[13]

Bentley was the most educated person Josiah had ever befriended, and he enthusiastically embraced all the guidance he offered. Each letter from Bentley was a gift. 'You cannot think how happy you make me with these Good, long affectionate & instructing letters,' Josiah would write. 'They inspire me with taste, emulation & everything that is necessary for the production of fine things.'[14] Bentley gave Josiah the confidence to believe that he too could be as capable of digesting the 'new philosophy' being espoused by *philosophes* and elaborated on by his new friends. Josiah said that Bentley's letters acted as 'my Magazines, Reviews, Chronicles, & I had allmost said my Bible', he laughed, reflecting on the irony.[15]

Josiah had gained new insights into the views long expressed by Dissenting preachers, including his brother-in-law William Willets, about the corruption of traditional education in society. The Anglican Church denied those who disagreed with some of its tenets the privilege of receiving degrees at the two English universities, Oxford and Cambridge. Furthermore, authorities even quashed the efforts of churchmen to print their own prayer books to 'instruct the ignorant' due to, as Josiah complained, 'motives that do no honour to the cloth'.[16] The corrupt politics of education and self-improvement were hidden under the cloak of 'providential design' – that God created all in the place they were most useful to serve. To the discomfort of those who upheld the traditional pillars of society – Anglican religion and the authority of the Crown – the secret, dishonourable 'motives' of subjugation were being more openly challenged.

Josiah thought about much of this in a letter to Bentley on 26 October 1762, the day after the second anniversary of George III's accession to the throne – a day when Anglican preachers across the country read from the Book of Common Prayer, when echoing throughout chapels was praise for 'our most gracious Sovereign Lord

King George' whom God was beseeched to grant 'health and wealth long to live, strengthen him that he may vanquish and overcome all his enemies'.[17] This was the time when the established Church preached that the authority of government was decreed by scripture and all Christians were obliged to submit to it. 'Submit yourself to every ordinance of man for the Lord's sake', read the first epistle general of St Peter, which taught one to guard against doubting the faith, 'whether it be to the King as supreme; or unto governors'. Do not, it continued, use 'your liberty for a cloke of maliciousness', but act 'as the servants of God'.[18]

The uncomfortable juxtaposition of 'liberty' and a required servitude is what troubled Josiah and his friends. Their scepticism over the Church's, and the state's, motives for educating and improving the poor was born from witnessing the way Dissenters' freedom to disagree with authority was blindly condemned as malicious. Anyone who 'altered to his own liking' the message in prayer books (which William Willets had just written an 'excellent little essay' about, according to Josiah and Bentley), was not, as Josiah sarcastically declared, showing 'ample effusion of such a truly Christian spirit amongst all professed teachers of the religion of the benevolent Jesus'.[19]

No one had an easy time defining, let alone defending, the concept of individual 'liberty' in the eighteenth century, though many people proffered their views. To some Tory historians writing in the Restoration period, liberties were regulated by laws, and the laws of England originated in the sovereign power of the King. There were no 'inalienable rights', argued Robert Brady, author of the *Complete History of England*, published in 1685. 'There is a clear demonstration, that all *Liberties* and *Privileges* the people can pretend to, were the *Grants* and *Concessions* of the Kings of this Nation and derived from the Crown.'[20] This was an influential argument which the Tory politicians of the 1760s relished and which Whig modernisers and dissenters found insufferable.

Bentley, though, found a refreshing rebuttal in his favourite author, James Thomson, famous for penning the epic nature poem *The Seasons* (1726–30) and writing the words to *Rule Britannia* in 1740. It was Thomson's poem *Liberty* (1735), where his 'Goddess of Liberty' travelled to ancient lands concluding on her return to Britain, that

> *On Virtue can alone my Kingdom stand,*
> *On public virtue, every Virtue join'd.*
> *For, lost this social cement of mankind,*
> *The Greatest Empires, by scarce felt Degrees,*
> *Will moulder soft away; till, tottering loose,*
> *They prone at last to total Ruin rush.*
> *Unblest by Virtue, Government a league,*
> *Becomes a circling Junto of the Great.*
> *To rob by Law; Religion mild a Yoke*
> *To tame the stooping soul, a Trick of State*[21]

When Josiah read Thomson's 'fine poem on Liberty' after listening to Bentley's encomiums, he was duly impressed, saying it had 'more than answered my expectations'. Josiah detected the author's 'goodness of heart' and 'zeal' for his subject. 'Happy would it be for this island,' thought Josiah, 'were his three virtues the foundation of British liberty: independent life, integrity in office, & a passion for the common weal more strictly adhered amongst us.'

Of the three, he knew full well that there was no 'common weal' amongst the people, particularly regarding their educational welfare. This was why philosophers were challenging fundamental models of education by promoting freedom of enquiry and, as a result, their works were being banned: Rousseau's *Emile*, for instance, was condemned by the Archbishop of Paris for its dismissal of the Bible as a source of education, and he ordered it to be burned in public. This prompted Josiah to be more interested in reading it than ever before, 'notwithstanding his Holiness has forbid its entrance into his domains', he said defiantly. Rousseau soon became a favourite amongst Josiah's friends, who would talk about how they 'formed a strong desire to educate' their children 'according to the system of Rousseau', where natural sciences, such as astronomy or chemistry, can serve their independence.[22]

While Josiah's Liverpool friends such as Dr Turner and Joseph Priestley were helping him to see new ways that experimental science could contribute to the improvement of business by enhancing the quality and novelty of his products, he was now beginning to see ways that empirical philosophy could reach out to the improvement of people.

Like Locke before him – whose empirical approach to education appealed to the experimentalist in Josiah and his friends, and who espoused the idea that nine out of ten people were 'good or evil, useful or not, by their education' – Rousseau's prescription for an education directed by the exploration of Nature, where he said 'we make scientific instruments of ourselves', saw 'value' as both moral and economic. Business, enlightened entrepreneurs were beginning to see, was a moral enterprise. The idea that the 'improvement' of minds and manufacturing processes could *both* be driven by the pursuit of experimental philosophy – which was also held responsible for posing a challenge to the King's divine right to rule – was one that would rest heavily in Josiah's mind when he contemplated how quickly 'our young folks . . . enter the busy world'.

Life was far more complicated when engaged in Enlightenment philosophy, not least because of the many paradoxes it revealed within contemporary society relating to ideas of freedom and justifications for servitude. These issues would reverberate in Josiah's ears and enrage discontented citizens who suffered the inequalities in society. Josiah would long struggle with these problems, addressed by many but articulated so poignantly by one of the first he read, Rousseau, in the famous opening to his *Social Contract*, published nearly simultaneously with *Emile*, in a phrase that would remain famous for centuries: 'Man is born free, and everywhere he is in chains.'[23]

ELEVEN

'Grief of Griefs'

D ESPITE JOSIAH'S BELIEF that fireside discussions of current affairs and philosophy had the *potential* to improve both
business and mind, Josiah also had bills to pay – rent to Long John
and cousin Thomas (which was months behind), and wages to his
workers. Consequently he never ceased the conventional grind of
producing as many crates of marginally profitable stock-in-trade
wares, such as butter cups and saucers, as possible. The war was
posing endless challenges to transatlantic trade and Josiah was forced
more than ever to concentrate his production on common pieces,
simple agate, enamelled salt-glaze and redware, the 'pretty but not
expensive' items, in the words of one retailer.[1]

Each day Josiah supervised his team of around fifteen workers
and children – the throwers and turners, the painters, glazers and
flowerers, the firemen and the packers who were under strict instructions to place nearly a hundred pieces of pottery per crate in such
a way as to keep them dry and safe during delivery.[2] No one found
this easy, and no one more than Josiah knew that the deplorable
condition of the local roads was the main cause of damage to the
goods. The local economy relied on travel. Josiah himself needed
to travel to see his agents and understandably dreaded it. He decided
that something needed to be done.

One day in 1762 Josiah, now thirty-two, arranged to meet with
a few other potters in the area who all agreed that living at the end of
a muddy, miry trail served no one's interest. Despite John Wesley's

disparaging remark a couple of years earlier that the potters lived
in a 'scattered town on top of a hill', Burslem was, they pointed
out, home to 'near one hundred and fifty separate Potteries' which
'find constant employment and support for near seven thousand
people', working in teams around a forest of new brick bottleneck
ovens. It was a busy hill. The two-year-old open-air market in the
town centre, next to the new town hall, was packed every Saturday
and Monday with merchants selling meat and vegetables, fish and
linen. The potters were making money. 'The Trade flourishes,'
Josiah and the others observed, 'so much as to have increased Two-
thirds within the last fourteen years.'[3] The earthenware and china
potteries in their region of North Staffordshire were the largest in
the country, employing on average more people than potteries in
Manchester, Liverpool or London.[4] Yet still no roads led to Burslem.

Josiah declared that they needed to start a campaign, that they
should petition Parliament for a turnpike between Burslem and
Cheshire, at least. To make clear the benefits to everyone and
marshal support for the scheme, Josiah gingerly stepped onto a stage
at Newcastle-under-Lyme town hall, leant against a crutch, and
addressed the gathered audience. It was his first public speech and
a tough audience. The gentlemen of Newcastle objected to the
proposed turnpike, fearing that the new 'bypass' road would affect
the tolls paid for access to the road currently leading through their
town. But Josiah rose to the occasion, pleading impartiality and
arguing the advantages and importance of working together with
one's neighbours.

'It might be asked,' Josiah said, 'from whence does Newcastle
derive its principal advantages, as a market & a trading town? Is it
not from the populous villages & manufactories in her neighbourhood?' Thousands of tons of raw materials yearly pass by the road,
'which puttith bread into the mouths & findeth employment for
many thousands of poor people ... And you know what sort of
road it is!' The great need to improve it, argued Josiah, was to
'enable us to bring our goods to *foreign markets* as cheap as the

manufactories setting up in other parts (which are endeavouring to rival us & thereby deprive us of a trade so advantageous to these parts)'.[5] This was the first time Josiah had made a public pronouncement warning of the threat that rivals 'in other parts' posed to their economy and highlighting the importance of servicing the 'foreign markets', but it was far from his last. Josiah had never felt so engaged with politics as he did as he nodded appreciatively at the applause he received at the end of his speech before being helped off stage.

The petition eventually sent to Parliament by the potters reiterated the points Josiah had made: it stressed that clay, flint and salt needed to be brought to Burslem from across Britain by land carriage, and that 'the ware in these Potteries is exported in vast quantities from London, Bristol, Liverpool, Hull, and other seaports, to our several colonies in America and the West Indies, as well as to almost every port in Europe'. Their businesses linked together a long chain of employment. 'The manufactures, sailors, bargemen, carriers, colliers, men employed in the salt-works, and others who are supported by the pot-trade, amount to a great many thousand people.' Surely, the petition humbly added, they were 'not unworthy of the attention of Parliament'.[6]

Josiah had been encouraged in his political activities by his good friend John Bentley, whose suggestion it no doubt also was that Josiah should visit Parliament for himself before sending the petition there. The capital was one of Bentley's favourite cities, a vibrant model, as Josiah knew, for the sorts of institutions and societies that he patronised in Liverpool. Westminster was also remarkably accessible to electors, and in the radically spirited season of 1763, rowdy merchants and pot-wallopers (or pot-*wabblers* as certain borough householders were called from 'having boiled their pots therein' as residents) regularly turned out in large numbers for political rallies waving their copies of John Wilkes's *The North Briton*, a weekly rag containing various allegations of government and royal corruption.[7] It was an interesting time for merchants with a strong interest

in foreign affairs, such as Josiah, to be visiting London: in February
the Treaty of Paris was signed, finally ending the Seven Years War
and inaugurating a new period of debate in British politics.

By the end of March, Josiah was willing to make the journey,
which he thought could serve different ends. It would be an opportunity to see at first hand which new products were being sold at the
merchants' stalls in Cheapside, where his friend and former agent
William Greatbatch (now fully set up on his own as Josiah's supplier
of slip casts) formerly delivered Josiah's wares to retailers. Items of
all sorts from manufactories across Britain were sold here and it
was the ideal place to see emerging trends and get new ideas for
the trade. A few shillings spent on a teapot or china plate that could
be used as a prototype might yield a tidy profit once Josiah had
trained his workers to copy the product. However creative Josiah
strove to be in the chemical enhancement of clay or his glazes, the
reality of the business remained that the potter's craft was fundamentally one of imitation and reproduction. Remembering that
would eventually prove very rewarding for Josiah in the long term.[8]

Besides his dealings with the trade, he had long heard stories
about life in London from his older brother John, who had moved
there from Burslem before their father died in 1739 (he would
eventually become a successful merchant in his firm Wedgwood &
Bliss on Cateaton Street). Josiah had been in regular contact with
his brother of late, and now, with Greatbatch out on his own, he
persuaded John to act as his London agent. It seemed a good
arrangement all round. Josiah found lodgings not far from John's
warehouse, at the 'Swan with Two Necks' on Lad Lane, a coaching
inn with a balustraded gallery with rooms overlooking a dirt yard
with stables and storage rooms.

In London one could fade away into the bland grey of the fog
and the simple dress of the city dwellers; it was too sprawling,
busy and anonymous for Josiah's liking. However from a business
perspective it was an essential entrepôt. The quality and diversity
of its shops was unrivalled: upholsterers, gold- and silversmiths,

instrument makers, perfumiers, jewellers, drapers, corner coffee shops, stationers, chemists and florists all packed into street upon street. Josiah shopped for shirts and linen for himself and as gifts for his sister's children, otherwise 'sister Willet's little lasses will go to bed without their nightcaps', he joked to his brother.[9] But even the spectrum of shops seemed to be fading into the stonework. The previous year an ordinance was passed prohibiting hanging trade signs, which were being made larger as aggressive shopkeepers vied for the air space above crowded streets. But as they swung above the heads of passers-by, gusts of wind sometimes tore them off the façades of the jerry-built Georgian terraces, injuring, or in some instances, killing prospective customers.[10]

Remarkably, London's streets seemed to be in no better shape than those of Burslem. When the King travelled from St James's Palace to Westminster to open Parliament, faggots had to be laid in rutted lanes to assist the passage of the royal carriage. And when Josiah made his way to Parliament to listen to the debates he arrived with his boots caked in mud. 'This day I had the mortification to hear the royal assent given to the odious Cyder Bill,' he wrote to Bentley on the evening of 31 March, from his room above the pub. 'The City of London petitioned the House of Lords against it, but to no purpose. Lord Bute harangued a long time in favour of the Bill & his own administration.'[11]

The Earl of Bute was the main subject of Wilkes's invective in *The North Briton*, which criticised the King's decision to appoint him the previous year as Prime Minister. Lord Bute was, in the outspoken opinion of Wilkes and other Members of Parliament, not only incompetent, but a crony of the King, appointed to help break the power of the Whigs. This was already enough to make the man distasteful to Josiah and his friends (those 'with candour equal to' Bentley's), but his 'lofty strain' of support for what became known as the 'Cider Bill' generated outrage among the mercantile community.[12]

The war had cost the country dear: the national debt had risen from £70 million at the start of hostilities in 1756 to £150 million by 1763. Emerging from arguments that the Colonies should be made to pay for some of the cost of the war (possibly in the form of a stamp duty on legal documents and newspapers) was Lord Bute's proposal to tax cider, wine and other commodities at 4 shillings a hogshead. Such an act would extend the powers of excise officers who already operated an oppressive system of household inspection without warrants, and would increase prying into people's lives in ways unprecedented before the introduction of income tax.[13]

The passage of the bill, Josiah reported, 'gives universal disgust here & is the general topic of every political club in town'. The problem, as Josiah saw it, lay not in the type of commodity being taxed, but in the disputes that would arise 'betwixt the importer & the Custom House officers' regarding the classification of goods for certain rates of taxation. Josiah mentioned the problems of distinguishing between 'grease' and 'Irish butter' when Parliament debated the passage of the 'Grease Bill' the following week. Not only did these bills complicate trade, creating hindrances that no one who relied on exports and imports wanted to see, but they provided alarming new powers of authority for customs and excise officers, who would now increase in number and extend the tentacles of a covetous government. 'The extension of the excise laws,' Josiah remarked, 'are most certainly calculated in their very nature to abridge the liberty of the subject.'[14]

Ironically, it was the potters' declaration of how much annual duty they paid to the government – purportedly amounting to £5,000, about as much as the country would gain through Bute's additional taxes – that may indeed have made them 'worthy the attention of Parliament', which voted to pass the bill for building a turnpike road between Burslem and Winsford, Cheshire, marking the first improvement in the landscape to help the potters' trade. But this was no compensation for the risks to free trade.

Bentley, to Josiah's surprise, did not react as bitterly as Josiah and his 'friends of liberty' had to the new customs laws, which, they feared, might not be tethered to any legitimate principles. 'I do my dear friend,' Josiah confessed to Bentley, 'for the first time differ somewhat from you in my sentiments on that subject.' But the issues were too weighty to deal with in a few sentences scrawled in late-night letters. Their differences of opinion would have to wait to be resolved until Josiah could call on his friend on his way back from London.

The trip had been trying with little to see in the state of the economy that would offer comfort to an ambitious small business-man. London manufactories at the heart of Josiah's interests were struggling. The porcelain factory at Bow had just declared bank-ruptcy, and Nicholas Sprimont, who sold figures and decorative vases for the higher end of the market, was chronically ill, leaving the future of his Chelsea factory in doubt.

Josiah, nevertheless, had reason to feel confident. His cam-paigning to improve the local roads had made him prominent within the local community and he was already being associated with its success. His dedicated work at Ivy House over the past year was also yielding surprising results: the business was performing well, supplying as much as it was capable of producing to both the dom-estic and West Indies markets, and he had managed to save enough to expand a little, signing the lease of a second pot-work just before he left for London.

For £21 a year, Josiah rented Brick House – a pottery inherited by the minor William Adams, to whom Josiah paid rent through the boy's legal guardian, John Shrigley.[15] It was one of three potteries owned by the Adams family in Burslem. An early seventeenth-century house, it was unique for being built of brick when timber was customary, and it sat on a sizeable plot of land on the road leading away from Burslem's market square to the south-west. It may have lacked the picturesque charm of Ivy House, but, with its end gables, attic dormers and transomed windows it had an elegance of its own. Most importantly, it was proven by the successful Adams family to be a productive pottery.

Brick House would be where Useful Tom would now live and here he would personally oversee the production of what Josiah referred to as his 'useful wares', the every-day, staple products that were so reliable, though not spectacular, in sales. Meanwhile, to help him at the Ivy House, Josiah brought back from London another family member who needed work: his fifteen-year-old nephew Tom Byerley.

Byerley was one of three children of Josiah's eldest sister Margaret, a widow who, with the help of her brothers and Reverend William Willets, had opened up a drapery shop in Newcastle-under-Lyme and paid to send young Tom to school. He had been working as a shop assistant for some years for Josiah's brother John in Cheapside, but the arrangement was not proving a success.[16] It may have been that the boy had other things on his mind. When Josiah and Byerley arrived back in Burslem, the boy's 'trunk came down with all his papers, &c.', Josiah told Bentley, and 'these unravelled a part of his history we were strangers to'. The boy yearned to be a writer, with a talent that Josiah found difficult to articulate, and so he stuffed a few sample pages into the parcel which he sent to Bentley. 'What can be done with so young a subject of authorism so terribly infected with the cacoethes scribendi as to take possession of a garret at fifteen!' cried Josiah, feeling an odd sense of avuncular responsibility. 'What we shall now do with a lad of his turn of mind I cannot tell.'[17]

Perhaps all was not lost, Josiah reasoned. After all, the boy clearly had a creative flare and was not ignorant, just a touch eccentric. Being bookish, Byerley was put to work on the business accounts, and was encouraged to learn French so he could translate foreign works for Josiah. Perhaps he would provide a valuable asset to the reading group. He was, as Josiah told Bentley, 'a very good boy & I hope will make a usefull member of Society'.[18]

For now, Byerley's role would be to take on some of the daily management responsibilities of the firm, allowing Josiah to focus on what had been distracting him for years: a certain matter of the heart.

The admonition in the first epistle general of St Peter to 'abstain from fleshly lusts, which war against the soul' and instead engage in 'good conversation', was not meant to encourage conversation *about* fleshly lusts, but that did not seem to discourage Josiah and Bentley from having late-night port-fuelled tête-à-têtes about such erotic pleasures. It would have, however, offered them a chance to laugh that, for once, they were following the Book of Common Prayer at its word.

Hidden somewhere in the depths of Bentley's study was a sampling of 'lascivious erudition', an amorous repository churned out by those 'pimps of literature' that enjoyed so much popularity.[19] It could easily have reflected the experiences Bentley gained from his days as a Grand Tourist (if he was anything like the debauched youth he travelled with) and which now, in his premature widowhood, provided a sinful source of tales with which to regale the less worldly Josiah. Even coming from the rather strait-laced and dutiful upbringing of the rationally minded Dissenting community, it was difficult to overlook the flood of Georgian sex advice manuals that dispensed with the Augustinian notion that erotic pleasures were driven by mere lust and insisted instead that they be treated seriously. Discussions relating to emotions and sexual conduct surfaced in tracts of all kinds – in pamphlets, magazine articles, satirical prints, or leather-bound books.

The sensation of the moment was the scandalous publication just produced by Josiah's new political hero, John Wilkes. His poem, *An Essay on Woman*, was one of the first parodies of Pope's *Essay on Man*, which Wilkes wrote with a pornographic twist, pondering:

> *Say first, of God above, or man below,*
> *What can we reason, but from what we know?*

Wilkes preferred to ask,

> *Say first, of Woman's latent charms below,*
> *What can we reason, but from what we know?*

Later, Pope's

> *Presumptuous Man! the reason wouldst thou find,*
> *Why form'd so weak, so little and so blind?*

was turned into

> *Presumptuous Prick! the reason wouldst thou find,*
> *Why formed so weak, so little and so blind?*

Wilkes's concluding moral:

> *Since Life can little more supply*
> *Than just a few good fucks, and then we die.*

The bawdy poem did no favours for Wilkes's political career, which was soon swiftly ended when he was charged with seditious libel after alleging in the *North Briton* that Lord Bute only became Prime Minister following an affair with the King's mother.

A more conventional and immensely popular tract that was widely distributed and discussed was *Aristotle's Master-Piece*. This was an anonymous compilation of folklore and medical ideas about sex and reproduction, first published in Britain nearly a hundred years earlier and reprinted in various editions and versions. Read by young men and women, even given to new brides as a gift from discerning relatives, it offered instruction on how to make sex enjoyable and efficient. When a couple is ready, it read, 'and if their imaginations were charmed with sweet and melodious airs, and care and thought of business drowned in a glass of racy wine, that their spirits may be raised to the highest pitch of ardour and joy, it would not be amiss'.[20] But all such advice was proffered only to married couples and was sure to instruct men that real pleasure was found only after vows had been exchanged, offering a glimpse of post-marital bliss:

> *Now, my fair bride, now will I storm the mint*
> *Of love and joy, and rifle all that isn't;*
> *Now shall my infranchis'd hand, on ev'ry side,*
> *Shall o'er thy naked polish'd ivory slide.*
> *Freely shall now my longing eyes behold*
> *Thy bared snow, and thy undrained gold;*
> *No curtain now tho' of transparent lawn,*
> *Shall be before thy virgin treasure drawn,*
> *I will enjoy thee now, my fairest, come,*
> *And fly with me to love's Elysium.*

Bentley knew that his good friend longed to have 'enfranchised hands', and took the opportunity to tease him about the prospect of marriage. 'His head is turned,' Bentley would say; he's going to be 'noosed'. 'I suppose,' Josiah said, those 'are synomims with you wicked Batchelors & Widowers . . . The case you suppose your head being Corrupted is a very possible one, it is a kind of Original Sin of which you are not thoro'ly clear.'[21] But when Josiah lowered the tone and asked Bentley 'Are your *last* & *first* thoughts ever employ'd on these subjects?', the air of frivolity and innuendo cleared as Bentley's thoughts solemnly turned to the memory of his wife, who had died in labour three years earlier – after only two years of marriage – along with their only child. She remained dear to his heart, and he was thankful to have her caring sister to form a platonic family. He hoped, he said, that Josiah would find the courage to seek out the one he loved.

That Josiah was still a bachelor at thirty-three was not remarkable. For those raised with strong craft or mercantile interests, late marriages were usual, though his older brother Thomas, feeling secure in the knowledge that he at least had a home and a workshop if not much money, was the exception to the rule. But for Josiah, as with many other younger siblings in labouring families, a life of thrift and asceticism was encouraged, leading to rationalised celibacy. Remaining single was good for business.[22] Along with pleasure – if that is what one was after, for the aristocracy was more often interested in creating economic unions – marriage brought children, and Josiah had long known the economic implications of familial growth. There was, however, another reason that might have played on Josiah's mind and reined in his marriage plans: the woman he regarded as the love of his life, his cousin Sally, was from a different station in life. She was rich.

The £5 Sally inherited from her Aunt Katherine would not have been treasured in the way Josiah treasured his £10 legacy, indeed she may hardly have noticed it. Sally's widowed father, Richard, possessing the same entrepreneurial energy as his brothers – Long John and cousin Thomas – divided his time between being a successful cheese factor and a banker. By 1763 his income was upwards of £1,800 a year, enough to grant him the lifestyle of a Squire Western.[23] In Richard's eyes, Josiah was someone who belonged in a potter's shed rather than a parlour. This mattered to Josiah, as much as it mattered to men of his position across class-conscious Britain. The vast majority of agricultural labourers, husbandmen and artisans married women of similar station and from their own town or village. It was practically unheard of to marry a woman who lived over twenty miles away and from a different social background, but this is what Josiah set out to do.[24]

Josiah was confident that Sally's father, Richard Wedgwood Esq., had reason to be satisfied with his accomplishments. He enjoyed good professional relationships with Richard's brothers (exchanging numerous orders a year with them), and he had worked hard to progress from working as an assistant in a muddy hovel to be in control of two pot-works.[25] He even had a hand in getting Parliament to build a new road between Burslem and Richard's backyard – Sally could visit her family with ease.

Richard saw things differently. Twenty-nine-year-old Sally was his only daughter, a living memory of his wife, and with only one other sibling – her older brother John – she stood to inherit a considerable fortune, in the region of £20,000 (upwards of £1.4 million today).[26] He had not envisaged that she would ever marry a mere potter. He was willing, however, to give Sally a say in the matter. For years she and Josiah had flirted with one another, and every other Sunday Josiah had ridden the twenty-odd miles to visit Sally on her father's seventy-five-acre estate.[27] Josiah was captivated by her wit and sensitivity. She was attracted by his naïve charm and bright-eyed visions of the future. Perhaps she saw in him the kind of warm-hearted dedication and commitment that had served her own uncles so well. Whatever it was, she had faith in Josiah and an attachment she wished not to lose.

Richard, a tall man with a fondness for velvet and bookkeeping, deliberated what to do with the couple. He would allow them to marry, he declared, but only when, or if, Josiah could offer him £4,000 jointure money.[28] Josiah was devastated. His early savings of about £20, half of which was gained by an additional inheritance from a cousin, had been reinvested in his business and was certainly far short of the demanded sum.

Josiah turned frantically to his account books. Every possibility of raising, borrowing, or promising the money had to be explored. One possibility lay in the lingering débâcle of the *Racehorse*. He was still administering the estate of 'Reid the bankrupt', and the insurance money was outstanding, though hundreds of pounds was being raised through china sold at auction and the collection of bills.[29]

More so than for Josiah, however, the complications were running Reid and his family into uncomfortable depths of humiliation, news of which placed Josiah in a moral dilemma. He received a letter from Reid himself pleading for help: 'Consider my case,' Reid begged, 'it's most melancholy thing that I, my wife & children must be most miserable if I cannot have my liberty in going about my affairs which would tend to the good of the creditors . . .'. Pleading for a certificate that would allow him to resume his trade, he wrote that it was never his intention to mislead anyone. 'I know my owners insurance', he said, '& despise the authors who' refused to honour their policies. Josiah and his co-executor, Dobson, assisted Reid with some money and a public collection, but it could never be enough. 'God knows what a melancholy tryall I have gone through,' Reid continued, but he was not the only one to have suffered.[30]

Josiah had tried to stretch out his lines of credit by following a conventional, if also ethically questionable, business practice of delaying payment for services until income from his own sales was realised. The person who this affected most was his friend William Greatbatch. Typically Greatbatch would visit Josiah in Burslem to deliver models and slip casts, take new orders and pick up monies owed; but Greatbatch had problems of his own. 'I intended to come over to Burslem on Friday next,' wrote Greatbatch in late May, 'but my little boy is so very ill that I am doubtful.' A week later he reminded Josiah about his bills: 'Desire you'l Remit what cash is Convenient for you ... I could not possibly come over myself for my Dear wife was taken so ill this morning.' The next day, Josiah received another letter. 'Desire you'l Remit me some cash by the bearer on the present occasion, for the Lord has been pleased to take my Dear Boy this morning.'[31] Josiah finally paid the bills. It seemed that for every stride forward – for every black entry in his account book – something intervened to set him back a yard.

With the year drawing to an end Josiah was obsessed with what bills he could collect on and what improvements he might make towards raising the jointure money for Sally's father. Scribbling as if in a daydream on the back of a list of debts owed to him, he wrote the word 'glazing' some twenty times, and in the middle of the page wrote one simple word: 'Love'.[32] In a last act of desperation he approached Sally's father again. He offered a compromise, a mixture of promises of future income, a commitment to engage in business with Richard and the Big House brothers, and some loans. It was not exactly what the merciless Richard wanted, and Josiah held his breath.

Days passed in uncertain silence as Josiah waited anxiously to hear from Richard. It was the most emotionally unsettling Christmas he had experienced since the winter following his father's death. Even a seasonal missive from Bentley lay unanswered on his desk. 'I [would have] acknowledg'd your very kind letter before now,' Josiah finally wrote, languidly, early in the New Year, 'but hoped by waiting a post or two to be able either to tell you of my happiness or at least the time I expected to be made so.' However, he continued, there was nothing to report:

> *O grief of griefs* that pleasure is still denied me & I cannot bear to keep my friend in suspense any longer, though I own myself somewhat asham'd & greatly mortify'd to be still kept at bay from those exalted pleasures you have often told me (& I am very willing to believe) attend the Married state.

Thoughts of 'virgin treasure' and 'bared snow' in 'loves Elysium' flowed from his pen . 'If you know my temper & sentiments on these affairs you will be sensible how I am mortify'd when I tell you I have gone through a long series of bargain making of settlements, reversions, provisions, &c, &c.' It was like no other business arrangement he had been engaged in.

'Gone through it, did I say! Would to Hymen I had – No, I am still in the Attorney's hands, from which I hope it is no harm to pray *"good Ld deliver me"*.' If it was left to young lovers' hearts to decided rather than the insidious 'marriage marketplace', then they would already be celebrating. Josiah despised the fact that love was being reduced to numbers like a chemical formula, that it was being transformed into a business practice. Did Richard think Josiah could 'improve' himself the way a product is improved, with a new glaze? 'Miss W and I are perfectly agreed & could settle the whole affair in three lines & so many minutes,' Josiah complained. 'But our Pappa, over carefull of his daughter's interest would by some demands which I cannot comply with, go near to separate us, if we were not better determin'd.'[33]

Then, after another meeting of 'great form' and three weeks of negotiation between Josiah, 'Mr W', and each of their attorneys, January's gloom lifted. 'All things being amicably settled betwixt my Pappa elect & myself I yesterday prevail'd upon my dear girl to name the day, the blissful day!' He announced to Bentley the prospect that 'Wednesday next' held for him: 'When she will reward all my faithful services & take me to her arms! To her Nuptial Bed! To pleasures which I am yet ignorant of, and you my dear friend can much better conceive than I shall ever be able to express . . . .' Bentley no doubt followed Josiah's recommendation that 'on that auspicious day, think it no sin, to wash your philosophic evening pipe with a glass or two extraordinary, to hail your friend & wish him good speed into the realms of matrimony.' Josiah then prepared himself for one of the very few weeks in his life when 'no business may intrude on my pleasures'.[34]

TWELVE

Recipe for Success

JOSIAH AND SALLY solemnised their marriage in the ancient parish of Astbury in Cheshire on 25 January 1764.[1] The occasion was blissful, and, 'for a handful of the first months after Matrimony' he said, he wished 'to hear, see, feel or understand nothing' but Sally.[2] This was the first time he had experienced the intimate sensations of another's flesh, much in the mind, he ruefully commented, of his impertinent 'Gossiping friends'. Some couples 'bundled' before marriage, a courting custom whereby the two spent the night together in bed while retaining an 'essential part of his dress', sometimes separated by a wooden board for good measure, but he and Sally had not. Neither had Josiah ever been tempted to turn to prostitution, as prominent as it was in London or Liverpool, not only because of the risk of disease, but because he was a romantic, not a rake, and could see no rationale for anonymous liaisons.[3]

For most of his life his own flesh, marked with traces of his childhood disease, was driven from his consciousness. His right leg, from the knee down, was a sore encumbrance. The most personal touch he experienced from anyone was therapeutic – his mother's hand on his hot forehead, the cursory squeeze of a physician's fingers on his calf. His physiology was so adapted to feeling pain that cosseting sensual pleasures was as more, he remarked to Bentley, 'than I shall ever be able to express'.

Sally and Josiah set up home in Brick House as it was larger than Ivy House and offered them the potential to grow as a family. While clearly not matching the grandeur of her father's or uncles' homes, Sally was as anxious to settle in as Josiah had once been to establish himself in his own affairs. She knew what to expect: the adjoining pot-work would be messy, not like the green lawn outside her previous chambers, and she would be woken up by the foul blast of a horn before Josiah would meet his team of artisans in the workshops. But she settled straight in. She was, after all, raised a Wedgwood. As Josiah beamed to Bentley, already they were 'two married lovers as happy as this world can make them'.[4]

Josiah was beside himself with pride. He had enormous respect for Sally, who in many ways reminded him of his own sister, Catherine. Beyond being well educated and exhibiting a reasoned temperament, she had a sharp intellect and varied interests. All were qualities that Josiah knew well in his sister, who never shied away from presenting her thoughts in the smoky evening debates with the men. It was no surprise, therefore, that Sally and Catherine soon became as close as sisters.

Besides devouring the impassioned political discussions that formed the principal social diet each time she and Josiah met with the Willets or Bentley, Sally was also committed to being part of her husband's professional life. Neither she nor Josiah ever saw their marriage merely as convenient for companionship. It was a partnership from the beginning, and she was dedicated to doing what she could to help Josiah by learning the intricacies of his craft.

Like many other struggling young men who would ultimately find success, Josiah benefited throughout from the support of the women around him. Being fatherless since nine, Josiah received from his mother Mary a physical and intellectual nurturing that few others had the occasion or inclination to offer. When he was young, she was committed to bestowing in 'Jos' sound, rational principles which she believed would help him deal with any of life's knocks. Though she was unable to give Josiah any money – that went to his older brother Thomas in return for her provisions and lodging – what she offered him proved an invaluable gift, and he would always remain close to her. The beneficent Aunt Katherine, who gave so substantially to charity and poor relief (even spending £200 on a new house for the rector), had also given Josiah a crucial start in life, the £10 which helped him to start out in his own career.[5] And his sister, Catherine, always offered her younger brother emotional support. When he ventured out on his own she invited him to be part of her life with her husband William, from whom Josiah learned fundamentals about chemistry and experimental philosophy. She had helped stimulate Josiah's creative and critical thoughts in their reading-group discussions, and always offered their own home as a welcoming retreat for Josiah and Sally.

Although this was an era in which an emerging capitalist order was so outspokenly fraternal in form, and when women were considered legally and politically *as* property rather than as owners of property or business, women did play a pivotal role, both in public and in private, in promoting business. Because of the property laws which naturally extended to financial marriage settlements, men could benefit by marrying into wealth and thereby boost their own enterprises. The Birmingham iron master Matthew Boulton, soon to be a friendly rival of Josiah's, gained the initial bulk of his wealth which he invested in his manufactory by marrying two sisters sequentially.[6] But women also acted as investors: the fact that they 'made up 20 per cent of loan capital traded in late eighteenth-century towns', and their wealth often supported the joint stock companies behind municipal utilities underlined just how lucky many (male) entrepreneurs were to have such support.[7] Josiah was one such lucky man. Upon marrying Sally, he had what three generations of his cousins had been denied by birth – what he was likewise denied by being born last – and what he so desperately sought to obtain through improvement of himself and his business: wealth.

'What forlorn Animals the best of us are,' Josiah once wrote to Bentley, when his sister-in-law was away, 'when destitute of a Female head of a Family.'[8] Josiah would soon grow more dependent on Sally than he could have imagined. In the evenings, from a well-worn habit, he would often withdraw to his workshop, open up his coveted notebook and resume his chemical experiments in the hope of improving on the quality and colours of glazes. For years he had done this alone, working in silence in a laboratory often filled with the smells of fused alkalis and smoking arsenic. Now Sally joined him, and under candlelight they sat night after night, perched on a bench, recording in the notebook chemical combinations – those that failed and those that looked promising.

It was a valued collaboration. 'Sally is my chief helpmate,' he proudly wrote to his brother, John, in London, informing him that he was on the verge of success in obtaining a purer white-glazed finish.[9] 'She hath learnt my characters, at least to write them, but can scarcely read them at present' – referring to the secret code Josiah used to record each chemical experiment and protect treasured formulas (such as that which yielded his 'good White glaze' in 1761, and which he and Sally were now trying to develop further). Secrecy was essential. Local potters could vary the appearance of wares by glazing with certain metallic ores, but these were expensive and the clay still often held a dirty and stubbornly unalterable tinge. It was therefore easier and cheaper for local potters to rely on the customary 'grass-green' and brownish, yellow glazes whereby they created tortoiseshell plates and earthenware vessels, in the shape of popular fruits such as pineapples. Any improvement in the appearance of products – achieved by introducing a new colour or a unique preparation of the raw materials – was valuable knowledge and could result in rival potters paying workers to snoop around their workplaces in search of such secrets.

This was all part of the business which Josiah and Sally worked at together. Sharing secret codes, writing recipes for potential success, moving between different rooms to monitor the progression of a product from conception to preparation to kiln firing: it was satisfying, even exciting. 'I often think if you could but once enter into the *spirit* of it,' Josiah wrote to his brother John, it 'would be the prettiest employment for you imaginable.'[10] But John was unconvinced, recalling that people in Burslem were always covered in clay dust and flint grime – it was why John had left for London in the first place – but Sally understood exactly what Josiah meant.

While Josiah excitedly praised the efforts of his 'chief helpmate', Sally's wealth – or at least until his death, her father's wealth – enabled Josiah to expand and improve on the quality of pottery he was able to produce. Soon after their marriage, Richard Wedgwood began giving Josiah hundreds of pounds of cash, which – whether following the 'negotiations' of the marriage settlement or on his own initiative – Josiah funnelled straight into the improvement of his pot-works.[11]

One of the improvements at Brick House Works was instrumental in introducing a new kind of discipline amongst Josiah's workers.[12] He had a bell rigged to a turret on one of his workshops across the yard from his house and every morning at quarter to six he rang it to tell his employees it was time to start work. Not every potter in Burslem worked on the same schedule, but every one of them (and even the postman) sounded a horn to summon their workers. It apparently took a dedicated ear to distinguish each tone, so Josiah eliminated possible confusion, or entreaties thereof, by establishing his own sound. From then on the Brick House Works was also known as the Bell Works.

Installing the bell was Josiah's first management innovation. He had long known the importance of discipline in the workforce, especially when it came to regulating working hours and distracting dilatory workers from the allure of the alehouses. Gone were the days when the rise and fall of the sun dictated the potters' working day. The day had to begin and end for the team in unison, or time and productivity was lost; it was up to Josiah to set times, shortening lunch breaks or prolonging the working day according to demand. 'Time wasted is existence, used is life!', was the adage of Bentley's neighbour, John Wyke – the watchmaker who attended the evening soirées with the rest of the Warrington circle. He would etch his maxims on the back of his watches – well out of the range of affordability for Josiah's workers – including 'O time! Than gold more sacred.'[13] Josiah, who got along well with Wyke, knew more than most that time was money, not having yet caught his breath from making up the time he had taken off in order to marry Sally.

Other improvements were also on their way. He had recently purchased 'an excellent book' published in Paris by Charles Plumier entitled *L'art de tourner*, a book on engine turning, or lathe working, which promised to teach one how 'to make all works of the turn to perfection'.[14] Conventional lathes – parallel lathes – had been first introduced in Burslem by the innovative Elers brothers at the end of the seventeenth century.[15] A pot or vase, usually 'Tea & Coffee Ware', was turned on the lathe (by 'lathe-treaders', usually children) and the turner would use a series of sharp instruments to thin, shape and incise uniform patterns – ridges and stripes, for instance – onto the rotating object. Lathes such as these were extremely useful and were celebrated for rendering precise, regular cuts in the pieces. More recently other improvements had been pioneered, notably by a Birmingham 'machanik' named John Taylor and an engineer named William Cox: they inverted the process enabling the creation of more complicated patterns. Now the cutting tool was fixed, stationary, and various shafts altered the motion of the rotating object making it eccentric, so that geometric, fluted and rose-like patterns could be repetitively inscribed on a piece of pottery.

Josiah had spotted one of these new engine lathes while passing through Birmingham in 1763 and stretched to make the investment to obtain one. Now, inspired by some of the ideas in Plumier's book, which contained a number of illustrations showing how other mechanical changes in the machine's design could produce more elaborate and detailed patterns, he was anxious to make further improvements via the 'hobby horse', his nickname for the engine. 'This branch hath cost me a great deal of time & thought & must cost me more,' Josiah wrote, '& am afraid that some of my best friends will hardly escape.' He had already spent almost £4 on a mechanic to work on his lathe, 'forming a big hoop' which would pull a rope to spin the shaft to which the piece of pottery was fixed,[16] but now his main obstacle to progressing with Plumier's ideas was that he could not read French. Tom Byerley was learning French in order to help with such matters, but he had a long way to go, and Josiah could 'not wait his time'.[17] So he sent a chapter of the book to Bentley, 'which if you can get translated for me it will oblige me much, & will thankfully pay any expense attending it', he wrote.

While Josiah waited for the deciphered plans for the enhanced engine lathe, he and Sally worked on in the laboratory, where they had 'just begun a course of experiments for a white body & glaze which promiseth well'.[18] He was still eager to improve the quality of his creamware by experimenting with the body and glaze of it, hoping to make the pieces whiter with more consistency, so that they could accept sharper images in Sadler & Green's transfer-printing process. This was especially important as he had just received a prestigious order from a client whom he wanted to impress: Sir William Meredith.

Meredith, a Whig whose main residence was in London, was MP for Liverpool and a Lord of the Admiralty.[19] He had done some banking business with Richard Wedgwood, who provided Meredith with a substantial £1,900 loan, and had learned of the promising career of Richard's new son-in-law. Meredith was also a patron of the arts, a collector of prints, vases and antique artefacts. In late 1764, he had the idea of commissioning a set of tableware embossed with his family coat of arms, and he approached Josiah's London agent, John Wedgwood, to place the order.

As a consequence of the temporary downturn in foreign trade during the war, Josiah had been busy 'sorting out my 2nd red-ware' – his packing crates of pottery seconds. These were the blemished items that were produced whenever Josiah was trying to perfect a new process, but which he could not afford simply to smash and throw into shard piles. Right now, as he and his turners were trying

Portrait of Josiah Wedgwood approaching his fiftieth birthday by George Stubbs. This portrait was completed 1780 and painted on Wedgwood earthenware.

Collection of early Staffordshire wares, saltglazed stoneware, typical of production *c.* 1750s.

The Churchyard Works, the family potworks built by Josiah's great-grandfather along
Church Lane on the southern edge of Burslem, where Josiah was born.
St. John's church is behind the house. From a nineteenth-century engraving.

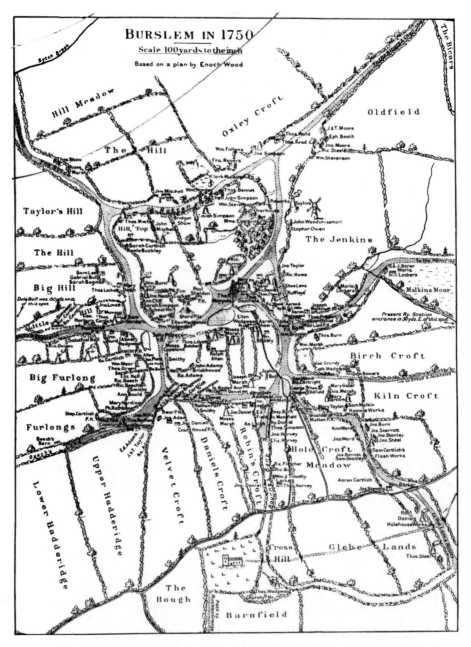

Plan of the town of Burslem, *c.* 1750, showing St. John's church to the south.
Overhouse Estate is in the north, while the site of Big House, next to the Red Lion Inn,
is at the junction to the right of the maypole.

Left Portrait of
Thomas Whieldon,
artist unknown.
Josiah was taken into
partnership with
Whieldon in 1754, and
began a series of
chemical experiments
that would revolu-
tionise pottery.

Below Cauliflower
teapot, *c.* 1763, so
popular and widely
produced during
Josiah's Whieldon
years.

Opposite A page from
Josiah's guarded
'Experiment Book'
(begun in 1759), where
he recorded chemical
formulas for new
glazes in secret code
to defend against
espionage.

Process to make the prussian lixivium

Take fixed vegetable alkali which consists of caustic
alkali represented by the yellow, & fixed air
represented by the blue in this figure ————————

————— Prussian blue, consisting of iron, the
brown part, & phlogiston the red part
of this figure ——————————————————

Mix them all together ————————

Make them boil & the result will be Fixed air expell'd
                                     Caustic alk & phlogist. united
                                     Iron precipitated

I shall remember this process my self much longer for having
seen it, & for my own use would contract it in some such way as
this.
Let this be chemical union or   Caustic alk.
  this precipitation   Fixed air
  this dissolv'd in air   Iron
  volatile. ∴ & signify diferent colours Phlogist.   Prussian lixivium
                            Nothing that

IVY HOUSE WORKS. BURSLEM
WHERE JOSIAH STARTED ON HIS OWN ACCOUNT IN 1759

The Ivy House Works, Josiah's first independent potworks, which he leased
from his relatives 'Long' John and cousin Thomas in 1759 for £15 a year.
From a drawing by a descendant *c.* 1864.

Above Thomas Bentley, Josiah's close friend from their meeting in Liverpool in 1762, who later joined as partner and managed the London showrooms (1769–1780). Attributed to Joseph Wright.

Right Joseph Priestley, radical chemist and dissenting philosopher. Priestley shared his experimental findings with Josiah who in turn equipped Priestley's laboratory with ceramic apparatus.

Above The Brick House Works, known as the 'Bell Works' after Josiah installed a bell to call his labourers to work. Josiah's second independent potworks which he leased from the Adams family in 1763. It was here that his wife, Sally, would join him after their marriage the following year.

Right Dr. Erasmus Darwin, great-grandfather of Charles, and close family friend and physician to the Wedgwoods. Darwin and Wedgwood met at the 'Lunar Society' – whose members gathered during the full moon to discuss philosophy and politics – at the industrialist Matthew Boulton's house in Soho, near Birmingham.

out new lathe techniques, there were lots of imperfect pieces being produced and he sent these on to to London in the hope of getting 'something' for them. 'I have no orders for them,' he told his nephew, Byerley, who had returned to London having grown restless in Burslem, 'but hope they'll suit the Gentlemen named on each crate & believe they will find them cheaper than any they can buy as the faults of most of them are small.' Byerley had instructions to travel door to door, showing the ware to former customers '& wait upon the Gentln to know their sentiments'. It was, Josiah conceded, a rather inelegant way to create a market for his goods and it was also risky since direct sales in this manner violated the agreements Josiah had with his London retailers.

'You must not mention them to such shops as Lambden & Woods, Veres &c,' Josiah warned Byerley, knowing this was bad practice, 'but as they are lowering value so fast', he had no choice. 'If any of them refuse having the crates now sent then you must try elsewhere for they must be sold, but remember,' he added, 'some of these pots are unavoidably much worse than others, so they must not be sold on return, they may open the crate before they buy them if they insist upon it, but they must take or leave 'em altogether.'[20] Reversing this rule of sale would later gain Josiah much admiration amongst his customers.

The Meredith order, however, marked the beginning of a rapid turnaround in Josiah's business which came at a time when foreign trade was happily regaining lost ground. 'If you can spare Tom I should be glad you wd send him down [to Burslem] immediately,' Josiah wrote to John. 'Our London orders & some foreign ones just come to hand and are very large, & require my constant attention in ordering & seeing got up &c &c, for that reason I shall send no more 2nd Eng[ine]d T pots to be dispos'd of by him.'[21] Tom was needed in Burslem particularly to deal with mounting paperwork and accounts, 'I am confined more to writeing than is anyway consistent with my interests,' complained Josiah, hoping to be free to concentrate on the Meredith order.

It was not often, if at all up to this point, that Josiah received an order from the titled, such as Meredith, a baronet. Those had usually gone to Long John and cousin Thomas, still by far the wealthiest and most prestigious potters in Burslem (accounts show they had spent £13,000 on acquiring property in Staffordshire over the previous twenty years, with sales hitting a peak of £800 in 1765), with nobility and the titled among their regular customers.[22] Josiah was thrilled to receive such patronage, writing to Meredith 'with my humble thanks for the honour of your two last Letters & your obliging offers'.[23] He had high hopes for the quality of the service Meredith would receive. 'I wish Sir William would give me a copper plate with his Arms suitable for Table plates & a Crest (if he would like it) to fill up one of the compartments in the dish rims,' he said to John, confidently adding that 'it would then be in my power to present him with one of the completest services of Staffordshire Ware, ever got up in the County.'[24] Josiah was determined to outshine all others.

His claim that he could provide 'the completest' as well as the most attractive service of earthenware ever produced in Staffordshire was not an empty one. He and his turners were becoming well practised in the use of the engine lathe which was giving accuracy and consistency of design and the creamware was now looking whiter and better than ever. It was no small accolade that the potter and retailer Enoch Booth, who had made the first innovations in creamware in the 1740s, was now placing orders by the dozen for Josiah's 'Cream Colour teapots', often urging him to be prompt as 'we aut to foyer this week & must have them to do foyering [firing] as it will disappoint us of filling 2 orders if not'.[25] Josiah's wares were beginning to look distinctive, at least to the trained eye of potters and retailers who handled them every day.

However, they were still not distinctive enough for some: this Josiah discovered when Tom Byerley confused some pieces of one of Josiah's competitors – a potter named Baddeley – with their own. Was Tom 'trying a trick upon us?', asked a shocked Josiah, when he saw a crate of goods bound for London containing a mix of the two. 'These are the worst I have seen,' he said, holding one of Baddeley's teapots. 'If Tom does not know the difference betwixt Mr Somebody's T Pots & mine, he is upon par with Mr Whites customers,' referring to one of his London retailers.[26] What was uncomfortable for Josiah, who decided that this incident was worth telling John about, was that customers could not easily see the difference in his much improved products either, despite all the work that went into them. To many, pottery was more often than not an unremarkable vessel with which to pour tea and serve biscuits. This indifferent perspective needed to be changed. Josiah, 'every night forming schemes' to impress the customers, wanted John to pitch the wares more aggressively, to *educate* the London consumer about why his wares were the best.

Sir William Meredith, who had, to Josiah's amazement, ordered another 'small service of printed dishes &c &c', had decided that he would personally take up the mantle of salesman and was 'promising to recommend them' to his company in London.[27] It was Josiah's reward for devoting his resources to getting the first order out in so timely a manner, and he felt humbled to be recognised in such an honoured way. 'You have heaped your favours on me so abundantly,' Josiah wrote to Meredith,

> that though my heart is overflowing with sentiments of gratitude & thankfulness I am at a loss where to begin my acknowledgements. Your goodness is leading me into improvements of the manufacture I am engaged in & patronising those improvements you have encouraged me to attempt, demand my utmost attention. With such inducements to industry in my calling, if I do not outstrip my fellows, it must be oweing either to great want of Genius, or application.[28]

How valuable it was, he thought, to have such a prestigious and influential patron. He did not know the half of it.

THIRTEEN

Fit for a Queen

'S UKEY IS a fine sprightly lass,' Josiah informed his brother John, doting on the arrival of his first child, Susanna, at the beginning of 1765. As soon as her uncle could break away from London and join them, Josiah wrote, he would find that Sukey 'will bear a good deal of dandleing & you can sing – lulaby Baby – whilst I rock the Cradle'.[1]

Josiah was enchanted with his baby daughter: her soft rosy cheeks and her blooming smile. 'The finest Girl!' he cried. 'So like her father!'[2] On a Thursday evening in late January, Josiah and Sally were joined by the Willets, Josiah's mother Mary, and 'my Daddy', Richard Wedgwood, for a lobster dinner celebration. It was Sukey's baptism, but since 'the weather is too bad to carry her to our Abby at present', she would be christened at home, '*privately* Churched', said Josiah, satisfied with the domestic arrangements.

In front of a roaring fire at Brick House, the family dined and drank the finest port from Richard's cellar. The 'extremely good' lobsters were an unexpected gift from John, which pleasantly satisfied Richard's demanding tastes. 'Tell John Wedgwood,' rumbled the 'old Gentleman', 'that I drink to his health & thank him for the Lobsters, they are very fine & a creature that I like.' This broke the ice on the occasion, and during the three days that Richard lodged with his son-in-law and daughter, he was, Josiah was relieved to report, 'unusual very merry & very good company'.[3] With scarcely enough time to digest the food and absorb the moment, Josiah was out the door, 'mounted upon my hobby-horse again', to address pressing issues of business. 'I shall hardly find time for nursing', he admitted, revealing a candid desire to be closer to his family than he could afford, especially as he had another debate which threatened their 'scheme of navigation'.[4]

For generations, potters in North Staffordshire had relied on three river routes for their trade. Clay from Cornwall and Devon, notable for being whiter than the local, reddish-clay, was shipped up to the River Mersey, at Liverpool and continued its journey up the River Weaver to Winsford, in Cheshire; wagons and packhorses then took the raw material the remaining thirty miles to Burslem, returning to Liverpool with loaded crates of the finished product. Almost thirty miles in the other direction, just south of Derby, was Willington, on the River Trent (which had been made navigable in the seventeenth century), where flint stones arrived from the north-east coast and wares were shipped out to London. Some forty miles south-west was Bridgnorth, just west of Birmingham on the River Severn, where one contemporary noted 'about eight tons of pot ware to be conveyed to Bristol', with return deliveries of 'white clay for Burslem'.[5]

The wet trade routes that spilled in from the coasts dried up within a thirty mile or so radius of Burslem, and the potters' new scheme was to extend them to make the movement of their goods and supplies easier than any road would allow. As Josiah put it, their inspired aim was 'the Uniting of Seas & distant countrys'.[6] Given Josiah's experience with the turnpike scheme a few years earlier, he was a natural choice for the potters to turn to as their representative. But unlike those debates, where a few Newcastle innkeepers objected to the plans for an improved road to Cheshire (fearing that the north-westerly route out of Burslem would take travellers away from their south-west-lying town), this project had the potential to provoke far more complex and troublesome interests.

For almost ten years Liverpool merchants and local landowners had been engaged in a grand project to build a network of canals for dependable navigation. In 1755 a survey was commissioned to explore the possibility of connecting the Mersey to the Trent. The rough, contorted landscape made this no easy task and the Liverpool interest died away, focusing instead on a less ambitious, localised plan. Three years later, through an initiative of the Staffordshire landowner Granville Leveson-Gower (1st Earl Gower) and Master Potters including Thomas Whieldon and the Wedgwood Big House brothers, the ingenious engineer James 'the Schemer' Brindley, known around Burslem for his landmark flint mills, was hired to survey the land to build a canal between Stoke and the River Trent. The next year, 1759, a separate canal project, inaugurated by the twenty-two-year-old Duke of Bridgewater (whose brother-in-law was Lord Gower) to connect the coal mines on his estate in Worsley to Manchester, eight miles south, received parliamentary approval.

To the public's fascination, the canal – which included Brindley's construction of a spectacular aqueduct where sixty-three-foot high stone arches carried the canal forty feet above a river – was completed in 1761. Despite a rugged landscape and competing political interests, it was clear that canals could work, and by the end of 1764 Josiah and his fellow potters, once again including his old boss Thomas Whieldon and the Big House brothers, were preparing the way to build the 'Grand Trunk Canal' to connect the Trent and Mersey rivers.

It would, however, be a hugely expensive endeavour. Josiah conservatively estimated that it would cost £80,000, money which had to be raised by subscription. Josiah took to canvassing support from anyone along the route who would stand to benefit from it. They had been willing to offer to pay for Brindley's original 1758 survey; now, Josiah explained, if they offered what they could, they could own a share of what was sure to be a profitable venture.

On a Friday evening in early March, Josiah met Brindley for dinner and drinks at the Leopold Hotel, a new public house run by a distant cousin of Josiah's, Ellen Wedgwood.[7] 'Our Gentlemen seem very warm in setting this matter on foot again,' he wrote, '&

I could scarcely withstand the pressing solicitations I had from all present to undertake a journey or two for that purpose.' Josiah's role would be to travel the length of the proposed route, rallying support for the project and identifying those who might object and calm their fears that the new canal might damage their own interests. Josiah brimmed full of enthusiasm for the project, writing that it was 'undoubtedly the best thing that could possibly be planned for this country', and, after learning as much as he could from Brindley about canal digging, set off to canvas support.[8]

First he went to Birmingham, to meet 'with one Mr [Sampson] Loyd in the Banking business' (Lloyds Bank, the result of a business partnership between Lloyd and John Taylor would open that year), who, it seems, 'is one of the Proprietors in the Burton Navigation which will be injured by our intended Canal', but who, he hoped, would see the overall benefit to business in Birmingham if their canal was built.[9] 'We made it appear pretty evident to the Gentlemen of Birmingham that £10,000 per annum would be immediately sav'd to them in the Article of Land Carriage to and from the River Trent, so soon as the Canal was brought to their Town', offering great advantage especially to the merchants who shipped iron and flax to Russia.

One merchant who became particularly interested in Josiah's ideas was Samuel Garbett, an accomplished chemist and later chairman of the Birmingham Commercial Committee which oversaw local business interests. He owned a manufactory servicing the iron industry and was convinced of the benefits that such a navigation system could bring. He had already been in communication with an agent of Lord Gower's to enquire about the Duke of Bridgewater's canal system. Garbett offered some advice to Josiah, recommending that to guarantee the success of their project, they needed to obtain the patronage of the wealthiest landowners they could. Lord Gower, he suggested, might be a good person to start with.

Josiah did not savour the idea of prostrating himself in front of the leisured class and begging for support, but he recognised that

Garbett, who seemed 'a very intelligent Gentleman', was right. After writing a carefully crafted letter of introduction on behalf of 'free-holders, tradesmen, & principal inhabitants of Burslem and the parts adjacent', Josiah 'had the honour of waiting upon Ld Gower with a plan &c &c and a petition from the Pottery praying his Ld Ship to take the intended navigation under his protection & patronage'. And in the grandiose surrounds of Gower's estate Josiah presented their proposal. To his relief, if also mild surprise, it was 'very graciously received'. Lord Gower was sensible of the utility of the scheme and, Josiah was assured, was willing to promote its execution. It seemed everything had gone as well as could be imagined, 'so far as the mind of a *great Man* can be known by its Countenance & professions', Josiah wrote.[10]

The praise was sarcastic, repeating what he had read from Samuel Garbett who enlightened Josiah to the fact that Lord Gower's '*Countenance* is of extreme consequence', more so, he implied, than Josiah could ever recognise, and that 'if He engages the Duke of Bridgewater, I don't see any alarming opposition, for all the Arguments from common Landholders are no more than general arguments against all inland navigation, and will be laughed at unless supported by a few such as Lord Gower & the Duke of Bridgewater, who have great ministerial weight'. There was, Garbett concluded, only one thing that could serve the cause better: 'if the King should patronise us, as I hope, there will not be any great Men warmly against us whose interest is not injured by it'.[11]

Having a royal patron would undoubtedly be most beneficial, but this was out of Josiah's hands. The young Duke of Bridgewater might be worth a visit, Josiah reasoned, and this is what he did a few months later. 'I have been waiting upon his Grace, the Duke of Bridgewater with plans &c respecting Inland Navigation,' Josiah told his brother, John, with a nonchalance which tried to underplay the hauteur of the occasion. Josiah, Master Potter of Burslem, spent 'about 8 hours in his Grace's company'. After being told that he would offer his patronage, Bridgewater surprised Josiah by giving him 'an order for the completest Service of Table service in the Cream Colour that I could make'. He asked whether Josiah might be interested in seeing his collection of antiquities acquired on a Grand Tour of Europe as well as some curiosities discovered closer to home. He 'shewed us a Roman Urn 1500 years old at least, made of red china, & found by his workmen in Castlefield near Manchester'. The day ended elegantly: 'sailing in his Gondola nine miles along his Canal, through a most delightful vale to Manchester'.[12]

If Josiah had ever doubted it, he had every reason now to be confident in his own 'Genius & industry'. Others, no doubt, were also impressed by his exploits, which identified him as yet another Wedgwood on the ascendancy. Shortly after this, Mr Smallwood, an acquaintance of Josiah's from Newcastle, unexpectedly stopped by at the Bell Works, willing to interrupt his day's routine work for a chance to see Josiah's reaction to a letter he was delivering by hand.

Josiah cursed the hot July weather that made their baby daughter uncomfortable and all of his employees languid. The heat from the kilns in the workshops was intense, made worse by the heavy steam from the arks, where a blanket of wet clay was being warmed to eliminate excess moisture. Still, it was better than London.

Josiah was worried about his brother John, who for months had been struggling with an unremitting illness. Back in the spring, Josiah had encouraged John to take a break, 'for I do not think that that close, smoaky place will ever agree with your constitution, & I do very earnestly intreat you to come & take the benefit of your native, salutary, country Air'. John said that he was too busy, but Josiah was insistent, knowing that business was useful to serve human interests, not the other way around. If 'you have not set the finishing hand to your affairs there, you may leave an agent to do it for you', he advised. 'Whatever inconvenience you may suffer by doing so, it cannot be put into competition with that invaluable blessing – Health!'[13] Eventually, John agreed with his brother, but felt France might be more salubrious than Staffordshire. Josiah had to concede that much, and signed off the letter wishing his brother 'bon voyage'. Shortly after finishing the letter Mr Smallwood appeared at the workshop door.

The letter that Josiah promptly read drove him from his bench on a hasty retreat to his office, shouting for his post boy to follow him at once and leaving Smallwood to find his own way out. Josiah quickly penned a letter to John about a change of plans.

'Dear Brother', he wrote, and getting right to the point: 'I do not believe I can spare you out of London this summer, if business comes in for you at this rate, for instance – An order from St James's for a service of Staffordshire ware'. It was an open invitation, issued from a Miss Deborah Chetwynd, 'Seamstress and Laundress to the Queen' and daughter of the Master of the Mint, for potters to offer designs in a competition to provide a 'compleat sett of tea things, with a gold ground & raised flowers upon it in green'. It was a large order: a dozen tea cups and saucers, the same number of coffee cups, six pairs of candlesticks, and with an assortment of matching cream pots, sugar dishes, and fruit bowls. He asked his brother to procure some 'gold powder' from a shop in Soho, London, so he could begin experimenting with it immediately.

Just as he was about to seal and hand the letter to his post boy, a flood of other concerns came to mind. He unfolded the letter and added a postscript. 'Does Miss Chetwynd,'

> Expect the gold to be burnt in, as it is upon the Chelsea china, or secured with a varnish only, like the Birmingham waiters & other Japan ware. If the saucers must have a gold ground both inside and out, & what colour the cups & other articles must be within, if a fine cream colour will do, whether the flowers upon the cups &c must be in also relievs or bass relieve, if the former, whether that will not be very inconvenient for the saucers, it will be extremely difficult to execute. What size will

be most agreeable too for tea cups, & Tea pots, & if there should not be a cream jug & Jarrs. If the hand candlesticks & Melons must have gold ground to match the Tea Things, or what sort of colour they must be.[14]

Josiah wanted 'to ask a hundred questions', and fortunately he could trust John to ask them on his behalf. He knew his brother was unwell, but this was urgent. 'Pray put on *the best suit of cloathes you ever had in your life* & take the first opportunity of going to Court,' he begged. John dutifully followed his instructions.

The excitement at the supper table that night at Brick House was overwhelming. The letter delivered by Mr Smallwood could change everything. He was given the chance to do what, he imagined, 'nobody else would undertake'. Perhaps no other potter in Staffordshire had self-assurance and ambition enough to do so. It was an immense gamble: it would be expensive, but more poignantly, one ran the risk of offering something to the Queen that might be judged inadequate. But Josiah would meet the challenge with characteristically obstinate determination.

In the sweltering London heat, John piled on layers of clothes suitable for a gentleman visiting Court, from the bagwig that laid rolls of curls on his head to the finery of his stockings. After his appointment with Miss Chetwynd, he sat at Windsor Lodge and wrote all the answers to Josiah's questions, ending with a note from Miss Chetwynd, hoping that Josiah would be able to accommodate the Queen's wishes. This is the line Josiah was waiting for: his brother's research had won him the chance to provide the Queen with her tableware. 'You may be sure', Josiah wrote back, 'my best endeavours will not be wanting to make the articles she orders as complete & elegant as possible,' adding, 'I shall be very proud of the honour of sending a box of patterns to the Queen' for her enjoyment.[15] And as an added gift – already playing the patronage game like a seasoned politician – 'I intend sending two sets of Vases, Creamcolour engine turn'd, & printed'. As an afterthought, he remembered what John must have gone through to have this meeting, confessing that 'the pleasure of your letter was more than ballanc'd with the fear I had, least the heat of the weather, the bustle of the Company & situation you were in should be too much for you.' Indeed, John was feeling worse than ever, but he was proud that his visit to Miss Chetwynd might potentially procure a patron beyond all expectations.[16]

A service for Queen Charlotte. Josiah wanted to show Her Royal Highness a sample of his new cream-colour glaze, of the fine crafts-manship produced by his engine lathe, and the new designs he had drawn up so that each item of the set would 'appear to be made for each other, & intended for Royalty'.[17] He sketched out some patterns and sent them to John to be transferred to a copper engraving so he could have elegant pictures printed of his proposed products. Meanwhile Josiah spent 'night & day' in his workshop 'preparing sprigs, handles, spouts, shapes, making experimts in burning gold &c &c for the tea service . . .'.[18] Once engaged with the project, his nerves began to show. Of course he would ensure that his 'best endeavours' would be given to provide an excellent service, 'but suppose we fail in burning the gold on, must we in that case stove it on . . . Must the saucers & other articles be gilt any farther on the outside than from the top edge to the foot?'[19]

There was no time to relax – no time to read the paper or raise support for the canals or play with Sukey. Sally had even become his amanuensis to help speed through correspondence. What made things especially trying was that July brought the infamous Burslem wakes, the festival allegedly linked to the feast of St Peter, but which had become a tradition of gaming, drinking and decadence.

This year Josiah cursed 'the foolish wakes' more loudly than before.[20] Although the workers received no wages during their revelry, since they were paid either by the day (the more skilled artisans) or by the number of good pieces produced, each day they spent at play was a day's less production for Josiah and all the other Master Potters. No manufacturer liked the holiday, or any such holidays. To his mind, they made no trade sense, a point made some sixty years earlier when a barrister named Sir Henry Pollexfen estimated that '2 Millions of Working People at 6d. per day comes to 50,000l', which translates into so much revenue lost to the nation 'by every Holyday that is kept'.[21]

'I am just teased of my life with dilatory, drunken, Idle, worthless workmen which prevents my proceeding with the tea service,' Josiah complained, 'to which more sorts of workmen are necessary than one would imagine.'[22] It was no use grumbling as he sweated away in his workshop, burning inches of candles faster than ever before, preparing samples and patterns for the Queen's review. 'You cannot think how busy all these things together make me,' he wrote to his brother from whom he quickly needed to know 'what patterns I shall send to Court'. Adding to the pressure was the arrival of another letter informing him 'that the Queen was impatient', being anxious to have the special service for a dinner she had planned. Yet practical problems with the production of the service were slowing things down.[23]

Cutting corners to save time was not an option for Josiah: 'From experience I can tell you, that the sooner' they are fired 'the more imperfect they will be'. He had not finished experimenting with the detail on the 'sprigs in green & gold ground', and was 'mortifyd to find it does not look so well as I expected . . . Powdered gold wld do the best for me if I knew how to polish it after it was burnt', but he lacked the knowledge. It was, as a formula on paper, simple enough. Josiah's useful handbook, Robert Dossie's *Handmaid to the Arts* (1758), instructed the craftsman to 'take any quantity of leaf gold, and grind it with virgin honey, on a stone, till the texture be perfectly broken', then 'put it into a china basin with water and stir it so that the honey be melted'. The steps then became more complicated, involving a pungent concoction of 'gum animi' resin, 'asphaltum', 'red Lead', and 'litharge of gold', mixed, boiled and strained through a flannel, with Josiah, as skilled a chemist as he was, not knowing how to apply the substance to the pottery.[24]

Someone must know how to decorate with gold the way the

Queen wanted it, he thought, and he urged John to search the Chelsea works or the Bow China works for someone who will 'perhaps tell you how it is polished for a little money'. Josiah suspected that it was 'neither a secret or a very curious art, for women [only used in the most menial roles] are employ'd in it at Chelsea'.[25] If only, he wished, some of those women – whose employment in manufactories across Britain was increasing and who helped to double the incomes of Staffordshire potters with their specialised skills in 'flowering' and painting items – were working for him.[26] Failing that, he turned to his chemical library, being advised that some European chemist had worked on the problem of combining different substances, though he could 'not find any French book on Chymical affinitys', he wrote with frustration.[27]

For the first time Josiah became noticeably despondent about the task at hand. 'For some tryals I made today I hope to be able *in time* to accomplish it, but not I fear in time for the Merry Meal,' he confessed to John. 'If you should see Miss Chetwynd again, pray do not say anything more that may lend to raise her expectations of the T. service, as that may help disappoint her.'[28] After three more days and nights split between his laboratory and workshop, Josiah asked for more gold powder to be sent up from London, 'as a great deal of it is gone in experiments'. Literally burning through gold in an effort to perfect the Queen's service was costing him dear, but he was prepared – not for the last time – to sacrifice a profit on one order for the sake of securing such a prestigious patron. Maybe more in hope than in expectation he wrote: 'I will forward the Creamcolour services as desired I hope the next week.'[29]

It took slightly longer but by the end of August, after nearly two months of exhaustive and costly work, Josiah was able to catch his breath and tell his friend Bentley with relief that 'I sent a crate of patterns off for the Queen last Saturday & desire your best wishes for their success.'[30] Now Josiah had only to wait for the verdict.

FOURTEEN

The Vexed & the Virtuosi

THE CREAMWARE SERVICE Josiah sent to St James's Palace was a remarkable achievement. Its ivory white, smoothly glazed surface created a decorative effect that was strikingly different from the common brown or rust-coloured wares locally produced. The tureens, *compotiers*, sauce bowls, and coffee cups had unusual but elegant curves; the conventional 'scroll handle' (S-shaped) on coffee pots and mugs was adapted to more ornamental 'cross-over' (two intertwined straps) handles. The plain plates introduced a new design – the round rim subtly altered to the shape of a flower's petals – which became known as the 'Royal Pattern'.

Before Queen Charlotte had the chance to comment on the delivery of Josiah's service, the rumour had spread that an innovative manufacturer was supplying quality 'cream ware' pottery that even the King had expressed admiration for.[1] It marked the end of the search for a form of pottery that could compete with porcelain. Nothing excited aristocrats more than the early hint of a new trend, and pampered dining rooms were soon filled with the chatter of new orders.

'Dr Swan dined with Ld Gower this week,' Josiah had heard on the grapevine, and 'after dinner your Brot Josiah's potworks were the subject of conversation for some time, the Cream Coloured table services in particular, I believe it was his Lordship who said that nothing of the sort could exceed them for a fine glaze &c &c.'[2] The idea that a small manufacturer from the provincial hills of

Staffordshire could receive such high praise from people of such 'great ministerial weight' Josiah found bemusing; it was also met with a degree of scepticism by the well-heeled gentlemen who combed Europe for the finest items of commerce. Some wondered whether Josiah Wedgwood's pottery matched, for instance, the quality of the wares produced by the French manufactory at Sèvres, owned for the last twelve years by Louis XV, samples of which could be found in the finest collections of England's landed gentry. 'His Ld Ship said that the late Ld Bolingbroke collected all the curious modelled earthen ware he could in France which were brought over to England & that it would be worth my while to go to London on purpose to see it.' Josiah took this less as a challenge than as an intriguing opportunity to collect more ideas about what to copy when manufacturing his own wares, especially since the sources of inspiration at Cheapside were drying up.[3]

One Wednesday morning in August Josiah looked up in amazement − as, no doubt, did his neighbours on Burslem's hill − as a chain of carriages pulled up in front of the Brick House Works out of which stepped the Duke of Marlborough, Lord Gower, Lord Spencer, '& others'. These, among the richest gentlemen in the United Kingdom (Lord Spencer alone owned 100,000 acres of land stretching across twenty-seven counties), had come to see Josiah's works for themselves.[4] They walked across the dirt yard, past squawking, flailing chickens, to the dusty workshops where they had been told the much discussed 'cream ware' originated. Josiah's home had become a national curiosity, an attraction for the aristocracy who had a 'madness to gaze at trifles' in the new manufactories.[5] Unsure of what to make of the visit, Josiah wrote to his brother that 'they have bought some things & seem'd much entertain'd & pleas'd'.[6]

For every new order that went out following the delivery of the Queen's service, twice as many seemed to come in. 'I sent a parcel to you which I hope is come to hand,' Josiah wrote to his brother, who was still struggling to regain his health and longed for a little relief, but 'I cannot promise you that it shall be the last of that sort.' On his desk Josiah had orders 'from the Duke of Grafton & Richard Hopkins, Esq, for services of Cream colour the same as Sr Charles Cootes, in a former letter from Sr Wm [Meredith] are ords for the same to General Honeywood – Mr Stevens & another Gentln in all with which I recd from him in Town eight services amount of the whole about £60 . . . Lady Broughton had a desert service . . . .'[7] It was an effort to stay on top of all the orders, not only in terms of filling them in a timely manner, but of organising the accounts, the invoices and payments.

Josiah had an idea. He drafted a template for orders and a template for bills, leaving blank lines for filling in with variable pieces of information, such as the quantity ordered, the customer's details, and the date. He wanted John to have the forms engraved so that numerous copies could be printed off on demand 'to distribute as occasion serves'; this would save John or Tom Byerley time and effort. He also had a new strategy for receiving monies owed.[8]

Traditionally, orders, which were usually small and relatively inexpensive, were delivered to retailers or customers on credit, often on the exchange of promissory notes or 'trade tokens'.[9] But now, business was booming – 'I have this year sent goods to amount of about £1,000 to London all of which is owing for,' Josiah told his brother, '& I shall not care how soon I was counting some of the money.'[10] Each order had its own price, varying in part as to whether it was for export, shops or a private family. For exports, Josiah added 5 per cent discount on orders 'for ready money', the goods 'being paid for here at the time of packing'.[11] Shops still dealt on credit, but aristocrats were notoriously bad at paying bills. Josiah's first and continuing patron, Sir William Meredith, offered some frank advice: 'You had best get your Brother to take the bills and receive the money on delivery.'

'This advice,' Josiah wrote to his brother, 'I think is too wholesome to be slighted & indeed I do not want these great folks to know that the Potters ever do give any credit at all. A word to the wise is enough.' Reviewing his accounts, he discovered one further problem. Since his services 'have been mentioned at St James's', he noticed that certain services that he had used – some engraving and delivery work, in particular – had suddenly become more expensive. 'I am very suspicious,' Josiah wrote, of certain people 'over charging [their] work especially in the spoon moulds', and he asked John 'therefore to know his charge before you pay him'. Celebrity, it was becoming clear, had hidden and unexpected expenses, and he needed to find ways to start protecting his profits.

Profits was exactly what motivated the Duke of Bridgewater's agent, John Gilbert, and his brother, Thomas Gilbert – MP for Newcastle-under-Lyme and agent for Lord Gower, when he decided to become directly involved with the proposals to build the Trent & Mersey Canal. The scheme to 'Unite Seas & countrys' was discovered by Gilbert, and seeing the chance to make a quick profit for his employers, launched their own scheme for financing the canal so that the Bridgewater-Gower interests would reap the largest profits.

When Josiah heard about this, he was 'astonish'd, Confounded & vexed'.[12] For months he had scarcely 'thought of anything at all but Pottmaking & Navigating', being conscious not to let the many new orders take him entirely away from the long-term plan of connecting the potteries to the rest of the world. Thomas Gilbert, whom Josiah had learned was the principal author of the opposing plan, was full of 'dark, mysterious & ungenerous' ideas that could undermine the dedication of 'the Persons who had hitherto lent their heads, hands & purses in planning & forwarding our scheme of Navigation'. Josiah was not going to let such a travesty occur. With a boldness and bravado that he never knew he possessed he rushed to Lichfield with Brindley to see Lord Gower in person, whereupon he 'intruded unasked upon a junto' of Thomas Gilbert and none other than Samuel Garbett, the Birmingham manufacturer, who received him with frozen glares that made it quite clear that 'they did not want my company'.

Josiah would not be deterred from upsetting their 'chimerical plan'. Holding his ground he declared that 'I had thought more on this subject than most of our people had', and therefore they 'placed me in the forefront of the battle'. Josiah faced up for a 'skirmish' with Gilbert, who with political legerdemain 'did not choose to answer *point blank* to some questions which I had prepared for him'. Samuel Garbett then piped up with an argument which Josiah patiently listened to before counter-attacking. 'The consequence of which was that in 10 minutes time he found his *baseless Fabrick* tumbling down to the ground & deserted it immediately.' Josiah was relishing his conquests.

In the midst of their debates, 'we were called to sup with Ld Gower' so that he could hear both parties' points of view. Never before had Josiah dined in the company of such dignitaries, nor had he ever been permitted to discourse on equal terms with, and in the company of, politicians. The civility of his host touched him. He was surprised that such an influential man, a 'great Man' – a former MP and Lord of the Admiralty, and now lord chamberlain of the royal household – could be so '*sensible & Humane*'.

As Gilbert – who spoke first – presented his ideas on behalf of the Duke of Bridgewater, Josiah could easily have lost his nerve, intimidated by the company and surroundings. But his eyes and mind never drifted and he listened steadfastly to the speech. 'Think my friend how I was delighted to find that he had not one argument, inference, or flourish to make in the whole harangue,' he told Bentley. Each point 'I *felt* myself able with the greatest clearness to confute'. He emphasised his emotional state. 'My *heart* was ingaged in the cause, & that I believe made my thoughts & expressions obedient to my wish.'

When he was called upon to make his reply he was direct, bluntly posing a question to his lordship. 'When a set of men had employed their time, talents & their purses for ten years together in the

execution of a design by which the Public would gain 300% . . .
what is their reward? Would it not be very cruel,' he asked, exposing
Gilbert's plan of creating a monopoly, if 'a new sett of Masters are
raised up to controul both them & their works?' 'Gilbert,' Lord
Gower said, after a moment's reflection on Josiah's words, 'I do not
think their plan can be rejected by Parliament.'

Josiah had clashed with titans and won. Josiah rode away from
Lichfield feeling he had arrived at a new station in life. 'I scarcely
know without a good deal of recollection whether I am a Landed
Gentleman, an Engineer or a Potter,' a dazed Josiah told Bentley,
'for indeed I am all three & many other characters by turns.' Boost-
ing his self-image even further, he had just learned that he was also
about to meet the Queen, a rendezvous that would make dinner
with Lord Gower pale by comparison.

Josiah was understandably nervous as he dressed for his meeting with
Queen Charlotte. After securing his brand-new, light brown dress
wig, he buttoned up his scarlet and lace waistcoat, eased on a blue
velvet jacket and strapped on his new sword, a proud gift to himself from Great Newport Street in London. It was a stylish touch – a
decorative accessory he knew was requisite when visiting the most
fashionable people in the country. Primed and feeling more confident
after indulging in an expensive shave, Josiah climbed into a coach and
was taken to Buckingham House at St James's Park, otherwise known
as the 'Queen's House', London's most opulent residence.[13]

Josiah had been told that the Queen was much impressed with
the service he had so frantically worked on. The pieces were finished
in his unique cream colour, with green and gold decorations as
requested, but, best of all, the engine-turned cups fitted the saucers
perfectly and the lid fitted the pot. As he had promised, it was
craftsmanship fit for a queen. Charlotte was so satisfied with her new
service that she bestowed a great privilege on Josiah. For posterity, he
recorded his version of how he earned a special place in history.

Having already introduced several improvements into this art, as well with respect to the forms and colours of the wares, as the composition of which they are made, [I] invented a new species of earthenware for the table, quite new in its appearance, covered with a rich and brilliant glaze, bearing sudden vicissitudes of heat and cold without injury ... To this manufacture the Queen was pleased to give her name and patronage, commanding it to be called Queen's Ware, and honouring the inventor by appointing him Her Majesty's potter.[14]

Queen Charlotte's command that Josiah should rename his cream ware 'Queen's Ware' was, more probably, an assent to an offer he made – the gift of naming the service in her honour, linking its uniqueness and 'brilliance' to the image of Her Majesty – in return he would use her assent to gain credibility in the marketplace for fashionable goods. It was a formula that Josiah studied as much as the chemistry of his glazes. As he said to Bentley: 'if a Royal or Noble introduction be as necessary to the sale of an Article of *Luxury*, as real Elegance & beauty, then the Manufacturer, if he consults his own interests, will bestow as much pains, & expense too, if necessary, in gaining the former of these advantages.'[15] In June 1766, in a stroke of marketing genius, Josiah placed an advertisement in *Aris's Birmingham Gazette*, announcing simply that 'Mr Josiah Wedgwood, of Burslem, has had the honour of being appointed Potter to Her Majesty.'[16]

He was, however, not the first to receive such an honour. In the early seventeenth century a merchant trader named Thomas Browne in Herald's *Visitation of London* (1634) referred to himself as 'Potter to King Charles', but Josiah nevertheless boldly seized the moment.[17] Not only would it serve Josiah's reputation well, but, as Bentley pointed out, it showed the Tory-loving royalty 'to have the success of all our manufactures much at heart, and to understand the importance of them', though 'Farmer George' never showed an interest in visiting the workshops of industry.[18] Indeed, seemingly not content with royal and elite patronage, Josiah would soon be writing to Bentley that he wanted to become not only Potter to Her Majesty but the 'Vase maker General to the Universe'.[19]

After Josiah left Buckingham House he strolled along Pall Mall where he passed 'large shoals' of Ladies endlessly seeking, it seemed to him, fashionable entertainment and objects of attention. If only he could draw their attention, he thought, but how? Each visit to London reaffirmed his impression that the new concept of 'show-rooms' was the key to turning 'the dirt under our feet into *Gold*', as he sanguinely promised Bentley, whom Josiah was trying to persuade to enter into a formal partnership. The idea was first given to him when Lord Gower and the other gentlemen paid a visit to the Bell Works, when, possibly frustrated by having to endure the treacherous roads, they wondered why Josiah had 'not a Warehouse in London where patterns of all the sorts may be seen'.[20]

For months he had been thinking about expanding his business beyond Burslem to London, with rooms and staff to cater to the whims of his new customers. Having his brother John there as an agent was not enough; he was too busy with his own warehouse to keep on top of Josiah's trade. 'I have often mentioned having a man in London the greatest part of the year shewing patterns, taking orders, settling accts &c &c,' he told John, '& as I increase my work, & throw it still more into the ornamental way, I shall have the greater need of such assistance.'[21] He sought his brother's advice about how much this was likely to cost, 'would £50 a year keep such a Person in London & pay rent for 2 rooms'?

While scouting for new premises in London, Josiah ducked into a coffee house to pen a progress report to Bentley. He was not having the best of luck. 'What I have seen is too small & not the most convenient situation,' he sighed. But roaming through London while he 'set out upon a large plan in writing to you', one thing was becoming clearer: Pall Mall – with its Restoration buildings and regal residents – 'is the best situation in London. It is convenient for the Whole of this Great Town, the avenues to it open, & everybody comes there some time or another.' It was in this wide street, with colonnades and clubs (Almack's, Boodle's and the Carlton among them), where, as the poet John Gay wrote in his *Trivia; or the Art of Walking the Streets of London* (1716):

> *Shops breathe perfumes, thro' sashes ribbons glow*
> *The mutual arms of ladies and the beaux.*

As an address, it was the perfect place to set up shop.

While writing about one of the rooms he had visited, he told Bentley about his meeting with the owners, 'a very good old Gentleman [who] has a young wife, & to her I am making my Court'. Josiah was always looking for a sale, and he knew a chance personal meeting with a young, wealthy woman of the house might be turned into a potential order. He was especially hopeful since, he observed, 'they are both of the Virtu species' – meaning they were amongst the 'Virtuosi', also known as the 'Dilettanti', the eighteenth-century collectors of ancient antiques. It was a rather new 'breed' to appear amongst the less noble ranks of society, though the Virtuosi had enough wealth to collect anything that was in fashion, most of it gathered whilst gallivanting around Europe on their Grand Tours.

Josiah told the couple about his pottery wares, that he was 'Potter to Her Majesty'. The gentleman was immediately interested and he invited Josiah to take a look at his personal cabinet of antiquities, 'a fine Collection of Raphael, Etruscan, & other very Curious Earthen wares'. It was a curious collection indeed – crude, dirty, cracked pieces of ancient pottery – typical of the sort of thing now being brought back in crate after crate from the shores of the Mediterranean.

What eccentric and infectious interests the leisured class had, Josiah thought, as he sat in the coffee house writing to Bentley. He took the last sip from his saucer, put the folded letter into his pocket, and set off exploring once again.

Some time later, he stopped to rest in St James's Park and watched the 'Ladies and Gentlemen of Quality' take their airings. Each one, he thought, was a potential customer, if only he could get them to walk through a room stocking his wares. But tea cups and snuff boxes, however well crafted, were as wearisome to the fashionable as wool. He remembered well his experiences when working with Whieldon: tastes change quickly and it was essential to be one step ahead. But a year after he delivered the service to the Queen he was shocked to find that 'the demand for this said *Creamcolour*, Alias, *Queen's Ware*, Alias, *Ivory*, still increases. It is really amazing,' he told Bentley, 'how rapidly the use of it has spread almost over the whole Globe, & how universally it is liked.'[22]

Happily for Josiah, the spread of popularity of his tea services corresponded to the exponential growth in the consumption of tea. In 1765, over 7 million kilograms of tea were exported to Europe, double the amount shipped twenty years earlier.[23] Josiah needed to expand his sales to America as quickly as possible. Even he was growing wearied of the 'green and gold' imitation of the Queen's Ware. 'I am quite clearing my Wareho. of Colour'd ware', he said, adding that he was 'heartily sick of the commodity & have been so long but durst not venture to quit it 'till I had got something better in hand'.[24] He needed something new to show and sell to the fashionable people parading along Pall Mall, and, remembering a recent conversation with his 'Virtuoso' friend, it dawned on him that he might just have something that would catch their attention: a story from history that stretched back to the beginning of civilisation.

FIFTEEN

Exquisite Models

EVERYONE KNEW it was a catastrophe, but as Goethe said, it curiously 'yielded so much pleasure to the rest of humanity'. On a hot August afternoon in AD 79, Mount Vesuvius erupted, burying the towns of the region of Campania, a seaside resort for wealthy Romans. A witness to the event from across the trembling Bay of Naples was Pliny the Younger who wrote to the historian Tacitus describing how blackened, burned pumice showered into the sea; dust permeated the air emanating a stench of sulphur and rocky debris blocked the escape of Vesuvius's victims, including his uncle, Pliny the Elder. Those who perished, said Pliny, would have thought that the world was perishing with them. Towns were left buried under up to seventy-five feet of ash and mud. Shocked survivors stared at the distant smouldering, molten mass. 'The mind shudders to remember,' wrote Pliny.[1] Over time much was forgotten, the Roman Empire collapsed and new towns were built along the Bay.

Nearly 1700 years later, a peasant digging in a well found building fragments and pieces of marble. The new Bourbon rulers of the region descended on this find with enthusiasm. In 1738 the Campanian town of Herculaneum was uncovered; a decade later workers reached a second town, identified as Pompeii when an inscription was found there in 1763. Bronzes, statues, jewels and even paintings were unearthed. Tourists as well as residents were fascinated; connoisseurs were captivated. 'There might certainly be collected great light from this reservoir of antiquities,' huffed Horace Walpole, 'if a man of learning had the inspection of it,' referring to men such as himself.

Travellers to the ancient lands and 'enlightened' scholars argued in their publications and clubs that their artistic and archaeological researches were crucial to understanding the historical development of society in general. 'While the antiquary investigates the origins of the Arts,' explained the historical painter and tutor in drawing, Thomas Burgess, 'he is led back to the first dawnings of civil life, and the progressive rise of political institutions. It is obvious, therefore, how wide a compass of human learning is subject to the researches of the Antiquarian.'

Here Burgess echoed popular sentiment: the public imagination was enraptured and there was no chance of keeping the tourists and the antiquarians away. While Josiah's workers were digging up clay and forming it into tableware, the plundering of buried cities had begun.

British Grand Tourists had always been excited by excavation. In England antiquarians such as William Stukeley combed parish grounds, uncovering ancient landscapes and studying sacred ruins. But a different kind of history was emerging in Italy and from its uniquely preserved scenes from the past. Evidence suggested that their art and culture had been influenced by both the Greeks and the Etruscans – that mysterious ancient civilisation that once thrived just north of Rome. History was beginning to reveal more about classical heritage than ever before and this was a lesson that classically educated Europeans were eager to learn.

Attention turned to the north, to the Tuscan mountains and to a landscape that hid even older secrets. This was also familiar ground to Grand Tourists who would pass each year through Tuscany on their way to Rome and Naples. The ancient Etruscans, made known through the writings of Livy and Virgil, had been a formidable

people – fighting off the Greeks for domination of the Mediterranean, and then the Romans, who eventually conquered and subjugated them. But they were enigmatic. No one knew how their home
– Etruria – originated. No one could understand their language.
The discovery of burial chambers, covered by mounds of earth or
set in hillsides, showed that they buried their nobility with great
splendour – in chambers with vaulted roofs often decorated with
coloured murals depicting scenes of dancing, banqueting, hunting,
fishing and horse racing.

Renaissance artists, such as Michelangelo, are thought to have
copied the few Etruscan frescoes that were then known. But the real
impulse to penetrate the vaults of antiquity came with the Age of
Enlightenment and the belief that through the study of inscriptions
and carved or painted images, a richer narrative of the past could be
revealed. As excavations spread into the Neapolitan south, remnants
of life in Pompeii and Herculaneum were uncovered.

Under the brilliant blue skies of Tuscany, over the rolling Floren-
tine mountains, along roads hedged with festoons of vines, mulberry
trees by the thousand and broad-leafed pollarded poplars, travellers
passed excavation sites being etched into the landscape, veiled by a
thin haze of dust from hundreds of peasants digging deeper into
the 'cities of the dead', the necropoleis. By the mid-eighteenth
century a host of British artists had become permanently resident
in the region with papal permission to superintend their own excavations.[2]

In 1748, the Scottish artist Gavin Hamilton arrived in Tuscany,
first earning a living by painting portraits of touring patricians, then
acting as a dealer in the trade in Etruscan antiquities. A party of
Grand Tourists gathered on horses and mules to be led by Hamilton
to see the digging at the ancient tombs and temples. Gazing down
from a sandy ridge they could glimpse pediments protruding from
the tiered ground, while workers emerged from tunnels hauling
decorative bas-reliefs, funerary steles and, most enticingly, ornamental vases. They spied artists sketching the artefacts in situ and dealers

carefully protecting their sites from prying eyes, concerned only with smuggling their finds into the unofficial art market. The enthusiastic visitors hurriedly made offers on the latest discoveries while Hamilton and his fellow dealers fast established an eager clientele.

One specific client, William Hamilton, British ambassador to Naples from 1767, possessed not only wealth and the desire to collect, but also enjoyed great political clout and the friendship of the King of Naples. Hamilton was perfectly placed to link together an alliance of artists, agents and connoisseurs in orchestrating a profitable trade in antiquities. He was also preparing a publication illustrating his personal collection that would help establish 'neo-classicism' as the eighteenth century's greatest fashion and, by chance, provide a blueprint for an unlikely empire in the making created by a little-known entrepreneur in Burslem.

William Hamilton's home, the Palazzo Sessa, set on a steep hill overlooking the spectacular Bay of Naples, quickly gained a reputation among Neapolitan high society and passing Grand Tourists as the place to go for vivacious assemblies. 'It is the custom,' explained one British visitor to Naples in 1768,

> when neither the Opera, nor any particular engagement prevent
> [us] to meet at his house, where we amuse ourselves as we are
> disposed, either at cards, the billiard-table, or his little concert;
> some form themselves into small parties of conversation, and
> as the members of this society are often Ambassadors, Nuncios,
> Monsignoris, Envoys, Residents, and the first quality of Naples,
> you will conceive it to be instructive as well as honourable.[3]

The King of Naples commented how he too enjoyed visiting Hamilton's house, where 'an interesting group of lovely women, literati, and artists were assembled'.

Hamilton also had a home, named Villa Angelica, south of the city, at Portici, near the Royal Palace and two miles from the base of Mount Vesuvius, not far from Herculaneum. It was equally picturesque, surrounded by a fertile vineyard with lava-baked paths leading up the mountain. Here, Hamilton and his wife, Catherine, entertained guests more intimately than at the Palazzo Sessa. One guest, Charles Burney (father of the future novelist, Fanny), was travelling through Naples collecting information for his *General History of Music* and had been invited with his friend Captain Forbes to dine with the Hamiltons.

The guests arrived at the Villa Angelica on a crisp autumn afternoon and immediately found the household convivial, indulging in one course after another, washed down with copious amounts of Neapolitan wine, punctuated with concerts performed by two of Hamilton's pages 'who play very well one on the fiddle and the other on the violoncello'.[4] Late afternoon was siesta time and the Hamiltons set up a field bed for Captain Forbes, who, originally planning to bow out, 'was easily prevailed upon to pig in the same room with me', wrote Burney. The party awoke after sunset for more musical entertainment and stories of Burney's research – 'musical talk' as he called it.

All such chatter stopped, however, when a loud explosion was heard from the direction of the 'very busy' volcano. The party ran to the veranda while William Hamilton fumbled with 'glasses of all sorts' with which to focus on the mountain – his own passionate subject of research. But even without any apparatus everyone clearly saw 'showers of immense red hot stones' raining down on the mountain; 'we were certain that they mounted near 1000 feet above the summit'. The rumble was deeper than thunder, wrote an astounded Burney, and the sight 'very awful and beautiful, resembling in great the most ingenious and fine fireworks I ever saw'. 'It was,' confirmed Catherine, who was by no means unfamiliar with the volcano's activities, 'an astonishing sight.'

The turbulent mountain kept Burney awake much of the night, even though he was fatigued from all the music and dancing. After the pages retired, Catherine sat at the harpsichord and William took the violin and played Vivaldi, Handel, and the more regional Piccini, Manna, and Paesiello. Burney was anxious to rise early and follow one of the paths up the side of Vesuvius to take a closer look at the activity, but William Hamilton advised against it, while such 'quantities of sulphurous smoke' emanated and uncertainty remained as to 'where the stones will drop'. Burney took a chaise instead, visiting 'the lava of former eruptions and to coast round the foot of Vesuvius as far as we could with safety by keeping always to the windward'. He had come prepared, putting on his flannel waistcoat, leather stockings, 'old good-for-nothing shoes' and a great coat – ready to climb ('sometimes on all fours') over the rugged lava, cinders, and ashes, feeling sorry for Captain Forbes, who emerged for a second time from his makeshift field bed ready to go with only the previous day's elegant silk suit to wear.

It was a privilege to go with a guide as knowledgeable and enthusiastic as William Hamilton, who was once even spotted in a back street of Naples in full court dress, complete with his star and ribbon, being helped by a local peasant carry home some recently excavated dusty vases which he had just purchased. That is why Charles Burney was so interested in crawling on all fours around the mountain. The blanket of ash and debris hid great potential treasure. In Burney Hamilton recognised a kindred spirit and he suggested that if he wanted to see some of the treasures, then he should come to look at his collection at the Palazzo Sessa, which he did a few days later.

According to one visitor, it was no secret that the Neapolitans were 'more suspicious and jealous' of Hamilton than anyone else for having amassed such a collection – over 2,000 antique objects, including over 700 ancient vases and 600 bronzes, alongside a separate collection of over 6,000 coins. However in Britain his efforts to promote the study of the classical past were celebrated. In the second half of the eighteenth century, Grand Tourists returning to Britain on the rising tide of neo-classical interest, led, as early as 1734, to the founding of the Society of Dilettanti, formed, as one contemporary explained, by some of the gilded youth 'who had travelled in Italy and were desirous of encouraging, at home, a Taste for those objects which had contributed so much to their entertainment abroad'.[5] The Dilettanti worked to achieve their ostensible goals by putting themselves forward as exemplary artistic patrons – they zealously collected and encouraged others to follow suit, supporting publications that sought 'less to dazzle than instruct' future students of classical antiquity. Charles Burney was one such student. When he returned to London, he was welcomed by the Dilettanti, who supported his nomination to the Royal Academy of Arts, the new institution opened by George III in 1768 after vigorous canvassing by the Dilettanti. Burney was a perfect candidate. In the view of Sir Joseph Banks, the president of the eminently prestigious Royal Society – he was 'one of the most learned men we have among us'.

The numbers of such men were growing, and Burney's new friend, William Hamilton, was fast becoming the doyen of fine taste – the 'head of the Virtuosi', in the words of the artist and president of the Royal Academy Sir Joshua Reynolds, who was honoured to join some of the Dilettanti on the day that Hamilton, during a visit to London, was ceremoniously inaugurated to the Society. Six members gathered around Hamilton who sat at a table with an Etruscan vase from his collection placed in front of him. Reynolds faced them, sketching the scene for a group portrait. The Society's president, Sir Watkin Williams Wynn, downed a glass of red wine and toasted Hamilton's health, gesturing towards the vase. It was a gesture that acknowledged his promotion of certain Enlightenment ideals – the advancement of the science of 'taste' by example, through rational instruction. Hamilton had now been inducted into the 'cult of connoisseurship'.

Some critics, such as Horace Walpole, dismissed the club. While he agreed in principle that there was virtue in antiquarian study, he doubted whether the Dilettanti would set a good example. After all, he jested, 'the nominal qualification for membership is having been in Italy, the real one, being drunk'.

But it was the Society's financial support for the publication of others' antiquarian researches that would earn its members recognition. Their latest member, Hamilton, was well aware of this. His own enormous collection had received widespread admiration since, between 1766–7, he had published four sumptuous folio volumes illustrating his collection, offering 'exquisite Models' that would aid future artists in the development of their skills of observation and drawing. Sir Joshua Reynolds was among the first to offer praise, writing a warm-hearted letter telling how much he admired the work and how confident he was that it 'will tend to the advancement of the Arts, as adding more materials for Genius to work upon'.

Hamilton appreciated the comment. 'Good models,' he affirmed, thinking of the elaborate engravings in his publication, 'give birth to ideas by exciting the imagination . . .'. Aspiring to fulfil the Dilettanti dream, his lavish volumes were not intended to provide 'merely the objects of fruitless admiration', but rather to 'revive an ancient Art'. Little did he foresee what a Master Potter from the Midlands with a bountiful imagination and mountains of determination would do when he encountered those illustrations.

SIXTEEN

Creators of Beauty

'I HAVE NOW BOUGHT the Estate', Josiah eagerly told Bentley, confident that his offer of £3,000 would be accepted by Mrs Ashenhurst, the elderly owner of Ridge House Estate.[1] He anticipated that the deal would be completed by next spring and quickly set about having the land surveyed for the construction of a grand factory and a new home for his young, growing family: Sally had just given birth to their second child, a boy they named John. Josiah hoped that Bentley would take a break from his duties and visit their 'dirty spot of Earth', a description given to Burslem by their mutual friend, Ralph Griffiths, editor of the *Monthly Review*.[2]

Josiah was particularly keen to have Bentley visit since they had just 'increased their connections'. Bentley had agreed to open his Liverpool warehouse to Josiah's goods and 'be a Pot merchant', acting as an import and export agent for Josiah's business and managing the sale and stock of the wares at his discretion.[3] Whatever goods Josiah bought from other suppliers for export, he and Bentley would split the profits 'evenly betwixt us'. If Josiah sent him 'goods of my own manufacture, I allow you a 10% commission as before'. Bentley had in the past sold items for Josiah and arranged for their shipment abroad, on commission, but this move marked the beginning of a closer professional partnership, and one that Josiah hoped would grow stronger after he had managed to lure Bentley to Burslem for good.

'My Sally says your *fat sides* require a good deal of shaking &

would recommend a journey on *horseback*, not in the Coach, to Burslem,' Josiah joked.[4] What's more, 'she will not fix upon a spot for either house or Gardens no nor even the Stables 'till you have viewed & given your opinion of the premises', flattering him that he should think of himself as 'Capability Brown' and thereby softening his teasing of his friend's portliness. 'Ten Guineas if I remember is the price of a single call, with or without the advantage of his direction, to make a lawn & piece of Water here – Cut down that wood & plant it there, level that rising ground, & raise yonder valley &c &c.' Why would they need to hire a Brown, Josiah asked, when Bentley had 'a hundred times the genius', and at the expense of a mere fifty mile ride, so much more could be accomplished. 'As our connections are to become extensive in the Potting business,' Josiah said, with a glint in his eye, 'it is absolutely necessary you should visit the Manufacture, see what is going forward there, make your bargains accordingly, & lend your assistance towards its farther improvement.'

Bentley's proposed visit to Burslem instigated a discussion with Josiah and Sally about the plans for the house and factory that would weave through their correspondence for months. They also talked about increasing the sales of pottery to America and the West Indies, hoping that the post-war political unrest would not interfere yet again with their lucrative trade. For months Josiah had been clearing out the recesses of his warehouse, sending 'Cargoes of Creamcolour & perhaps a little green and Gold for hot climates', asking Bentley to organise a shipment to the capital of British West Florida, to 'sell all the green and gold for Pensacola, [and] the new discover'd Islands', adding that 'Green desert ware is often wanted, *in reality* for the West India Islands.'[5]

Josiah also wished to pursue an idea of his, which, he told Bentley, he had been reminded of by a comment made by Lord Gower after one of his visits to the Bell House Works. He 'asked me if I had not sent Mr Pitt over in shoals to America'. They had done it almost a decade earlier when Admiral Vernon became a national hero, so why not Pitt (the Elder); Josiah knew the Colonies were enthusiastic supporters of the Whig Prime Minister. 'What do you think about sending Mr Pitt upon Crockery ware to America?' he continued. 'A Quantity might certainly be sold there now & some advantage made of the American prejudice in favour of the great man.'[6]

This time, there was no sarcasm in Josiah's use of the term 'great man'. Josiah and Bentley, as well as so many other merchants involved in the foreign market, cheered Pitt's campaign to protect national trade and his staunch opposition of damaging government proposals such as the Stamp Act. 'It is my opinion,' Pitt had declared to Parliament, 'that this kingdom has no right to lay a tax on the colonies. Trade is your object with them and taxing was ill advised. If you do not make suitable laws for them, they will make laws for you, my Lords.' In the face of fierce American resistance to the Stamp Act, and following another impassioned speech by Pitt in January 1766, the Act was repealed.

But before Josiah and Bentley had a chance to execute the design for Pitt's portrait for their plates, the climate of colonial trade changed once again. 'The American business is in a critical condition,' a gravely concerned Josiah wrote a year after Pitt's speech, '& I do not know what to determine upon without you, for you will be concern'd in the event as well as myself.'[7]

Pitt had fallen ill, and his nemesis, George Grenville, a protégé of Lord Bute (and ironically Pitt's brother-in-law), was once again arguing that 'the troops to be kept up in America shou'd be Paid by the Colonies' through new taxes. The Chancellor of the Exchequer, Charles Townshend, agreed and began drafting an 'American Import Duties Bill' to raise revenue. Of particular concern to Josiah was Article Seven of what became known as the Townshend Act, which discontinued 'the drawbacks payable on china earthenware exported to America', eliminating the refund on the duty manufacturers such as Josiah were liable to pay.[8]

Since George Grenville's first speeches when he was Prime Minister in 1763 – which led to the passing of the Stamp Act – and his persecution of Wilkes for publishing the *North Briton*, Grenville had aroused the wrath of most of those who looked out for Britain's mercantile interests, Bentley and Josiah included. In December 1766, when debates between Pitt and Grenville on the quartering of troops and new taxes were at their height, Bentley wrote an anonymous (as was customary) article in the *Monthly Review*, attacking the book *Trade and Finances* written by Grenville's former secretary to the Treasury, Thomas Whately.

'Tho' the subject of commerce has been frequently investigated, it is far from being so well and universally understood as to render the illustrations of future Writers unnecessary,' Bentley wrote in the article. 'Indeed many of our commercial laws are so extremely absurd, as to injure those manufactures and branches of trade which they were intended to encourage, to retard improvements, and prohibit invention; so that they stand in great need of general *Review*.' The book, Bentley bluntly put it, was full of 'circumstantial enumerations' and 'written in favour of a party'. 'It must be confessed,' he continued, 'this noble work would require a knowledge of facts, a clearness of understanding, an impartiality of judgement, a love of the public welfare; and a *portion of undisturbed leisure for deliberation*, which rarely fall to the lot of any man; and never to one of our bustling financiers, or Ministers of State.'[9]

Josiah unwittingly read his friend's diatribe while reading the *Monthly Review* out loud one evening to Sally (for the 'amusement of Deary' as he put it). 'Why Joss!' Sally shouted out, shrewdly recognising their friend's brand of argument and prose style, 'one would think thou wast reading one of Bentley's letters.' This suddenly struck Josiah as being 'very certain'. 'I shall not wonder to hear,' Josiah later joked to Bentley, 'that George Grenville has sent to inquire of the Publisher, who it was that wrote that letter.' It was such intrepidness to 'set our *Great* & *Little* folk right' that Josiah and Sally so admired in their friend.[10]

Josiah was gripped by the debates over taxation and colonial unrest every evening as he read the papers. They brought back an anxiety that had haunted him for years. At the beginning of 1765, in the midst of debates affecting colonial trade, a concerned Josiah had written to the only politician he then had contact with, Sir William Meredith. 'The bulk of our particular manufacture you know is exported to foreign markets,' explained Josiah, 'for our home consumption is very trifleing in comparison to what is sent abroad, & the principal of these markets are the Continent & islands of N. America . . . .' 'This trade to our Colonies,' he continued, 'we are apprehensive of losing in a few years,' if not from strangling trade regulations, then because the colonists 'have set on foot some Potwork there' to compete with the mother country's manufacturers.

Josiah was referring to a story that had caused him particular alarm. A Master Potter from Staffordshire named Bartham had recently emigrated to America and had set about 'hireing a number of our hands for establishing new Pottworks in South Carolina'. As the 'necessaries of life & consequently the price of labour' was 'daily advancing', making the management of a manufactory more expensive and stressful, Josiah thought it 'highly probable' – no, he changed his mind categorically – there is 'no question but more will follow them & join their Brother Artists & Manufacturers of every class who are from all quarters takeing a rapid flight'. By impressing 'the evil' of 'these emigrations' upon Meredith, a great patron 'of the arts & Commerce of your Country', he hoped something might be done.[11]

But two years later, there was still no relief. 'Mr Grenville & his party seem determin'd to *Conquer England in America*,' Josiah reported during a visit to London in 1767, echoing Pitt's own proclamation when he added that 'the Americans will then make Laws for themselves & if we continue our Policy – for us too in a very short time'. Bartham's example, Josiah teased, might yet prevail. 'If we must all be driven to America you & I shall do very well amongst the Cherokees.'[12]

Ironically, a possible resolution to Josiah's immediate concerns came with an unexpected order for his wares. 'Would you think it,' he exclaimed to Bentley, 'I am this morning going by Command to visit your old friend George Grenville. You may make yourself easy about America, we will settle their affairs whilst his Lady is giving her order for Crockery ware.'[13] Josiah had in the past overcome personal aversions for the sake of a sale or promoting his own interests, and this curious encounter was no exception, as he gained another aristocratic patron. This was also the case when, in a further attempt to enrich his manufactory and draw on the potential that America had to offer, Josiah contemplated contacting none other than the Chancellor of the Exchequer, Charles Townshend.

The idea came up during a discussion with the Duke of Bridgewater, when Josiah enquired about the prospects of obtaining a patent granting him exclusive rights to the import of 'Cherokee' clay, or kaolin, from America. He had been conducting routine experiments on different kinds of clay bought from clay merchants which included 'a lump' from South Carolina, 'which surprised me a good deal'.[14] It had some unusual qualities: it was whiter than most clay and remained so after firing at high temperatures, taking on a translucent, glossy quality. After consulting his chemical friends, including Joseph Priestley and a new acquaintance, the engineer James Watt, Josiah learned that 'kaolin will come out of the fire perfectly white' because it lacked 'phlogiston', a substance (according to contemporary theory) that allowed other substances to burn.[15] This might, Josiah thought, be the secret ingredient he needed to make real Chinese porcelain – a commodity that was so sought after it would be like being able to 'turn dirt into *Gold*'.

Josiah immediately asked Bentley to enquire about importing more of it, which 'must be got as clean from soil or any heterogenius matter, as if it was to be eaten & put into Casks or Boxes' which recorded exactly the place, and depth, from which it was mined.[16] Later, he bought a map of North America by the traveller, cartographer, and geologist John Mitchell, who Josiah also personally visited in London to talk about clay deposits. He even 'kept incognito' at a meeting with 'three Gentlemen who had resided long in South

Carolina, one of whom gave me a small sample of the Cherok earth, by way of Curiosity, not knowing who, or what I was'. He discovered information about its location – the main source was 300 miles inland from Charles Town – and some practical details about how to transport it abroad.[17] What he was hoping for from Charles Townshend was no less than a monopoly on its use in Britain.

The Duke of Bridgewater was sceptical about Josiah's plan. 'The Chancellor of the Exchequer might be applyd to grant it to me Duty free, & to lay a duty upon all imported by others,' but, the Duke explained, as it would need to be a Parliamentary affair, it 'very probably would not pass, but would inevitably lay the whole affair open.'[18] Drawing attention to the scheme would work against Josiah, he continued, since 'Mr Townshend and Ld Shelbourne' are friends with none other than Samuel Garbett, the Birmingham merchant who had interfered with the plans for the Trent & Mersey Canal, who they had intimated 'is sure to be advised of it'.

Given the political climate, created not least by Townshend, it would certainly be a coup if Josiah managed to get his way. However he was realistic about his chances and decided to act on the Duke's prudent advice and 'send a Person over immediately without applying for a grant, a Patent or anything else'.

Josiah thought about who he could send to America as an agent. One possibility was Thomas Griffiths, the brother of his literary friend Ralph, whom Josiah discovered, 'hath resided many years in N.A. & is seasoned to the S.C. Climate by a severe fever he underwent at Charles Town & has had many connections with the Indians'.[19] He had bought into a share of 3,000 acres of land with two partners and planned to produce sugar from maple, 'which secret he had learned from the native Indians', but had been frustrated in his scheme for lack of money. He replied that he would be happy to offer his services to Josiah, who worried a little that the entrepreneur might 'take it into his head to redeem, with my money, his share of the improvements his partners have made on their grant of land'. He knew he came from a respectable and friendly family, but had 'known such instances of Persons changing their sentiments & principles with the Climate'. Still, Josiah concluded, it was worth the risk. One way or another, Josiah wanted the Cherokee clay.

Meanwhile another issue offered Josiah little relief from apprehension about his 'downright serious business' plans.[20] Bentley was still resisting Josiah's inducements to enter into a more formal and committed partnership, which would require his permanent removal to Burslem. Bentley meditated on the difficulties of the move, which Josiah picked apart one by one:

'I have total ignorance of the business,' claimed Bentley. 'That I deny,' Josiah riposted. 'You have taste, the best foundation for our intended concern, & which must be our *Primum Mobilie*, for without that, all will stand still.' Bentley emphasised that he did not know the practical side of the craft, but Josiah assured him that you 'will soon be learned by so apt a scholar. The very air of this Country will soon inspire you with the more Mechanical part of our trade.' Bentley foresaw many difficulties in quitting his current position and ending his prospering partnership with Samuel Boardman, only established two years earlier, in 1764. Josiah agreed that it was a risk, a 'matter of Calculation, in which there is no data to proceed upon, but probabilities of future contingencies, which we cannot investigate'. However, Josiah was emphatic that it was a risk worth taking: 'I have, it's true, a great opinion of the design answering our most sanguine expectations with respect to profit,' he said.

But one of Bentley's concerns, Josiah wrote, 'staggers my hopes more than anything else': Bentley did not want to leave his friends and the pleasures of Liverpool.

Josiah trod cautiously. 'Can you part from your Octagon, & enlightened Octagonian brethren, to join the diminutive & weak society of a Country Chapel? Can you give up the rational & elevated enjoyment of your Philosophical Club, for the puerile tete a tete of a Country fireside?' Could he prise himself away from his evening soirées with all those 'learned & ingenious friends' in town 'to employ yourself amongst Mechanicks, dirt & smoke?'

Josiah paused. However true, perhaps this was not the most attractive way to put it – no Gainsborough elegance in this portrait of provincial, manufacturing life. But there was a deeper sense of satisfaction to be derived from it. 'I have some hopes,' he wrote, that if you 'fall in love with & make a Mistress of this new business, as I have done in mine, I should have little or no doubt of our success.' He implored Bentley to think of the power one had as a manufacturer, who with 'raw Materials, the infinite ductility of the Clay' can 'be the Creator as it were of beauty, rather than merely be the vehicle, or medium to convey it from one hand to another'. Things were progressing slowly with the purchase and development of Ridge House Estate, and so he beseeched Bentley to take his time to think things over.

Part of the delay at Ridge House was due to the Derbyshire architect Joseph Pickford, whom Josiah had hired to develop plans for the new houses and factory. Josiah had been introduced to Pickford through friends of Bentley's, but after one quick look at his first drawings, 'Sally and I pronounce'd its doom', as did Bentley, who was becoming increasingly interested in ideas concerning their proposed partnership.[21]

Josiah wanted everything to be just right, and 'proposed to Mr Pickford an alteration or two' on, for instance, what he now tantalisingly referred to as Bentley's new home. He enlarged the rooms here and there, so that Bentley would be able to 'sup in *comfortably*'. He liked some of the exterior details, but thought 'three outside doors are too many for your small house, & would render it very windy, cold, & uncomfortable'. The brew house was 'abominable', but these were 'trifling alterations', which he and Bentley mutually worked on during one of their meetings at what Josiah now referred to as 'Etruria'.[22]

The development was not progressing as smoothly as they had hoped. 'This building of houses my Friend so far as we have hitherto gone is very near akin to *Building Castles in the Air*,' exclaimed Josiah in desperation. 'The old Mansions are all swept clean away! & you see a totally new one erected in their stead' – the whole project stretching above a staggering £10,000 (£700,000). 'So help me – Bentley,' cried Josiah, 'to create new Vases for the payment of my Architect!' Thankfully the 'new mansion' that Josiah preferred to Pickford's original Palladian plan was '5 to £700 less than the former', and was designed to be 'more in the Modern, & I think *true* taste'.[23]

On top of this Josiah received the unsettling news that old Mrs Ashenhurst was not satisfied with his £3,000 offer for the estate, and was willing to accept a competing offer. 'Indeed,' he wrote to Bentley, hoping to assuage his friend's anxieties about the whole affair, 'I am not in possession of the land you know to build you either a House or Works, but am with the Old Ladys Steward & you have furnished me with a very strong inducement to comply with almost any terms they shall propose.'[24] But this would take more time.

Wanting to progress with his plans in other ways, Josiah travelled to London in the hope of finding a shop to rent, where he envisioned 'setts of Vases should decorate the Walls & both these articles may, every few days, be so altered, revers'd & transform'd as to render the whole a new scene', a showroom strategy where 'business & amusement can be made to go hand in hand'. He also continued the more pleasant conversation he had earlier begun with Bentley about 'anything curious in the Pottery branch' relating to 'antiquities'.[25]

When he returned to Burslem, at the beginning of June 1767, he felt rejuvenated, with 'a heart perfectly at ease & rejoicing with my family & friends at our meeting together again in health and safety'. He excitedly wrote to Bentley, telling him of all the 'designs, Models, Moulds, Clays, Colours &c &c for the Vasework by which means we shall be able to do business *effectually* 12 months sooner than we could without those preparatory steps'.

But as Josiah gave the post boy his cheery letter for Bentley he was given another in return: it was from William Hodgson, a London merchant and friend of his brother John, containing news that Josiah could hardly take in.

SEVENTEEN

An Afflicted Heart

I T TOOK JOSIAH a day to gain enough strength to inform Bentley of the terrible news from London: 'Your friend & My poor
Brother is Dead.'[1]

John was forty-six years old, nearly ten years older than Josiah,
yet it was only recently, when John agreed to help his younger
brother engage with the London marketplace, that the two had
become so very close. He had entirely dedicated himself to Josiah's
welfare, squarely confronting his increasing responsibilities despite
suffering various severe bouts of illness over the years. Whether it
was attending Court or knocking on doors to collect outstanding
bills, he had never failed his brother. Josiah was in disbelief, unable
to accept the news that John 'is no more, is no longer the warm &
benevolent friend, affectionate Brother, or chearfull Companion,
but is now a lifeless, insensible Clod of Earth'.

What made the shock all the more severe was the mysterious circumstances surrounding his brother's death, as pieced together by
his friends and described in Hodgson's letter. On the ill-fated night,
four days earlier, John had gone to watch fireworks at Ranelagh,
the public gardens on the banks of the Thames in Chelsea, where
fashionable crowds frequented concerts, balls and masquerades.
Afterwards, he went to the Swan Inn at Westminster Bridge, ('where'
Hodgson wrote, 'we used to dine & get a little refreshment') and
where he stayed until about midnight. He asked for a room 'but
unfortunately they were unable to accommodate him, so that he was

obliged to go see for one elsewhere, & in passing the River side, tis supposed he slipped in.' His body was found floating in the Thames at 5a.m. the next morning.

Those were all the particulars that Mr Hodgson could relay. 'It is indeed too much for me,' Josiah confessed: 'I can scarcely think at all.'[2] But however much he tried not to Josiah found himself tortuously retracing and replaying the last hours of his brother's life in his head. 'Many things if you were here I should ask you,' he wrote to Hodgson, '& yet I am afraid to know them.' Josiah could not shake the feeling that there was some foul play or devious cause involved. 'I know you will do everything in your power to preserve the memory of your Deceased friend from censure,' he continued, but 'I shall be very unhappy till I know some further particulars'. A brief report in London's *Lloyd's Evening Post* would only have fuelled Josiah's suspicions:

> Monday evening a man threw himself into the River near the White Swan at Chelsea and was drowned, and yesterday his body was thrown on shore by the tide near that place; the cause of his committing this action is said to be a disappointment in a love affair.[3]

Whatever else, if anything, Josiah or his brother's friends learned about John's death, appears to have been buried with the past.

Despite his grief, Josiah expressed his thanks to Hodgson that in him John had a good friend to 'perform the last offices of humanity', and who could advise 'what is to be done on this melancholy occasion'. He asked the merchant to retrieve 'a little box' from a desk at the warehouse that Josiah used 'in which I put the notes he had for his money, & other papers' and to think about 'my late Brothers Connections & who to invite to the funeral'. Their elder brother Thomas was preparing to travel to London for the funeral, but Josiah needed to stay at home – for Sally was pregnant with their third child and was expected to go into labour any day.

As the executor of John's will, Josiah was determined that his brother would have a fine send-off. 'Everything is to be done in a handsome manner, he has left enough behind him to do it with,' he announced. 'As a small Testimony of the Esteem my poor Brother had for you,' Josiah wrote to Bentley, 'he hath left you five Guineas to buy a mourning ring. I know he always wished to be remembered by you.' Now more than ever Josiah was thankful to have such a 'dear friend' as Bentley.

> I know you will sympathise with me in my distress, & I need not tell you how doubly welcome a few lines will be at this time from a real, affectionate, & sensible friend, such a one as you have ever been to me since I had the happiness of being known to you. Let us now be dearer to each other if possible than other, let me adopt you for my Brother & fill up the chasm this cruel accident has made in my afflicted heart – Excuse me, my dear friend, the subject is too much for me.

'I am,' Josiah signed the letter faintly, 'your miserable friend.'[4]

A month passed and Josiah remained 'in distress', re-reading letters through 'a Valley of Tears' from friends that were 'a Cordial to my afflicted heart'.[5] 'The loss of a Brother, a sensible, Benevolent, & truly affectionate Brother' tore a breach in 'a heart rather too susceptible of grief'.

This was the longest period that Josiah had spent away from work since his accident on the way to Liverpool five years earlier. But business, he knew, must go on or he and his family would face further distress. He became alert to his lethargy when Bentley travelled to London for pressing issues connected to his own affairs – addressing debates connected with new legislation on bankruptcy on behalf of the Corporation of Liverpool, and in late July 1767, supporting a friend in a court case. When Bentley's friend lost his case, which appeared to have some residual effects on Bentley's own business affairs, Josiah was quick to offer consolation. 'Besides all pecuniary considerations' in this 'unlucky turn in your affairs,' Josiah wrote, 'you have too much Philosophy . . . to be deeply, or too long affected by a mere accident.' Bentley should turn to his friend, and 'infuse into his bosom a portion of that cheerfulness & flow of good spirits, you are so largely possessed of', and remember to 'look forward & be happy'.[6]

After writing this, Josiah seemed to take his own advice. He recognised that he needed to return to work, and he began a course of experiments to refocus his mind – 'Labour I will not call it,' he said, preferring to use the term 'entertainment' – travelling to local mines to collect materials for his experiments and obtaining various fusible substances to mix with clay and analyse for their chemical properties and suitability as glazes.

But what lifted Josiah's spirits most was that they had a new arrival to their family, whom they named Dicky, and it was with some joy that he informed Bentley of the news that 'Mrs Wedgwood & her Wedgwoodikin are both well'.[7]

'I am now sunk over head & ears into business again, & have now, at this present time of writing, a Warehouse full of Gentlemen & Ladys,' Josiah reported to Bentley a month later.[8] Whether it was to make up for lost time or discharge the pent-up anxieties about work, he was now busier than he could remember: experimenting, travelling, selling and sketching. 'Why you never knew so busy a Mortal as I am,' he exclaimed. 'Highways – surveying Ridge House Estate – Experiments for Porcelain, or at least a new Earthenware, fill up every moment almost of my time & would take a good deal more if I had it.'[9] He had a catalogue of orders at hand and a range of products that were flying out of his warehouse in crates. 'Creamcolor Tyles are much wanted,' he noted, '& the consumption will be great for Dairys, Baths, Summer Houses, *Temples* &c &c.'

This was the sort of stock-in-trade ware that always provided the bedrock of Josiah's business. His experimental triumphs, such as cream (or Queen's) ware, provided a welcome windfall, but as always Josiah was anticipating a change in consumer taste. 'Every rarity soon grows stale,' he wrote, which is why he was still drawn to work in the laboratory each night.[10] 'Many of my experiments turn out to my wishes, & convince me more and more, of the extensive capability of our Manufacture for further improvements,' he confided to Bentley, encouraging him to share his dream about future success. 'It is at present (comparatively) in a rude, uncultivated state, & may easily be polish'd & brought to much greater perfection. Such a revolution, I believe, is at hand, & you must assist in, & profit by it.'[11]

Josiah thought that the 'revolution' was not only linked to the production of new kinds of products, but to the way people shopped. He had seen the new phenomenon of conspicuous consumption, and he believed he had 'a mode of introducing this article amongst that sort of Customers who can afford to pay for anything they like, though the price is a little too high for People in the middle station'.[12] It was, Josiah felt, time for change.

'We will,' he proclaimed, 'COMMAND SUCCESS, if you can make this branch of business worth your pursuit.'[13] 'I have some tryals that will do you good to look at,' he pleaded, which will 'make you an Etruscan' yet! 'Leave off trimming your old skiff, come & assist in putting a new one upon the Stocks.'

Ironically, it was the present boom in business that was keeping him one step away from entering this new world. 'My present business is too good to be neglected for uncertainties,' an unusually cautious Josiah determined, '& I must, so long as that is the case, be content without arriving at those improvements in my Manufacture, which a little application would bring within my reach.' 'However,' he wrote, drawing attention to one piece of progress he had made which he used to whet Bentley's appetite, 'I have improved bodys enough for Vases, & ornaments are really an inexhaustible field for us to range in.' The 'field', Josiah believed, of 'ornaments' – decorative, rather than 'useful' wares – was where he and Bentley would find their first 'hidden treasure'. His next visit to London convinced him of this.

Since Josiah's chance meeting with the Virtuosi couple in London over a year earlier, where he was first shown Etruscan vases in the gentleman's cabinet of curiosities, Josiah had been seeking out all the information he could on ancient antiquities, particularly the decorative, 'ornamental' vases that Grand Tourists proudly displayed as souvenirs of their travels. He asked Bentley to enquire about 'a volume or two' that he could read that 'may be of use to me in the Antiquities', wanting to study everything from colours and textures to design. 'Who knows what you may hit upon, or what we may strike out betwixt us?' he wrote, but 'you may depend on an ample share of the profits arising from any such discoveries.'[14]

Bentley advised that Josiah should visit the British Museum, where over the past decade since its foundation, curiosities and literature of that sort had increasingly stocked the shelves. As Josiah prepared for his London trip, he dashed off a letter to Bentley, asking for '*written instructions* what books I am to buy, & what Books I am to see at the Museam &c &c'.[15]

In London Josiah stayed at a two-bedroom flat in Charles Street, very near the fashionable Grosvenor Square, which he had rented from a shoemaker just before his brother's death. It was cramped and cluttered with his wares, which were essentially sitting in storage, wanting 'nothing but arrangement to sell them'.[16] He dreamt of a larger place, which would

> enable me to shew various Table and desert services, completely set out on two ranges of Tables, six or eight at least; such services are absolutely necessary to be shewn, in order to *do the needful* with the Ladys in the neatest, genteelest and best method. The same, or indeed a much greater variety of setts of vases should decorate the Walls, and both these articles may, every few days, be so alter'd, revers'd & transform'd as to render

the whole a new scene, even to the same Company, every time
they shall bring their friends to visit us.

Besides scouring museums and bookstores, Josiah also took the
opportunity to find new staff, and he spent his days talking to
modellers, 'enamellers', 'carvers', and other artists to work on his
ideas for producing ornamental pottery. One Thursday, however,
he had a particularly stimulating day, and that evening he excitedly
updated Bentley on developments.

'One of the objects' of the day 'was seeking after a house, or
rather Warehouse in which I have at last succeeded to my wishes,
& quite beyond my most sanguine expectations'.[17] It was a new,
large house on Great Newport Street, around the corner from
Charing Cross Road near Soho, and, better yet, he had reached an
agreement with an enameller named David Rhodes who was to
move in and begin working on new patterns. He 'work'd several
years at a China work' and 'is a perfect master of the Antique stile
in ornaments, Vases &c'.[18]

This was a happy coincidence, for just that day, he wrote, he
had been discussing details of the 'Antique stile' with some new
acquaintances, a certain Sir William Schaw Cathcart and his wife
Lady Jane Cathcart. Sir William had recently been appointed
British ambassador to the Court of the Empress Catherine II in
St Petersburg, and was preparing for his commission when he
ordered a dinner and dessert service from Josiah which was to have
each piece marked with his family's coat of arms. The Cathcarts
were members of what Josiah recognised as 'the Virtu species' –
Lady Jane's brother was none other than William Hamilton – and
Josiah acted as quickly as possible to promote his services to the
couple. They spent 'several hours' together that Thursday. Lord and
Lady Cathcart were clearly intrigued by Josiah's enthusiasm and
commitment to his craft, as well as by the fact that Queen Charlotte
topped an impressive list of clients.[19] The Cathcarts left the meeting
confident that they had just met someone worth knowing. Josiah

felt the same, telling Bentley that 'we are to do great things for each other'.

It was clear to Bentley from Josiah's name-dropping, in this and in other letters, that his friend was beginning to acquire many valuable contacts around the world, which suggested even greater future success. Josiah, for his part, hoped such stories would act as inducements to Bentley, for Josiah now believed that his friend was on the verge of agreeing to their partnership.

At the same time Lord Cathcart had been deliberating on presenting Catherine the Great with the kind of gift that the King and Queen of England themselves enjoyed, perhaps a tea set or some dinner ware. Perhaps – even better – his new friend could design a unique set especially for the Russian Empress. Both parties would benefit: Catherine would be honoured by Lord Cathcart's gift, and Josiah Wedgwood's reputation would flourish. In fact, it would fulfil an ambition that Josiah had already declared to Lord Cathcart, who remembered his plans to manufacture a novel product with which he hoped to 'surprise *the World* with wonders'.[20]

The surprise came in the form of the ornamental vases Josiah was now obsessed with, which 'almost overwhelm my patience', and which delighted the Virtuosi, including Lord and Lady Cathcart.[21] Josiah had explained to them that he was thinking of producing something that was not necessarily functional, or 'useful', but rather an item purchased specifically for display; something that would take pride of place on a mantelpiece or in a cabinet. Lord and Lady Cathcart knew exactly what the potter was talking about, knowing well the market for such fashionable items. Lady Cathcart, it so happened, had been reading about such ornamental vases in a book her brother was just about to have published. It immediately struck her that one of the first 'great things' they could do for Josiah would be to lend him some of the lavish plates from her brother's illustrated volumes, which showed in the finest detail ever the richness of Etruscan art.

A few months earlier, Sally had excitedly observed Josiah 'leaving home in a great hurry' to '*finally* settle the plan' on the design of Etruria with the architect Mr Pickford and later, with equal relief, to finalise the purchase of the land.[22] The troublesome Mrs Ashenhurst had died suddenly before being able to reject Josiah's offer and her executor had wanted a quick sale.

Josiah now spent his days with 'about 50 people' – builders, workers, visitors, and family.[23] 'We were making sagars at Etruria, building the steps, Glazeing the Windows, & getting forward as fast as possible; your [Bentley's] house' – for his friend had now agreed to join Josiah as a partner in the new works – 'is tiled and the sash frames come.'[24] They had also taken on a new apprentice 'with good fingers' as a modeller, since 'we shall want many festoons & other ornaments upon Vases', and labourers were stopping by the Bell Works, attracted by all the noise of construction coming down the valley, wanting 'to know when they must begin' work there.[25]

Josiah, meanwhile, worked late into the night on new patterns for 'Root flowerpots . . . Essence pots . . . Vases & ornaments . . . Toilet furniture . . . Elegant teachests' and 'Ten thousand other *substantial forms*'. In dim candlelight in his workshop, with 'hands so cold I can scarcely hold the pen', he updated Bentley on his progress: he was seeing very little of Sally or his children; Dicky is 'a Charming boy . . . [or so] his Mother tells me . . .'.[26] It was all becoming too much.

Months of inclement weather had been scraping away at Josiah's health, leading him to complain about its 'hazardous state'. 'This return of my Complaint sunk my spirits, & dishearten'd me greatly in the prosecution of my schemes,' he wrote, but 'I have now begun a course of Exercise which I intend to continue, & consists in riding on Horseback for 10 to 20 miles a day, & by way of food & Physick, I take whey & yolks of Eggs in abundance, with a mixture of Rhubarb & soap.'[27] Despite his attempts at improving his regimen, the frantic months of extensive travelling and long days supervising the works at the pottery – tiresomely climbing up and down ladders and stairs to various workshops and offices – had inflamed a 'bilious complaint'; more precisely, he had, as he told one of his employees, 'over-walk'd & over-work'd my knee lately'.[28]

The pain in his knee was acute, and Dr James Bent, a local physician, prescribed an emetic to cause vomiting – the theory being that it might release some of the rotten bile irritating his leg. It offered temporary relief but, Josiah complained, 'the pain had no soon left my knee than I was very ill in other respects, attended with great heat & difficulty of Breathing', leading him to feel perversely relieved when the pain returned to his knee and the other symptoms ceased.[29] After a brief consultation Josiah knew there was only one solution. It was time to have the leg removed.

No one had any doubts about the dangers of the surgery, and no one was more aware than the patient of the fact that there was no way to deaden the pain. A few drops of laudanum might help calm the nerves but it required phenomenal fortitude to survive what was nothing less than torture beginning the moment the saw scraped the skin. Some patients chose to have their vision obscured from the operation, but Josiah was one to confront the ordeal face on. A month earlier he had declared that 'I am in no fear of the event' – referring to an imminent council meeting to face objections to his plans to build his expansive 'Vase works' on Ridge House Estate, 'I know my conscience is good, & I feel a match for them all.'[30] It was an attitude that could also describe the manner in which he approached the operation.

Josiah sat in a chair with at least four other people in a room at his home at the Brick House: two surgeons (one to saw, the other to stitch), a physician of whom Josiah was growing increasingly fond, Dr Erasmus Darwin, and Bentley, who had stepped in to look after the business and whose 'brotherly love & affection' helped soothe Sally's nerves.[31]

It was not long after the door closed for the procedure on that Saturday afternoon, 28 May 1768, when Sally, anxiously sitting in another room with Sukey, little John and ten-month-old Dicky, received the reassuring news that all passed without alarm. Josiah's surgeon, James Bent, had proved his skill with the curved lance – slicing through the skin with one quick rotating movement – and the saw, which severed the leg just below Josiah's right knee.

That same day, Josiah's new in-house bookkeeper, Peter Swift, while writing an invoice of goods, took a brief moment to relay the news to the staff of the London showroom.

> Sir,
> Your favour of the 26th is just come to hand, but can make no reply to the contents. Mr. Wedgwood has this day had his leg taken off, & is as well as can be expected after such an execution. The Revd Mr. Horne's goods are packed, and one Crate for the ware-house, the particulars of which I shall insert at foot, or as much as time will permit.

Peter's commitment to getting on with business would doubtless have made his employer proud.

But Josiah would have known little of this. For days after the operation he lay in an opium-induced oblivion, cared for by Sally, who changed his bandages and administered his medicine. This would prove to be the most physically and emotionally consuming week of Sally's life ('I think Mrs. Wedgwood has had severe tryals of late,' Peter Swift would write in his typically understated manner.[32]) While Josiah slept in his recovery room, their baby Dicky was becoming ever more ill, 'violently seized with a Complaint in his Bowls'.

Like his older sister and brother a year before, Dicky had been given a smallpox inoculation, on the advice of Erasmus Darwin. He was sure of the benefits of the procedure to keep at bay the disease which 'walketh in darkness'. 'One grain of variolous matter, inserted by inoculation,' Darwin wrote , 'shall in about seven days stimulate the system into unnatural action; which in about seven days more produces ten thousand times the quantity of a similar material thrown out on the skin in postules!'[33]

Josiah and Sally, brought up as they were to appreciate such prescriptions for the rational management of health, were quick to sign their children up for the treatment. Josiah, of course, was especially committed to try the wonders of 'the experiment' if it promised to save his children from 'that terrible disease' which had caused him so much trouble. It was a controversial decision – many Anglicans and Catholics condemned the procedure, accusing doctors of playing God, 'that it is bringing a Distemper upon our selves, and thereby usurping the sacred Prerogative of God, who kills and makes alive, who wounds and heals, as he pleases'. In his *Case for Receiving the Small-Pox by Inoculation* the outspoken Dissenter Philip Doddridge dismissed such attitudes as pandering to superstition: If everything was God's will, he wrote, it would be 'as rational to conclude, that our Lives should be preserv'd without eating and drinking, and that we shall be delivered from Danger without a prudent care for our own Safety.' With no 'Divine oracle' to consult, 'Observation and Experiment must guide us'.[34]

This had long been Josiah's sentiment: 'Everything derives from experiment.' Science and medicine should be embraced, used to promote the improvement of humanity. Experiments, Josiah was convinced, were risks worth taking. After some 'Convulsions at the first appearance of the eruption', Josiah had written, and after a period of becoming 'so very Ill that I confess I repented what we had done', each of the children had recovered.[35] But now, five months after his inoculation, Dicky was gravely ill.

During the week after Josiah's operation, the surgeons returned to remove his bandages and inspect for any sign of infection. 'Wedgwood continues in a good way,' Peter was relieved to inform his London associates, 'his Leg was opened on Thursday for the first time, & both the Surgeons said it could not possibly be better, & he has every good Symptom, so that we have the greatest hopes of a perfect cure.'

But the bright outlook for Josiah and his family was quickly shrouded with grief. Dicky had not been able to resist the 'terrible disease', and on that same day God received their ten-month-old baby.

EIGHTEEN

The Arts Reborn

W ITHIN A MONTH of his operation Josiah was up and back to work having 'left off my laudanum . . . am better without it', visiting the workshops and taking therapeutic 'airings' in a chaise. He wrote to Bentley that the skin on the upper part of his wound had healed, and that Sally sent her 'love & respects' for all his support and kind words. 'Mrs. Wedgwood says you are a sad flattering Mortal,' he teased. 'Give over Joss!' Sally finally yelled, frustrated that her patient was overworking again, 'and tell our friend Bentley that I command it.'[1]

Josiah squared up again to the chores of business, dealing with the plans for his new factory and a growing team of employees, both in Burslem and in London, at the showroom on Great Newport Street which his staff were in the process of moving into. 'Now I am recover'd so far as to be able to write, I find myself head & ears in debt in that way, & every post is increasing the heavy load,' he complained.

> It is this which confines me to the house, & retards my perfect recovery more than anything else, & though I put as much of this business off me, as I decently can, yet I have very many letters which, *when I am able to, & at home*, must be wrote by my own hand, or they wo'd give offence.

With typical philosophical curiosity, Josiah, even when trying to get on with business, found himself drawn to studying his altered limb. 'My leg is almost healed,' he observed, commenting that his wound was now precisely two inches by one and a half, 'I measured it with the compasses this morning when I dress'd it – yes, *when I dress'd it*, for I have turned my surgeon adrift & Sally & I are sole managers now.'

As part of his convalescence Josiah tried out for the first time a wooden prosthesis strapped under his right knee and a few weeks later decided to go rambling with it in Cheshire. It was there that he met 'another artist'. 'He is a Mathematical instrument maker,' he told Bentley, adding that he was considering hiring him 'in making & repairing Engine Lathes, punches & tools of Various sorts'. A talented 'mechanic' was always a welcome contact, especially when he showed Josiah that he too wore a wooden leg and that he had turned his wood-working skills to being 'a wooden-leg maker'. 'His name is Brown,' Josiah informed Bentley, and before he knew it this jack of all trades was 'at present making me some legs'. Josiah wanted his prostheses to be carefully crafted to look as much like his previous leg as possible, capable not only of wearing his stocking and shoe, but of being mechanically jointed so the foot could move. It was an ingenious design which would be worked on and improved by later instrument makers who maintained the mechanical equipment in the factory. Rarely it seems did Josiah rely on a simple 'peg leg', and with one or two later exceptions, all portraits and statues show him with a fully-formed right leg.[2]

In the midst of catching up with correspondence, Josiah remembered that 'a long time ago' he requested William Cox, who in 1765 Josiah had made the manager of his London premises then at Charles Street, to 'ask Ld or Lady Cathcart if I should return the prints I had from them & so learn how I could be supplyd with the three volumes of them which are publishing abroad'. He recalled that Hamilton was in the process of publishing his elaborate multi-volume presentation of the excavated vases from ancient Etruria and was eager to see the full treasure trove of designs and patterns. He wanted Cox to pay his respects to Lord and Lady Cathcart, since, in his words, 'I shall be very glad to see the fine Etruscans you have set my mouth a watering after.'[3]

His wishes were answered with the arrival of a package. Lady Cathcart had sent a carefully wrapped parcel containing bundles of her brother's engraved illustrations. Josiah was as excited and overwhelmed as when Mr Smallwood delivered the letter from Miss Chetwynd on behalf of the Queen three years earlier. He pored over the illustrations and was immediately flooded with ideas. He eagerly drew up some sketches for his own designs and sent them to Bentley hoping he could find time to 'dip into them'. Josiah was keen that his friend realise the importance of reproducing objects that were so sought after by the virtuosi. He talked about 'the colours of the Earthen Vases, the paintings, the substances used by the Ancient Potters, with their methods of working, burning, &c.' – all details were relevant if one was to gain the appreciation and respect of the connoisseurs whom it was so important to impress.

Virtuosi, such as Hamilton, had pronounced that their illustrations and collections would aid future artists to, in Hamilton's words, 'revive the arts' in Britain. When classicists, historians, artists and art patrons studied the antiquities, they believed they could learn the academic principles upon which 'modern' art – their own neo-classical productions, should be established. As the French *philosophe* Montesquieu remarked in his *Voyage d'Italie*, 'there are some statues which the connoisseurs have established as examples and rules . . . it is from them that the Moderns have built up their system of proportions, and it is they which have virtually given us the arts'.[4]

However, it was unlikely that the virtuosi ever considered that a potter would be the one to revive the arts through studying the images of antiquity. Potters were not artists, they were crude artisans who produced items of utility, nothing more. In the eyes of the members of the Royal Academy of Arts (founded just months after Josiah received Hamilton's illustrations, in December 1768) the highest forms of art were drawings of historical scenes and land-scapes, and plaster modelling from live nudes. Pottery was akin to the work done by engravers, a group who were, to their frustration, excluded from membership of the Academy.

Josiah hoped that by imitating the 'chaste simplicity' of ancient antiquities he could elevate the status of pottery. He was determined to refashion himself and his craft, to shake off the bigotry that high-minded artists had against artisans. To accomplish this he knew he had to persuade the connoisseurs, the self-styled arbiters of taste whilst also engendering some metropolitan respect for the marginalised provincial potter. This was no easy goal, for the divide between these two worlds was as wide as the gulf between Pall Mall and Gin Lane. Josiah was aiming for an identity somewhere in-between.

He and a group of acquaintances assembled at the home of the literary editor Ralph Griffiths which met 'as a Society of Artists'. 'You will easily perceive the use we may make of such an institution,' he wrote to Bentley.[5] Josiah remembered how the aristocratic collec-tors had found it hard to conceive that his creamware, coming out of a muddy hovel in the Midlands, could be more attractive than the wares produced at, for instance, Sèvres. Indeed, it had been difficult enough to convince his good friend Bentley to give up his cultural connections at Liverpool to live in this 'dirty, smoky place', and he had found it near impossible to get London artists to take up employment in Burslem. Indeed when he asked Bentley whether anyone could 'prevail upon any [artist] to settle 150 miles north of the great Metropolis?', he learned that it was probably impossible.[6]

After an awful year of personal tragedy and business difficulties, Josiah was once again enthusiastic about the future. No one had ever tried to apply the potter's skills to the ornamental production of the antique in the way he was planning to. A decade earlier some Staffordshire potters had attempted to produce salt-glazed figurines modelled after Spinario but these were crude products, never praised for their beauty.[7] He intended that his replica vases would provoke a radically different reaction.

He believed he could change the image of pottery by allying it to the vogue for a sentimental view of heritage and civilisation. Connoisseurs and virtuosi saw how the raw material of the earth itself created an intimate bond with the past, hiding ancient treasures that had been formed of the very earth to which they returned, buried in rubble and ash. By resurrecting 'Etruria' to rework the raw materials and encourage potters to aspire towards recapturing 'universal beauty', Josiah and Bentley had enrolled history on their side. Bentley, who had formally signed a partnership with Josiah, 'in making ornamental Earthenware' (with the partnership books officially opening in November of 1768), reiterated that it was 'in the original works of the ancients, to which our artists can have access, that they must expect to find just and beautiful ideas', and it was in Hamilton's own collection 'that they must search for hidden treasure'.[8]

Of course, Josiah had not merely stumbled on the name Etruria: it was a deliberate act of branding, of giving a new identity to his wares, and to his employees whom he called his 'Etruscans', on their learned quest to recapture the ancient principles of grace and beauty. Going one step further to prove his dedication to Hamilton's call for a successful 'revival' of the ancient arts, Josiah even began experimenting with techniques and materials in order to recreate what it was like to be an ancient potter, claiming as he did so that he now breathed 'Etruscan air' (dropping references to this 'smokey place' in favour of images of Tuscan blue skies and gentle breezes).

The raw materials used by the ancients, he believed, had distinctive qualities. 'I apprehend the Etruscan body owes its lightness to a mixture, either natural or artificial, of volcanic ashes,' he wrote. Attempting to replicate the substance, he took 'a good red clay' and would 'mix with it as much ground charcoal as can be conveniently worked in'.[9] He also questioned his chemically minded friends about how the different climate of Italy and England might affect the product, since different gases – the subject of Joseph Priestley's investigations – in the atmosphere might alter the colour of the wares during firing. It was a fantastically innovative way of using experimental science to understand history, predating the scientific methods of excavation and analysis developed in nineteenth-century archaeology.

Time was once again of the essence, especially as Josiah was alert to the fact that other manufacturers were plotting to steal his ideas. In August 1768 he was told by a reliable source that a London china merchant had sent one Humphrey Palmer, a potter based near Burslem, copies of 'all my patterns as they arrive at my rooms in London'. He asked William Cox to be vigilant when receiving goods and displaying the new items.

> You must try if you can recollect any particular Persons repeatedly buying a few pairs, or single articles of yr new patterns as they arrive, very probably it may be some sham Gentleman or Lady equipped for the purpose with their footman or maid to carry them home to prevent discovery. That they do get my patterns from you in some such way I am certain, but the further particulars you must endeavour to discover.[10]

Even if the design of the 'Etruscan' wares had not yet been discovered by others, Josiah learned that other craftsmen were expanding their ranges to include ornamental objects such as vases.

'What do you think of that!' he exclaimed to Bentley after meeting one potential competitor in London, adding – in a playfully condescending tone: 'Do you not tremble for our Embryotick Manufacture?' At least this particular competitor was a 'Stone Manufacturer', and unlikely to tread on their commercial toes. But other more sinister rivals were bound to be close behind. He might have even learned that other manufacturers were, at that precise moment, doing what he most feared by producing their own imitations of ancient figures. The Sèvres factory had just made its first batch of biscuit statuettes after the antique, and, more alarmingly, given the swarms of British Grand Tourists, the Capodimonte 'china' factory in Naples was known to have produced a porcelain figure of Laocoon being strangled by green snakes as in the description in Virgil's *Aeneid*.[11] Such fears filled Josiah's dreams and left him restless on many nights.

'I have had many *Visions* since you left us,' he reported to Bentley at the beginning of 1769, after finishing a suite of experiments to improve the quality of his Etruscan ware whilst also overseeing the completion of the factory and the new homes. 'Some of which are so *strange & fore-boding*, that I have even been so weak as to write them in a book.' The fine-tuning was proving frustrating. He was producing the pieces by the crate load but the colours were off, the proportions were wrong, and there were other irritating imperfections. Besides this, he was not even sure what to call the pieces: were they urns or vases? A semantic detail, perhaps, but integral to their promotion where authenticity was crucial.

Josiah attempted to remain philosophical, reminding himself and his partner that 'in the manufacturing of these delicate compositions, & the disappointments you must expect to meet with when you become a Potter so that if you can be picking up a little patience & storeing it against a time of need, there may be no sort of harm in it'. Yet such calm considerations were again punctuated by bouts of excited anticipation and restless, anxious nights. 'I have lately had a vision by night of some new Vases, Tablets &c with which Articles we shall certainly serve the *whole World* . . . We are far enough before our rivals, & when ever we apprehend they are *treading too near our heals*, we can at any time manage them.' It was essential to maintain belief, especially since money was running low and only the official opening of the new factory could rescue their finances.

Foul weather over the summer of 1768 had slowed down progress on Etruria. The foundations for the houses had been laid but the buildings only stood at 'plinth height' because the workers had been unable to make bricks amidst all the rain.[12] But Josiah was equally concerned that his architect, Mr Pickford, was coming down too hard on the workmen. He 'does not seem to consider their having any feelings at all', wrote Josiah.

> I have seen a great many instances of it & may perhaps some-
> time or other find a mode of conveying a lecture to him upon
> a proper treatment of our inferiours & to prove that our humble
> friends, as somebody beautifully calls them, have like passions
> with ourselves & are capable of feeling pain or pleasure nearly
> in the same manner as their Masters – but this must be done
> obliquely.[13]

While building work was on hold, Josiah and Bentley continued with their plans for the factory. One of Josiah's central concerns was to make sure that it was erected in exactly the right spot to take full advantage of the forthcoming Trent and Mersey Canal, the precise route of which was being carefully plotted by the engineer Hugh Henshall. Some 600 men were busy working on a northern segment of it; 10 miles had already been dug out, and it would not be long before the workers would be making their way down by Burslem.[14] Josiah had known that the canal would pass through the lands of Ridge House Estate when he bought the property; its lower elevation on the base of the large ridge of moorland that led to Burslem provided the natural geography for the canal's path. But Josiah now needed exact plans. As soon as Henshall surveyed the land, Josiah obtained a copy of his drawings and sketched the desired position of his factory, being 'accurate with respect to the dimensions being off-traced from Mr Henshall's plan of the survey'.

Josiah showed Bentley the sketch. Along a thick black line run-ning north to south, at the corner where the canal intersected the road leading south-west to Newcastle-under-Lyme, Josiah perfectly positioned his 'Vase works'. The manufactory was to be a 150-yard long, rectangular building with numerous rooms built around two courtyards and eight 'hovels', or kilns. Each room and yard would have a different function. The building was to be architecturally anchored by a round, domed room, 'for plates and dishes only' – probably intended as drying and storage room (the dome is today the only remaining fragment of the original Etruria factory).

There were to be three covered buildings, separated by two walled-in, two-storey courtyards. The first building was a warehouse; the adjacent walled courtyard was for storing coal, with a section for 'clay & rubbish, that nothing may be seen or exposed on the outside of the building'; the higher, three-storey, central building, between the two symmetrical courtyards, housed the main rooms for the production of every sort of 'useful ware', the sort of stock-in-trade plates and pots that Useful Tom had manufactured at the Ivy House Works. Through the second courtyard, where more clay was stored and where rejected items were buried, was 'the ornamental work', where the revolutionary 'Etruscan vases' were to be manufactured. Everything was contained within these protective walls, and all aspects of the production of the wares would take place in separate rooms, working around precision machines like the engine lathe, finely balanced throwing wheels and large mills for mixing clay – arrangements which both reflected the need for security. Josiah had drawn up plans for the largest and most specialised pot-works ever designed, and arguably the most efficient and best situated. As he described it, it was the most 'modern' factory in the world.

During Etruria's construction some of Josiah's 'brethren', the other Staffordshire potters, began to grow suspicious of Josiah's intimacy with the engineers of the canal and the grand plans for his new factory. His hard work to raise subscriptions and canvass political support for the canal had at first been rewarded with praise and with his non-stipendiary appointment as treasurer of the company established to build the canal, but now it seemed he had always intended to use inside knowledge of the canal project to unfair advantage. After all, while Josiah was the most outspoken regarding the advantages of the canal to the *'country's* trade', all the Staffordshire potters owned a stake in the project, raising £20,000 amongst themselves for its construction (£6,000 from the Wedgwood clan itself, including Long John and Cousin Thomas; a figure which, however, still paled in comparison to the more than £140,000 contributed by local gentry).

'Some of my good Neighbours have taken it into their heads to think I shall have too pleasant & valuable a situation by the side of the Canal as it is plan'd & executing thro' my Estate,' he reported to Bentley. 'This has raised a little envy in their breasts, & as they are Proprietors they have represented to the Committee that the Canal ought to be made along the Meadows, as that is the shortest, & most natural course for it. That it will receive more water & retain better what it does receive as the upper course is over sloping banks & sandbeds.'[15] A committee was set up, and Josiah, feeling he 'was a match for them all', argued forcefully, defending his integrity and enrolling the support of the canal engineers to give a 'true state of the case'.

Josiah's arguments prevailed, allowing him to press on with his plans, aggressively buying more land around the estate, partly as elbowroom and partly to keep away his competitors. 'I believe you will think me almost out of my senses for thinking of buying more land,' Josiah said to Bentley, '& indeed it is not because I shall have money to spare that I would make this purchase . . .'. But, he explained, 'it is full of limestone which I shall unavoidably lay dry in guttering for my own,' it would allow him the potential to expand in the future, and, above all, 'if I do not buy it for those purposes somebody else will who may be very disagreeable neighbours'. Sensibly, given the recent local reaction to his development plans, he noted that 'my application is at present a secret'.[16]

Josiah's concerns about not having 'spare money' to risk were rising, as, throughout the summer of 1768, his business finances dwindled. His wife's capital was most likely the source of payment for the first stage of building work (approximately £2,000) but Pickford's bills were piling high. One unexpected, and rather spectacular, expense was a bill for over £600 incurred on his suddenly receiving six tons of 'Cherokee clay' which Thomas Griffiths had procured and shipped from America. Josiah was shocked by the bill, though he had yet to learn of the extraordinary circumstances in which the clay had been obtained.

To compound the problem, the person whose job it was to knock on doors and collect debts, Tom Byerley, had yet again been struck with wanderlust and had decided to set off for Philadelphia in search of stardom. Despite disapproving of this venture, Josiah had a soft spot for his nephew and did what he could do pay Byerley's way, advancing him £70 for his trip, but asking him 'to ship himself in the cheapest way'. 'He promises to be very good,' Josiah told Bentley, '& I hope for his own sake, as well as his friends, that he will perform his promises.'[17]

Josiah was now forced to rely on William Cox in London, whom he implored to *make hay whilst the sun shines* and collect the outstanding debts. Josiah also asked him to take along with him examples of his new wares when calling on clients, the first pieces produced in the 'antique' style, showing customers what was soon to be available if they paid up promptly.

As a result of Cox's door-to-door visits, interest soon began to spread throughout London. 'Mr Cox is as mad as a march Hare for Etruscan Vases,' an exalted Josiah wrote to Bentley from London in November, on his first trip there since his operation. 'Pray get a quantity made or we shall disgust our good customers by disappointing them in their expectations. But raise no dust at home though about them, for that will make our antagonists open all their eyes & ears too & push them forwarder than they would perhaps move at their own natural rate.'[18] Josiah followed this up by visiting as many members of the nobility as he could manage, and was advised by one, Sir Henry Chairs, that 'they are vastly admired (the Vases) but the Ladies think them dear' at Josiah's suggested price of between 7 and 9 shillings each; 'however he says *they will sell*'.

His idea of reproducing Etruscan vases was, he was now sure, the key to unlocking the consumer 'revolution' he had discussed with Bentley. His samples, though still 'rude' in his opinion – since he still lacked the ability to replicate with consistency the ancient 'grace' – were proving the perfect prelude to the grand opening of Etruria.

Having whetted the appetite of the aristocracy for ornamental pottery, Josiah now wanted to push at the boundaries. He was sure that as word spread, he could encourage them to buy even more expensive vases by making the items appear limited and exclusive. Josiah prepared four 'serpent handled antique vases, part of which have the handles twisted & are finished in a more elegant manner than the others'. Josiah asked his book-keeper in Burslem, Peter Swift, to send these to William Cox in London with instructions that they 'not let be seen till the others are all sold, & then raise the price of them 1/ each for being higher finished'. At the last minute Josiah amended the instructions, bumping up the price. 'Those charg'd 9/ must be 10/6, and those 7/6 be 9/, never mind their being thought dear,' Josiah briefed Cox, 'do not keep them open in the rooms, shew them only to People of Fashion.'[19] It was a principle of consumerism that Josiah himself helped define: deny the majority the ability to purchase art then use their lack of means as proof of inadequate taste.

Meanwhile Josiah scoured London for more ideas. 'I am collecting some figures (antique) to be made in Etruscan earth,' he reported, adding that the Dilettanti Sir William Chambers '& many others have a high opinion of them to mix with the Vases, by both these articles I hope we shall make a revolution in the chimney pieces & strip them of their present gaudy furniture of patch'd & painted figures'.[20] Before long, Josiah was happily informing Sally that 'new cabinets are opening to me every day', and he had just received an invitation to visit with Sir Watkin Williams Wynn at his home in

St James's Square 'to shew me some things for the *improvement of Vases* he has brought home from his Travels' – one of the finest collections made in the eighteenth century.[21]

In order to capitalise on the interest generated by his and Cox's visits, Josiah decided that a catalogue comprising illustrations of his vases (the modern equivalent to Hamilton's pictures of the antique) should be produced and put on show at the Great Newport Street showroom 'as they will be looked over by our customers here, & they will often get us orders & be a pretty amusement for the Ladies when they are waiting which is often the case as there are sometimes four or five different companys.' '& I need not tell you,' he continued to Bentley, 'that it will be our interest to amuse, & divert & please, and astonish, nay & even ravish the Ladies. But who am I writing to! – Not to my wife I hope, no she must wink here, this is all under the rose, to my good friend, Vase maker General to the Universe.'[22]

The strategy of visiting nobility, inviting only select 'Fashionable' to glimpse the rare 'backroom' pieces, and displaying a catalogue with spectacular, coloured engravings of a range of vases (to 'prevent the *sameness* which must be rather disgusting if we confin'd the shew to one sort only') paid off. Before Josiah had barely articulated it, his 'revolution' was in full swing. 'Etruscan Vases are the run at present,' he declared at the beginning of February 1769.[23] 'The great demand here may not be baulked. I could sell £50 or £100 worth per day if I had them!' Lord Bessborough, who had travelled in Europe with his wife (who was in fact much more interested in Grand Tourism), paid Josiah the greatest compliments that he could imagine. The 'fine old Gentleman, a very fine old Gentleman,' Josiah stressed, who 'admires our vases & manufacture prodigiously, says we shall exceed the Antients, that friezes & many other things may be made, that I am a very ingenious man (theres for you now, did I not tell you what a fine old Gentleman he was) & that he will do me every service in his power', starting with an order for three vases.[24]

It was imperative that the new factory was opened before competition could emerge. 'Pray do exert yourself to get the works at

Etruria finished,' he urged both Bentley and Useful Tom from London; 'in the mean time let all the hands that can be spared & can work at Vases be imployed in them.'[25] By end of 1768, just as Josiah and Bentley's formal partnership books were opened, it seemed that Etruria would finally come to fruition. Josiah (now back in Burslem) was able to report that the 'works are cover'd in, & they are beginning upon the Cellar arches, & the Chamber & ground floors, as soon as these are finish'd I shall order them to be fitted up & put some men into them to make sagars, prepare clay, build ovens, &c &c that we may begin to do something *in earnest* as soon as possible'.[26] Over the next six months a large blanket of land was transformed into a grand building site. Josiah and Sally's modest manor house, Etruria Hall, was taking its symmetrical Georgian form on the east hill overlooking the site of the works down the slope to the west. What was intended as Bentley's house, the Bank House, was going up on the land further south. There was a barn, offices, the ornamental and useful works, an inn and forty-two houses next to an orchard which would be rented out to the workers. Josiah called it 'Etruria Village', a model community which was Josiah's improved version of his old partner Thomas Whieldon's commitment to provide affordable and convenient housing for his employees.[27]

In April 1769 Josiah assured Bentley that 'I am getting things forward at Etruria as fast as possible'.

> The slip kiln is nearly finish'd upon our friend Mr Whitehurst's plan, the Sagars are got ready to fire, & I have sent some fired ones from hence to support the new ones in the oven. Two mills are nearly finish'd, & your house is going on as fast as the Works. The Joyners have left mine to finish yours, which Mr Pickford assures me shall be completed in seven weeks at farthest.[28]

At long last, Josiah and Bentley had decided on a date for a ceremony to mark the official opening of Etruria. While the works were still under construction, they built a platform on which a hand-turned potter's wheel was placed with a tub of prepared clay.

The hot sun on that Tuesday, 13 June 1769, dried out the muddy fields of the seven acre construction site. A crowd gathered, the workers and potters relieved to have half a day off. Sally, who was eight months pregnant (with their son, whom they would name Josiah, or 'Joss', Junior), stood with Sukey and little John, her father and her brother. Long John and Cousin Thomas, with their children, soon arrived, as did the Brindleys, the Henshalls, and the Whieldons. One conspicuous absence was Tom Byerley who, in his wild enjoyment of America, had run out of money and been thrown into a debtors prison in Philadelphia. (Tom would eventually be bailed out, after receiving over £800 in help, probably from Josiah, who kept the matter a secret from Byerley's mother, his sister Margaret, daring not to 'acquaint her with this last instance of his incurable madness'.[29])

Josiah gave a brief speech, then he and Bentley put on a show that would become legendary. Josiah donned the potter's 'slops', the leather apron and cap, and formed one mound of clay after another into elegant Etruscan vases, while Bentley cranked the shaft to spin the wheel for Josiah. He threw six vases in black basaltes, fashioned after Hamilton's *Etruscan Antiquities*, which his artist David Rhodes painted with red figures depicting 'Hercules in the Garden of the Hesperides', with the inscription:

June XIII M.DCC LXIX
One of the First Day's Productions
at
Etruria Staffordshire
by
Wedgwood & Bentley
Artes Etruriae Renascuntur

The last line of the inscription said it all: 'The arts of Etruria are reborn!'[30]

NINETEEN

Ingenious People & Formidable Opponents

Amid the hoary Ruins Sculpture first,
Deep-digging, from the cavern dark and damp,
Their Grave for Ages, bad her marble Race
Spring to new Light. Joy sparkled in her Eyes[1]
JAMES THOMSON, *Liberty* (1735–6)

THE SENTIMENT would not have been lost on Josiah or Bentley, both admirers of the poetry of the Whig and minister's son, James Thomson. Etruria, Wedgwood & Bentley's (as the firm was now officially called) factory, had been unveiled as a proud monument to the pursuit of freedom, to trade and to creating a new future from a buried past.[2]

The landscape and status of industry was attaining new levels and the world now looked to North Staffordshire as the source of a manufacturing revolution. 'In general,' commented Arthur Young, whose survey of industrial and agricultural experiments across the country was published in 1770, 'we owe the possession of this most flourishing manufacture to the inventive genius of Mr Wedgwood, who not only originally introduced the present cream coloured ware, but has since been the inventor of every improvement, the other manufactures being little better than mere imitators.' Recognising Bentley's valued role, Young added that Wedgwood 'has lately entered into a partnership with a man of sense and spirit, who will have taste enough to continue in the inventive plan ... in case of accidents' – an acknowledgement of the many risks to life from working in the workshops of industry and from ill-health. This was one of the main reasons why entrepreneurs were eager to engage in partnerships: if something happened to one of them, it should 'not suffer the manufacture to decline'.[3]

What was notable about Josiah and Bentley's partnership, and some others forged at this time, was that it was between two unrelated people. Looking outside of the family for partnership had, up until now, been extremely rare – largely because it was practically impossible for a family to build up its own wealth if a large share of the business was owned by another family. The change, personified in Wedgwood & Bentley, was made possible by the phenomenal growth in revenue and assets generated by modern processes of industrialisation which in turn required recruiting the best talent, 'sense and spirit', whoever they might be.

At Etruria's opening ceremony, the partnership itself was less the focus of celebration than the bricks and mortar of the rising works and the potter's raw material of clay; it celebrated the 'ancient' craft itself, the workforce – numbering now over a hundred – who represented a commitment to the highest standards of craftsmanship. They shone out amongst a community that had grown immensely since Josiah's childhood. Arthur Young estimated that there were now '300 houses, which are calculated to employ on an average of 20 hands each or 6,000 on the whole', but that the total 'variety of people' involved with all aspects of the trade 'cannot be much short of 10,000 and it is increasing every day'.[4]

Once when Josiah excitedly wrote to Bentley about successful improvements to his engine lathe which his 'ingenious' smith promised to keep secret and 'make them for no one else', he suddenly paused and recognised the need to forsake what he called 'narrow selfish views' of the benefits the improvements could bring to one's business and 'to let our improvements take a free cause for the benefits of our *Brethren* & *Country*'.[5] Although as a businessman Josiah was obviously happy to have the lead on his competitors, he also remained true to a moral code – as preached by his Unitarian 'brethren' such as William Willets or grandfather Stringer – that wealth became 'valuable' when it enriched not merely the individual but the community as a whole. It was a sentiment succinctly expressed on another occasion when Bentley bantered Josiah about his 'doctrines of *money getting*', to which Josiah replied sincerely: 'I do not expect my Pupils to divest themselves of Humanity, to make, or amplify a fortune'.[6]

Of course Josiah hoped that the scientific and mechanical improvements would benefit the business financially, but this success would amount to nothing if it did not reflect the improvement in the condition of life for *all* provincial, disenfranchised manufacturers, whose position in society was – Josiah and Bentley both believed – unjustly subjugated because of their Dissenting religious and political beliefs. Their accomplishments in designing new materials and products, and the money they made for their products, amounted to nothing if it did not generate broader social change; the principles of mercantile freedoms should extend to social freedoms, to create, in essence, a more egalitarian society.

Josiah and Bentley were not alone in believing in the 'usefulness' of enterprise, indeed it was a belief held by many manufacturers across the world. In Britain, the founders of the Society for the Encouragement of Arts, Manufactures and Commerce in 1754 had made explicit links between industrial pursuits and the growth in wealth and power of the state.[7] In self-congratulatory terms, the Society associated the innovative work of its rapidly rising membership – it had grown from seventeen members in its first year to over 2,000 a decade later – with Britain's coeval military and economic successes. They represented the culmination of centuries of struggle 'against foreign despotism and false religion'. 'No truly benevolent or public spirited Briton can hesitate' to support the Society, announced one of its early members, Charles Powell. 'It will not only unite in one common Bond all real Patriots, or as I should call them the Patrons of the Nation, but will in time, I hope utterly extirpate all Party distinctions, the Bar of Society and Civil Government.'[8]

It was because they purported to have national rather than purely personal interests at heart that manufacturers felt they should be 'encouraged' and not marginalised in society. Robert Dossie, a founder member of the Society, developed the point in his *Handmaid to the Arts*, which the Society sponsored and which Josiah for one (among many manufacturers) found essential reading for practical tips on japanning, gilding, glazing, and such.

> That the national improvement of skill and taste in the execution of works of design is a matter of great importance to any country . . . [and] of the commercial advantages resulting from it, will be allowed by all . . . The strong disposition that prevails not only in the European countries, but in the respective settlements of their people in Asia and America, for using those decorations and ornaments in dress as well as buildings and furniture . . . gives at present the foundation of several of the most considerable branches of trade: which are daily increasing, with the luxury, that seems removing from the East, and spreading itself over these Western countries and their colonies.[9]

New ornamental items and artistic or craft designs – which made even mundane items such as snuffboxes or heat screens for fireplaces appealing – generated wealth for manufacturers, but, Dossie pointed out (and as others including Josiah echoed to politicians), manufacturers faced international competition, and even in something as seemingly straightforward as the skill of varnishing, 'there is a rivalship betwixt ourselves and the French, [which] renders the cultivation and propagation of this art of great importance to commerce'.[10]

A large part of the problem was the unfair system of taxation. Manufacturers increasingly saw their output contributing to the strength and power of the nation but, frustratingly, they were not being given any greater political say vis-à-vis the powerful landed peers and aristocrats in 'civil government'. When Josiah and Bentley opened Etruria's trading books in 1769, government revenue from taxation totalled £11 million, only £1.7 million of which was generated from local property or assessed taxes, that is, from the aristocracy's (and MP's) capital wealth. With the introduction of income tax thirty years away, the main source of state revenue was through customs and excise and the taxation of raw materials (Staffordshire potters, for instance, paid on average an annual duty of £5,000 for salt used in the glazing process).[11] With George III's government's penchant for introducing new mercantile taxes (which Bentley so bitterly attacked in the pages of the *Monthly Review*) the manufacturers clearly felt they were being penalised, not 'encouraged', in their efforts to improve the economy. Manufacturers across Britain were prepared for a long hard battle.

In such circumstances organisations like the Society for the Encouragement of Arts, Manufactures and Commerce provided an important collective voice, and both Josiah and Bentley, unsurprisingly, became closely involved with their campaigns, as did other manufacturers Josiah was beginning to watch closely. One was Matthew Boulton, who – while sharing the 'common Bond' for promoting British industry – Josiah soon saw as a formidable rival to his own interests.

In 1759, the year Josiah established his independent Ivy House potworks with Long John and Cousin Thomas's help, a thirty-one-year-old Birmingham buckle maker named Matthew Boulton inherited his father's metal-works manufactory and began dreaming up plans to expand his business to include other 'mechanic inventions, toys and utensils of various kinds in gold, silver, steel, copper, tortoiseshell, enamels, and many vitreous and metallic compositions'.[12] Boulton had already started producing philosophical instruments, including thermometers and scales, and had been voicing his interest in producing electrical machines.

It was this part of his business that attracted the attention of fifty-two-year-old Philadelphia *philosophe* and representative of the Pennsylvania Assembly, Benjamin Franklin, who was sent 'Home to England' to petition the Crown for more equitable treatment regarding matters of taxation. But Franklin also took advantage of his foreign residence – his third out of a total of eight trips to England during his life – to tour the manufacturing regions of the Midlands, from where his ancestors had originated, and where he found a band of 'industrious, ingenious working people [who] think themselves vastly happy that they live in dear old England'.[13] Franklin set about collecting linen, snuffboxes, 'something from all the China Works in England', and other items which he sent home 'to show the Difference of Workmanship' between the different crafts.[14]

One of his stops in 1758 was at Boulton's Birmingham manufactory where Franklin not only picked up some buckles, but was introduced to some of Boulton's new friends, such as the robust, highly innovative, free-thinking, radical physician, Dr Erasmus Darwin, who had recently set up his medical practice in nearby Lichfield. For Franklin, unaware that he would return to England on several other occasions, this was only a shopping spree. But the friendships he forged during this trip provided the foundation of a long-lasting association with Midlands manufacturers and innovators, which soon came to include Josiah, with whom Franklin shared a transatlantic vision of industrial progress and profitable trade between England and America. One of their common complaints, of course, was the British government's policy on colonial affairs, against which Franklin and his friends were beginning actively to voice their dissenting opinions.

Besides sharing general thoughts about the potential progress of colonial trade, Boulton also had his own vision of becoming a world-leading manufacturer, but he was being held back by a prob-

lem that would take the better part of the next decade to solve. Much
of his manufactory, like so many others in the 'age of invention'
(as Samuel Johnson marvelled), relied on machine production –
mechanically operated engines performing tasks such as turning
lathes and stamping sheet metal. His engines were driven by a water
mill, but the water source was always running dry, either from
drought or diversion to the demanding Birmingham Canal. Boulton
called on Darwin and Franklin to help him tackle the problem by
improving on one of his own primitive designs for an engine
powered by steam. But first, a flurry of questions needed to be
addressed, from the chemically oriented – such as the temperature
at which evaporation is most effective (prompting Darwin to engage
in a series of experiments on sulphurous and saline 'vapours', 'Food
for Fire-Engines!' he called it) – to issues of craftsmanship, with
Franklin at one point writing to Boulton: 'Query. Which of the
steam valves do you like best?'

One day, years later, Boulton received another visitor, this time
at his new, state-of-the art manufactory in Birmingham (completed
at a cost of £10,000 with finances gained through two successive
marriages[15]). Boulton had heard that the engineer James Watt had
been working on his own design of a steam engine at an ironworks
in Glasgow. He was already preparing drawings of his unique steam
engine for a patent application but was being frustrated by 'villainous
bad workmanship' in the actual production of his engine. Boulton
invited Watt to Birmingham. The 'Soho' workshops were a stark
contrast, having a well-ordered, disciplined, and highly skilled workforce. Boulton had a proposition: if they worked together to build
the steam engine, they could solve each other's problems. But
perhaps even more might be accomplished.

According to Boulton: 'My idea was to settle a manufactory near
my own, by the side of our canal, where I would erect all the
conveniences necessary for the completion of engines ... from
which manufactory,' he added grandiosely, 'we would serve all the
world with engines of all sizes.' But why be modest? After all, he

was convinced that he and his new partner had a technology that would revolutionise industry by turning fire and steam into mechanical muscle. In the future when people such as James Boswell would ask him what business he was in, he had a proud answer, which would later (and to this day) be emblazoned on the walls of museums of science and industry: 'I sell here, Sir, what all the world desires to have – POWER.'

Boulton's achievements, and the well-timed collaborative efforts that went into making them, particularly caught the attention of ambitious industrialists such as Josiah and Bentley. Josiah had first been introduced to Boulton through a mutual friend, Erasmus Darwin, while in Birmingham en route to London in 1767, and from that point on began thinking about his own use of power at the pot-works. Josiah toured Boulton's Soho works and was particularly taken with a well-crafted lathe which produced a 'crown' motion which he had never before encountered. 'I intend to ask him if he would like to part with his lathe,' he cheekily told Bentley. But with the factory's 500-plus employees which, Boulton claimed, gave him an annual turnover of £30,000 (compared at this time with Josiah's workforce of around a hundred and an annual turnover of perhaps £5,000 or £6,000), Josiah was clearly impressed and not a little envious. 'He is I believe the first – or most complete manufacturer in England, in metal. He is very ingenious, Philosophical & Agreeable,' he concluded.[16] It was this visit, combined with the inspiring idea he was soon to have in London relating to ancient vases, that would provide Josiah with a fresh blueprint for the future.

In the years before going into partnership with Bentley and the opening of Etruria, Josiah had become all too aware of the benefits of collaboration. He had been introduced to Erasmus Darwin years earlier by Matthew Turner, the experimentally minded surgeon who had treated Josiah's leg injury on his trip to Liverpool in 1762 (and who, of course, introduced Josiah to Bentley and all the others connected to the Warrington Academy, including Joseph Priestley, from whom Josiah solicited help for his own experiments).

Josiah and Darwin's relationship gelled in 1765, when Darwin proved an enthusiastic supporter of the Trent and Mersey Canal scheme. Josiah, like most people, was bowled over by Darwin's robust character and snappy wit (tempered in public speaking only by his stammer). He told Darwin 'you . . . have public spirit enough to be Generalissimo in this affair', and asked for his comments on Bentley's draft pamphlet which explained the benefits of the proposed canal.[17] Darwin, always outspoken, but as likely to lambast as to heap praise, was very critical of the piece which placed Josiah in an awkward position between two talented friends. Darwin's marginal comments included the accusations that Bentley's sentences were 'formal and parsonic', 'very garrulous', and of 'sad language', adding the complaint that he mentioned the benefits for 'China again! Is not this Hobbyhorseycal'.[18] Bentley, however, remained diplomatic and unruffled, allowing them to move on to other concerns.

One issue they discussed in February 1768, just a few months before Darwin and Bentley travelled to Burslem to attend Josiah's amputation. Josiah's problem was much the same as Boulton's: he needed to harness power so that he could operate his flint mill and grind enamel colours. Darwin, ever an enthusiast for coming up with solutions to mechanical conundrums, thought he had the answer. He called it a 'Horizontal Wind-mill', which he believed would generate a third more power than any vertical windmill with sails of the same dimension. He thought it would be a perfect improvement for Josiah's 'elegant manufactory' because, he said, in an elaborate explanation accompanied by diagrams of how the wind blows,

1. there are no Wheels or Cogs
2. no moving parts but the Sail and its upright Shaft
3. Much less friction in this way

4. The power may be increas'd after the mill is built
5. it goes with all winds night and day

The fifth point amused Josiah, who asked Bentley, 'What windmill does not?' Darwin added that 'there is a large room under it for the convenience of the work', and invited Josiah to 'send some ingenious people over to Lichfield to pass a day and observe this model' he had constructed.[19] Darwin was so excited with his Horizontal Wind-mill that he also wrote to the Society for the Encouragement of Arts, Manufactures and Commerce asking for one of their awards in recognition of his invention's contribution to advancing commerce, but one was not forthcoming. Josiah was nonetheless keen to bring the windmill to Etruria, even though it would take 68,000 bricks, 4,000 feet of wooden planks, a 30-foot long (one foot thick) shaft, and two large sails, to build. Etruria, Josiah felt, was worth it. Darwin's novel windmill was finally finished in 1779, where it remained in operation for thirteen years until being replaced by one of Boulton and Watt's steam engines.[20]

Long before the steam engine found its place at Etruria, Josiah had had other ideas about how he could benefit from befriending Boulton. In March 1768 he went to Birmingham and spent a whole weekend with Boulton, talking shop and hammering out a mutually beneficial deal. The idea was that Josiah would supply plain ornamental vases which Boulton would finish by applying colourful gold and purple metal works – ormolu – to vases. Boulton declared that he was going to 'supplant the French in the gilt business', and Josiah was seduced by his confidence. By the end of the weekend Josiah was able to assure Bentley that they had 'laid the foundations for improving our Manufacture, & extending the sale of it to every corner of Europe'.[21] It seemed a promising collaboration, making them 'Patrons of the Nation', uniting forces to quash all threats of foreign competition. 'Mr Boulton tells me I should be surprised to know what a trade has lately been made out of Vases at Paris,' Josiah told Bentley.

The Artists have even come over to London, picked up all the old whimsically ugly things they could meet with, carried them to Paris where they have mounted & ornamented them with metal, & sold them to the Virtuosi of every Nation, & Particularly to Millords d'Anglise, for the greatest raritys, & if you remember we saw many such things at Ld Bolingbrokes which he brought over with him from France.[22]

However such ideas of collaboration were shelved when Josiah was forced to stop work for the operation on his leg and lengthy convalescence, during which time he received a friendly, though brief, visit from Boulton, who looked around the Brick House Works with Bentley. Later in the year, in November 1768, Josiah bumped into Boulton again, this time in London.

'Mr. Boulton is picking up Vases, & going to make them in Bronze,' Josiah informed Bentley, who was in Burslem overseeing the construction. Again, Boulton 'proposes an alliance betwixt the Pottery & Metal branches, Viz., that we shall make such things as will be suitable for mounting, & not have a *Pott* look, & he will finish them with the mounts. What do you think of it?' Josiah wondered, guessing that Bentley would probably think it best if left alone. 'Very true,' pre-empted Josiah,

> but he will be doing [it], so that the question is whether we shall refuse having anything to do with him, and thereby affront him, & set him off doing them himself, or employing his friend Garbett. If we join with him in this scheme, I apprehend we can always bind him to us by making him such things as nobody else can, & thereby make it his interest to be good.

Before long, Josiah discovered more about Boulton's character, his business strategy, and his confidence. 'Mr Boulton has not sent any of his things to St James's', Josiah commented, thinking it odd not to offer gifts to the Royal household in the hope of receiving more orders. 'He soars higher, & is scheming to be sent for by his Majesty!' But Josiah admired his audacity. 'I wish him success,' he wrote, 'he has a fine spirit, & I think by going hand in hand, we may in many respects be useful to each other.'[23]

But however enticing the idea that innovation might be nurtured by collaboration, Josiah and Bentley also knew (and Bentley appeared to be acutely aware) that capital expansion was driven by competition. So while it was clear that Josiah and Boulton were capable of helping each other, it was not long before both sides were investing everything in order to steal markets from the other.

Boulton started the skirmish by doing some quick calculations. Since he was planning to expand his business, and he liked the idea of putting ornamental detail on plain pottery vases, then why go to an external source for the base product? Boulton imagined that he would profit more if he collaborated with Josiah only on specialised pieces – such as setting Wedgwood's cameos and intaglios in cut-steel mountings. But vases he could manufacture himself. It did not take long for Boulton to convince himself of this, especially as Wedgwood and Bentley were dragging their feet, and he soon made his intentions known.

Josiah reacted philosophically to what he immediately interpreted as impersonal but nevertheless dangerous competition. Needing to think things through, he dispatched a long letter to Bentley echoing his friend's oft-repeated sentiment that resolution on reflection is real courage. 'If Etruria cannot stand its ground, but must give way to Soho, & fall before her, let us not sell the victorie too cheap but maintain our ground like men, & endeavour, even in our defeat to share the laurels with our Conquerors.'

Josiah wrote a further letter to Bentley reflecting on the latest challenge to his ambition. He took pride in competing with someone he admired so much as Boulton, he said, declaring: 'It doubles my courage to have the first Manufacturer in England to encounter with.' This was a noteworthy tribute from Josiah: an acknowledgment not only that Boulton had beaten him to the mark in building his grand new manufactory – twice the size of the yet-to-be completed Etruria – but also recognition that Boulton possessed rare qualifications. 'I like the man, I like his spirit,' he continued. 'He will not be a mere snivelling Copyist like the antagonists I have hitherto had, but will venture to step out of the lines upon occasion, & afford us some diversion in the combat.'

It was a competition to see who could best capture the market, which included creating consumer demand for special objects. Both parties knew that unique ware – something that would fashion taste and establish the vogue – would win the day, and Josiah knew that Boulton would be a tough competitor. He had a lean labour force of hundreds who followed a disciplined regimen in the sixty specialised workshops and vast warehouses of his new Soho factory.

Boulton was confident from the outset and quickly set about researching the market, sending an agent, Wendler, on a mission to Italy to scout the local market for fashionable art. Wendler was given a wide remit, encouraged to purchase anything that would help Boulton 'to know the taste, the fashions, the toys, both useful and ornamental, the implements, vessels &c. that prevail in different parts of Europe, as I should be glad to work for all Europe in all things that they may have occasion for'.

Josiah had high hopes for his Etruscan vases, but was nevertheless wary about the competition on his heels, telling Bentley:

> I have got the start of my Brethren in the article of Vases farther than I ever did in anything else, & it is by much the most profitable branch I ever launched into. 'tis a pity to lose it soon – there is no danger – true, not of losing the business, but the prices may be lower'd by a competition, & if the imitations are tolerable, the demand from us may be diminish'd, for all our buyers are not, though many of them are, qualified to discern nice differences in forms & ornament.[24]

But before Josiah could become too concerned about others in-truding on his scheme, he received exciting news. His sister, Margaret Byerley, had just returned from visiting the new show-rooms in Great Newport Street. 'No getting to the door for coaches,' she exclaimed, 'nor into the room for ladies & Gentn & Vases . . . Vases was all the cry.'[25] Josiah now knew that the Etruscans would provide them with the success they needed to propel Wedgwood & Bentley to a new realm of success.

TWENTY

French Frippery & Russian Husks

L ORD AND LADY CATHCART assumed residence in St Petersburg in 1768, with Lord Cathcart taking up duties as British
envoy to the Court of the Empress Catherine II. Before they
departed London, however, Josiah took advantage of one last opportunity to meet with his patron. 'I have waited upon Ld Cathcart,'
Josiah informed Matthew Boulton, when they still intended on
collaboration, 'to bring about the plan we settled of introducing
my manufacture at the Court of Russia.' Once again they proved
invaluable patrons, and Josiah excitedly reported that 'the Ambassador, but particularly his Lady, came into my measures with the
utmost readiness'. They had ordered 'a large service' of crested dinner
ware which they wanted delivered to Russia.[1]

By using diplomats' homes as showrooms Josiah had a wonderful
opportunity to gain exposure in distant markets, a strategy Josiah
had stumbled on a few years earlier when 'an East Indian Captain
& another Gentleman & Lady from those parts' ordered 'a Good
deal of my Ware, some of it *Printed & Gilt*, to take with them for
presents to their friends, & for their own use. They told me it was
already much in use there, & in much higher estimation than the
finest Porcellain, the Captain said he had dined off a very complete
service just before he left India.'[2] Now Josiah had reason to hope
that, through the example of Lord and Lady Cathcart's dinner
parties, the Russians would also acquire a high estimation of his
wares.

One practical problem which Josiah faced increasingly was how to get payment for goods delivered abroad. He already had problems collecting debts from his wealthy customers in relatively nearby London. One possible solution was to offer free delivery if the goods were paid for in cash on delivery. But while that would pay the bills, 'I cannot raise the prices in proportion,' he determined, '& if I pay the Carriage without altering the prices it will make near £500 per annum difference in my profits. Besides some of my customers (if I sell goods at deliver'd prices at all) will want them deliver'd at all lengths from 20 to 300 miles.'³ Eventually Josiah compromised according to his customers' demands, offering free carriage for cash-on-delivery orders in London only and replacing any item that was damaged in transit anywhere else in the world.

Delivering goods outside the United Kingdom was complicated. For his American market, Josiah employed third-party retail agents to deal with the particular issues of selling the goods to colonists. The risk here was less from Josiah's perspective since the main market here was for his reject pieces. It was all that consumers in America and the West Indies could afford, since Josiah's seconds and even thirds cost the same as most Staffordshire potters charged for their primary pieces. Exploiting his reputation as much as poss-ible, Josiah was now charging up to three times as much for his wares (even 'stock-in-trade' useful wares) than anyone else.

Wedgwood & Bentley was also receiving orders direct from across Europe from nobility and needed to find ways of insuring the goods in transit and of securing payment. Lady Cathcart offered a sugges-tion. 'If the Bills are sent to me with all the charges of packaging, shipping, & exchange of money included, address'd to any Merchant here, as soon as the goods are Delivered I will take care that the same be duly honor'd.' She added that there was really no other way. 'I have no commd of money in London, & can do no other-wise.'⁴ Josiah then asked Bentley to find a Russian merchant through whom they could do business. It would be a headache, but Lady Cathcart promised it was worth it. She even followed up her letter with another, promising Josiah that 'anything of Gildin & shew is liked best at St Petersburg'.

As exciting as it was to have business expanding at such a pace abroad, the demand for ornamental wares was adding immense pressures to the pot-works. Etruria was not yet operational, and Josiah found himself complaining to Bentley that he was receiving orders which he could not fill. 'We have a large ordr from yr house for abot 50 crates all of thirds, but cannot possibly complete it,' said Josiah. 'It is all for Jamaica.'[5] He was also having problems meeting orders for his primary clientele, the London elite. 'Ld Barrington is angry with me for neglecting to send a table service he ordered a long time since at my Rooms in Town,' he wrote, 'he has had a great deal of Company & nothing to eat off.'[6]

Josiah was desperate for more help. Useful Tom was proving as valuable as ever and had redoubled his efforts at the 'useful works' after the departure of Tom Byerley. Bentley, meanwhile, had moved to London, but had no intention of returning to Burslem. He had gently explained to Josiah that even the new estate of Etruria, where his home, Bank House, was still under construction, was not the best place to employ his talents. He needed the metropolis, and it made more sense that his education and connections were put to use by engaging with the fashionable customers in London and where he could also scout for artists to work on the wares. So at the end of 1769, Bentley bought a house with a large garden in Chelsea (after being guided in the purchase by Sally, who believed it to be a fair price for such an elegant property), and assumed a new role managing the showroom and overseeing the all-important finishing stages of the decoration of the ornamental vases.

With the London side of business in Bentley's capable hands, Josiah summoned William Cox to Burslem to 'take a little of the weight of business off my shoulders'. Josiah was now free to concentrate on 'a list of the workmen' employed in nearby potteries from which he 'intended hiring such as will suit us at Etruria'.[7]

Josiah was keen to build up an army of his own workers fast. 'I shall hire all the Men that offer & I think likely to do us any good,' he wrote.[8] Once under his command, he was sure that he could train them to perform to his standards. The amenities at Etruria also meant that Josiah could attract the most talented people available, who 'several others would fain to hire' but who 'chose to come to me'.[9] 'A Porter has offer'd himself who I think is likely, he is abt 50, can write, is a stern morose or rather resolute Character, & wants a fix'd situation for the remainder of his days,' Josiah told Bentley. 'The worker in metal I mention'd to you in my last has try'd various schemes but never could succeed *as a Master*, he is pretty well stricken in years & will now be content with a place that will procure him food and raiment for life.'[10]

A few years earlier in London Josiah had mooted the idea of 'making habitations for a Colony of Artists – Modelers, Carvers, &c', and he had imported the idea to Etruria, where a workers' 'Village' was under construction.[11] The homes, as well as the plan to provide education, training, and even health care for the workers, made it appealing to those who were particularly concerned about their quality of life after retirement (a comprehensive retirement scheme, where a fraction of workers' salary was withheld, would be introduced later in a plan devised by Josiah's friend Joseph Priestley).[12] Josiah was delighted that his investment in Etruria might solve the problem of the 'Lazy & fickle & not likely to stay long in any one place' labour force that so frustrated him.[13]

While the staff and the factory continued to grow, Josiah returned to the issue of providing Lord and Lady Cathcart with their service: he thought of sending them some additional, unsolicited, patterns that he hoped would be received with the implicit understanding that Lady Cathcart might display them for her visitors. Not sure how he could convey this clearly – and without offending her – he consulted Bentley. 'They must not be *presented*, & we must not pretend to charge for them, so that they must neither be *given* nor *sold*, – but we must borrow a pair of her Ladyships chimney pieces to shew them upon . . . May not you give Ld Cathcart a hint that we are preparing to paint the Etruscan Vases after Mr Hamilton's Book.'[14]

But Lady Cathcart was far more astute than Josiah gave her credit for, and as soon as she began receiving his wares, she engaged the interest of her Russian acquaintances. 'I am on the spot to be of Service,' she told Josiah, and true to her desire to promote trade between England and Russia, Josiah immediately had orders from Russian gentlemen.[15] All too predictably he also quickly encountered more practical difficulties of delivering and protecting his orders. In one instance, there was a misunderstanding over the cost and conditions of insuring a service about to be sent to Russia. 'I was not order'd to insure,' Josiah explained, '& I know the risque is the gentleman's who order'd the Goods,' but he anticipated that if anything happened, 'if they do not *receive* the goods, they will not pay for them.' If only '*gentlemen* were *Merchants*, & *knew the rules of trade*', then life would be much simpler.[16] In this instance, Josiah was forced to insure the order at his own cost.

To Josiah and Bentley, these were minor frustrations. They were thankful for their connections in helping them enter a new market, and optimistic that their foreign trade would flourish. Bentley particularly, in a reversal of roles from the pre-partnership days when Josiah was so sure of their future profits, felt confident of their situation, and assured Josiah in no uncertain terms that they would outperform any competitors. It was a belief that comforted Josiah, especially when he discovered that Matthew Boulton had abandoned all ideas of collaboration and had set himself up as a direct rival.

Sukey was now four, little John three, and their 'bantling', little Joss, a month old. The children missed their father, and neither he nor Sally had much time for weekend relaxation or family play. Josiah dined virtually every night of the week at the pot-works. 'Saturday is the busiest of my busy days,' he complained to Bentley, to whom he spent hours writing on Sunday mornings, his children

tugging at his elbows as he tried to catch up on the week's developments, 'if these Bratts will let me', he added wryly.

On the last Sunday of September, 1769, Josiah had much to say
on the nature of the competition.[17] On his way up to Burslem, he
reported, William Cox had stopped by Boulton's in Birmingham,
'to look at their Manufacture'. It was intended as a friendly visit, and
Boulton had taken his guest on a tour, showing him how they made
buttons, watch chains, and toys, 'but would not permit him to see their
Vase work'. Cox asked Boulton why. 'I find,' Josiah continued, 'they
are affronted at my not complying with their orders for the Vases to
be mounted,' and that subsequently 'they had been offer'd the Vases
for mounting by several Potters, but were now determined to make
the black Vases (Earthenware Vases, they took care to tell him)
themselves, & were building works for that purpose!'

Josiah was rather stunned by the news that the metal worker had
suddenly decided to become a potter. Josiah joked to Bentley that
he expected them to start recruiting his labourers for the princely
sum of £200 or £300 a year to manage their new works, but Cox
– who was rather reserved and somewhat shy – seemed more concerned by Boulton's behaviour. 'They talked to him in the stile &
manner of Rivals to us,' Josiah reported, 'big in their own conceits,
with some mighty blow their uplifted hands were prepared to let fall
upon us. So stand firm my friend,' Josiah sarcastically commanded
Bentley, '& let us support this threatened attack like Veterans
prepar'd for every shock or change of fortune that can befall us.'

Bentley had, in fact, already anticipated Boulton's manoeuvre and
he wrote to Josiah repeating his belief that they were capable of
capturing the foreign markets, especially the French market which
Boulton had earlier made such a fuss about.

'Do you really think that we may make a *complete conquest* of
France?' Josiah asked,

Conquer France in Burslem? – My blood moves quicker. I feel
my strength increase for the contest – Assist me my friend, &

the victorie is our own. We will make them (now I must say *Potts* & how vulgar it sounds) I won't though, I say we will fashn our Porcelain after their own hearts, & captivate them with the Elegance & simplicity of the Ancients. But do they love simplicity? Are you certain the French nation will be pleased with simplicity in their Vessels? Either I have been greatly deceive'd, or a wonderful reformation has taken place amongst them – *French* & *Frippery* have jingled together so long in my ideas that I scarcely know how to separate them, & much of their work which I have seen *cover'd over with ornament*, had confirmed me in the opinion.[18]

Bentley patiently answered Josiah's questions, providing a list of reasons 'for the *Virtuosi* of France being fond of *Elegant Simplicity*', which further convinced Josiah of the brilliance of his own idea of imitating the ancient arts and of anticipating the rejection of rococo in favour of neoclassicism.[19]

But Josiah could never have foreseen that the taste for his wares would catch on to the extent that they did, further afield, particularly in Russia. 'The field is vast indeed!' he exclaimed as he set about devising ideas for capturing markets in Ireland, Germany, Holland, and even China.[20] Most significantly another 'Avenue into the Russian Empire' had opened up.[21] In 1770, Catherine the Great, who so eagerly bought Western productions, considering 'foreigners as a kind of superior beings, in regard to the arts and sciences', commissioned from Wedgwood & Bentley a Queen's Ware dinner service that was decorated with a border of continuous wheat husks painted in purple. The 'Russian Service', as Josiah referred to it, was painted by artists under Bentley's supervision at the Chelsea Decorating Studio, one of the back rooms of their Great Newport Street showroom.

Not dissimilar to the reaction following Queen Charlotte's commission of the Queen's Ware, as soon as the Empress received her creamware 'Husk' service the Russian aristocracy sought to acquire dinner services of their own. Josiah had received some more letters from Lady Cathcart that promised more 'Ords from Russia this Spring [that] may do great things'.[22] 'What is good will sell here,' she told him, 'what is new will be greedily sought after, & more bespoke ... If you send good Merchandise, I think the Sale is certain.'[23] She advised Josiah of an English merchant who was resident in Russia, who spoke the language and was 'remarkably sensible' and in her estimation likely to be the best person to act as an agent for Josiah's trade to that country. 'I flatter myself I can be of great use forwarding among the Russians' knowledge of his wares, but warned Josiah at the same time not to inflate his prices – 'for that has often destroyed our trade'. 'I hope you won't lose the opportunity of this spring as your ware is now in fashion ...' she added, 'and with the confidence that what is offered is as Cheap as it ought to be I shall speak of it to all my acquaintance without fear or reserve.'

'What shall I say to this good Lady?' Josiah asked Bentley. 'Her Goodness to us beggars all thanks.' With Useful Tom working to supplement the labour to manufacture the Etruscan vases, which were 'the run' at the moment, they had fallen behind in their sales of 'useful wares', and Josiah had begun to worry that the demand for the stock-in-trade wares was slowing down. Therefore, he wrote to Bentley,

> the Russian trade comes very opportunely for the useful ware, & may prevent me lowering prices here. The *General trade* seems to be going to ruin on the Gallop – large stocks on hand both in London & the Country, & little demand. The Potters seem sensible of their situation, & are quite in a pannick for their trade, & indeed I think with great reason, for *low prices* must beget *low quality* in the manufacture, which will beget *contempt*, which will beget *neglect*, & *disuse*, and there is an end of the trade.[24]

While the ornamental wares remained a huge success (in 1770 accounts showed profits upwards of £4,000) and with business expanding into new markets for his useful wares, he was able to weather the fluctuations in consumer demand with greater comfort. He was, after all, many paces ahead of his 'brethren'. 'How many Lords and Dukes Visit your rooms, praise your beauties, thin your shelves, & fill your purses,' Josiah playfully asked Bentley in 1771, '& if you will take the trouble to acquaint us with the daily ravages made in your stores, we will endeavour to replenish them.'[25] His monthly trade with his Liverpool printers Sadler & Green now stood at £650, a huge increase from the meagre £30 a month at the start of their collaboration a decade earlier.[26] Wedgwood & Bentley's strength was such that Bentley flattered Josiah by dubbing him the 'Generalissimo' of trade, which Josiah humbly thought 'over rates my powers in War'.[27]

Before Josiah could think about enjoying the new prospects for Russian sales, he received word of competitive moves on the part of Matthew Boulton. About the same time as Lady Cathcart arranged for Josiah's spring sales, Boulton had packed up a collection of his ormolu vases – those decorated with gold and other metals in the manner he earlier discussed with Josiah – and sent them to Russia for the attention of Lord Cathcart. It was a strategy worthy of Josiah himself, and it worked. Lord and Lady Cathcart, being solely interested in promoting trade with Russia from *any* of England's entrepreneurs, while providing the Empress with unique products from the West, showed them to the Empress who, declaring them 'superior in every respect to the French', bought the lot. For Boulton, it was a masterstroke.

But the victory celebrations were soon halted by news that saddened all and reminded Boulton, Josiah and Bentley of the humanity that tied their interests as 'Patrons of the Nation': Lady Jane Cathcart had passed away in St Petersburg, and Lord Cathcart was preparing to return to Britain.

TWENTY-ONE

Wanting Air for Sally

O VER THE LAST YEAR Josiah had been spending less and less time with his family – the few hours he spent at home each day being used to update Bentley on events, with 'Sukey & Jack at my elbows' ('little Jos says ta ta', he added when signing one letter).[1] While Josiah always talked to Sally with regard to business developments, and relied on her judgment in many matters of 'taste' – in the decoration of their wares, for instance – it is also clear that Sally had many other concerns to occupy her.

As the business grew, so had the family, and while they were always anxious about what Josiah deemed 'evaporating cash reserves' (mainly due to heavy reinvestment in the business, recruiting labour and updating tools), their standard of living was in fact rising fast. As well as being frequently asked by Josiah to finish business correspondence as he rushed out to meetings in the mornings, Sally also took on the task of managing their personal affairs, overseeing the education and health not only of their own children but also of her nieces, Catherine and William Willets' children. Two of their girls, Kitty and Jenny, were close in age to Sukey, and had become good friends, especially after the Willets moved into 'Bentley's' Bank House. Josiah and Sally agreed to pay for the education of all the children, continuing the family tradition of ensuring the 'improvement' of future generations.

Sally had also become closely involved with helping their employees settle into their new environment. They had hired many

243

men and some women as artists for Bentley – sometimes married couples – from all over England. Sally took a personal interest in getting to know them. It was important, she felt, to understand their character and concerns in order for the business to succeed and for the employees to feel loyal and committed to the job. Josiah, though more concerned with the workers' technical skills, also believed in the principle of creating as agreeable an environment as possible. It was this philosophy that had led him to build houses for his workers, to attempt improvements in their physical working conditions and health care, and eventually to implement Priestley's insurance scheme.

As complementary and distinguished as both Sally's and Josiah's efforts to manage their (and others') lives were, Sally occasionally grew restless at being at the Brick House Works. She, like Josiah, longed to move into their new home, Etruria Hall – the design and furnishing of which she had taken command of – but, unlike Josiah, she did not have much opportunity to get out and travel about. He was frequently on the road – spending increasing amounts of time in London, sometimes stopping at Lichfield or Birmingham en route to visit Darwin or Boulton, and Sally now needed some respite, something amounting to a holiday. So, being as passionate as she was about politics, when the chance presented itself at the end of 1768 for a long vacation in London, she leapt at it.

In November 1768, Josiah and Sally, accompanied by Catherine Willets and a maid servant, set off for the capital. William Willets remained in Newcastle to watch over their children, while Sally and Josiah's children remained at home, under the care of Bentley who had come to Burslem to oversee matters at Etruria. With Josiah bound to be 'on the commercial ramble' in London, Sally and Catherine would be left to their own devices. It suited them fine: 'we have all things in common', said Sally; this was going to be *their* trip.[2]

Sally and Catherine would be staying at the rooms above the showroom at Great Newport Street, Soho. They were not large, and they were simple, with some select pieces of tasteful furniture to make a comfortable stay for Josiah or Bentley when their presence was required in London. The main chamber room had a four-poster bed and a mahogany night table. There was a large mahogany dining table with twelve hair-bottom mahogany chairs, more often covered with bills, books and catalogues than chinaware. Another room had a simple feather bed and a walnut bureau. The inventory which William Cox drew up of the rooms before his move to new premises in Chelsea otherwise noted only a 'glass frame' for the dining room, a kettle, and four pairs of blankets.

In preparation for the ladies' arrival, Josiah ordered that the simple, guest-quarter feel to the rooms be improved upon. 'New grates are put up in some of the rooms; new beds and fenders are bought; a glass bookcase is set up in the drawing room; and a wealth of comfortable bedding comes up by wagon from Staffordshire,'[3] he wrote, though neither Sally or Catherine realised that such efforts had been made to make the rooms more acceptable for their arrival.

'We have a variety of weather,' Sally informed Bentley, to whom she wrote with news of their trip and to acknowledge Bentley's reassurances that the children were doing well. 'Wet mornings & fine afternoons which makes the Streets so dirty it prevents our rambling so much as we wish either by Moon or by Sun however we omit very few Oppertunitys, & I can assure you are right busy on Saturday night.'[4] They headed for Drury Lane '& were very much entertained' with theatre. They dined with Mr and Mrs Hodgson who had looked after the final arrangements for brother John's funeral, and met with Ralph Griffiths, where the group debated politics. Sally stressed that they *debated*; 'it is,' she declared, 'nothing uncommon for Gentlemen & Ladies to differ in their Politicks'. And at present there was much to debate.

John Wilkes had just returned to London from Paris, where he had fled when facing prosecution for libel after the publication in

1763 of his *North Briton*, in which he notoriously attacked the King and Prime Minister. Wilkes, the son of a malt distiller and champion of middle-class and Dissenting desires to reform Parliament, stood as a candidate for the relatively poor constituency of Middlesex in the general election of April 1768. Wilkes hoped that his candidacy would generate enough publicity and support amongst his followers to protect him from prosecution. Indeed, he swept the poll, a pronounced victory in part attributable to the barricades his supporters – including local labourers dissatisfied with their wages and working conditions – erected in roads leading to the polling station in Brentford, allowing through only those who wore Wilkes's colours.

Despite his popularity and success at the polls, he was immediately arrested, sentenced to twenty-two months in prison, fined £1,000, confined to the King's Bench Prison and expelled from the House of Commons. It was a move that Wilkes, an extraordinary self-propagandist, used as proof to the world that Britain's constitutional principles were being grossly violated by the government.

'If ministers can once usurp the powers of declaring who *shall not* be your representative,' he thundered; 'the next step is very easy, and will follow speedily. It is that of telling you whom you *shall* send to Parliament, and then the boasted Constitution of England will be entirely torn up by the roots.'[5] Radical Protestant reformers and 'Rational Dissenters' (including Josiah and Bentley's close friend, Joseph Priestley) used the opportunity to spread the philosophy of man's natural rights, to stress personal virtues and 'qualities of industry, sobriety, frugality, enterprise', self-improvement, and careers being opened to people on a meritocratic basis.

Less philosophical protesters took to the streets. A riotous crowd descended on St George's Fields near the prison in protest at Wilkes's punishment. A magistrate who was trying to read out the Riot Act was struck on the head with a brick, and troops opened fire on the crowd, killing several people. The repercussions of this lasted for months, leading to more riots and demonstrations. Sally was gripped with the news as it unfolded in London. 'As I am

deeply enter'd into politicks', she wrote in one of her many letters
to Bentley;

> & you was so kind to encourage me in that most *Laudable* study
> by enquiring who was next to be murder'd, I could not forbear
> giving you the earliest intelligence of 14 that have suffer'd Mar-
> tyrdom for their Countrys good this day at Brentford. This
> afternoon Mrs Willett & myself have been to hear the debates
> at the house of Commons. No Male Animals were admitted
> so my good man cou'd not attend us.[6]

While Sally cheered the crowds who supported Wilkes, Catherine
found the debates and riots overwhelming. She shared the beliefs
and the political principles of her husband, Sally, Josiah and their
friends, but, as William Cox told Bentley, 'the Middlesex Election
hath Frightened Mrs Willets so that she wisheth herself at home
Again', where, safely removed from the ruckus at 'Whitfields Parliament' and 'Westminster', they could debate without risk of injury.
Sally, however, felt energised by the passion of the people.

'Mrs Wedgwood is pushing me off the stool,' Cox scribbled to
Bentley, whose 'inch of Time' at the writing desk to pen his daily
bulletin was over. Sally was eager to update Bentley on another day's
political developments. Josiah was somewhere in London collecting
ideas, and Sally wished that Bentley was there to see all that was
happening. Alas, she could only 'hope to smoak a pipe with you
very soon' and discuss the country's affairs.

When away from politicking, Catherine was happy to report that
'we are hurried to & fro in this great Metropolis', paying 'a dozen
Visits in the City & bin entertained very agreeably'. Bentley wrote
to them eliminating any worries they might have had about their
children's conduct. Sally heard 'such fine things of my Lad [two-
year-old John] & I will thank you again for conveying that *Smile*
to me. I have seen it ever since & you do not, cannot, know how
much good it has done me.' Bentley similarly told Catherine that
he had been to visit 'Mr Willets & the Children', and he commented

on the youngest. 'Jack's smile Pleased me much,' Catherine said to Bentley, 'but,' she teased, 'why did not Polly smile too?'[7]

All 'the Ladys' engagements in London exhausted even Josiah. 'I will not trust to writing in the evening any more,' he told Bentley, having as much difficulty as William Cox in keeping his seat at the writing desk.

> I find it impracticable, engagements of my own, or the Ladies are always filling up those hours, indeed we are under the necessity of encroaching upon regular bedtime, to have an hours rest, or enjoyment of ourselves in peace & tranquility & not-withstanding every moment is employ'd & we are in a constant bustle, I have for my own part got very little done yet & the Ladies have business enough cut out for them to employ them a month longer...[8]

Sally thought Josiah's complaints about how busy they were making his life quite unjustified. 'My good man is upon the ramble continually,' she retorted, 'and I am almost afraid he will lay out the price of his estate in Vases [which] he makes nothing of giving 5 or 6 guineas for', but – and here was the rub – 'if we do but lay out half the money in ribband or lace there is such an uproar as you never heard'.[9]

Their month-long stay in London concluded as hectically as it had begun: by the end of December Sally was able to send a message to Bentley from Newcastle-under-Lyme saying that they had 'just arriv'd, in good health & tolerable spirits' upon 'completion of their peregrinations', but 'as the chattle of the Bartts seems so ingaging after this long absence, they propose spending the evening here before they come to Burslem'.[10]

Life quickly returned to its familiar rhythm: Josiah was once again on the road while Sally held the fort in Burslem. But on one homecoming, a year after their London vacation, Josiah was met with a particular surprise. He had suffered a difficult journey back from London by carriage, meeting 'with several accidents on the road, such as springs snapping, shafts breaking, &c, which delay'd us something in our journeying', taking him three days to make it back to Burslem. But as his chaise descended the final hill from Newcastle leading to the valley and the site of Etruria, 'I was rewarded for all the risques & pains I had undergone in a tedious long & dirty journey'.

> I found my Sally & family at Etruria! Just come there to take possession of the Etruscan plains, & sleep upon them for the first night – Was not all this very clever now of my own dear Girls contriving. She expected her Joss on the very evening he arriv'd, had got the disagreeable business of removing all over, & I wo'd not have been another night from home for the Indies.[11]

Sally had inaugurated their new lifestyle in their home at Etruria. The design of the house was much admired by all who had seen it – a mutual friend of theirs and Erasmus Darwin's called it 'fit for a Prince'. It was a substantial country house, three-storeys high, in a well-proportioned style that was becoming very popular in the Georgian period. The lofty entrance hall met a large staircase. The rooms to either side were large, with multiple windows. It was not perfect – yet. Josiah was unhappy with the pointing on the brick-work, a fence needed to be finished, and the garden was a disaster with a mud pit where the pond should be – but Sally was determined to be in her new home and Josiah was happy to comply. She had also arranged a 'company' dinner to be held at Burslem's town hall for 120 of their workmen, a prudent gesture in recognition of the completion of the first stage of the massive construction project.

Josiah had always been immensely proud of his wife's skills in managing the practicalities of life. Many a time Sally's level-headedness and willingness to engage with the various dimensions of the business had provided Josiah with essential support. And now, again in 1770, Sally's resourcefulness was called upon as Josiah was struck down with another illness.

Josiah was convinced he was going blind. He saw spots when he looked at the sky or at blank paper when he tried to write, and clouds appeared when he looked at any distant objects or landscapes. 'They are near, or farther from the Eyes in proportion to the distance of the object I am looking upon,' he said.[12] He consulted a doctor who it was claimed had cured the Duke of Bedford and the Duchess of Norfolk of a similar disorder, who 'hopes he shall be able to set me to rights but says there is always *some danger* in these cases'. Josiah was ordered to wash his eyes three times a day with a medicinal cocktail, but after some weeks following this prescription Josiah's fears only grew worse. 'My *life*, as well as my *sight* is at stake,' he said, in a fit of hypochondria, since he was told that two 'miserable patients' near Burslem had died from the disease, which was 'seated near the brain wch is often the case, Vertigoes convulsions &c put a period to life & sight together'.[13] In the meantime, 'I am often practicing to *see* with my *fingers*, & think I shld make a tolerable proficient in that science for one who begins his studys so late in life, but shall make a wretched walker in the dark with one single leg.'[14]

But gradually the symptoms subsided and Sally was relieved of the burden of acting as his amanuensis once again. In May 1771, Sally gave birth to their fifth child, 'little Tom, for so they call him', as Josiah announced to Bentley. The next day they were visited by the Willets and Erasmus Darwin and his boys – five-year-old Robert and eleven-year-old Erasmus, Darwin's wife having died the year earlier. Sukey got along with the boys well, and would grow increasingly fond of Robert.[15]

Throughout the next year, Josiah remained 'nailed down here as fast as a rock', suffering 'a vast deal of *hard weather* as we call it here'. 'We poor villagers neither escape a blast or a drop of rain,' he wrote to Bentley, especially as he had no mature trees on the moorland ridge to help break the bracing winds. But, in early 1772, he was at long last relieved to be 'removing our Wheels, & Lathes, & all our furniture & hands from Burslem to Etruria', to the new factory, '& this makes us very busy'.[16]

As early as 1769 he had been given notice to leave the Brick House (Bell) Works since its owner, William Adams, had come of age. 'My Landlord is married and will come to them himself,' wrote Josiah. 'Here's a fine piece of work cut out for me!'[17] Sally's initiative in moving into Etruria Hall had helped matters, but without the use of the Bell Works there had been added pressures on production. Now the bell from the old works was hung proudly in its own turret at Etruria and struck for the first time to call workers to their new workshops.

'The sun shines, & the birds sing so finely,' an elated Josiah wrote, celebrating the brief relief from the harsh weather they had of late, 'that it goes against the grain to be confin'd in a room, when every living creature ought to be in the open Air swelling the chorus of universal praise for the chearing influence of the Sun, & the prospect of a returning Spring.'[18] But the severe winter weather had taken a more severe toll than he had realised.

'Mrs Wedgwood is Ill of Rheumatism, quite laid up at present,' Josiah told Bentley.[19] She became so weak, she had to be 'Carried to & from her bed'.[20] For weeks, her health had been fluctuating, and with occasional brief blasts of sunshine, Sally was able to 'take an airing on Horseback', but more often than not Etruria was drenched in a cold rain, which did her no good and worried their friend and physician, Erasmus Darwin.[21]

'He says he is afraid her disorder will be stubborn,' said Josiah, 'they have bled her twice & are now going to blister her. She is very ill, not the least help for herself. Her wrists, shoulders, neck, Hips, knees, Ancles, & feet are all violently affected, & she is as complete a Cripple as you can imagine.'[22] Darwin recommended that Josiah take her to Buxton, in Derbyshire, where she might benefit from the mineral water which flowed tepid from the ground into baths (heated, Darwin explained, from the earth's 'central fires').[23] Here, as elsewhere in spa towns, patients soaked in tubs and drank from the springs. Such therapy was one of the current medical trends amongst doctors, such as Darwin, who believed that the waters had chemical properties (which they were trying to identify) beneficial to weak constitutions. Other doctors disagreed, believing that it merely provided a placebo effect, attributing imagined benefits to the pungent odour and distinctive taste of the waters, without which 'patients would have no confidence in their virtues'. Still, other physicians worried that the present lack of knowledge might lead to dangerous abuses. Buxton water in particular, argued one physician, 'is not to be trifled with, for if it be unnecessarily used, it will certainly do Harm'.[24]

Josiah and Sally were, as ever, inclined to place their faith in the rational, if experimental, system of medical knowledge, especially since they knew that Darwin had been working on the chemical analysis of Derbyshire waters; but Josiah also thought it prudent to seek a second opinion. He contacted Mr Bent, the surgeon who amputated his leg, to ask if the Buxton waters were the most beneficial, or whether, for instance, Bath might not be a better place to go.

While Josiah certainly had Sally's interests at heart, he nevertheless could not resist taking advantage of any trip out of Etruria to serve his business interests as well. For years he had been conscious of the effect that 'the Season' had on commerce in different towns, commenting to Bentley in 1769 that 'I believe London will, like Bath, extend her season through the whole year!'[25] Knowing that his fashionable customers spent so much time and money in Bath, he set his sights on opening a shop there as soon as he could afford to. By 1772, the plan was ready to materialise. By March, Bentley had settled on premises he thought acceptable, and had hired a couple, Mr and Mrs Ward, to manage the shop. Josiah had Useful Tom working overtime 'to prepare a sortment of useful ware, services, &c &c' to stock the new showroom.[26] Since Sally's fever had eased and it appeared she could indeed manage the journey, the thought crept into his mind that he might have the chance to be present when the showroom opened.

Josiah first approached Sally about the idea, and 'mention'd going to Bath with her, instead of Buxton, & I should be glad to give Mr & Mrs Ward a little assistance at their first opening if possible'. When she said she no objection, Josiah then consulted Bent and Darwin. 'Mr Bent is on my side,' said Josiah, but 'Dr Darwin is rather against me.' Darwin may have been worried about the length of the trip from Etruria to Bath, and may even have been influenced by the physician William Falconer's treatise (just published) on Bath's waters, with reference to their effects on rheumatism, where he provided twenty-five pages of contraindications to taking the therapy. Josiah, however, determined he would gently persist with the idea, reckoning that nothing would happen for at least a month, an inconvenience, since time was of the essence. 'Pray when does the spring season begin, & end, at Bath,' Josiah inquired of Bentley.[27]

A month later, Sally was feeling moderately better. 'Mrs. Wedgwood has been well enough to ride out for some days past, but cannot yet dress herself & her Arms are rather worse this morning.' She was hoping to gain enough strength over the next ten or twelve days to travel to Manchester, where Sukey and her cousins, Jenny and Kitty Willets, were being sent to boarding school; but another change in the weather quashed those plans. 'Mrs Wedgwood is again confin'd to her bed chamber,' Josiah informed Bentley toward the end of April. 'We have for some days past had very cold weather, a severe North East Wind, & snow ... I despair her being able to go abroad [out of town] anywhere without a few weeks of warm weather.'[28]

At the beginning of May, amidst enormous confusion at the Etruria factory, 'half remov'd, the men all unsettled, both in body & mind, nothing in a finish'd, settled, state', Josiah was needed to deliver 'the little Lasses' to a Mrs Holland in Manchester, with whom they lodged while attending school.[29] 'I have left them with a very good Woman,' he said, '& hope they will be happy, & improved.' He also took the opportunity to stop by the town of Bolton on his return, 'to look at the school intended for Jack [six-year-old John] when there is a vacancy for him'.[30]

It was like 'a man leaving his house on fire', but despite all the on-going difficulties of settling into Etruria, Josiah was off once again, this time with Sally by his side, en route to Bath. Sally was by no means perfectly fit – they estimated that a decent recovery would take roughly three weeks in Bath – but she was feeling well enough to socialise, drink to their distant friends' health each night, and enjoy the intimacy of the balmy, June nights.

In the day, Josiah helped prepare his Bath showroom, and scout the competition in the area. He considered the shop Bentley had opted for unsatisfactory since the street was busy with 'Coal Carts, Coal horses & Asses – & a great way from the Town & Parades & not very near the principal Pump Room'.[31] It seemed far from the fashionable city centre, near Market Place, where Josiah spotted 'a very rich shop' which was selling 'a large assortment of Mr. Boulton's Vases'.[32] The vases were ornamented with minerals which the shop's proprietor drew Josiah's attention to. He told Josiah 'of Mr Boulton's having ingaged at several £1000 expense the only mine in the World' that produced the precious stones, 'and that nobody else could have any of that material'.

Josiah listened patiently to this 'long tale' but then discreetly pulled the gentleman aside and advised him 'not to tell that story too often as many Gentlemen who came to Bath had been to Derbyshire, seen the mine, & knew it to be free & open to all the world, on paying a certain known mine rent to the Land owner'. The shopkeeper stared at Josiah, and 'assur'd me upon his honor' that he had only repeated what Boulton had told him was true.

'Well done Boulton, says I, *inwardly*,' Josiah laughed, taken with his rival's cunning sales tactics. He then asked the shopkeeper how well the vases sold. 'So so,' the gentleman replied. 'I am afraid,' a satisfied Josiah declared, 'they will never answer Mr Boulton's end as a Manufacturer.'

After a few weeks of therapy in Bath, Josiah was disappointed to report that 'Mrs Wedgwoods lameness continues'. He was especially concerned since her joints were badly affected, 'especially her knees' – they 'make a crackling noise like dryd parchment whenever she bends them' – and Josiah worried that she might face surgery, or worse. Moreover, Sally was growing uneasy and was developing 'a longing after home & for her Bratts', John, Josiah and baby Thomas, who were being cared for by a hired nanny and Useful Tom's wife.[33] Catherine Willets was due to give birth any day, but wrote to Sally to tell her that 'Mr Willets has just been at Etruria to look at your offspring', and all was well. 'Tom grows every way very fast, will almost overrun them . . . Sukey [now seven] likes Manchester very well & Mrs Holland is very kind to them all.'[34] She also had news of a housekeeper that Josiah thought of hiring to ease Sally's burdens. A letter of recommendation advised that the woman 'will be an advantage to the children as they will learn none of those evils to which they are subject to in the company with the generality of servants, she is particularly handy & useful about sick persons'. That sounded promising, and, the next week, when Sally learned that Catherine was 'safely delivered of a very fine girl' and that 'your son Tommy has four teeth', Sally became desperate to return home.

By the time they made it back to Etruria, a full month later, Sally was 'almost a skeleton, & has not strength to walk 20 yards'.[35] Mr Bent was of the opinion that her health was rapidly deteriorating once again due to a 'Breeding disease', since she was again pregnant. 'All hopes I had conceiv'd of her speedy recovery are all vanish'd,' said Josiah, getting visibly more anxious.

Her sickness & vomiting, with all the unfavorable symptoms are return'd, & as Doctor Darwin, who attended her yesterday, apprehends an inflammation of the Liver, & she is so extremely weak and emaciated I am really alarm'd for her safety, & in great distress.

He begged Bentley to refrain from writing about this in his return letters, hoping to keep his anxieties hidden from Sally as much as possible. Bentley had plenty of other things to fill his letters with, since Josiah continued to bombard him with particular questions about new sorts of wares they were hoping to sell.[36]

A month later, in early September, Sally miscarried '& nothing but the greatest attention in nursing & keeping everything quiet about her can save her life'.[37] She was emaciated and pale, '& does not seem to have a drop of blood in her body'. Erasmus Darwin was now regularly making the sixty-mile round journey from Lichfield to Etruria, and prescribed 'a course of steel, in the form of ten grains of fresh iron fillings mixed with quince marmalade taken twice a day (with four drops of laudanum added to each dose)'.[38] Darwin was particularly eager to help such good friends, especially since his own wife's death two years earlier, when, as he said, 'the dear Partner of all the Cares and Pleasures of my Life ceased to be ill – and I felt myself alone in the World'. He wished for nothing more for his friends than to remove the threat of death.[39]

Josiah supplemented the iron shavings with ripe plums and cider, 'but I believe I shall not gain much credit in my office amongst the female nurses here', he wrote. He feared the onset of autumn, and the change in weather, and hoped yet 'to fortify her against winter'.[40]

Josiah was in anguish, and unsurprisingly he noticed that he too had 'lost a great deal of flesh', prompting Darwin to urge Josiah to eat despite the trying circumstances.[41] To compound his distress he learned the shocking news of 'a scene of vilany amongst our servants in the House', who, while Sally suffered upstairs, were 'robbing us of everything they could carry off'. As if carrying on with business, organising the factory, and doctoring and fearing for Sally's life was not enough, he now had 'to sweep the House of every servt we have in it, Male & Female, some from the field Men & others from the works'. He was devastated to learn that the staff, whom Sally had tried so hard to befriend and help settle, were 'inclin'd to attack their Mistress' when so vulnerable. He again kept this quiet from Sally, and plotted to 'complete the revolution' in staff termination and replacement when she left the house to stay with her family in Cheshire.

Only she was not strong enough to travel, remaining bedbound 'in a very dangerous situation' for much of the year. Winter was once again descending on them like a scourge. 'I am almost distracted with my fears for her, & for myself, for I should, in losing her go near to lose myself also, & I fear, though I shudder at writeing it, that she has but a poor chance for recovering her present illness.'[42] Their surgeon Mr Bent 'thinks the only thing that can save her wod be going to Italy or the south of France', Josiah told Bentley, but that was an enormous risk.

Josiah took her to Lichfield to stay with Darwin for ten days, allowing him to deal with the 'revolution in our household' and 'hope that the chance of place, Air & company will have a good effect'.[43] But Sally remained sick. Darwin, her 'favourite Esculapius', optimistically told Josiah that 'if we can preserve her thro' the cold weather to April, she will do very well, & make a perfect recovery in the summer'.[44] The winter would be bleak.

TWENTY-TWO

All the Gardens in England

1772 WAS ALSO a difficult year for other members of Josiah's family. His eldest brother, Thomas, fell gravely ill. In the twenty years since inheriting the Churchyard Works and Overhouse estate (where he lived with his second wife, Jane, and five children, three from his first marriage) Thomas had not managed to improve the properties much, nor had he excelled as a potter – just as Josiah had predicted when he left to go off on his own, shortly after completing his apprenticeship.

Thomas struggled for years to recoup the losses incurred as a result of his and Josiah's father's poor management of the pot-works. He never did pay the £20 inheritance his father left to Josiah and his siblings – Josiah delivered that out of his own pocket after he married Sally. Although Thomas had worked hard at his pot-works, employing eighteen staff – accounts show a regular purchase of eighteen coats, which probably formed part of the workers' wages – he never managed to muster much business. When he fell ill he had a meagre £172 of earthenware stock – simple wares, such as baking dishes, blue and white cups and saucers, mustard plates, and 'sortables'.[1] His pot-works were serviced by four horses, two carts, four lathes, two throwing wheels, and some tools – in all amounting to a mere £130.[2]

Josiah had had infrequent and rather formal contact with his eldest brother, whom, Josiah wrote, 'has had vexations & fretting enough for ten years past to have destroyed half a dozen constitutions'. Finally in February 1773, Jane – a reserved and somewhat mysterious character – called on Josiah and asked him to visit Thomas who had been confined to the house for several months and whose health, like Sally's, was rapidly deteriorating.

When Josiah arrived at Overhouse he discovered that the family was 'in a deplorable way'. Josiah asked Erasmus Darwin to examine his brother, who Josiah said was suffering from 'Ailments of various kinds, which seem now to have resolv'd themselves into a Dropsy. His Legs & Body swell, his appetite is nearly lost, & he sleeps but little.'[3] Equally gloomy was the unsettled state of his personal affairs which, observed Josiah, 'Having Children by two Wives, one of whom you know is alive, & a sad Rakish Boy for his eldest son', meant that it would not be an easy matter to 'bring about a settlement' in the event of his death. He had to act swiftly. Darwin estimated that Thomas had no more than weeks to live.

To confound matters, the 'Rakish' eldest son from his first marriage, twenty-nine-year-old Thomas, was, according to Josiah, having a mental breakdown caused by the 'extreme narrowness & something rather worse' of his stepmother. For years he had been 'ill-treated & almost ruined' by her 'black misdeeds', which his sisters escaped through marriage.[4] At her husband's deathbed, Jane confessed to Josiah 'that it was her daily study to set his Father against him, in which, alas, she succeeded too well, that she has wrong'd him every way'. Even her younger son, who was in a state of shock at his father's demise, became overwhelmed with 'the foolish talk & behaviour of his Mother to him [which] made him for some time quite an Idiot'.[5]

Josiah managed to get his brother to write a will just in time. Thomas passed away at the end of February. The family was left with relatively little. Jane received £50 worth of furniture (a third of the value of all the furniture), and rental income from six houses they owned as part of his original inheritance, which she added to monies and furniture she had already stolen in anticipation of her husband's death, and which she had secreted at a neighbour's house.[6]

Thomas's four youngest children shared legacies totalling £1,100, while the eldest son, Thomas, inherited Overhouse estate and its pot-works. Josiah was kind to Thomas junior and did all he could to make him feel part of Josiah's own family. At times Josiah felt encouraged by his prospects. 'The improvement of my Nephew, & his reformation which is daily confirming gives me a very sensible pleasure,' he told Bentley. But this Thomas was no more suited to business than his father or grandfather before him, and he repeatedly asked to borrow money from his uncle.[7] Josiah soon found himself financially supporting Thomas, his younger stepbrother 'who is not one remove from an idiot', and 'the vilest wretch that ever lived', and Jane, the stepmother, who spent the next twelve years, until her death, 'deprived of reason, & overwhelmed with guilt & despair'.

Just after his brother Thomas's death, Josiah at long last had something positive to report. 'Mrs W has had a good night & is as much better this morning as one could expect from so favourable a circumstance.'[8] Spring had sprung and summer was on its way. Thinking of Darwin's prognosis, he was elated to report that Sally had pulled through and was smiling once again.

Spending time at Overhouse estate with his dying brother had been like stepping into the past for Josiah. Indeed, Burslem itself had begun to feel like a foreign land. Etruria was far more sophisticated than anything the community had seen before and Etruria Hall put his cousins' Big House to shame. Whether by coincidence or design, it was built just within view from the top of Big House, so Long John and Cousin Thomas could always gaze at Josiah's success. With all the family sadness, however – including the death of Long John's one-year-old son from smallpox in 1772 – Josiah was in no mood to boast.

About the only bright spot for Josiah amidst the gloom and worry of 1772 was the unexpected news that Bentley was 'upon the verge of the Holy Estate of Matrimony'. While working at the London showroom two years earlier he had met one Mary Stamford, the daughter of a Derbyshire merchant. 'How,' Josiah teased, 'can it be possible that you should meet' the 'Lady of your choice' at their rooms on Great Newport Street? 'Nothing surely can have more the Air of Romance,' he concluded. Bentley had kept the marriage plans rather quiet, no doubt finding it difficult to discuss them when Josiah's letters were so full of concern over Sally's frail health. 'While,' said Josiah, 'we all wait with great impatience for the remainder of the curious History which the good Lady has promis'd you,' he did have one slight, but immediate, concern: did Bentley have any plans to move from Chelsea, or indeed from London?[9]

Josiah still wished to expand their London showrooms, to encourage better sales amongst his fashionable customers. He had heard that the Society for the Encouragement of Arts, Manufacture and Commerce was taking up rooms in a new development called the Adelphi on the Thames Embankment. Designed by the architects Robert and James Adams, the development consisted of twenty-four terraced houses which were finished by some of the best painters and craftsmen available, including Angelica Kauffman, Cipriani, and Zucchi. Completed in 1772, its first tenants included David Garrick and Dr Johnson's famous friend, Topham Beauclerk, and later Richard Arkwright. Now Wedgwood & Bentley (for Bentley assured him that he and his soon-to-be bride were staying in London) wanted a presence in it.

With the opportunity to have their rooms custom built, Josiah and Bentley immersed themselves in the minutiae of design, putting to paper ideas that they believed would create the perfect suite of offices and showrooms. Different spaces were specifically designed to display different kinds of wares from both the useful and ornamental branches, including a Dessert Room with a 'dessert Table' in the middle, a 'Vase Room', and gallery with encaustic plaques and bas-reliefs 'suitable for large Halls and Stair Cases'. Ascending a large, gently rising main staircase the customer would be led to more rooms of vases, with 'cabinet drawers under, down to the floor, for pictures, Gems, Heads, &c'. A rear staircase would lead to offices for keeping accounts and writing, where Josiah imagined an ingenious communication system: 'a Tin pipe may be put to a note upon the Desk below when any particular account &c is wanted above & another convenience of the same sort from the back stairs into the Packing House'. Josiah also wanted to have the largest window possible in the front of the shop. Not only would this throw much light into the room, but, as it had never been done before (not least because the science of glassworks could not yet produce such windows), it 'should be rather Magnificent on the Outside to render it conspicuous'.[10]

But their plans to move into the Adelphi never materialised, largely because Josiah and Bentley concluded that the high rent – £400 annually – could not be justified given the problems inherent in the design of the whole complex (crucially, their new warehouses would be at risk of flooding from the Thames).[11] But they had another possible venue: Number 12 Greek Street, south of Soho Square. Portland House, named after the owner of the estate, the Duke of Portland, was the largest house in the street, having seven windows along a fifty-four foot frontage. It had the added bonus of requiring little work to transform it into a showroom space since a previous tenant was a medical man, who had built a large dissecting room in it. 'I like the idea of a dissecting room,' wrote Josiah, thinking that it would be ideal to convert into a gallery.[12] While Josiah had to sacrifice the idea of one large shop window, they did implement some of their other imaginative designs, including fitting a network of speaking tubes throughout the building to expedite communication.

The new premises, which Wedgwood & Bentley paid £300 rent per year for, came at an opportune moment. In 1772, Parliament approved the purchase of William Hamilton's collection of antiquities, deeming it 'simple, beautiful and varied beyond description', items 'far superior to any that have ever been collected', and it was to be put on public display at the British Museum.[13] Josiah wanted his shop to emulate the Museum displays, which, he was sure, would generate new levels of interest in his Etruscan wares. He also suspected that more competitors would move onto his turf and sensed the need to protect his innovations by more formal means. When his 'First Day's vases' were thrown at Etruria in 1769, he was the first potter to imitate the ancients by having his artists paint red figures in the antique style on his black basalt vases, and he hoped to remain the only one for as long as possible by patenting the technique of 'Encaustic Painting'.

The figures on the Etruscan wares were painted by Josiah's artists with an antique-looking smooth, matt finish, rather than the familiar glossy enamel. The secret lay in Josiah's formula for the pigment, which consisted in part of a chemical concoction including bronze powder, vitriol of iron, crude antimony, and exact amounts of other chemicals.[14] Josiah hoped that by taking out a patent he would protect not only the specific formula for his pigment but also the concept of imitating ancient wares. But he was to be disappointed.

Soon after Josiah disclosed his formula as part of the patent, which he obtained in 1769, a London merchant was discovered to be selling 'antique' vases with encaustic painting. Josiah traced them back to a potter named Humphrey Palmer, from Hanley, a village adjacent to Burslem. Josiah sued him for 'trespass' but was immediately concerned about his lack of evidence. 'The *selling* you can prove easily & clearly', he wrote to Bentley, 'the *Making* I cannot prove at all', and further, he could not prove that Palmer and the London merchant were partners, which he thought was the crucial link. 'That matter is kept a secret', he said, while encouraging Bentley to 'have a coffee with Neale, the London merchant selling the encaustic vases, to tell him what he's doing to judge whether "he sins willfully"'.[15]

Trying to avoid an expensive legal case which he might lose anyway, Josiah approached Palmer hoping they could settle out of court, using neutral potters and artists as arbitrators. 'But in short, after much talk & shuffling . . . he durst not agree . . . & had trifled with me exceedingly in the meantime'. Instead Josiah pursued his case by other means, gathering 'evidence' by soliciting expert opinion. He talked to two potters, '& they declare that they are certain whatever the Law may determine the country will universally give the invention of Etruscan painting to me', and he showed the specification of his formula to two 'clever' enamellers (they had read Hogarth's analysis of beauty and Burke on the sublime, he noted), who 'declare they do not prepare their colours in the same manner & likewise no one else does'.[16]

Josiah succeeded in obtaining an injunction, but the proceedings proved to be a drawn-out affair, and eventually, in return for an undisclosed sum payable to Wedgwood & Bentley, Palmer became 'a sharer in the patent'.[17] Josiah never bothered taking out a patent again, realising it would always mean revealing the secrets of his laborious experimental trials. The experience had left him immensely frustrated: 'There is nothing relating to business,' he wrote, 'I so much wish for as being released from these degrading slavish chains, these mean selfish fears of other people copying my works.'[18]

Josiah's solution was to use a marketing strategy that would keep him one step ahead of the competition. Bentley had often tried to encourage Josiah to produce a full range of different kinds of wares in order to add variety to the showrooms. Josiah thought this was too risky. 'If everything we do & produce must be instantly copied by the Artists – our rivals – should we not proceed with some prudent caution, & reserve, & not shew either one, or the other, *too much at once?*' Only when the fashionable item has 'had its day' should they then 'surprise the World' – 'keep the public attention awake' – by bringing out a new item. This was a philosophy that he had developed when working with his first partner, Whieldon, who was equally concerned about the limited term of consumers' interest in new products. So he flooded his correspondence to Bentley with ideas about possibilities for the next project. Perhaps, he thought, after Etruscan ware grew stale, he would produce figures after Raphael: 'in order of time he ought to do so'.[19] 'Variations', Josiah stated, 'will produce business enough for all the hands we can possibly get together.'[20]

This strategy might deal with the majority of his rivals – the 'sniveling copyists' he had no respect for, but dealing with 'the Boultons & . . . the great ones of the land', those with their own skills and original ideas, remained a different matter. Josiah was exasperated that Boulton had been gaining much attention by auctioning his ormolu wares. They had been fetching amazing prices. 'I am not without some little pain for our Nobility & Gentry themselves,' Josiah exclaimed, wondering why Boulton's 'glitter' of ornamental metal was proving so attractive. 'What heads, or Eyes could stand all this dazzling profusion of riches & ornament if something was not provided for their relief,' such as in the form of ancient simplicity. But, he wrote, he still had 'some hopes for our black, Etruscan, & Grecian vases'.[21]

Although Josiah remained in their present course of production, in early 1773 an unexpected order came through the Russian consul in London, Alexander Baxter, that would help to catapult Wedgwood to the apex of his fame, and help finish off Boulton as a rival in this field of industry. The order was from 'my Great Patroness in the North', Catherine the Great, who commissioned an extraordinary dinner service she intended to use at state occasions for up to fifty people at the new Chesmenski Palace in St Petersburg, in an area referred to as *La Grenouillière*, 'the frog marsh'.[22] The set amounted to over 950 items, including 680 pieces for dinner and a 264-piece dessert set, with additional tureens, decorative fruit baskets, and ice-cream 'glaciers'. The set was to be prepared 'in the Royal pattern', with a painted border upon the rims of the dishes similar to her previous Husk service, but this time with a symbolic green frog instead of a husk and with '*every piece having a different subject*' in the middle.[23]

Josiah quailed at the practical difficulties involved with preparing each item, 'tolerably done', with a unique view of British landscapes and buildings. 'Why all the Gardens in England will scarcely furnish subjects sufficient for this sett,' he wrote to Bentley. He knew that they had recently undertaken a lavish commission for the King of Prussia – a dinner service showing scenes of his own dominions for his own use, but it was not as large as this and Josiah shuddered to think of the cost of production.

He thought of all the artists involved, copying pictures from galleries or books. 'Do you think the subjects must all be from *real views* & *real Buildings*,' he worriedly asked Bentley, '& that it is expected from us to send draftsmen all over the Kingdom to take these views – if so, what time, or what money?'[24] He imagined it would take two or three years to complete. 'Suppose the Empress should die,' he remarked, 'it will be a very expensive business.'

He estimated it would cost in the region of £1,000 to £1,500 to produce. The Russian consul thought this a bit steep and asked Wedgwood if he could revise the figures downwards. 'If his Mistress heard him she would rap his knuckles,' Josiah complained.[25] Of course they could do them more cheaply, as low perhaps as £400 or £500, but it would 'not be *fit for an Empress's Table*, or do us any Credit'.[26]

Wedgwood & Bentley, of course, took the risk and faced up to the challenge. Josiah hired an artist to start with the landscapes around Staffordshire. He equipped him with a camera obscura and gave him instructions to 'take 100 views upon the road'. Josiah judged they could compromise to a degree with the source of their illustrations, which if they were all taken on site, would – the artists estimated – cost upwards of £3,000. Besides they could use 'the paintings in most Noblemans & Gentlemans houses of real views' and 'the *publish'd views* & the real Parks & Gardens' to keep costs down.[27] Since they were so willing to let Josiah use their collections of vases as models, he was sure aristocrats would allow his artists to sketch from other parts of their collection, especially when their estates would be depicted for the 'first Empress in the World'.[28]

Throughout the next year the artists painted over 1,200 different views representing, as Bentley described it, 'all of the centuries and styles, from the Huts of the Hebridean islands to the masterpieces of English architecture'.[29] Amongst scenes of St James's Palace, Kew Gardens, and splendid estates such as Chatsworth, Wedgwood & Bentley also included pictures of industrial progress, such as the dock-yard at Plymouth, a Bristol colliery, the Bridgewater Canal, and – framed within a large, oval service dish – a symbol of industrial achievement itself: Etruria. Nowhere amongst the 950-odd pieces was Wedgwood able to find room for Matthew Boulton's Soho works.

The good news was that the excellent team of artists they employed, led by three women landscape painters – Mrs Wilcox, Miss Glisson, and Miss Pars – finished the job in just over a year, well under the estimated time. The bad news was that the cost of production had far exceeded Josiah's original estimates, amounting to around £2,500. Given all the activity and engagement with the 'Noblemans & Gentlemans' in the early stages of production, when the service was nearing completion, Josiah and Bentley considered whether it would be beneficial to display the service to the public before it was sent off to Russia. Many of the ladies and gentlemen whose estates were represented were curious to see how their homes had been depicted. The benefit, Josiah thought, was that 'it would bring an immense number of people of fashion into our Rooms – would fully complete our notoriety to the whole Island, & help us greatly, no doubt, in the sale of our goods, both useful & ornamental. It would confirm the consequence we have attain'd, & increase it, by showing that we are employ'd in a much higher scale than other Manufacturers.' On the other hand, there was some danger. 'Suppose a Gentleman thinks himself neglected, either by the omis-sion of his seat, when his Neighbours is taken, or by putting it upon a small piece, or not flattering it sufficiently.' They then risked condemnation, 'he then becomes our enemy . . . & Damns it with the Russian Ambassador & with every one he is able to'.[30] Josiah left the matter to Bentley's prudent judgment.

Bentley decided it was worth the risk, but they decided upon a tactic of issuing tickets to raise interest by making the display of the Russian service an exclusive event. One of the ticket holders was the bluestocking Mary Delany, who declared herself 'giddy' after looking over the collection. 'It consists I believe of as many pieces as there are days of the year, if not hours,' she wrote.

> There are three rooms below and two above filled with it, laid out on tables, every thing that can be wanted to serve a dinner; the ground the common ware pale brimstone, the drawings in purple, the borders a wreath of flowers, the middle of each piece a particular view of all the remarkable places in the King's dominions neatly executed. I suppose it will come to a princely price; it is well for the manufacturer, which I am glad of, as his ingenuity and industry deserve encouragement.

However, she was briefly taken aback when she spotted an error on one of the plates, which wrongly attributed the ownership of her niece's home, Ilam House. She promptly pointed out the error, ensuring that they 'acknowledge its *true master* to her Imperial Majesty'.[31] Aristocrats' carriages soon crowded Greek Street to the point of creating a traffic jam, culminating in a personal visit from the Queen, who, according to Bentley, expressed 'her approbation in pretty strong terms'.[32]

As much as this magnificent commission did for Wedgwood & Bentley's pride and reputation, it was – in Josiah's view – a 'tedious business' conducted for little profit. Catherine, who was proud of the service, keeping it on open display for all visiting dignitaries to view, paid just over 16,000 roubles for it (approximately £2,700), giving Wedgwood & Bentley a meagre £200 profit.[33] Also, it was a one-off, which meant that, unlike the original Queen's Ware service or his Etruscan vases, it would not generate a flood of orders from those eager to emulate royalty.

Josiah realised that he needed to move on with new products. At the end of each day, after emerging from overseeing the production of 'Catherine's Ware', he would return to his experiment book. Catherine's service had certainly outdone Boulton's earlier triumph in Russia, but Josiah was pursuing another scheme to win the war. If Boulton thought that misleading the Bath merchant about the rarity of the gems he used in his ormolu vases was clever, he was about to learn a lesson in true one-upmanship. Josiah had been experimenting with the five tons of 'Cherokee' clay that Griffiths had brought back from America a few years earlier and was obtaining some remarkable results. Above all, Josiah planned to use the amazing story of how the clay had been obtained to full and powerful effect.

TWENTY-THREE

Deep in the Cherokee Backcountry

W HEN JOSIAH complained that it was going to cost him 25 guineas to send Thomas Griffiths from London to Charles Town, South Carolina, he had no idea what the physical and emotional cost of the journey would be.

Josiah begrudgingly obtained a ticket on the *America* in July 1767, and on the sixteenth, under the command of Captain Raineer, Griffiths sailed for Charles Town. Disagreeable weather made it a slow journey, and after two months at sea – enjoying the occasional meal of a shark and having witnessed a young woman in the steerage give birth to a baby girl – Griffiths finally arrived, at 'a miserable hot and sickly time'.[1] He rested and acclimatised for two weeks at the port, and after stocking up on tea and coffee, three quarts of alcohol, and a tomahawk axe 'for the journey', Griffiths mounted his rented horse, named March, 'and then went off for the Cherokee Nation'.

He headed out north-west, toward the southern Appalachian region, wandering through fields and forests, over meadows on serpentine trails, through hundreds of miles of 'very deep and daingerous Roads'. The weather was 'very hot and fainty', and at a tavern and inn a few days later he observed 'the People almost all dying of the ague and feaver'. Two nights later, his horse was too exhausted to go on, and he 'was obliged to sleep under a Tree with my horse, very near the place where five people had been Rob'd and Murder'd but two days before, by the Virginia Crackers and

Rebells; a Set of Thieves that were join'd together to rob Travillers and plunder and destroy the poor defensless Inhabitants of the New Settlements'.

On the trail the next day he happened to meet a trader, something of a rarity since travellers often covered twenty or thirty miles without seeing a person or so much as a hut. They joined company, and six miles later, as the sun was setting through the woods, his companion became agitated by the sight of two men ahead. He 'pray'd me to give him one of my Pisstolls and keep the other in my hand Ready cock'd', and as his companion anticipated, 'they soon gallop'd up a Deer Track into our Road, with a 'how do you do Gentlemen, how far have you come this Road? Have you met any horsemen?', and then wished us a good evening. After turning back to ask whether they had heard any news of robbers, 'which we anser'd in the Negative', they continued on their path. 'It was well we were together and that we had firearms,' Griffiths said, 'as he had knowledge of one fellow, and believed him to be concerrn'd in the late Murders', which proved accurate, as Griffiths later saw one of the men executed for his crimes.

After this, Griffiths parted company from his acquaintance, and days later, some two hundred miles from Charles Town by his estimation, he arrived at a plantation called Whitehall, where he was asked to accompany an Indian woman belonging to the Chiefs of the Cherokees. She had been taken and ransomed 'by our Indian deputy of the Illinois' and rescued by John Stuart, Superintendent of Indian Affairs (Stuart's life had been saved by the great Cherokee Chief, Attakullakulla at the time of the fall of Fort Loudon). After three nights on the road, Griffiths and the Indian woman arrived at old Fort Prince George, a trading post across the Little Tennessee River from Old Kowes (Keowee, or Cowee as it is spelled today), formerly the chief town of the lower Cherokees, just south of the present North Carolina border.

'At this Fort I delivered up my Squaw and Letters' to the commanding officer, and discovered that the commissaries for Indian affairs were meeting with a number of chiefs: Great Bear, the Rising Faun, Old Woolf, and *attaw kullucllah* himself. 'All these met at this Fort to call a Counsell and held a grand talk concerning a peace with the Norward Enemies.'

Happy to be off the trail and under a tent, Griffiths ate, drank, smoked and 'began to be famileer with these Strainge Copper collourd Gentry', and when the moment was right, he requested permission to travel through their nation, in search of 'curiosities', 'in particular to speculate [after] any White Earth'. Accordingly the commanding officer called over a linguist, who was instructed to be 'very particular on the subject' to the Chiefs, who, after a long hesitation and several debates amongst themselves, granted him permission. Two young warriors 'seemed to consent with some Reluctance,' Griffiths observed, 'saying they had been troubled with some young men long before, who made great holes in their Land, took away their fine White Clay, and gave em only promises for it'. They were concerned since 'they did not know what use the Mountain might be to them, or their Children'. However, Griffiths had behaved like a 'True Brother' by safely bringing the Indian woman home, and they 'did not care to disappoint me for that time'. He then departed the Fort with great formality, 'such as singing and shaking hands; besides making a publick show of their gifts and offerings for Peace'.

Heading north along the Savannah River into the valley, he passed small villages of Indians with old men, women, and conjurers, who offered him grapes and apples. The younger men were out hunting. In one village, he visited 'my old Consort', the Indian woman he had escorted to Fort Prince George. She had been obliged to undergo an eight-day confinement in the 'Town house' according to the Indian custom after returning from imprisonment 'by any enimy whatsoever', and after that she was 'to be stripp'd, dipp'd, wellwash'd, and so Conducted home to her husband', where bad distempers sometimes raged against the woman. He met another old Indian woman who had 'undergone that dreadful barbarity, of being shot thro the shoulder, Tomahawked in the breast, and then scalped' by her husband, but lived.

At the end of October, after nearly a month of travel, while 'in fear of every Leaf that rattled' in the forest, he had passed picturesque waterfalls, brooks, and springs into present day North Carolina. 'In my way I passed the spot where Coll Montgomery was greatly Repulsed by the Indians', he noted, reflecting on the battle of Echoe, and 'the place where Coll Grant gained complete victory over em'. He did not stop to gaze at the scenery for long. As November arrived, so too did strong north-easterly winds 'with cold and heavy Rain or Sleet' all day long.

'By that time there was scarce life in either me or my poar horse.' He spotted a faint glow of a fire in the distance and he stumbled to the cabin. 'Unluckily the master was gone out,' he said, 'but the poar old Squaw dried my Cloathes as well as she could, and wrapped me up in a blanket and a Bear Skin.' The next morning her husband, an Englishman named Mr Downy, returned, and stewed some fowls 'which made me a Glorious Repast'.[2]

Soon he arrived at 'Cowes Town' (Cowee), on the Little Tennessee River near Iotla Creek. 'I remained a few days, and furnished myself with a Servant, Tools, Blankets and Bear Skins', and on the third day of November they set off on the last leg of the journey, up to 'Ayeree Mountain', deep in the Cherokee backcountry. 'Here we laboured hard for three Days in clearing away Rubbish out of the old Pitt which could not be less than twelve or fifteen ton.' Once the pit was cleared, Griffiths picked up a spade of clay and examined it. The Cherokee clay, or 'kaolin' from the Chinese for Kau-ling ('high ridge'), was pure white and powdery – the kind of clay necessary to make real porcelain. To Griffiths this was the equivalent of finding a gold mine.

As he was admiring his find, the Chiefs of the Ayeree Mountain appeared and took him prisoner, 'telling me I was a trespasser in these lands', and that they had received private instructions not to consent to any of their clay to be dug unless they received 500 pounds of leather for every ton of earth. He sent for a linguist and argued that there was a misunderstanding with the gentlemen at Fort George, 'and after a strong talk which lasted for four hours', they settled matters and Griffiths was able to continue his work. To help with negotiations, 'I invited em together & treated em with Rum and such Music as I was capable of, which made em dance with great agility; especially when the Bottle had gone about well; which is the only way to make friendship with any Indians, provided they are not made Drunk.'

By the time Griffiths was allowed to return to work, four days later, the weather had turned, and heavy rains fell throughout the night, creating a torrent that flowed down the mountain with such force that not only did it fill his pit, 'but melted, stained and spoil'd all I had dug'; adjacent red strata bled into the pure white clay, and a mud slide had destroyed his wigwam, 'so that we were nearly perished with wet and cold'.

It took Griffiths at least another month, until 18 December, to re-dig and dry the clay he intended to take back to England, working frantically to finish before the ground froze. After taking the opportunity to 'hunt, fossil & Botanize', he loaded up his packhorses and began the return journey. He had only been travelling a few days when his own horse stumbled on a narrow, slippery path and rolled over. Griffiths was thrown to the ground and 'the boar Beast tumbled into a Creek & was spoiled'. 'This was an unlucky circumstance as I had then several hundred Miles to Travil, besides the loss of a fine young Cherokee horse.'

Reaching Fort George on 27 December, when 'I could gladly have kissed the soldiers for joy', he loaded five wagons with five tons of clay and set off for the last leg of his journey. On 4 February, 'I arrived once more at dear and long-wished for Charles Town', making it back to Burslem by the end of April, when he delivered the five tons of white clay to Josiah, along with an account of his journey and a three-page list of expenses totalling £615, 19 shillings and threepence.

TWENTY-FOUR

Poison & Porcelain

WHEN THE CHEROKEE CLAY first arrived in Burslem in spring 1768, Josiah had many other things on his mind, not least the imminent operation on his leg. His immediate reaction was to be horrified at the cost of the clay – which at the time he could not afford – but it was not long before he realised the immense sacrifice and peril of Griffiths's journey.

The white clay from America brought with it a fascinating history which, in Josiah's eyes, would be part of every piece of pottery manufactured with it. It was as if the Indian spirits were embodied in the earth, captured in the mound of covered clay now stored in the covered courtyard of his factory. Not unlike the way he had just 'revived' the ancient arts and recreated an Etruscan legacy, he wanted to use the exoticism of the Cherokee nation to highlight the uniqueness of his wares. But he also knew that the clay was valuable in other ways. Kaolin was the key ingredient in the production of porcelain.

Porcelain was a thousand-year-old Chinese invention that remained a mystery to Westerners until 1708 when the recipe for it was discovered by the alchemist Johann Böttger, leading to the establishment of the Royal Saxon Porcelain factory at Meissen. The production of this 'white gold' was one of the most closely guarded secrets in Europe. The reward for discovering the formula was the privileged ability to charge patrons exorbitant prices for such prestigious items. That is, if the manufacturer could be consistent.

The first manufacturer of hard-paste porcelain in Britain was William Cookworthy, a Quaker apothecary and chemist from Plymouth, Devon. In 1745 he was visited by Andrew Duché, a Huguenot colonist from Virginia, who brought samples of kaolin clay from the site at which Griffiths was later to dig. After studying the qualities of the clay, which Duché demonstrated could be turned into porcelain cups (today he is regarded as America's first porcelain manufacturer), Cookworthy discovered deposits of kaolin in Cornwall, at sites which would become famous in the history of pottery.[1]

Experimenting with the kaolin and gathering information about the manufacture of porcelain from other sources, Cookworthy eventually discovered the secret of producing hard-paste porcelain (by mixing kaolin with china stone, or petuntse, as opposed to soft-paste porcelain which is mixed with grit, or 'frit', to give it its durability). In 1768 he obtained the first patent for its manufacture, which gave him a monopoly on the use of some of the Cornish clay for which he paid certain landowners for mining rights.

At the time, Josiah, and indeed other Staffordshire potters, were not interested in manufacturing hard-paste porcelain. They saw too many complications in the manufacturing process and knew that some porcelain manufacturers had gone bankrupt. However Cornish clay was of value to them since they could use it to enhance the cream-colour of earthenware.[2]

Although Josiah had been advised that Parliament would not allow him his own monopoly on the American kaolin, and that the cost of importing it was in any case prohibitive, Josiah had still forged ahead and managed to acquire five tons of Cherokee clay. Now he turned his attention to producing a rival to the hard-paste porcelain that was being manufactured in Plymouth. The time was ripe. 'I apprehend our customers will not much longer be content with Queens ware,' he wrote in 1774, 'it now being render'd vulgar & common everywhere.'[3]

Josiah knew he needed to maintain the product image that he had worked so hard to establish. His primary customers were the rich who were prepared to pay exorbitant prices for exclusive items, which allowed for high initial production costs. By the time Wedgwood & Bentley developed the techniques, materials, moulds, and skills required to halve production costs, the craze for the products had usually died down amongst the rich, leaving the option to mass-produce and sell at a cheaper price. There was, after all, another market developing, which Josiah famously commented on in 1772, by which time his ornamental vases adorned most aristocrats' homes.

> The Great People have had their Vases in their Palaces long enough for them to be seen & admir'd by the *Middling Class* of People, which Class we know are vastly, I had almost said infinitely, superior in number, to the Great, & though a *great price* was I believe, at first necessary to make the Vases esteemed *Ornaments for Palaces* that reason no longer exists. Their character is established & the middling People would probably buy quantities of them at a reduced price.[4]

Josiah, now part of the 'middling class' himself (albeit in the upper division of it), recognised that this was a professional class which would respect the level of improvement in education and living conditions that they were generating. But as a class of aspirational consumers, wanting to emulate 'the Great', Josiah considered them no better than the 'seconds' and 'thirds' of his pottery. They simply did not have the spending power to be deemed 'legislators in taste', as Josiah called his preferred customers.

'Few Ladies, you know, dare venture at anything out of the common stile till authoriz'd by their betters – by the Ladies of superior spirit who set the ton,' Josiah told Bentley.[5] Such was the trend for emulation that the *British Magazine* had complained that the 'present vogue for imitating the manners of high life hath spread itself so far among the gentle folks of lower life that in a few years we shall probably have no common people at all'.[6] Josiah doubted that the 'high' and 'low' would ever amount to the same class, knowing that the *ton* – the fashionable society in London – could buy their exclusiveness while the middling sorts could not. He would exploit their 'superior number', but they were never his primary market.[7]

Josiah was especially adamant about this when he found that Mr Ward, his Bath showroom manager, had been placing adverts in the local press and delivering hand bills at the Pump Room, as most other shopkeepers did. This was 'a mode of advertising I never approv'd of', Josiah wrote crossly. 'We have hitherto appeared in a very different light to common shopkeepers, but this step, in my opinion, will sink us exceedingly.'[8]

But his worries about 'sinking' in the estimations of the elite were suddenly eclipsed in 1773 by a new concern: the public were about to be told that eating off Wedgwood's Queen's Ware might be hazardous to their health.

Physicians had long known about the dangers to health of working with lead. In 1745 an English translation of the 'father of occupational health', Bernardino Ramazini's *Diseases of Tradesmen*, placed potters alongside lead miners as workers most at risk. By then, the process of liquid lead glazing on earthenware was commonplace, making the wares waterproof and adding decorative colour by using a wide range of metallic pigments. One of the most innovative glaziers in Staffordshire was Thomas Whieldon, which was an important reason why Josiah, who spent most of his early career experimenting with new kinds of glazes, joined him in partnership.

The cream-coloured earthenware that Josiah developed during his time at Whieldon's, and which had given Josiah his early fame, required a transparent lead glaze. It presented a glossy, clean-looking surface, but preparing the glaze was hazardous. The lead first needed to be ground into a dust, which would then be melted and daubed onto a piece of pottery (in a biscuit – or once fired – state); the pot would then be sent to the kiln for its second firing. During this process, as Ramazini wrote, potters 'receive, by the Mouth and Nostrils, and all the Pores of the Body, all the virulent Parts of the Lead thus melted in water and dissolved, and are by that means frenzied with heavy Disorders'.[9] The symptoms were widely commented on. 'First of all their hands begin to shake and tremble, soon after they become paralytic, lethargic, splenetic, cachectic, and toothless; and, in time, we scarcely see a Potter that has not a leaden cadaverous complexion.'[10]

Lead, it was clear, had 'pernicious principles' for which there was no cure (though 'mercurial purges' were recommended) but commercially it remained a vital material to work with. Besides all of the other uses for lead, as a glaze in pottery it allowed people to eat and drink from the wares. 'What a great change would the world be put to,' observed Ramazini, if everyone was forced to rely on 'pewter and copper vessels'.

But in the 1760s, other physicians were wondering if the dangers of lead poisoning were limited to those involved in its manufacturing process. In 1767 the physician George Baker studied an endemic outbreak of 'Devonshire Colic', when some 300 people from the Exeter area were taken to hospital with complaints that, as Benjamin Franklin observed (whom Baker consulted), resembled symptoms shown by painters who suffered lead poisoning. He also noted that the outbreak – which had been seen in previous years – coincided with the apple harvest. With these clues, Baker examined Devonshire cider and found traces of lead. He also examined the cider presses and found that, unlike cider presses in other regions, their cisterns were made of lead, which, he claimed, contaminated the apple juice and affected those who drank the cider.

Even though some doctors rubbished his claim – rejecting the idea that a chemical reaction between the fruit's acid and the lead could cause contamination – and even though he faced outright hostility from the cider makers, Baker persisted with his claims, and published an article that linked the occurrence of 'dry stomach-ach' to lead poisoning. When he discovered that there was a colic outbreak in Spain, which some thought was caused by a bad batch of grapes from Madrid wine, Baker offered his own theory. 'May it not reasonably be imagined,' he wrote, 'that some part of this endemic evil may be owing to glazed earthen vessels, which are generally used at Madrid, for almost all culinary purposes?'[11] This was the first time that someone had suggested that the common lead-glazed pottery, used everywhere, not just Madrid, might cause those who ate or drank from it to fall ill, and possibly worse.

Baker went on to elaborate on his theory by comparing modern pottery to ancient pottery, working under the (false) premise that, unlike modern potters, the ancients did not suffer from colic. 'That part of the old earthenware, preserved in the British Museum, sup-posed to be of Roman manufacture, is not glazed,' he wrote. 'Those vessels, which are called Etruscan, and are supposed to be of greater antiquity than the Roman, have indeed a paint or polish on their surfaces, but that does not appear to resemble our modern saturnine vitrification.' By this stage Josiah had not yet produced his imitation Etruscan vases, or presented to the world his patented 'encaustic painting', which was different (more in the ancient style) from the common, shiny, lead glaze. Baker was convinced that the so-called 'modern improvements' generated by the 'age of chemistry' were in fact responsible for spreading disease amongst consumers. His conclusion was that because 'the ancients were ignorant of this art, it seems probable that their ignorance, in this instance, contributed its part toward securing them from the colic'.[12]

This argument, which Baker presented to the Royal College of Physicians in 1767, prompted other physicians to follow up on his claims with their own investigations. One of them was Thomas Percival, a leading Manchester physician, whom Josiah had met once while at the Buxton mineral baths in 1773. Part of Percival's research was analysing the mineral content of the waters at Buxton, because of the debate over the risks of consuming mineral water. When he met Josiah and learned they had mutual friends, including Joseph Priestley, Percival courteously gave Josiah his manuscript titled 'Observations and Experiments on the poison of Lead', drawing Josiah's attention to the section on lead-glazed pottery.

Josiah had not been aware of the debate up until this point, and on reading the relevant passage he became instantly upset. Percival seemed to have put Josiah himself under the microscope. 'The very beautiful polish of the Burslem pottery, commonly called the Queen's Ware, inclined me to suspect that lead, which is easily vitrified with sand and kali, enters into the composition of glazing,' wrote Percival. To determine whether his conjecture was true, Percival experimented on some of the pottery, discovering 'that lead is an ingredient in the glazing of the Queen's Ware', though in a small proportion, which Percival believed was harmless, but he warned against preserving 'acid fruits and pickles' in it, which could have the same effect as the Devonshire cider outbreak.

Percival asked Josiah if what he had determined was correct, '& I told him it was,' he answered, '& that Lead is likewise an ingredient in Flint & almost every other kind of Glass, at which he express'd his surprise, & I suppose will be trying his experiments upon Glasses before he publishes'. Josiah sent a copy of the paper to Bentley with the hope that he could find a way to 'mend' Percival's account by rewriting it to remove the association between themselves and lead poisoning, 'for though the Doctor is convinced that he may eat his pudding with perfect safety off our Manufacture, yet when whimsical & ignorant people read account of *Lead & Poison & Queen's Ware* in the same paragraph they may associate the ideas together as we do of Darkness & spirits, & never after see one of our plates without the idea of being poison'd by it'.[13]

Bentley immediately saw this as the crucial issue. He needed to know exactly what Josiah had said to Percival, since he worried that Josiah might have piqued a debate with the doctor about his results. 'I did not dispute Dr Percival's conclusion,' Josiah explained.

I only urged that Lead was an ingredient in all Glasses & Glazes for culinary uses, & that from examining a plate which had been in use for 5 or 6 years I was very certain a Person might eat every meal of his whole life off Queen's ware without a possibility almost of his taking in a grain of dissolv'd Lead from the Glaze if he lived to the Age of Methusalah.

Josiah's frustration was that, while Percival pointed out that he 'had taken care to express himself very cautiously' – in fact, he would later coin the phrase 'medical ethics' – the doctor seemed to have no sense of the commercial impact of his medical comment. Josiah hoped that Bentley would convince Percival 'that he was likely by publishing that paragraph to deprive some thousands of their daily bread & the nation of one of its capital Manufactures'. Which was the greater danger, asked Josiah, eating off of Queen's Ware or 'the fatal blow to the Manufacture' that such a suggestion might provide?[14]

Percival did not change his paragraph, but by the time his small book was published a year later, another physician, Dr Gouldson, who had less scruples than Percival and an apparent (and un-explained) vendetta against potters, published a pamphlet 'to shew how pernicious' lead-glazed earthenware was, which he circulated among the ladies and gentlemen at Buxton – that is, those people already concerned about their health. 'I believe,' Josiah remarked sarcastically to Bentley, 'we had better publish a pamphlet shewing the pernicious consequences of Lead in our Flint Glass, with some doubts whether it may be perfectly innocent in our Mirrors, Lustres &c &c', in order to jump on the bandwagon.[15]

Not that Josiah dismissed the problems lightly. He had always embraced every new invention or design that might work to save or improve potters' lives, applauding, for instance, Thomas Benson's solution to the problem of inhaling flint dust and his design of an engine to grind flint stones under water (patented in 1713). As Benson wrote, due to the high death rates among workers respon-sible for grinding flint, which was added to the clay to give the ware greater hardness, 'it is now very difficult to find persons who will engage in the business to the great detriment and obstruction of said trade'.[16] Even though flint grinding subsequently carried fewer risks, workshop labour remained difficult to find due to the prominence of other diseases, such as 'potter's rot', or silicosis. Josiah believed that new factories and machines could be built on principles informed by science and medicine, making them healthier places to work and generating a revolution not only in new products and consumer spending, but in the standards of living of the labouring classes. It was this utopian faith in the future of industry that was the drive behind Josiah's ambition to be the biggest and most respected entrepreneur in the world. He would, however, eventually consider the persistence of diseases amongst his workers one of the most disappointing failures of his career.

But at this time, 1773, following charges that his wares might cause those who ate off them to shake, become paralytic, and go toothless, Josiah decided the best strategy was to return to his laboratory. 'I will try in earnest,' he declared, 'to make a glaze without Lead, & if I succeed will certainly advertise it.'[17]

Managing the public image of the business – whether in terms of the safety of the products, their colour and craftsmanship, the design of the showroom, or mode of advertising – was always a central concern to Josiah. As the business became more successful, the number of threats to this image grew, and came now not only from doctors, but from unscrupulous traders. In 1774, for instance, he discovered that one of his former modellers, who had left his employ to go to work for Humphrey Palmer, was distributing seals and cameos fraudulently stamped 'Wedgwood & Bentley', and was therefore taking advantage of Josiah's innovative idea to 'brand' his own products. Dreading the expense and tribulations of a lawsuit, Josiah attempted 'to stop the Rascals career' through an announcement drawing attention to it, including 'a description of his Rogueship'.[18]

Josiah knew it was time to surprise the world with something new, something his competitors could not imitate. But not at any cost. Even if Josiah could get access to the Cornish kaolin, he would not do what Humphrey Palmer had done to him – flagrantly 'trespass' the patent and steal the idea. That would reduce him to the level of the 'sniveling copyists' he condemned. In 1766 Erasmus Darwin had written to Josiah with news that a French nobleman and 'Man of Science, who loves everything English', was seeking to sell 'the Secret of making the finest old China, as cheap as your Pots' for £2,000 (ensuring him that the materials were in England) but Josiah had not pursued it.[19] Again, years later, when the proprietors of the closing Bow manufactory approached Wedgwood in an attempt to sell their secrets of soft-paste porcelain (which they had patented in 1744), he responded unequivocally: 'I do not wish to purchase any English process, and much less the Bow, which I think one of the worst processes for china making.'[20] Rather, Josiah preferred to rely on his own chemical knowledge and embark on an experimental quest to invent something entirely new which would put his Cherokee clay to use. So as he was finishing Catherine's 'Frog Service' he was able to report to Bentley 'on some very promising experiments'.[21]

Discovering a new 'secret of nature' may happen in a flash, but the flash usually only occurs after an interminable period of non-eventful work. Tiring work, especially since the complaint in Josiah's eyes, which neither he nor his doctors could diagnose, was still causing him discomfort. He spent month after month systematically experimenting with new kinds and proportions of clay mixed with chemicals, and test firing the materials at different temperatures, using small, swatch-like samples. As always, he meticulously recorded each step in a secret code in his experiment books. Fatigued and under much stress, he lamented the inconsistent results he was getting and a sense of distress at not knowing where precisely he was going, or would end up. 'I am fairly enter'd into the field,' he wrote late one night, '& the farther I go, the wider the field extends before me'. In his usual way, Bentley responded with encouraging words, politely if pedantically reminding his partner that it was 'bad policy' to hurry things, but that was not what Josiah was worried about.[22]

He felt he was on the brink of discovery, but he faced constant problems with the unfamiliar materials he was using, and new problems were arising from being unable to ascertain the heat to which the experimental pieces had been exposed. 'Moorstone & Spaith fusible are the two articles I want,' he wrote, referring to china stone and spar (carbonate of barium),

> & several samples I have of the latter are so different in their properties that no dependence is to be had upon them. They have plagued me sadly of late. At one time the body is white & fine as it should be, the next we make perhaps, having used a different lump of the Spaith, is a Cinamon colour. One time it is melted into Glass, another time dry as a Tob:Pipe.[23]

One good result was not followed by another. 'I cannot work miracles in altering the properties of these subtle, & complicated (though native) materials,' he sighed, but he would not give up. 'If I had more *time*, more *hands*, & more *heads* I could do something'; but he had none of these things, and there were more pressing matters, family matters, to attend to which frustratingly were interrupting his concentration: 'A Man who is in the midst of a course of experiments *should not be at home* to anything, or any body else but that cannot be my case . . . I am almost crazy.'[24]

The difficulty was that Sally's only brother, John, had fallen gravely ill; Sally was pregnant again and unable to travel, and therefore it was left to Josiah to, among other errands, travel to his father-in-law Richard's home in Cheshire, where John lived, and call for Erasmus Darwin. The prognosis was not good. Josiah was there for two weeks, comforting his 'Aged & affectionate father' who could do nothing but watch his only son, bedbound, emaciated 'and in the last stage of a worn out constitution', quietly pass away.[25] Josiah worried about leaving his father-in-law alone in the house, where 'the place, & the scenes every hour bringing to his remembrance the loss he has sustain'd' – first his wife, then his son – and Josiah persuaded him to return with him to Etruria.[26]

Meanwhile, 'my dear Girl', Sally, 'bears this afflicting stroke of providence with that fortitude & strength of mind, which, from other instances, I have reason to say she seems indued [imbued] with the power of exerting upon every proper & trying occasion.' It was a good thing, for the next week, at half past four in the morning, 'she gave me a gentle notice to quit her Bed & call the Midwife' ('as usual', he said, it was 'very short notice of the approaching critical moment'). Fifteen minutes later 'news was brought me that I had another Daughter, & all was well'. They named her Catherine, and Josiah ordered 'two Barrels of Good Porter & a Barrel of Oysters' to honour the occasion.[27]

After the oysters it was back to the laboratory, where a frustrated Josiah was determined to make the different materials for his new ware bond successfully. Were he to accomplish this, it would be 'a metamorphosis we should endeavour to throw an impenetrable veil' over.[28] It was difficult for Bentley to understand exactly what Josiah was up to. Partly through concern for the protection of trade secrets, partly through paranoia, Josiah purposely kept Bentley in the dark about his research, fearing their correspondence would be intercepted. When Bentley requested particulars of what Josiah was doing, he was answered in code, with the information scattered in different letters, since, as Josiah said, 'it is too precious to reveal all at once'.[29] In these letters he frequently offered propitious hints and clandestine commands to discontinue some practices in London, such as enamelling certain pieces, because his new secret formula embraced that part of business. The problem was his new formula was still not yielding consistent results, and nothing could be made public before standardisation was achieved; 'uniform success', as Josiah called it.

On 18 December 1774 Bentley was given his first glimpse of the fruits of his partner's labours: '4 black & Blue onyx Intaglios'. Josiah had also made some medallions, seals and cameos – smooth pieces of pottery with an image carved (as in signet rings) or in relief (such as the cameos). What made these pieces particularly special was the preparation of the clay. It was hard and durable, but it possessed a translucent quality, like porcelain, and unlike all other pottery, it had not been painted or enamelled. Rather, the clay itself had been dyed blue or black with a metal oxide before firing, so that each piece was composed of clay stained all the way through with a particular colour. Josiah had just introduced a new coloured body, 'my porcelain', which in November 1775 he would name 'jasper'.[30]

On New Year's Day, 1775, he gleefully reported to Bentley that he was able to produce this ware in a number of colours in good quality. 'The blue body I am likewise *absolute* in of almost any shade, & have likewise a beautiful Sea Green and several other colours' for cameos depicting 'the heads of Eminent Men, Greeks, Romans & Moderns', themes of 'War – Hunting – Music – & the Arts & Sciences', or they could be catered for certain occasions or country's tastes. The market in Mexico was particularly religious, he had been told, so he wanted to produce pictures of 'Crucifixes, Saints, &c' for bracelets, lockets and so on.[31]

There was still some work to be done, but Josiah was now progressing in leaps and bounds. He ordered fifty tons of white clay from Bruges with which he hoped to confirm that he could successfully replicate the process with consistency, 'so you see a spirit is up amongst us which must have consequences, & I hope they will be desirable ones'.[32] Josiah's spirits in his newest endeavour were further raised when a visiting Austrian nobleman told him that 'the Manufactures of Dresden & Berlin Porcelain both of which he had visited were not, he said, to be compar'd with ours for taste, Elegance of designs, & fine modeling'.[33] Josiah then boldly declared that he was 'going upon a large scale' in preparation for the coming winter's show, where they would 'ASTONISH THE WORLD ALL AT ONCE, for I hate piddling you know'.

Josiah was feeling confident and proud with his jasperware, which 'nobody', he relished in saying, 'but W & B can make'. One potter claimed that he had discovered the secret, but, Josiah calmly said, 'I would as soon believe he had discover'd the Philosophers Stone'.[34] So confident was Josiah in his 'victory', that he was happy once again to explore collaboration with his friendly rival, Matthew Boulton, who, he noted, was 'very civil to me'.[35] The cameos he was producing were 'suitable for setting in boxes, Lockets, bracelets, &c &c' and Boulton, whose metalworks were well suited for this, told Josiah that he 'thinks he may have many opportunities for disposing of some this year', and wanted to discuss a strategy. Later they came to an agreement.[36]

It would take Josiah slightly longer to introduce his new ware than he anticipated, for he spent the winter on 'the completion of the Art of *Jasper making*', but his work, he felt, had paid off.[37] 'I believe I can assure you of a conquest,' he wrote, '& a very important one to us.'

While, in the long course of his experiments, Josiah used an array of different materials to obtain the special qualities that made 'my porcelain' unique from anything else available, he was sure to include one ingredient that made it even more distinct. 'I have often thought,' he wrote to Bentley,

> that it may not be a bad idea to give out, that our jaspers are made of the Cherokee clay which I sent an agent into that country on purpose to procure for me, & when the present parcel is out we have no hopes of obtaining more, and it was with the utmost difficulty the natives were prevail'd upon to part with what we now have, though recommended to them

by their *father Stewart* [James Stuart], Intendant of Indian Affairs. But then his Majesty should see some of these large fine tablets, & be told this story (which is a true one for I am not joking) . . . This idea will give limits, a boundary to the quantity which your customers will be ready to conceive may be made of these fine bass reliefs, which otherwise would be gems indeed. They want nothing but *age* & *scarcity* to make them worth any price you could ask for them.

Although his jasper was mainly made from the fifty tons of clay he had ordered from Bruges, and could in fact be made from English kaolin, for added authenticity Josiah made explicit that there was a real link between his wares and the Cherokee story. 'A Portion of Cherokee clay is *really used* in all the jaspers so make what use you please of the fact.'[38]

'A Portion.' Bentley was sceptical, not only since the portion would have been so small as to be irrelevant with the quantities he produced, but in Josiah's own formula for jasper, the number 23, the secret code for Cherokee clay, was notably absent.[39] Bentley, always confident that Josiah's jasper was comfortably in a class of its own without the tall tale, chose to keep 'the story' quiet.

TWENTY-FIVE

Mad Ministers

'I AM NO POLITITIAN,' Josiah declared in January 1775, but: 'All the world are with the Ministers & against the poor Americans. They are all gone mad, & have given them up for incurables.'[1] His outburst had been provoked by the government's preparations to bring in its 'New England Restraining Act', which would effectively restrict colonial trade and commerce to Great Britain, Ireland and the British West Indies. This was Parliament's response to the declaration of the Continental Congress the previous October, wherein colonial delegates attacked what they called 'cruel and oppressive acts' by a 'wicked ministry' in Britain which was discouraging the settlement of British subjects in North America. The Congress angrily declared that 'we will not import, into British America, from Great-Britain or Ireland, any goods, wares, or merchandise whatsoever', initiating a 'non-consumption agreement' that agitated diplomatic and commercial relations to an unprecedented degree.[2]

For decades Britain had ruled over a bountiful 'empire of goods'. Trade with the Colonies, the original thirteen states of the United States, had grown in proportion to the number of settlers in America – a population, as Benjamin Franklin explained in the wake of the Seven Years War, with a strong affection for the mother country, and 'a fondness for its fashions'.[3] Around one-third of British manufacturers' customers lived in the American Colonies and 'around half of all English exports of copperware, ironware, glassware, earthenware, silk goods, printed cotton and linen goods, and flannels were shipped to colonial [that is, American] consumers'.[4]

For over ten years, since the successful campaign to have the Stamp Act repealed, British manufacturers had been forced to the edge of their seats watching and hoping that their government would not try to introduce any further mechanisms to close down trade with the Colonies. Benjamin Franklin, arguing against the Stamp Act in 1766, outlined the potential fragility of this trade. Colonists, he explained, purchased three kinds of product: 'necessaries, mere conveniences, or superfluities'. The first, 'as cloth, &c with little industry they can make at home; the second they can do without . . . the last, which are much the greatest part, they will strike off immediately'.[5] British goods were ultimately expendable: Americans, if they had to, and if they felt less sentimentally inclined to the mother country, could and would do without them.

By 1776, Pitt the Elder (now Lord Chatham) emerged from retirement to rebuke the British government's rash actions towards the American colonies. 'To impose servitude to establish despotism over such a mighty continental nation must be in vain, must be fatal,' he said.[6] Along with the Americans, Josiah once again cheered his hero, but it looked as if Pitt's admonishment might be futile.

'I have got a whirl in my head', Josiah wrote to Bentley, as he travelled around on business, exposed to all the debates on the 'American problem'. In Manchester, he heard one outspoken gentleman who 'froth'd at the mouth' being 'exceeding hot & violent against the Americans'. His aim was to put an end to the distribution of petitions against the use of coercive acts in America – petitions largely supported by Dissenters who saw the government's aggression as another unjust extension of its corrupt powers. The man, who 'was so excessively rapid in his declamations, and exclamations' shouted that he would move 'Heaven & Earth either to prevent their petitioning, or to prevail upon them to *counter petition*, in which last', Josiah sadly reported, 'I believe he was successful.'[7]

Josiah learned that the speaker, whom American sympathisers

naturally assumed was an 'agent' of the British government, was energetically travelling from town to town, preaching about the wrongs of Americans taking arms against the King, and aggressively spreading his counter petition to drum up support for the British government. Josiah was alarmed to find 'that his labour has not been in vain'. 'His harangues, & even those simple queries have had a very considerable effect amongst many, Dissenters & others,' Josiah wrote. 'I do not know how it happens, but a general infatuation seems to have gone forth & the poor Americans are deemed Rebels.'

George III's Proclamation of Rebellion came a few months later, on 23 August, by which time preachers and spokespeople for and against the conflict had travelled widely, debating, petitioning, and publishing. Samuel Johnson wrote a pamphlet arguing that taxation was not tyranny, and, embracing the point, John Wesley issued a 'Calm address to the colonies' – half a dozen copies of which arrived at Josiah's home, 'to my astonishment', he wrote, from the 'House of a Noble Lord in our Neighbourhood' who strangely thought that he might sympathise with the minister's arguments supporting the extension of the government's powers over America. 'Wesley is not a bad *Cats Paw*,' Josiah quipped, but 'they seem determin'd to lay hold of him & use him to their best advantage'.[8]

Tired of what he saw as biased newspaper reports and the neglect of the 'friends of America' to publish prompt replies to the propaganda, Josiah asked Bentley to 'send me half a dozen of the answers & another book or two which you mention'd to me as the best things publish'd upon the American controversy'. One of the publications Bentley sent a few months later was *Observations on the Nature of Civil Liberty*, published by the Dissenting minister Richard Price, which Josiah devoured, calling it a 'most excellent pamphlet'. He agreed with Price's moral principles, which posited that 'liberty' was a natural and unalienable right to every member of society, and that the principle of liberty included self-direction and self-government. 'If the laws are made by one man, or a junto of men in a state, and not by common consent, a government by them does not differ from slavery,' Price wrote, going on to develop what became an immensely popular argument justifying the American Revolution/ War of Independence based on liberal principles of civic consensus and representation. He proclaimed that he saw the events in America as 'a revolution which opens a new prospect in human affairs, and begins a new era in the history of mankind'.

'Those,' Josiah announced, 'who are neither converted, nor frightened into a better way of thinking by reading this excellent and alarming Book may be given up for harden'd Sinners, beyond the reach of conviction.'[9] Josiah then delved into more literature on the concept of liberty and inalienable rights, re-reading John Locke and carefully reading Thomas Paine's *Common Sense*, a new publication which forcefully argued for America's complete separation from Britain. This was just the beginning. Over the next year, 1776, Adam Smith's *Wealth of Nations* would be published, which elaborated on Josiah's favourite theme of 'self-improvement' by linking it to the growth of commercial society, where (as Smith said) everyone 'becomes in some measure a merchant'. Also published was Edward Gibbon's *Decline and Fall of the Roman Empire*, which warned against the dangers of idle rulers overindulging in luxury and vice. Josiah and Bentley, with all their friends (and, no doubt, Sally, though she and much of the family were suffering from another 'tyrannical' fever), excitedly discussed the new commercial and moral order taking shape around them. It was probably the most intensive political discussion that Josiah and Bentley had engaged in since their correspondence and friendship began, and since Bentley had suggested his friend read Voltaire, Rousseau and the French *philosophes*, over a decade earlier.

This time, however, the philosophy of government and individual rights was not simply a subject raised for Josiah's own edification. The 'rebellion' had commercial implications that would certainly affect their business. But soon Josiah found himself placed in an awkward situation. As a well-known and respected manufacturer with a record of representing local interests, Josiah was asked to put forward arguments in favour of the government's position. He was approached by Lord Gower to solicit public opinion in the area about forming a militia to fight the revolutionaries. Josiah was exasperated. He had shown, and would continue to show, his gratitude to his valuable patron 'where I can do it without a sacrifice to principle', as he wrote to Bentley, 'which I hold too dear to part with at any price'. But why, he wondered, had he been approached in preference to the Gilberts, the Beards, the Sparrows – Lord Gower's own agents, lawyers, and associates, 'whose devotion is unquestionable'. But Josiah knew it was a moot point. 'I will not scrutinise into the motives that actuate the great ones of the Earth ... I will do what better befits me – Obey – & give the best information I am able.'[10]

He mulled over the question Lord Gower had posed to him. 'How will the people stand with respect to raising the Militia?' 'The *common People* I suppose,' Josiah said, 'Tradesmen, &c.' It was an 'evil' idea, he immediately concluded, and he doubted there would be much goodwill in Staffordshire since the last militia that was raised, during the Seven Years War, was told it would not be sent abroad, but, he recalled, 'this promise was basely broken, & the poor Fellows were sent to Gibraltar'. After spending a few days 'collecting intelligence', Josiah wrote to Lieutenant-Colonel Sir John Wrottesley, of Stafford, who was preparing to sail to America with the 1st Regiment of Foot Guards (later the Grenadier Guards). While the idea of raising a militia to fight in America, especially when many of the men would be his own employees, was against Josiah's principles, he found a way of stating his views diplomatically, stressing the economics of it, for Josiah knew that ministers were convinced that Britain's ability to win wars was largely attributable to its thriving economy: 'There is no doubt,' Josiah said,

> but every Parish would willingly be excused from the expense
> which raising the Militia will certainly bring upon it; and the

Manufacturing Parts, whose rates are already very high, will be the more sensible of any addition to them, especially, if at the same time they feel this new burden, their trade should be upon the decline.

That said, he recognised that he needed to tell the 'great ones' what they wanted to hear, and not to come across as unpatriotic himself. However admired he was as a potter and businessman, he knew that in situations such as this attention would focus on his being a Dissenter who probably had suspect connections to radical philosophers and revolutionary sympathisers. Knowing that the 'great ones' would carefully listen to what he had to say, Josiah added that if it became necessary 'to defend ourselves', he believed the local people 'will very readily acquiesce in it when call'd upon to perform that duty'.[11]

The economic point, though, was the crucial one. Josiah was not speculating that manufacturers *might* feel their trade 'upon the decline', they were *already* feeling it. The effect of the Seven Years War on commerce had been dramatic. In 1770, customs and excise officers recorded over 1.2 million pieces of glass and earthenware shipped to America. In 1775, under 139,000 pieces were sent.[12] Congress had authorised privateer raids on British ships, and, three months before the Declaration of Independence was signed, American ports were officially closed to British trading ships. Manufacturers worried that this was the end of a major artery of trade, but they were not all in agreement on the principles at stake. Boulton – who, in 1772, was in serious financial trouble following a credit scandal and only saved himself from bankruptcy by borrowing money – despised the American embargo on the grounds that it posed a threat to his business. But other entrepreneurs and manufacturers, particularly in Josiah's circle of Dissenting friends, including of course Bentley, Erasmus Darwin and Joseph Priestley, supported the 'poor Americans' in their cause, hoping to see liberty triumph over tyranny (Boulton, we should remember, was an Anglican). As they saw it, the American cause was only a problem to trade because the 'mad ministers' created insufferable conditions by trying unfairly to extend their rule. It was not dissimilar in principle to the grievances Dissenters had expressed for decades. Whatever the commercial considerations, Josiah was clear in his opinion of the 'absurdity, folly & wickedness of our whole proceedings with America'.[13]

One unexpected consequence of the war with America was Tom Byerley's return to Burslem. When he left for America in 1768, Josiah showed some frustration with his nephew's peregrinations – at fifteen wanting to be an author in London, at nineteen giving up as an actor in Dublin, then at twenty venturing off to explore America and ending up in a jail.

The year after Tom's release from prison, Josiah was relieved to learn that his nephew had settled on becoming a school teacher in America. Josiah implored him this time to use some 'good sense' to satisfy 'the Gentlemen who repose so much confidence in you as to place their Children under your care'. To help him along his more enlightened path, Josiah sent him two globes and a packet of books for his instruction, assuring him 'that I shall at all times receive a particular pleasure in doing everything in my power that may contribute to your real welfare & happiness'.[14] But in the gathering storm of 1775, when it looked as if he might need to take arms against his countrymen, Byerley decided it was time to return to England, to the great relief of his mother, Margaret. 'She had much rather he should run away,' wrote Josiah, 'than stay to fight in so disagreeable a service as he must have been engaged in.'[15] Upon his return to Staffordshire, Tom resumed his occasional position as general clerk.

Josiah was thankful to have Byerley back at work. With all the pressures of the war, and the demands of inventing new materials and designs (not helped by 'the Workmens *unhandiness* & *want of Ideas*'), it was a relief to have someone within the family who, until wanderlust struck again, could manage much of the paperwork. One of the first things Josiah asked Tom to do was act as the 'Clerk to the Committee of Potters' which had been set up to represent local concerns regarding the Prime Minister's enquiry as to whether lowering the duty on imported European earthenware – with the expectation of reciprocity in British exports to Europe – would help or hinder their trade.

Josiah was of the immediate opinion that abandoning *all* duties, which had long been the subject of his complaints, would allow free trade and encourage open competition. 'I should be asham'd to feel anything like a fear in having a free intercourse open'd between Great Britain & all the Potteries in the World,' Josiah confidently declared, 'we enjoying the like liberty of exporting our Manufactures to other States.' When preparing Byerley with the arsenal with which to convince 'our Fraternity' of potters to agree, Josiah had a second thought about lowering the duties of the 'Asiatic Porcelains', 'as we can have no motive or expectation of receiving any reciprocal advantages'. In essence, cheaper Asian porcelain would, Josiah feared, kill the home market for English porcelain and, more importantly, his own new jasper.[16]

Inspired by the prospect of uninhibited trade with Europe, if the Prime Minister, Lord North, could get reciprocal agreements with foreign governments, Josiah swiftly began jotting down ideas about what kinds of goods he could send into foreign markets. Bentley thought about inlaying snuff boxes with pictures of 'Kings and Queens', an ironic thought that did not escape Josiah's attention. They 'will be very good things *for England*', Josiah remarked, and elaborated on his friend's suggestion:

> We can make other Kings & Queens, & eminent Heads for other Countries & such subjects will be the most likely to go in quantities, for People will give more for their own Heads, or the Heads in fashion, than for any other subjects & buy abundantly more of them. Henry the 4th, & some others for France for instance & the proper Heads for the different European Markets.[17]

Josiah mentioned France because Bentley had just told him of his plans to go there, to see Paris, and Josiah immediately saw that his learned partner might do a great deal of useful research there.

TWENTY-SIX

The Philosophes *& Plaster Shops of* Paris

THREE WEEKS AFTER the American Declaration of Independence was signed, Bentley and 'my good governess', his wife Mary, arrived in Paris. They were there at the invitation of Elizabeth Montagu, one of the *ton*, and a regular customer at Wedgwood & Bentley's showrooms, who was on her first trip to Paris.

When the Bentleys arrived, they found that Lady Elizabeth had been showing her collection of Wedgwood & Bentley cameos and intaglios to no less than 'the Duke or Count of Rochefoucault, to the Popes Nuncio, & many other great personages, who', she reported, 'were highly delighted with them'. She enjoyed having Bentley on hand as an added attraction to the unique jasperware. 'She is pleased to say she is proud of shewing them,' Bentley told Josiah, '& always observes they are made by her particular Friend.'[1]

Bentley's trip was 'professedly a journey of expense and amusement' – a sort of belated honeymoon.[2] Like many travellers, he kept a diary, which Josiah for one was eager to read. Also like many of his contemporaries, Bentley was critical of the differences between London and Paris. Everything, he claimed, was 'black and dirty. The streets are narrow, dirty, and badly paved, without any side walk for passengers.' In the mornings, he ate breakfast at the English coffee shop and then sat by the Pont Neuf bridge by the Louvre and read English newspapers; in the afternoon, he assessed the architecture. He was disparaging of French ornamental design:

> Many of the buildings are *grand*, but few of them *beautiful*. The famous Louvre is an incomprehensible jumble of magnificence and meanness – of grandeur and bad taste – and ruins. The Seine at Paris is but a poor dirty river. Their bridges are not worth speaking of. Their gardens are in the old Dutch taste; Kensington gardens are infinitely superior either to the Tuilleries or Versailles. The palace of Versailles merits the same character as the Louvre. Some parts of it, both within and without, are very magnificent, while others are only fit to excite disgust. The insides of their houses and palaces are almost all in the same style; as much glass and gilding as they can either afford or contrive to put into them; and nothing can be uglier and more tasteless than their chimney pieces, which are all alike, from Calais to Versailles.[3]

Elizabeth Montagu, while finding French women 'better informed than the English in general' – since informed conversation was not banished 'under the notion of pedantry' – felt much the same as Bentley about the physical environment. 'Tell me,' she asked Bentley, 'whether Paris had more the appearance of a city rising or falling into ruin?' Bentley thought the latter, which unsettled Josiah when he read Bentley's account, thinking the worse of the future market for his goods. 'Your remark that everything is either unfinished, or going into decay, might furnish much speculation,' said Josiah. 'It seems to indicate great unsteadiness in the nation, & sudden transitions amongst the Great, from Riches to Poverty – from Court Favour to disgrace and obscurity.'[4]

Bentley agreed. 'The causes,' he said, 'must be looked for in the character and state of the nation. The French have very magnificent ideals, and it is their delight to be laying magnificent plans. They begin works with a degree of vigour and expense that exhausts both their patience and their finances. They are too lively, too volatile when they have been interrupted to return heartily to the same object.'[5] Such thoughts were wrapped up in both men's concerns over the uncertainty of the future world order, which swayed like a ship in a storm between opposed political and moral principles.

Bentley recorded his thoughts while watching Pigalle finish his statue of Voltaire, depicted as a naked, frail old man. Though Bentley called it a 'fine statue', public opinion was already condemning it as an aesthetic failure. Was it symbolic of the failure of the eighty-two-year-old's Enlightenment philosophy? Was it symbolic of the failure to create a Panglossian world amounting to 'the best of all possible worlds'? Josiah and Bentley both hoped not. They wanted desperately to believe in their friend Benjamin Franklin's optimistic prediction about the possibilities of improving standards of living in the New World (embodied in Franklin's own rise to fame) and his belief that, owing to the wonders of science and medicine, all diseases, 'even that of mortality', will be eliminated. They wanted to believe that Voltaire's own inspired writings promoting tolerance and individual rights still provided the clarion call for positive reform. But ideals, they knew, did not transfer to reality. The uncertainty about how the revolutions they were following would unfold unsettled people like Bentley who placed so much faith in the theories of the great philosophers. A meeting with one of France's greatest philosophers and one of Bentley's heroes would help him regain some confidence in the future.

Bentley claimed that he was 'not made of the stuff' to trouble a person of status without being summoned – very unlike Josiah, who would break in on any conversation in any home to sell his wares or his ideas. But Bentley could not resist the urge while in Paris to climb to the fifth floor of a house in the rue Plâtrière, near the gardens of the Palais Royal, uninvited, leaving his card four times, in the hope of meeting one of his favourite authors, sixty-four-year-old Jean-Jacques Rousseau. On his fifth trip up the stairs on a rainy afternoon, my heart expanded with joy when Madame his spouse opened the door and desired us to walk in. I found this great philosopher writing or composing music in a small and very homely apartment, and his wife working by his side. He received us very civilly, but as soon as I observed to him that I had the pleasure of bringing some letters and books for him from Mr Day and Mr Williams which I had left a few days ago, I began to fear our conversation would not be very agreeable, not of long continuance . . .[6]

Bentley had earlier delivered to Rousseau's home two publications by friends from England: one was Thomas Day's 1773 anti-slavery poem, *The Dying Negro;* the other, David Williams's *Liturgy on the Universal Principles of Religion and Morality.* Both Day and Williams were part of the loose circle of friends linked to the teachers of the Warrington Academy and entrepreneurs like Josiah, Boulton and others, who occasionally participated in the meetings of the self-styled Lunar Society, the moonlit, monthly gatherings of like-minded men who privately discussed religion, politics, and science.[7] Both were also founding members, along with Benjamin Franklin and Bentley, of the Margaret Street Chapel, the first Unitarian chapel in London, set up as 'a society for a philosophical religion'.

Williams, a translator of Voltaire and later the founder of the Royal Literary Fund, penned the liturgy to define and defend their mission to promote public worship, 'a form of social worship in which all men may join who acknowledge the existence of a supreme intelligence and the universal obligations of morality'.[8] Bentley, who it is suspected co-wrote the liturgy with Williams, thought Rousseau would appreciate their intentions. 'Ah yes,' Rousseau responded, 'that is a truly noble and respectable undertaking.'

'And sir,' said Bentley, 'it is not an *idea* or *theory* only. Mr Williams has begun a Church and a course of lectures upon these principles.'

'Why do you confine God within the walls of a house?' asked

Rousseau. 'Would it not be better to worship him in the open air under the canopy of Heaven?'

'Not in England,' replied Bentley, 'it rains too often.'

Rousseau smiled, saying it was a 'very good answer'.[9]

Bentley had also thought that Rousseau would appreciate Day's poem, which was dedicated to Rousseau: a man who 'prefers exile, poverty, and obscurity, to all the riches and the honours which ambitious meanness extorts from Kings'. The poem cried out against the disgraceful actions of 'Christian merchants' who were 'annually reducing millions to a state of misery still more dreadful than death itself':[10]

> *ARM'D with thy sad last gift – the pow'r to die,*
> *Thy shafts, stern fortune, now I can defy;*
> *Thy dreadful mercy points at length the shore,*
> *Where all is peace, and men are slaves no more;*
> *— This weapon, ev'n in chains, the brave can wield,*
> *And vanquish'd, quit triumphantly the field:*
> *— Beneath such wrongs let pallid Christians live,*
> *Such they can perpetrate, and may forgive.*

However, Day also logically extended his argument to condemn the hypocrisy of the American revolutionaries who were ostensibly fighting on moral principles of inalienable human rights. 'Such is the inconsistency of mankind!' Day argued:

> These are the men whose clamours for liberty and independence are heard across the Atlantic Ocean! Murmurings and rebellions are the first fruits of their gratitude . . . Let the wild inconsistent claims of America prevail, when they shall be unmixed with the clank of chains and the groans of anguish . . . But let her remember that it is in Britain alone that laws are equally favourable to liberty and humanity.

This was the passage that upset Rousseau. It was, he said, an 'unjust reflection' upon the Americans, who 'had not the less right to defend their liberties because they were obscure or unknown'.

Bentley learned that Rousseau thought it was important at this time to support the American cause, now 'that these Americans were able to defend themselves', in spite of the existence of slavery in the Colony. The problem of slavery was a moral issue being confronted in the courts of law, Rousseau said, and he condemned Day for writing 'upon subjects that he did not understand'.

It was an awkward position for Bentley, who defended his friend's intentions while acknowledging that Day's heated poem was written when 'he was something younger than he is now'. But, to Bentley's great delight, he and the philosopher continued to converse for hours, discussing the meaning of virtue and goodness, and systems of education reminiscent of those Bentley had learned of when reading *Emile* years earlier, principles which friends of his actively adhered to when raising their own children. Listening to the author, the great philosopher, Bentley was tremendously impressed. Meeting Rousseau was not only the most important aspect of his trip, but arguably the most notable event in his learned life.

When their conversation came to an end, Bentley became absorbed by the friendliness of Rousseau's expression and earnestness of his manner. When Rousseau said to Bentley that he would be glad to meet again, Bentley suddenly 'felt very foolish'. 'Something was the matter with my eyes, that I could not very well see how I got through his little antechamber to the stairs, and I quite forgot to take leave of Madame Rousseau.'

Josiah, no doubt, shared Bentley's enthusiasm for his discussion with the renowned philosopher. When Josiah and Bentley first met, fourteen years earlier, Rousseau's *Emile* had just been published. Bentley had urged his new friend to read it, thereby introducing him to the world of French philosophy. For years they had debated the concepts and tenets articulated within, but now, weeks after the Americans asserted a new identity for themselves, the discussions seemed to bridge the gap between the ideal and the real, the philosophy of reform and the revolutionary fighting. But Bentley's trip was not over, for he had more practical concerns to address.

Like Josiah's incognito discussions with travellers to America when he thought about obtaining Cherokee clay, Bentley discreetly dipped in and out of shops, taking notes, buying specimens, and scouting for casts which could be used for their own decorations. 'Upon examination,' he wrote, after stepping into a 'plaster shop' one afternoon, 'I found the things much worse than I expected; the honest man told me they were very good, but I spoiled them with looking at them through my glass. There are but very few *fine* things anywhere.'[11] At a shop in Rue St-Jacques, he spotted imitation Queen's Ware which he learned was manufactured at Montereau, a few miles down the road toward Auxerre, but they were no match for Wedgwood & Bentley's authentic wares. 'The models and glaze in general are very indifferent, and the workmanship bad.' One place he had to visit before he left was Wedgwood & Bentley's foremost continental rival – the factory at Sèvres.

It was a few miles outside Paris, on the road to Versailles. Supported by the King, the few hundred employees worked in a 'very magnificent building'. 'The workshops are very commodious and well fitted up, and there are several fine apartments left for his Majesty when he chooses to visit the manufactory.' Bentley took notes on their *déjeuners*, teapots, dessert services, terrines, and other table services.

They have an *immense* number of ornamental vases, highly enriched with enamel and burnished gold; and amongst *several hundreds* there may be about *half a dozen* very elegant forms. All the rest are neither antique nor gothic, but barbarous beyond conception. I must particularly distinguish a *new kind of vases*, intended for some of the royal apartments at Versailles, of which I saw but one. This was in a pretty good form, but its style, if I may use that expression, was charming. White biscuit with bas-relief bays, ornamented and not overdone with burnished gold. These vases are from a few guineas to 50 guineas a piece.

His note-taking continued. He spied biscuit medallions and figures – one a bust of Voltaire which Pigalle used to model the face for his own statue – marbled vases and miscellaneous pieces of ornamental and useful wares. He noted the workers' practices – painting, glazing, and pressing their moulds. 'They turn their plates upon a horizontal wheel,' he noted, 'very different from any I have seen in England.'

Bentley then pocketed his pigskin notebook and courteously bought a few small pieces to take back with him to England. He felt he had learned all he could from the French, which, he added in a condescending tone, was not much. As he looked around, he realised that they had more to worry about in England from French visitors than vice versa. English fashions, he concluded, were a bit of a craze. 'It is striking and rather flattering to an Englishman to see how fond they are of making almost every thing à l'anglaise,' he wrote. Indeed, a number of manufactures advertised their wares as 'façon de Angleterre' or 'a la manière d'Angleterre'.[12] Perhaps Josiah was not as paranoid as he sometimes seemed when writing in secret codes and separating the content of his letters to Bentley.

Josiah reminded Bentley that among his amusements he should engage in 'some useful pursuit' whilst in France, and urged his partner to visit foreign ambassadors and take out an advertisement for their wares in the papers (he ended up placing an advert in the *Gazette de France*). 'I [will] willingly refer myself to your journals,' Josiah informed Bentley, '& our future conversations for the particulars of your Tour, as I would wish you to see, hear & memorand all you can, as well for pleasure, & entertainment, as utility.' When Bentley and Mary returned from Paris, in September 1776, the partners 'discuss'd over a Pipe' the particulars of this useful pursuit.

TWENTY-SEVEN

A Poor Regiment

Smoking a pipe was, as Josiah exclaimed, 'doubly sweet' when it meant face-to-face conversation with Bentley. Anticipating late-night talks about the French trip, Josiah ordered no less than a crate of wine to celebrate his friend's return – some, no doubt, to be shared with Mary, but Sally, forty-two-years old and eight months into another pregnancy, probably desisted. This was the sort of indulgence that Josiah and Bentley, both now forty-six, relished. Bentley, with his curly brown hair descending further down the back of his head, was rounder about the waist than ever and was suffering from a near crippling case of gout. Josiah remained leaner, though his jowls were fleshing out and his fingers had become thick and coarse. The two partners still corresponded as quickly as the post could deliver their letters between London and Etruria, but with the business growing, there was often much more to discuss than a couple of sides of parchment would allow.

Sally was due to give birth for the seventh time. With five children already tugging at his elbows, Josiah struggled to find time for reading and writing after the workers left the factory and after he had finished his explorations in the laboratory. He had already resorted to writing 'before our people are up', but, impressively, he still put in long hours in the pursuit of new ideas.[1] 'Nay, you need not make such a face of wonderment,' Josiah wrote to Bentley in Paris, who was just promised some *'quite new' bas-relief* designs (referring to the slightly raised figures appearing on jasperware). 'I have many ideas & visions crowd in upon me, not only quicker than I can execute them, but faster than I can find time to lay them to rest a while in my Common Place Book.'[2]

While Bentley had been away, in the midst of what Josiah called his frantic 'visions' of the future, it had looked as if all production might suddenly grind to a halt. When he finally had a chance to contact Bentley, Josiah was relieved to be able to share his account of the new problems. Bentley, as usual, provided 'a healing Balsam to my mind which is almost distracted & torn to pieces with the Men, & things about me here'.[3]

The cry 'ere comes Owd Woodenleg' would alert the other workers at Etruria to an imminent inspection of the wares, and it never failed to send a chill up their spines. Josiah would emerge from his office, cross a bridge specially installed to connect his office to the first of a line of workshops, and descend a staircase to the factory floor. Scrutinising works in progress, he would sensationally smash with his stick any object that fell short of his standards, declaring that 'This will not do for Josiah Wedgwood.' 'My name has made such a Scarecrow to them,' he told Bentley, 'that the poor fellows are frighten'd out of their wits.'[4]

He certainly believed in stern discipline – his workshops were run like a military regime. 'It is *hard*,' he once said, 'but then it is *glorious* to conquer so great an Empire with raw, undisciplin'd recruits. What merit must a General have who achieves such wonders under such disadvantageous circumstances.'[5] He was always looking for effective ways of instilling that much-desired discipline among his labourers. He posted 'rules of conduct' on factory doors banning alcohol, 'obseen writing' on the walls, and gambling, and he made a spectacle of himself as the Master who ruled with an iron hand, or at least a hard wooden cane. While his performance of smashing imperfect pieces powerfully increased his authoritarian stature – something that rather took Josiah aback, since normally his workers were as willing to give as well as take – its purpose was not primarily to frighten them. All potters smashed up their trial and imperfect pieces, usually by throwing them into shard piles, thereby preventing others from stealing them as free samples of new products. Josiah, probably impulsively, one day decided to break a piece down on the workshop floor, and found it turned heads.

Josiah's relationship with his workers went beyond supervising their craftsmanship. He took on apprentices for whom he often had the responsibility of housing, feeding and ensuring their wellbeing, which included taking a personal interest in their development from boys and girls into men and women. Journeymen were intended to develop an intimate role in the running of the business, which required examination of their moral conduct. The factory workers formed a close community. Many lived in 'Etruria Village', in the rows of neat houses that were now taking shape adjacent to the factory, where their children would grow up and where retired workers could live out the rest of their lives. Josiah's authority was underwritten by an industrial paternalism, where his role was to teach obedience, humility, sobriety, and proper conduct.[6]

Josiah would become most upset and frustrated when his workers broke the rules. In the early 1770s, Josiah became aware that one of his senior employees, Ben Mather, who had been hired as head clerk to oversee the London warehouses, was corrupting a younger employee, 'taking & Keeping him out the Evenings', indulging in 'Gallantries & evening rambles'. Josiah immediately thought it time to 'introduce new regulations', but worried that Mather might also be involved in embezzling funds. 'What avails all our industry & care,' asked an aggravated Josiah, 'if we must finally lodge all the fruits of it in the hands of unprincipled Boys & spendthrifts, who we see are debauching & ruining themselves, & perhaps half a score of their acquaintance at our expence.'[7] Josiah volunteered to Bentley that he would be willing to sacrifice some profit in exchange for 'a more certain foundation' in the labour of their manufactory. Always committed to the principle of 'improvement', Josiah rejected the idea of abruptly dismissing the wayward employee in favour of offering him help. 'Charity may incline us to hope that after a little cool reflection & seeing the folly & danger of his past conduct, there is still some chance of his being reclaim'd,' he said to Bentley.

> If he is immediately turn'd adrift, with the total loss of his character, he may probably be driven to a degree of desperation beyond any effort of amendment. He should have *some hope left him* that upon a change of conduct he may still be restor'd to the favour & confidence of his friends.[8]

It was such hope for the future improvement of moral, mental, and even physical health that was the main driving force behind the vigorous growth of Wedgwood & Bentley. Rooted in their devotion to Enlightenment theories of progress was a utopian belief that the money Josiah and Bentley made would, after being reinvested in their business, provide for the research and development of a better standard of living for those for whom they were responsible. According to this philosophy, conducting chemical research to eliminate lead from glazes, starting a school for the children of Etruria Village, and training the workers with new skills were all part of the panoply of responsibility of 'enlightened' entrepreneurs. Essentially growing up without a father and discouraged in his prospects by the replacement patriarch (his older brother) in his family as a boy, Josiah was determined to provide what he could for the community that he believed could also be improved, just as he had been through his own efforts.

But there was responsibility on both sides. The workers had to cultivate a resistance against the evils and vices in society. They had to learn a new way of life. 'They seem to have got the notion,' Josiah said after his workers began to live in their new houses, 'that they are to do what they please.'[9] Part of their reform involved being trained in new ways of working, as well as living. When Etruria opened and Josiah had to recruit new labour, he faced the time-consuming task of training them how to make wares that their apprenticeships elsewhere had not taught them. Every new type of product that Josiah invented required new methods of production – successful jasperware, for instance, required a new kind of kiln to fire it properly. The problem was, complained Josiah, 'we have too many *fresh* hands to take in at once, though we have business enough for them, if they knew how, or would have patience to learn to do it, but they do not seem to relish the idea of a second apprenticeship.'

This problem never fully went away. New levels of skill were developed with every experimental achievement. Standardisation was crucial for product 'quality assurance'. If the colour of the wares varied – especially in the item of creamware, where the colour was its most desirable aspect – their customers complained. Josiah himself had a difficult enough time with consistency, but to train all his workers to follow suit was a nightmare which needed addressing.

'A *Waking notion* haunts me very much of late which is the beginning of a regular drawing, & modelling school to train up Artists for ourselves. I would pick up some likely Boys of about 12 years old & take them apprentice 'till they were twenty or twenty one & set them to drawing.'[10] He had a similar 'scheme for taking Girls into paint', a crucial aspect of his skilled labour force that women excelled at, as they did with 'flower dressing', a skill which a certain Mrs Southwell, a regular visitor to Etruria, demonstrated to Josiah. 'I am more & more in Love with her every time I see her,' he declared, excited about having 'such a Mistress in the Science of flower dressing' to share her talents with his women employees.[11] Whatever resources he created for his workers, though, he needed some assurance that they would be willing and committed to learn new techniques.

Like any other forward-looking business, Wedgwood & Bentley had to adapt rapidly to changing fashions to stay afloat and this often required a new specialisation in the workforce and diversification of skills. Techniques such as lathe operating, glaze mixing, slip-casting, and firing at controlled temperatures were performed with that unwritten know-how that distinguishes the skilled from the novice, leading in turn to more specialised workshops and a more particular division of labour. Since workers eventually improved their skills and the particular ware they were manufacturing, they naturally felt they should be rewarded with higher wages. This was what had led to Josiah's latest headache.

Josiah was not averse to rewarding his workers as they grew more skilled, even doubling the pay of some from 7 or 8 shillings a week to 14 or 15 shillings for finely executed designs; 'improved in their *wages* as well as in their *workmanship*', as he put it.[12] On the other hand, he drove a hard bargain when he felt his 'hands' were not performing to the required standard, especially his painters who – he had occasion to lament – 'have shamefull prices & done shamefull work for it'. This reflected a hierarchy amongst the arts, where painters customarily demanded more for their work, feeling that their status should be elevated above cruder crafts.

But Josiah, like many other manufacturers, was cautious about the wages he was prepared to pay. At face value he could be accused of merely wanting to keep overheads down to maximise profit, but this was not the case. He had little problem raising the prices of his wares to earn more, since the bill was paid by the rich, but he would not penalise the poor for profit. Nor did he fall in line with Arthur Young's assessment (repeated by numerous contemporary economists) that 'everyone but an idiot knows that the lower classes must be kept poor or they will never be industrious'.[13] Rather, he worried about whether the workers recognised the value of money, about what *useful* ends it could be put to, instead of using their higher wages to spend in the pub. This caused resentment amongst workers who considered it an intrusion in their lives which were already uncomfortably regulated by bells and clocks at the factory. That was because Josiah (and an increasing number of other manufacturers) wanted workers to recognise the value of time, by which they were now paid rather than for piece-by-piece productivity.

'Expenses move on like clockwork,' Josiah wrote to Bentley, wondering how he could create incentives for his workers, '& are much the same whether the quantity of goods be large or small.' Producing as much as possible in a given time was, of course, the desired effect, but expenses persisted regardless.

> Wages to Boys & Odd Men, Warehousemen & Book-keeper who are a kind of satellites to the Makers (Throwers, Turners, &c) is nearly the same whether we make 20 doz of Vases or 10 doz per week, & will therefore be a double expense upon the latter number. The same may be said in regard to most of the incidental expenses, Coals for the workshop fires (no small expense) which must be rather increas'd than diminish'd when the men are idle, in order to keep them warm.[14]

One emerging economic theory that Josiah did appear to sympathise with (while struggling to determine the best means of correlating work with wages), was that pay itself was not a good incentive to work. In what later became known as 'backward bending labour supply', economists reasoned that workers would do less work with more money since they could attain the standard of living they wanted with less labour. Those 'who can subsist on three days' work will be idle and drunken the remainder of the week', one government report on taxes concluded in 1764. 'The poor in the manufacturing counties will never work any more time than is necessary to live and support their weekly debauches.'[15] Josiah's alternative incentive schemes provided a guarantee of a higher standard of living for his employees. If they remained in his employment, they could have a home to live in, education for their children, and – a new idea at the time – a share of a collectivised plan of health insurance offering financial security for them or their family in the event of illness or death. It had a long way to go, but Josiah believed in its progressive tone. His workers, however, were more difficult to persuade.

One Monday morning in mid-July, 1776, just as Bentley and Mary were heading off to Paris, Josiah arrived at Etruria's front gate at half-past six to open up the factory and found 'all the Men at the Ornamental work were assembled to meet me'. They wanted to expostulate about their wages, which at the end of the previous week Josiah had complained 'were exorbitant & must be reduced'. The men had been brooding on this all weekend.[16]

'They determin'd not to begin to work on Monday morning till they had settled this matter with me', arguing that they were doing their best work, that they 'work'd late & early & could not work any lower &c &c'. It was, Josiah coldly remembered, exactly like the complaint he heard repeatedly from the painters at their Chelsea workshops. Josiah talked to them for fifteen minutes, standing his ground, then losing his temper. 'I told them we would *make a new sett of hands* which they must be sensible was in my power to do rather than submit to give such prices as must in the end ruin the Manufacture both to us, to themselves & their Children after them.' He suggested that they return to work and that he would review their wages and the prices of the products to see if anything could be done, but he made it clear that 'if they meant to frighten me into their measures by assembling together in that way they were very much mistaken in their measures'.

The workers shuffled but remained in front of him. One of the younger men who 'seem'd to take the lead for the rest, talk'd very pertly', demanding to know why, if the Master was unhappy with his work and unwilling to reward him money, he had not been dismissed from duty. 'The reason,' Josiah calmly stated, leaning forward, 'was my hopes that he would, as he had often promis'd me, do better', but since the boy suggested he would rather leave his place than mend his work, Josiah gestured to the road. 'This stopp'd his mouth', he reported, and prompted the others to go quietly about their work, '& there the matter rests at present'. Josiah knew the matter was far from settled.

The tension at the factory sometimes worried Sally. She was concerned it might turn ugly, that the workers' restlessness might be directed against Josiah or the managers. As the size of the workforce increased, it had become harder for her to acquaint herself with all the employees, and reports of such events made the business feel strange, distant and somewhat dangerous. Etruria Hall was only two hundred yards up the hill from the factory, but Sally seemed to be casting it further from her mind. As Sally listened to Josiah recounting these latest incidents one late September evening, Josiah noticed that 'Mrs Wedgwood was not frightened at all', and later that night, Josiah learned why.

'A little before 12 she talked of some pains which I thought it would not be in my power to remove, so I immediately sent for better assistance & amongst them they presented me with a fine Girl in her Cap &c before two.' Sally was fine, and so was the baby, a girl. They named her Sarah, the latest addition to their growing army of Etruscans.

TWENTY-EIGHT

Arrivistes

IN May the following year, 1777, the Trent and Mersey
Canal was officially opened. Ninety-three miles of calm water
now cut through the crags and chasms of the rugged Midlands
landscape that had previously made travel and the transportation of
goods so difficult. The tunnels, locks and associated works made it
the greatest civil engineering work built in Britain.[1] At a cost of more
than £300,000, it was a crowning achievement for the industrialising
world and a project in which Josiah took a small measure of personal
pride.

Josiah had already taken the opportunity of enjoying 'a very pleasant expedition' along the canal from Cheshire to Manchester, where
the 'Canal Duke', Bridgewater, was running two passage boats: 'one
carries Passangers at a shilling each – the other is divided into three
Rooms & the rates are 2/6 per head for the best Room, 18d & 12d
& it is the pleasantest, & cheapest mode of traveling you can conceive'.[2] The canal ran right through the heart of the estate of Etruria
on its route south to Derby, where it met the River Trent. Josiah's
sprawling factory, red-brick walls with large windows, was perfectly
located only yards away, parallel to the bank of the canal, with a
level, flagstone embankment where the warehouse men could wheel
the crates of goods onto the long wooden boats. It was every bit
as dramatic a transformation in the operation and appearance of
manufacturing life as Josiah could have envisaged. It was the epitome
of the reformation of life in what was now the industrial Midlands.

John Wesley, who once commented on the small hill that was scattered with potters, did not recognise the place. 'The whole face of this country has changed,' he said, twenty years after his first visit. 'The wilderness is literally become a fruit field. Houses, villages, and towns have sprung up.' As much as the landscape had changed, however, so too had the atmosphere. With factories and houses came more ovens, workshops and 'prodigious piles of coal burning to coke', as another traveller remarked of the nearby metalworks at Coalbrookdale, Shropshire, shocked by 'the furnaces, the forges, and the other tremendous objects emitting fire and smoke to an immense extent, together with the intolerable stench of the sulphur', giving him the uncomfortable feeling 'of being placed in an air pump'.[3] The sky no longer carried steel-coloured clouds. It was now, as Josiah called it, 'the Blacklands'.[4]

The Burslem potters struggling to make a living up the hill gazed down on Josiah's situation with envy, land-locked and unable – for lack of wealth to build and available land to build on – to follow his example and relocate along the canal. He stood alone as a symbol of the new order of things. He had eclipsed all other potters whose manufactories were only incrementally developing, falling well short of the scale of Etruria. Some potters were still proving strong – Spode for instance, Whieldon's talented apprentice who left shortly after Josiah arrived as a partner, was one of the best of Josiah's local competitors, but with the war and the cost of keeping ahead of fickle consumer tastes, the broader level of competition was growing thin.

Now and then Josiah sympathetically reflected on the fate of his competition. After a quick trip to Cornwall in 1775 in search of kaolin, Josiah expressed his surprise that the pot-work of a manufacturer named Nicholas Crisp, who had moved to Cornwall from London to manufacture porcelain, was 'not in a more flourishing and improved state than we saw it', considering its prime location. Despite the apparent advantages, Crisp died almost penniless. 'Poor Crisp haunts my imagination continually,' Josiah wrote to Bentley, as he was struggling to perfect his jasperware. 'Ever pursuing – just upon the point of overtaking – but never in possession of his favourite object. There are many good lessons in that poor Man's life, Labours & catastrophe if we schemers could profit by example.'[5] A similar example was presented in the story of Richard Champion who had engaged in expensive litigation to ensure his rights to the monopoly of the Cornish kaolin when he bought Cookworthy's patent, but failed to extend its life. 'Poor Champion, you may have heard, is quite demolished,' wrote Josiah, who was active in getting the court to quash Champion's application. 'It was never likely to be otherwise,' he continued, 'as he had neither professional knowledge, sufficient capital, nor scarcely any real acquaintance with the materials he was working upon.'[6]

Without those three qualities – money, professional skills and scientific knowledge – one was, Josiah was sure, doomed to fail in the modern world of industrial manufacturing. The symbol of success for the previous generation – Long John and cousin Thomas's Big House – was a remnant of a world that was now lost. It was, literally, a dying family craft. Cousin Thomas had passed away in 1776, after a life devoted to his and his brother's pottery. Following in his brother's footsteps, he had finally married at the age of sixty-two, and died eleven years later without children. His gravestone in the churchyard of St John's in Burslem is succinct: 'Here lies the body of Thomas, brother of John Wedgwood.'

Josiah probably realised that his own place in history was already secured, that his name would mean much more than an association with the rest of the Wedgwood family. Each new product was, in a sense, a commemorative piece capturing the progress of the art of pottery for which he was responsible. 'I have often wish'd,' Josiah wrote in reply to Bentley in 1774, 'I had saved a single specimen of all the new articles I have made to be left as a sacred deposit for the use of our Children & Children's Children with some account of what *has* been done & what *may* be done, some *hints* & *seeds* for future discoveries, might perhaps be the most valuable treasure we can leave them.' He had not done this before, but now 'resolv'd *to make a beginning*.[7] He wondered if there was something more he could do to tell the story of his accomplishments, something artistic. If he did, it would also help to set the record straight about who the real innovators were, which one person, who in 1777 was inundating Josiah with requests for a particular jasper portrait medallion, was working hard to distort.

Paul Elers was the son of John Philip Elers, one of the Dutch brothers who had made such an impact on Staffordshire pottery manufacture at the end of the seventeenth century. He had learned that Wedgwood & Bentley were producing portraits of 'Illustrious Moderns' for those 'in all the Courts & Countries of Europe to be immortalised'.[8] Elers thought it would be appropriate to have a portrait of his father produced, who, he was sure, belonged to the list of illustrious moderns by virtue of the innovations he made in the world of pottery, and also it would be particularly appropriate to have his father portrayed in this medium. Wedgwood & Bentley happily complied, but soon Josiah discovered that Mr Elers desired a bit more.

Since his 'friends are pretty numerous', Elers repeatedly wrote asking for more and more copies of the portrait (he '*begs without ceasing*', Josiah said), suggesting some improvements to it, namely that an inscription be engraved on the copper frame in which the portrait was set to read: *Johannes Philipus Elers – Plasticis Britannicae Inventor*, declaring that his father was the 'inventor of British pottery'.[9]

'This inscription,' wrote an irritated Josiah, 'conveys a falsehood, & therefore can do no honour to the memory of his father, who was not the *inventor* but the *improver* of the art of Pottery, or forming clay in Britain.' Josiah then told Bentley the story of the Elers brothers, and how they eventually moved to Burslem because 'Pottery was carried on there in a much larger way & in a much improved state than in any other part of Great Britain'. When they arrived, they had made a spectacle of themselves by glazing their wares by using salt, but Josiah was uncertain if even this was their own improvement. He asked Bentley to 'obtain some intelligence amongst the Potters near London' to see if this was already being practised there, or perhaps in Bristol.

The one 'improvement introduc'd' by the Elers brothers that Josiah was prepared to acknowledge 'was the refining of our red common clay, by sifting & making it into Tea & Coffee Ware in imitation of the Chinese Red Porcelain'. But even Josiah would not concede 'invention', only 'improvement', 'refining' and 'imitation'. They were 'ingenious', said Josiah, 'but the sum total certainly does not amount to INVENTING THE ART OF POTTERY IN BRITAIN'.

Bentley, as usual, suggested ways that Josiah could write to Paul Elers and delicately break the news that he was not prepared to assert such a claim in their portrait, but Josiah was determined to drop the issue altogether, particularly when Paul Elers kept suggesting ways in which Wedgwood & Bentley could rise above producing 'trifling trinkets' to manufacture 'Bomb proof fortifications' and water pipes, 'for London first & then for all the world'.[10]

Josiah did not waste much more time in correspondence with Elers the younger, instead funnelling his annoyance over the issue into creative energy. He began to wonder just what the origin of pottery was, and whether he could represent it in his own way. He had an idea of what kind of story it would be.

Under the glowing light from a hanging lantern she watches as her lover sleeps, slumped in a chair, head and shoulder resting against the wall. He will soon be gone, off on a long and perilous journey to fight a war in foreign lands. The Greek maiden begins to trace her lover's shadow. His silhouette on the wall will preserve the moment. The woman's father, a Corinthian potter by the name of Dibutade, will use her drawing to model a clay relief, which he will bake in his furnace to create for her a ceramic memento.

This legend of the origin of painting and the invention of the art of modelling bas-relief sculpture was the basis of Joseph Wright's allegorical painting the *Corinthian Maid*. Josiah commissioned the painting from Wright in 1778, the year that a mutual friend, William Hayley, retold the story in his poem, *An Essay on Painting*. Josiah wanted the work to depict the antique origins of his craft, and the progress he had made in the art. The painting would also help illustrate to Wedgwood & Bentley's customers that their pottery, decorated with low reliefs, was the aesthetic descendant of ancient attempts to preserve a precious memory.

Wright thought it was a good idea to include pieces of pottery 'to mark [the maiden's] father's profession', and Josiah lent the painter some antique vases for him to copy, though he did wonder how his vases 'could be supposed to exist in the infancy of the potter's art'. But the painter made it a subtle allusion. In the corner of the ancient pottery stood an earthenware vessel while in an adjacent room, embers crackled in a fiery kiln.[11]

Wright was already well known for painting scenes of scientific experiments, philosophical lectures and industrial work. Throughout the 1770s he produced a series of paintings depicting industrial progress and entrepreneurial pursuits, capturing scenes of skilled craftsmanship in Midlands metal works and textile mills, such as *The Iron Forge* (1772). His paintings illuminated the dusty corners of workshops and the candlelit smiles of satisfaction on the faces of natural philosophers and inventors. He showed England's entrepreneurs at work, chasing dreams of literally manufacturing a better Britain. Wedgwood's choice of artist established Etruria among the triumphs of the new age.

The artist himself was an experimenter, a 'mechanical genius' who tested different pigments and materials to render light sources and shadows more effective or dramatic – borrowing technical methods from studies of old masters, such as Rembrandt, to discover the secrets of their colouring.

From a blacksmith illuminated by the white-hot metal on an anvil to a portrait of Richard Arkwright resting next to a model of his patented spinning frame, Wright captured the resourcefulness and versatility in pursuit of the Enlightenment, diminishing the sense of provincial insignificance for humble family manufacturers. His portraits showed that the world owed much to the lives of ordinary people outside the metropolis. He himself gained an international reputation as 'Wright of Derby'.

His art also told the story of the triumphs of the entrepreneurial and enquiring Enlightenment industrialists like Wedgwood. He masterfully used light sources in his paintings to reveal moments when those toiling to uncover the secrets of Nature unlock one of its secrets. Josiah was fond of such images, and he considered commissioning Wright for a work to capture another of his triumphs – a painting that he hoped would inspire in his children a love and passion for science.

As his children grew older, Josiah gained new company in his coveted laboratory, where he still conducted his experiments each night, where 'I can be instructing them, even by way of play & amusement, in the rudiments of chemistry & give them a turn to such studies, & enquiries as are most likely to be of use to them in their particular occupation'.[12] Josiah envisaged a portrait of his sons, the future talent of his trade, engrossed and enthralled by experimental enquiry. His oldest son, twelve-year-old Jack, would be standing at a table conducting a chemical experiment, 'mixing fixable air with the glass apparatus &c.; & his two brothers accompanying him'. The youngest, seven-year-old Tom, would be 'jumping up & clapping his hands in joy & surprise at seeing a stream of bubbles rise up just as Jack has put a little chalk to the acid'. The other, nine-year-old Joss junior, would be sitting 'with the chemical dictionary before him in a thoughtful mood, which actions will be exactly descriptive of their respective natures'.[13]

The portrait of his sons would have emblematised his motto that 'everything comes from experiment', a philosophy that was shared by many of Josiah's friends – his collaborators in scientific experiment as well as his entrepreneurial competitors. It also represented a flair for the kind of work that would make the next generation of Wedgwood potters as successful as their father, or at least that is what Josiah hoped. He had a vision of the future for them which was very different from his own childhood. 'Jack,' he predicted, 'is to be settled as a gentleman farmer in some desirable situation, with as many acres for himself & his tenants to improve as I can spare him. Joss & Tom to be potters, & partners in trade. Tom to be the traveler, & negociater, & Joss the manufacturer.'[14] The children, however, were developing their own ideas.

In 1778 Sukey turned twelve. She was developing into a 'womanly, affectionate' daughter, with an excellent education which Josiah was soliciting help from all his friends to further improve. At seven she had been sent to a boarding school in Manchester, but returned home for a summer break so 'full of pouks, & boils & humours' that Josiah needed immediately to take her to the Buxton baths to recover. This is what happens 'after sitting & sewing at school for 12 months', he spat, agreeing with Sally never to send her to such a place again.[15]

Instead, it was to be home tutoring with vetted teachers that would be better 'than any common Boarding school Master'. Sukey spent the next few years learning music, drawing, and geography. She wrote plays with roles for her brothers and sisters, and she played her harpsichord while her sister Kitty sang (another scene which Josiah wanted captured in a painting). At times, Sukey stayed with the Bentleys in London 'who would support her mind' (Josiah was slightly worried about her 'journalist' tendencies, thinking that it had led her cousin Byerley astray for so long), and to enhance her character. 'We know our dear Sukey to be a good & affectionate

Girl,' Josiah wrote, 'and hope, nay are fully perswaded she will deserve this character as well from her Father & Mother Bentley, as she has done from her Father & Mother Wedgwood.'[16] Her younger sisters were looked after by a nurse whose 'language & manners are very well, & she keeps the children in great order'.[17] Sally warmly welcomed the nurse, for keeping control of her Etruscans was getting more difficult than ever, now that they had yet another new daughter. The previous summer, in 1778, forty-five-year-old Sally had given birth to Mary Anne, their eighth – and final – child. (Always amazed at Sally's fortitude, Josiah described how, after preparing a pot of tea for the family, she 'slipt upstairs just before supper', delivered the baby, then 'eat her supper, went to sleep'. It was all the proof anyone could need, said Josiah, of the 'enlightn'd age' they lived in.[18])

Jack, being the second eldest after Sukey, was also sent to boarding school, in Bolton, and showed bookish interests, which inspired his younger brother Joss. 'My dear boy,' Josiah wrote to his eldest son when he first went off to school,

> Your brothers often talk of you & seldom omit drinking your health at dinner. Joss wants much to go to school with his brother Jackey, that he may learn to read & learn so many things out of books which he is very earnest to know, but finds there is no other way of gaining the knowledge he wants, but by becoming a scholar and reading & studying for himself. 'Oh I wish I could take up the book, & read the story out myself, papa,' he cries.[19]

Like Sukey, however, Jack fell ill while at school and Josiah had to rush to Bolton to retrieve him. He was sure that it was owing to too much of what his friend Joseph Priestley referred to as 'phlogisticated air' (hydrogen), which contained harmful acids when breathed in close quarters. 'I am convince'd,' stated Josiah, 'that if they are confin'd again to school air, with school discipline, their healths & bodily strength must be diminish'd very considerably, if not totally lost.'[20]

Above Sarah Wedgwood, who preferred to be called Sally, in a portrait by Sir Joshua Reynolds in 1782, when she was forty-eight.

Right Selection of 'Queen's Ware' – creamware – pieces so named after Josiah impressed Queen Charlotte with the quality of the dinner-service she ordered in 1765. Its ivory-white glaze was unique at the time, the fruit of Josiah's tireless chemical experimentation.

Above A 'Queen's Ware'
teapot manufactured by
Josiah *c.* 1770 – one of many
pieces of pottery with transfer-
printing by the Liverpool firm
Sadler & Green that depicted
a political or commemorative
scene. The pot shows the likeness of John Wilkes, whom
the Wedgwoods and Bentley
admired for his support of
parliamentary reform in Britain
and the liberties of the
American colonies.

Left A portrait medallion of
Josiah's patroness, Queen
Charlotte, (white cameo on
blue jasperware), part of a series
depicting 'Heads of Illustrious
Moderns', which Josiah and
Bentley produced after Josiah's
invention of jasper (unique for
its colors and porcelain-like
translucence) in 1778.

Above The *virtuosi* – aficionados of the antique – shopping for ancient vases in Naples, Italy, after which Josiah not only fashioned his reproductions of 'Etruscan' vases, but gleaned ideas about displaying his own wares in his London showrooms. Sir William Hamilton is the tall, thin gentleman at the right of the picture.

Right Lady Jane Cathcart, wife of the British envoy to St. Petersburg, Lord Cathcart, and sister of Sir William Hamilton. She inspired Josiah to imitate the ancient vases her brother collected in Italy, and introduced his wares to the aristocracy in Russia: Catherine the Great placed two extensive orders with Wedgwood.

One of six 'First Day Vases' Josiah threw to mark the official opening of Etruria Factory,
near Burslem in Staffordshire, on 13 June 1769. The vases were made of black basalt,
with classical figures painted in red encaustic enamel.

Etching of Etruria Factory, conveniently built along the Trent & Mersey Canal.
Josiah campaigned aggressively to have the canal dug. Completed in 1777,
it added a critical trunk to the inland navigation system in Britain and eased
the transportation of raw materials and finished products.

Above Etching of a throwing room in Etruria, where throwers formed pieces on the potter's wheel. This was one of many rooms in the factory – among modelling, glazing, moulding, flowering, and finishing rooms – where work was highly specialized. Wedgwood was careful to prevent anyone – even his employees – from being able to understand, and so steal, his methods.

Left Matthew Boulton, the Birmingham 'buckle maker' – a friendly rival industrialist to Wedgwood & Bentley's production of 'ornamental' pottery and organiser of the 'Lunar Society' meetings at his home next to his Soho metal factory.

The 'Portland Vase', a 10 inch high exact replica of the ancient vase sold to the Duchess of Portland by Sir William Hamilton in 1784, and copied in limited numbers by Josiah in black and white jasper in 1790. This vase, rare for not being discarded for its imperfections, was blistered because of a slight miscalculation in its firing temperature – a common frustration for Josiah before he perfected the firing process.

英國の宅地烏德へ幼き時
疾を得て不具と成一が其
國の陶器の粗なるを憂ひ
數年工夫して精巧の品を
造り出一國の大益を成す
或人之を譽て此人きの疾ある
故に心を内に用ひ此術を
得るよ...

Left A wood engraving depicting a one-legged Josiah as conceived by a Japanese artist, *c.* 1880. While Josiah's leg was amputated in 1768 following an infection related to a childhood disease, he had specially-manufactured prostheses formed in the shape of a normal leg and never had himself represented with a straight peg leg.

Below Portrait of the Wedgwood family on the grounds of Etruria Hall by George Stubbs, 1780. Left to right: their children Mary Anne, Sarah, Thomas, Catherine, Susannah ('Sukey'), Josiah II ('Joss'), John ('Jack'), and Sally and Josiah. A discerning eye might detect a small puff of smoke in the distance over Josiah's left shoulder – the only allusion to the industrial basis of the family's new wealth.

Josiah's final words in his distinctive handwriting
in one of over a thousand letters to Bentley.

While Jack was recovering at home under the medical advice of Erasmus Darwin, Josiah avowed that he would keep the boys home and have Tom Byerley 'give them some lessons in Latin, & for English, French, writing, accounts & drawing, we must make the best shift we can amongst ourselves. Riding, running & other bodily exercises make a considerable part of our schooling & entertainment.'[21] Josiah felt comfortable knowing that at home his children could receive proper attention to their minds, morals and physical health (since, he noted, 'their constitutions were not of the Herculean stamp').

Thinking about the future of his seven children (in order of age: Sukey, John – known as Jack, Joss, Tom, Catherine or 'Kitty', Sarah and now Mary Anne) Josiah, in collaboration with Bentley, Darwin, and a new acquaintance introduced through Darwin, the educational writer Richard Edgeworth, developed a detailed plan for their education.

Darwin was strongly supportive of the idea, as was Edgeworth, who had already asserted his plan to raise his own children on Rousseau's principles. But Darwin gave Josiah some advice about the content of their education, considering it 'a very idle waste of time for any boys intended for trade to learn Latin, as they seldom learnt it to any tolerable degree of perfection, or retain'd what they learnt'.[22] Josiah was not so sure, even though he felt that modern translations of classical works were adequate in order to gain classical knowledge. The 'Etruscan education', however, drew on more familiar resources.

> Before breakfast we read English together in the newspaper, or any book we happen to have in the course of reading. We are now reading Ferbers travels [*Travels through Italy in 1771 and 1772*], with the globe and map before us. After breakfast they go & write an hour with Mr Swift & with this small portion of time, & writing their French exercises & entering some experiments which they make along with me: all of which I insist upon being written in a fair legible hand, they have

improv'd more in writing in these few weeks here, than they did in the last twelve months in Bolton.[23]

Jack, Joss and Tom then went to stay at Darwin's house in Lichfield for a month, where he had hired a French prisoner to teach them French. 'Your little boys are very good,' Darwin reported to Josiah, 'and learn French and drawing with avidity . . . Josiah is a boy of great abilities and little Tom has much humour.'[24]

While they were away, Josiah took the opportunity to draw up a schedule which all his children, as well as Useful Tom's and the Willets's children, could follow.

> Susan, John, Josiah, Thomas & Kitty Wedgwood.
>
> With three boys & a girl at our Mr. [Useful] T. Wedgwoods . . . One day of schooling for our own five scholars.
>
> Rise at 7 in winter when I shall ring the school bell, & at 6 in summer.
>
> Dress & wash half an hour.
>
> The boys write with Mr. Swift one hour along with Mr T. Wedgwoods (if I approve of company) in some room fitted up for the purpose at the works.
>
> The little girls an English lesson with their nurse *in the school*, which happens to be a room near the nursery. I would instill an early habit of *going to school at stated times* in the youngest of our scholars as it will make it so much easier to them by as much as it seems a necessary & connected part of the routine or business of the day. My young men are quite orderly in this respect since I let them know that it was indispensable, & they are very good in keeping my eleventh commandment – *Thou shall not be idle.*
>
> Breakfast – as school boys.
>
> From 9 to 10 French.
>
> From 10 to 11 Drawing
>
> From 11 to 1 Riding or other exercise which will include gardening – Fossiling, experimenting, &c &c.
>
> Susan fills up these intervals with music besides her exercise.

From 1 to dinner at half past 1 washing &c in order to be decent at the table.

Half past 2 Latin one hour.

Then French one hour and conversation in the same, in the fields, garden or elsewhere as it may happen half an hour, to 5 O' Clock.

From 5 to 7 exercise, bagging, &c.

At 7 Accounts one hour – Supper, & to bed at 9.

The little lasses I had forgot they must have two more English lessons in the school, & Kitty as much French as she can bear.

Josiah's twenty-year career of developing schedules to discipline his workers had clearly rubbed off on his (rather unrealistic) plan of schooling – it was a kind of miniature factory for his miniature Etruscans. One difference, of course, was that they were not learning the tools of the trade yet. They were not undergoing apprenticeships. They were not regulated by a pre-determined division of labour to train them with specialised skills. The opposite was true. Theirs was to be a rounded education, a *liberal* education that previously was reserved only for the gentry and above. Josiah's children were the first generation of the entrepreneurial class to be able to afford and desire the gentrified education.

Josiah wanted another portrait to show this, and commissioned George Stubbs to do it. While Stubbs was an eminent painter of horses, he was becoming well known for depicting aristocratic families in leisurely rural settings with their horses and for the last couple of years had started oil painting on ceramic plaques for Wedgwood & Bentley.

It was a large family portrait, four feet by five, on a wood panel (which Stubbs preferred to canvas). Josiah and Sally sit on a white wooden bench that encircles a mature tree on their lawn near Etruria Hall. Josiah, in a beige suit with an orange silk waistcoat, rests his arm on a small, round mahogany table with a black basalt vase on it. Sally is sitting next to him, dressed in an elegant, flowing yellow silk dress, gesturing toward their seven children, the eldest four of whom are on horseback. It is a graceful and tranquil portrait, and it takes an acute eye to spot the small puff of smoke in the background, beyond Josiah's left shoulder, where a kiln is burning – a discrete allusion to the source of the wealth that had elevated the family to a gentrified lifestyle that surpassed even Sally's own family.

Josiah's growing preoccupation with his children's education throughout 1779 occurred at a transitional moment in his life. He was approaching his fiftieth birthday, when 'a man is either a fool or a physician', he laughed to his friends. No, answered Darwin, 'a fool is a man who never tried an experiment', and while Josiah was no physician, Darwin and all their mutual friends knew that Josiah was no fool.

Sadly, the person who had taught him his early experimental skills, his brother-in-law the Reverend William Willets, had recently died. Josiah and Sally were relieved they were there to comfort Catherine, Josiah's beloved sister, who had been so encouraging and supportive of Josiah and Sally in their younger years. Catherine looked forward and onward, and with Josiah's help, opened a milliner's shop in Newcastle. He had also recently heard that their brother Richard, who fought with the British army in the Seven Years War, had died. Josiah never talked of him, but knew that his brother's death was the result 'of a long course of drinking & irregular living'.[25] Richard was Josiah's last living brother.

At about the same time, Josiah's early partner, Thomas Whieldon, retired. With savings of about £10,000 he was nowhere near as wealthy and accomplished at the end of career as Josiah already was, but he was comfortable in his neo-gothic estate which he had built near his pot-works. His wife had died seven years earlier, and Whieldon had since occupied himself by getting involved in local affairs, later becoming High Sheriff of Staffordshire.

Josiah was now at an age and stage of his career where he could begin to think about other aspects of life. After years of neglecting the children to spend time in his workshop and laboratory, they were now all of an age when he could look forward to 'Fossiling, experimenting, &c &c' with them. For the first time he took up a hobby. 'In turning my back on the pottery,' he said to Bentley, 'I have got my face over a shell drawer, & find myself in imminent danger of becoming a connoisseur.'[26]

He enjoyed being outdoors, digging for fossils and shells with his children, but he longed for the time when, 'retir'd from this bustling World', he and his dearest friend Bentley 'will enjoy a few of those quiet hours which it has hitherto seem'd impossible for us to find', when they could read books and discuss all that happened in their lives.[27] Every summer for years Josiah had implored Bentley to break his routine and take an excursion into the country. 'It is not good for man to continue too long in one place,' he wrote, lest suddenly they find they have become '*an old man*'. 'So take care of yourself, & run away in time, as I do often, & by that means intend to continue young a long time to come.' But the 'quiet hours' with Bentley would never come, and Josiah would soon learn that time had indeed overtaken them.

TWENTY-NINE

Renewed Grief

1780 BEGAN WITH great distress. 'My dear affectionate father,' as he referred to his father-in-law, Richard, passed away. His portrait, also painted by Stubbs, was just finished. Josiah thought it 'a very strong likeness'. It depicted Richard as a frail man in an oversized coat wearing a fine white wig. His face is lined and his eyes fading, but he possesses a faint, easy smile. At seventy-nine-years old, he seemed remarkably untroubled by thoughts of illness or his own demise, even though his death was brought on by increasingly severe bouts of rheumatism.[1]

Sally was only comforted in her grief by the knowledge that her father had lived a successful and long life. Her sadness grew, however, when, shortly after, her uncle, Long John of Big House, also died. She was now the only one remaining on her father's side of the family.

Many children attended the funerals – Long John had six children, Josiah and Sally had seven, and Catherine Willets had three. One of Catherine's daughters, Sukey's best friend Kitty, could not attend due to an increasingly severe case of consumption. Josiah called in Erasmus Darwin to examine the fourteen-year-old, but Catherine's letters to her brother and sister-in-law painted a grim picture.

'Dr Darwin has bin here,' Catherine wrote to Sally, who was in London with Josiah briefly visiting the Bentleys, 'but did not say anything comfortable about her, indeed I was afraid to ask, my own fear suggested enough for me.'[2] For the past few days Kitty had been 'seized with a violent spitting of blood', which the local surgeon, Mr Bent, hoped would help turn the humours to her advantage, but her pulse remained extremely weak and low, and she was unable to rest without opium.

Opium was the only drug that Darwin had any confidence in, and he prescribed it as if there were no other options. 'All the boasted nostrums only take up time,' he declared, always warning others to look out for quacks, '& as the disease is often of a short duration they have gain'd credit which they do not deserve.'[3] But Kitty's illness did not look like it would be of a short duration.

'Her Breath is so very short & the Weather continues so bad she cannot get out' for some fresh air, Catherine reported a few days later. A bitter February fog had descended in the valley, crawling along the canal and enveloping the Willets' home. 'She is now taking Dr Darwin's prescriptions twice a day.' Opium, buttermilk, and chamomile tea was all she could consume, while she continued to spit up blood.

On Mr Bent's advice Josiah paid for a two-week treatment at a hospital in Norwich, where Kitty was wrapped in towels and soaked in cold water, which, as uncomfortable as it sounded, led Catherine to believe that it might have an agreeable affect on her daughter. After two weeks, however, Kitty was complaining of the soreness in her bones, her mother was at breaking point. In the carriage on the way back to Etruria, Catherine cried in a letter to Josiah. 'I am sure your ears are open to such & your Heart ready to relieve, I have suffered so much this fortnight at Norwich that it has made me quite low, I found my poor girl in such a low poor way so emaciated & altered that it shocked me & I never got over it.' Kitty died before they reached home.

'I have this morning been mingling my tears with my family and friends,' Josiah wrote to Bentley.[4] A young man named Caldwall who had been courting Kitty with the hope of one day marrying her, was there also, mourning 'with almost fantastic sorrow'.

I hoped to have been firm & not to have renewed their grief
with my unavailing tears, but the attempt was vain, we yielded
to nature and wept over the remembrance of our dear niece &
the amiable dispositions of her mind to which we had fondly
hoped for a longer date.

Sukey was equally devastated. 'I scarcely ever saw her look worse,
& am greatly afraid of a course of illness.' Sukey, alas, was not the
only daughter he was worried about.

Two-year-old Mary Anne was suffering terribly. It had started a year
earlier, when, due to what Sally and Josiah assumed was difficulties
teething – since several of her teeth were 'pushing forward at the
same time' – she suffered 'convulsions which lasted thirteen hours
without intermission'. This attack was followed by more over the
next few days, when one morning 'we found she had lost the use
of her arm & leg on one side'.[5] Darwin was promptly called in,
who 'order'd our little girl to be electrified two or three times a day
on the side affected, & to be continued for some weeks'.

This was a new experimental practice. Electric currents were
linked theoretically to the concept of 'animal electricity' – a vital
force that animates the living – and to fire, reasoning that electricity
was a 'fluid' form of fire which, as a vital element in the body,
provided the heat in living things. Though predating Galvani's
invention of what became known as the galvanic battery, medical
researchers, particularly in France, were already experimenting with
electric currents, generated through the use of an apparatus, such
as the Ramsden hand-cranked plate electrical machine, which was
connected to Leyden jars – specially constructed canisters – which
stored electric charge. When a thick conducting wire protruding
through a cork on the Leyden jar was brought into contact with a
friction device, a spark from static electricity was discharged.

Electrical experiments with affordable equipment had become
immensely appealing to entrepreneurial culture – inventors and

entertainers alike. As many experimentalists discovered, lightning flashes were difficult phenomena to analyse, but 'drawing lightening from the clouds to a private room', reproducing electric sparks on command, literally stunned spectators.[6] In France, one doctor sent an electric shock through a row of 180 royal guards, much to King Louis XV's amusement. But it also allowed experimentalists to claim control over the hidden powers of 'Nature'. 'The fable of Prometheus is verify'd,' proclaimed one to another self-styled 'electrician', 'what after this can mortals find difficult?'

Such experiments were what had largely driven Benjamin Franklin to conclude a decade earlier that 'all diseases, even that of mortality' will be eliminated, and they were why Joseph Priestley was so interested in writing a history of experimental progress in this field. It is therefore not surprising that Darwin, their mutual friend, was one of the first to experiment with the use of electric shock treatment in physiological disorders.

'I am the electrician upon these occasions,' said Josiah, who was given some charged Leyden jars and instructed to run a current through the right side of Mary Anne's tiny body, treatment which 'the Doctor gives us great hopes of our poor little girls limbs being restored'. The electricity, they hoped, would not only give her back movement, but stimulate the growth of the limbs, preventing them from being shorter than the others, which they believed would result from paralysis. Josiah also lanced her gums with the sharp end of an ivory modelling tool and kept them open, waiting for the teeth to appear.

'I am in great pain for my dear little girl,' Josiah wrote, after two weeks of treatment. 'She recovers very little use of her hand & leg, & is not quite clear of the spasms in the diseased hand & foot.'[7] Josiah could no longer bear to administer the electric shock treatment, and remained disconsolate. After a month, Mary Anne's condition grew worse. Opiates had no effect, and her 'convulsions became so incessant, & so violent that we could scarcely hold her in the warm bath'. One evening, Sally and Josiah were horrified to find that Mary Anne was completely motionless, that she could not make a sound, and 'did not know any of us, but seem'd quite in a fright when we came near her'. From this point on, a morbid pattern emerged. The infant suffered from convulsions, paralysis, slight recovery, then more convulsions. She would never much improve.

In late 1780, George Stubbs was nearing completion of the Wedgwood family portrait when Josiah wrote to Bentley asking him to find someone in London who could make a suitable frame for it. For the past few months Josiah had been more prolific than usual in his barrage of letters to Bentley, relaying detailed reports of the 'scenes of blood & carnage' that returning soldiers witnessed in America, where battlefields had become 'the grave of thousands & tens of thousands of our fellow-citizens'. In the wake of this, he described at length the debates in Staffordshire regarding the controversial decision to raise a local militia, the sudden dissolution of Parliament, and the widespread 'Gordon Riots', the anti-Catholic riots that had erupted following the passing of the Catholic Relief Act. His letters were long, but Bentley's were getting shorter.

Bentley had been complaining of headaches, recurring bouts of gout, and a persistent cold for weeks, but he managed to stay on top of business, writing succinct updates on the stock of wares and offering his usual encouragement for Josiah's latest design ideas for jasperware. At the end of October 1780 Josiah was looking forward to a trip down to London to see how Bentley and Mary had settled into their new house near Chiswick. 'As soon as I think [Stubbs'] picture is finished, I will hie [hurry] away to kiss your hand at Turnham Green,' he wrote.[8] He never received a reply.

THIRTY

'Half myself'

'OUR POOR FRIEND YET BREATHES,' Ralph Griffiths, their mutual friend and Bentley's neighbour, wrote to Josiah, 'but alas! It is such breathing as promises but a short continuance. Almost every hope seems to have forsaken us! I dread the thought of what will be the content of my next.'[1]

Josiah was stunned. Nothing had given him any indication that Bentley's illness was as serious as it was, nor, for that matter, was anyone prepared for the worst. Josiah immediately set out that wintry day for London and arrived the next, Sunday, 26 November. But he was too late. Bentley had died at his home hours earlier, after collapsing from an 'apoplectic seizure',[2] his wife, Mary, and their friend Ralph Griffiths at his side.

Josiah had frequently expressed his deep affection for his friend and partner, letting him know how much his encouragement and sage advice meant to him. He was moved when Bentley expressed much the same. 'I have not any friend,' said Bentley,

> By whose side I have been accustomed to engage & conquer; & who had the same Energy that you constantly possess, when there is occasion for it, either to promote the public good, assist your Friends, or support your own rights. I fancy I can do anything with your help, & I have been so much used to it,

that when you are not with me upon these occasions I seem to have lost my right Arm.[3]

Now, with Bentley gone, Josiah felt 'but half myself'.

Consolations poured forth from grief-stricken friends. 'Our esteemed friend,' wrote Bentley's Liverpool partner, Samuel Boardman, 'during the short time he was with us, spent a happy and useful life. He has left us a noble example of virtue and goodness which I hope will never be forgotten in our actions, both in public and private life.'[4] Others were worried about the severe effect this would have on Josiah. 'Your letter communicating to me the death of your friend,' wrote Erasmus Darwin, 'and I beg I may call him mine, gives me very great concern; and a train of very melancholy ideas succeeds in my mind.'[5] He recommended to Josiah 'exertion' to help dispossess 'the disagreeable ideas of our loss', and asked him to read the consolatory letter which the great Roman orator Cicero received from a friend upon his daughter's death. It began:

> I was indeed as much grieved and distressed as I was bound to be, and looked upon it as a calamity in which I shared. For, if I had been at home, I should not have failed to be at your side, and should have made my sorrow plain to you face to face. That kind of consolation involves much distress and pain, because the relations and friends, whose part it is to offer it, are themselves overcome by an equal sorrow. They cannot attempt it without many tears, so that they seem to require consolation themselves rather than to be able to afford it to others. Still I have decided to set down briefly for your benefit such thoughts as have occurred to my mind, not because I suppose them to be unknown to you, but because your sorrow may perhaps hinder you from being so keenly alive to them.[6]

Darwin hoped that Josiah would accept that he was not alone in his grief, and that his friends were available to offer him much-needed support. He was especially sensible of what loss could feel like, since Darwin was still experiencing difficulties coping with the death of his young son two years earlier. 'Pray pass a day or two with me at Lichfield,' Darwin begged, 'I want much to see you.'

Bentley's death was, as Darwin exclaimed, 'a public calamity'. His role as the public face of Wedgwood & Bentley had gained him many friends and much attention from people of a variety of backgrounds. A day after his death, the *St James's Chronicle* reported the news, stating that

> For his uncommon ingenuity, for his fine taste in the arts, his amiable character in private life, and his ardent zeal for the prosperity of his country, he was justly admired, and will long be most seriously regretted by all who had the pleasure of knowing so excellent a character.[7]

Sir Walter Scott, writing an account of the life of Bentley's niece, the novelist Ann Radcliffe (whose parents were Wedgwood & Bentley's Bath showroom managers), summed up the Wedgwood & Bentley partnership: 'Mr Wedgwood was the intelligent man of commerce, and the able chemist; Mr Bentley the man of more general literature and taste in the arts'.[8] It was an overly simplistic dichotomy, but it captured the essence of a well-balanced partnership that had worked wonders.

Bentley's death meant that the business would suffer. Everything Josiah had done for the previous eleven years had been conducted with Bentley's advice and assistance. No one could simply step in and assume Bentley's role. Now, all that they had developed was reduced to a list of the current stock of ornamental wares that was being catalogued so that Mary, Bentley's widow, could realise Bentley's share of the partnership which was bequeathed to her. Josiah decided the most prudent action was to sell the stock and divide the money accordingly. Over a thousand lots of items, ranging from cameos, intaglios, medallions, busts and statues were auctioned the next year at Christie & Ansell in Pall Mall, raising over £2,000 which kept Mrs Bentley's property 'preserved from a considerable diminution'.[9] But this was the official end of Wedgwood & Bentley.

After the sale, gossip spread speculating on the future of Wedgwood's pottery. Tom Byerley later explained that 'a great many discriminating people were so captivated by [Bentley's] intelligence and animated conversation that they believed & propagated the opinion that he was the origin of all the fine works of taste & all which they saw exhibited in our rooms'.[10] Perhaps, they thought, with the educated and talented Bentley gone, the business would not survive.

Josiah, though sunk in spirits and in a state of depression not felt since the death of his brother John, was not concerned. He knew he had something ready that would answer the customers' expectations and 'surprise the world' once again. In Josiah's last letter to Bentley he mentioned that he was 'contriving some vases for bodies & bodies for vases', referring to his attempts to make ornamental vases with jasper. Despite the difficulties in forming vases with 'the most delicately whimsical of any substance I ever engaged with', he had managed to succeed shortly after. It was too late, of course, for Bentley to see the ornamental item that would sell better than anything else that Josiah produced.

Bentley was buried 'in a new vault close to the west door of the added aisle' within the parish church of St Nicholas at Chiswick. Josiah, Joseph Priestley, and two other friends all wrote epitaphs for a marble plaque and passed their versions back and forth. When they decided on the inscription, they commissioned the Flemish sculptor Thomas Scheemakers (whose father had made the famous sculpture of Shakespeare at Westminster Abbey) to carve a neo-classical marble mural and bust, above a plaque engraved by the famous architect James 'Athenian' Stuart. It read:

THOMAS BENTLEY,

Born at Scrapton in Derbyshire, January 1, 1730
He married Hannah Oates of Chesterfield in the year 1754,
Mary Stamford of Derby in the year 1772,
Who survived to mourn her loss.

He died November 26, 1780.
Blessed with an elevated and comprehensive understanding,
Informed in variety of science,
He possessed
A warm and brilliant imagination,
A pure and elegant taste.
His extensive abilities,
Guided by the most expanded philanthropy,
Were employed
In forming and executing plans for the public good.
He thought
With the freedom of a philosopher,
He acted
With the integrity of a virtuous citizen.

THIRTY-ONE

'A Most Riotous and Outrageous Mob'

AFTER BENTLEY'S DEATH, Josiah lost his reason for carving out extra time to pen long, informed and energetic letters. Those that he did compose were not written with the same bold, clean and confident penmanship that he proudly developed in his youth: his script began to look thin and unsteady, and his letters became empty. He himself looked tired and aged. In 1782, he commissioned two portraits from Sir Joshua Reynolds, one of Sally, one of himself. Both are distinguished, but sombre. His eyes, black as the background, look forlornly into the distance, and he makes no effort to smile.

Thanks largely to Useful Tom's reliability, the business managed to maintain a steady output of useful wares, and Josiah took on Bentley's role of commissioning artists, such as John Flaxman junior, to design new relief medallions and experiment with new ornamental styles. When Jack, his eldest son, turned fifteen in 1781, he began working at the factory, learning various aspects of production and accounting. The factory had twenty-two separate work stations, with skilled artisans supervising the work of each. Over the years, Josiah had invested in improved machinery and increased the number of engine lathes, throwing wheels, and grinding mills.[1] Each year, the workers had become more efficient and specialised – more focused on a particular aspect of production.

Josiah still worked in his laboratory to improve the machinery and practices of production, aiming to optimise efficiency and standardise production. His latest pursuit was to perfect a method for accurately measuring the high temperatures in kilns, which had always been one of the most crucial, as well as skilled, aspects of the craft. No thermometer existed which could withstand such extreme degrees of heat (above 1,000°C), so the regulation of the kilns' temperature depended upon the tacit knowledge of the 'fireman', and his ability to observe the colour and quantity of the coal.

Josiah was working on a solution with what he first called the 'colour thermoscope'.[2] He believed that heat could be measured by the changes in the colour of clay specimens during firing, and designed a glass tube with a graduated scale that could hold small clay pellets, which, when fired at different temperatures, yielded colours from beige to dark brown. Josiah tried to calibrate this range of colours to a particular temperature of the oven. His interpretation of the oven's temperature was based on examining the colour of the clay pellets.

He submitted a paper explaining his method to the Royal Society (the oldest and most prestigious scientific society in Britain) in December 1781, but its president, Sir Joseph Banks, criticised the technique for the difficulties of distinguishing different shades of colour and the loose correlation between that and particular degrees of heat. But Josiah was not discouraged. He returned to his laboratory, sought help from Joseph Priestley, James Watt and others, and after many trials and experiments, invented a new measuring device, which he called the 'pyrometer'. It was made of a porcelain gauge of his own construction which held specifically sized clay pellets that shrunk during firing according to the degree of heat that passed through them, a correlation that yielded acceptably consistent results.

In May 1782, Josiah submitted a revised paper to the Royal Society describing his new invention. This time, Banks, who praised Josiah for having 'turned the art of Pottery into a Science', accepted its scientific conclusions, and almost exactly on his fifty-second birthday, Josiah was elected a Fellow of the Royal Society.[3] It was the most prestigious appointment of his life – a perfect reward for a career committed to the scientific improvement of his craft, and his enduring quest to discover through experimentation the hidden principles of nature.

Josiah felt honoured to receive this appointment – not least since he had found in Sir Joseph Banks a new friend and enthusiastic patron (sending Josiah samples of earth he collected during his travels with Captain Cook). But he was equally pleased to have come up with a device that further mechanised production. Anything to remove the unreliability of human judgment, any way of transferring skill from a person to a machine, was beneficial in the eyes of the master. The workers, however, feeling their jobs more at risk with each technological improvement, reacted differently to such innovations.

On a chilly October morning in 1779, 'a most riotous and outrageous Mob' gathered outside Richard Arkwright's cotton mill in Matlock, on the west bank of the River Derwent, 'armed in a warlike Manner', according to a witness who testified in front of Parliament. They broke down the doors of the workshops, stormed in and smashed the new spinning machines and retreated only after torching the buildings.[4] They then left to hunt down and destroy other manufactories.

Josiah happened to be in Lancashire at precisely this time. From Bolton, to the north-west of Manchester, he heard the distant beating of a drum leading the march of, he was told, a force of rioters now 8,000 strong. They had spent the last few days gathering more firearms and ammunition, 'melting their pewter dishes into bullets'. Already there was bloodshed. During an attack on another mill, in nearby Chorley, 'two of the mob were shot dead upon the spot, one drown'd, & several wounded'. Reinforcements from the militia in Liverpool and Yorkshire were called in, but one factory owner, Sir Richard Clayton, attempted to defend his property with fifty hired men. They were no match, and were forced to watch 'whilst the mob completely destroy'd a set of mills valued at £10,000'. This was a determined mob, barrelling down the road just behind Josiah as he hurried back to Etruria. Their 'profess'd design', he learned, 'was to take Bolton, Manchester & Stockport in their way to Crumford, & to destroy all the engines, not only in these places, but throughout all England'.

The workers' situations had already been badly affected by the downturn in trade caused by the war with America. The local landowners – it was alleged in a later newspaper report – may have been slow to come to the defence of the manufacturers since they feared that the poor rates would be burdened with unemployed workers displaced by new inventions. In despair, the labourers assembled to destroy the machines that caused them distress.

The government demanded answers as to what was happening and set up a parliamentary committee to weigh the arguments of the workers and industrialists. The industrialists won, arguing that the economic advantages of the new machinery not only benefited the state, but would in turn benefit the workers since the machines helped expand the trade, ultimately offering more jobs to those willing to work them. But this was precisely what had motiv- ated Wedgwood's men to strike. They may have been promised employment, but – the workers were beginning to feel – it was deskilled, and therefore easily dispensable, work.

The all-round worker, once trained to see the manufacturing process through from clod of earth to packaged product, was rapidly becoming extinct, replaced by the specialist worker who occupied a particular spot in the division of labour, now the basis of modern business. This approach also limited the scope for industrial espion- age since the specialist worker, knowledgeable only in specific aspects of the production line, was not worth bribing to relinquish secrets.

It was because factories were becoming mechanised that visitors were strictly limited in what they were allowed to see of the secret operations inside. While ever conscientious about protecting his trade secrets – especially surrounding the scientific formula of jasper – Josiah occasionally dropped his guard. Not long after finalising its composition, he sent jasper portrait medallions to the portrait modeller Joachim Smith, who had associations with William Duesbury, owner of the Derby porcelain works and the person Josiah felt was the biggest threat to the future success of jasper. How much, Josiah wondered, had Smith 'learnt from seeing our things, & the free conversation we have had with him upon these subjects'. And how much, he shuddered to think, was he telling Duesbury.

Suspicions were further aroused when, weeks later, 'a Man from the Derby China works' visited Etruria, ostensibly seeking employment, though Wedgwood was sure that he was 'sent to learn something from us'. His application was denied, and it became a matter of policy to carefully direct the gaze of all visitors to Etruria to designated areas. This frustrated the gentry, who had previously enjoyed their freedom to roam and see the ingenious processes at work, and gave some commentators even more cause to be suspicious about the origins of new wealth. Everything is 'wrapped up in mysterious darkness', complained Pastor Frederick Wendeborn, when later writing his *View of England* (1791), 'and I have been told, that even not all the directors themselves are admitted behind the curtain, or shewn the Caves of Plutus, where the treasures of the Company are deposited'. What were they hiding? What was so special about a machine, an engine, or any mechanical contrivance, such visitors wondered, not yet grasping that these were no mere nut and bolt items of furniture but devices with previously inconceivable capabilities to harness the hidden powers of nature. Others, of course, knew well that there was something special going on behind closed doors. 'We have had several foreigners here lately,' Josiah had written to Bentley the year before his death, '& most of them extremely anxious after the composition of the black of which we make our vases & busts, & quite hurt & disappointed when they are told we do not shew that part of the manufactory.'[5]

Workers meanwhile had their own reasons for being 'delusioned' (as Josiah put it) into thinking that there was a conspiracy against them. By some accounts, it might appear that they were correct: their freedom to move in the labour marketplace was being deliberately manipulated to protect industrial trade. The General Chamber of Commerce even advocated legislation to prevent the emigration of skilled workers who might be enticed by promises of a better life, in terms of wages and working conditions. This too concerned Josiah, who, following another outbreak of rioting, this time close to Etruria, in Newcastle-under-Lyme, in 1783, issued an *Address to the Workers in the Pottery on the Subject of Entering into the Service of Foreign Manufacturers.*

Lest anyone contemplate emigrating, enticed by seductive stories of life abroad, Josiah felt compelled to inform them of the terrible consequences that had befallen others. Consider John Bartham, the young potter who left Staffordshire to set up his own factory in South Carolina. He spent three months sailing the rough seas to America, arriving debilitated and capable only of watching his men fall sick and die around him. Englishmen, Josiah stated (following a medical theory expressed by the physician John Arbuthnot among others), susceptible to changes in weather and climate, would inevitably be struck down by 'a disease of the mind, peculiar to people in a strange land; a kind of heart sickness and despair, with an unspeakable longing after their native country'. That there was money to be made was a figment of the imagination; most workers were left in strange foreign lands facing the 'hard necessity of begging in the streets'.

Contrast this to life in Staffordshire, Josiah continued, 'a land truly *flowing with milk and honey*'. Life was rapidly improving thanks to the new factory system. 'Ask your parents for a description of the country we inhabit when they first knew it,' Josiah urged. 'Their houses were miserable huts; the lands poorly cultivated and yielded little value for the food of man or beast.' Today, look at the change. 'The workmen earning nearly double their former wages – their houses mostly new and comfortable' – a point to be particularly stressed and celebrated since he himself had built a model community for his employees. What could be the cause of complaint, considering that 'Industry has been the parent of this happy change – A well directed and long continued series of industrious exertions'? Of course, it was no gentrified life, as Josiah's now was; the employees could never afford to purchase one of Wedgwood's wares, they could only make them, which only contributed further to their sense of alienation. Things were getting better, Josiah argued. Could they not see what was happening, he wondered?

Not everybody needed convincing that the industrial landscape was bearing healthy fruit; one visitor even wrote to Josiah praising Etruria as 'that paradise'. This description chimed with Josiah's visions for the community he had set up at Etruria, for he, like many of his enlightened friends – industrialists, doctors or natural philosophers – believed that society was inestimably improvable, 'perfectable' even.

That was a sentiment that found expression in American republicanism after independence had been won, which translated into what was called 'republican technology', with people such as Thomas Jefferson and Benjamin Franklin insisting upon the interrelationship of freedom, industriousness and virtue. The revolutions – political, scientific and industrial – were fundamentally transforming the world into that utopian future that had been so passionately dreamt of decades earlier when Josiah, Bentley, Priestley, Franklin and all the others first set out on their respective journeys.

It remained a vision that Josiah was willing to articulate, but privately he was growing despondent. With all the success, wealth, and expansion of the factory, he knew that the spectre of disease still haunted the hills. 'Potter's rot', or silicosis, remained the principal cause of death amongst pottery workers, a sign that the air was contaminated with vile particles, whether from rubbing mould lines off dry figures, smashing imperfect wares, grinding flint and lead, or breathing in the thick atmosphere of coal smoke.

Josiah had hoped that Priestley's pioneering experiments on air might provide a remedy. In Priestley's 1782 book *Experiments and Observations on Air* – experiments which followed on from his discovery of the difference between different atmospheric gases, leading to the isolation (or 'discovery') of oxygen in 1776 – he announced that he could manufacture air that could be purified in such a way so as to 'prepare it for respiration'.[6] Erasmus Darwin, who had been following Priestley's experiments with much interest, had begun his own course of experiments with air, looking for ways it might be used as an antiseptic for the lungs to cure diseases (including consumption and potter's rot), and was soon prescribing '6 gallons of pure oxygene a day' to his consumptive patients.

When Josiah read Priestley's book, it started him thinking. 'May not Dr Priestley's experiments of producing pure air be applied to the improving or changing of the air of sick rooms or hospitals?' he wrote.[7] It was easy to imagine all the other places that would benefit from having pure air pumped into them: school rooms came to mind, as well as ships and factories. He even asked Priestley for the estimated cost of supplying air to Etruria, but they were stumped on the design of such an apparatus. One solution Priestley devised was to impregnate water with 'fixed air', creating carbonated water which he offered to the navy as a probable cure for scurvy (an idea that soon caught the attention of a Swiss gentleman named Jacob Schweppe).[8]

The 'aerial solution' to atmospheric pollution was an idea in gestation which would be pursued over the next decade. In the meantime, Josiah had to assure his workers that things would get better and until this time to rely on their 'sick club', the scheme by which workers 'lay by a little money whilst they are in health & can spare it, & receive it again in time of sickness', something which Josiah had seen in operation at Boulton's factory, as well as in the 'Female Clubs' when earlier travelling in Cornwall.[9]

In the spring of 1786, Sally and Josiah's faith in science and medicine and the 'perfectibility' of the world was soundly shaken. After emotionally taxing trials of electrocution and years of opium dosing to help ease her repeated convulsions, seven-year-old Mary Anne became very ill with a deep fever. On 4 April, Sally and Josiah called in Darwin, but even he seems to have been at a loss to determine what to do with the girl. 'If the ague does not weaken her very much,' he said, 'I should give her no medicine at all (not even a vomit), except she wants some natural evacuation, a stool daily. If it should continue a month I should then advise to put an issue in the thigh of the affected side.'[10] The ague did continue, but Mary Anne did not last a month. She died on 21 April 1786.

Sally and Sukey took the loss harder than Josiah, who seemed to have become stoical about death. He spent little time outwardly grieving, choosing instead to bury himself in his workshop, where he engaged in one last project.

THIRTY-TWO

'Some plan of life'

O N THE FRASCATI ROAD, a short distance from Rome, was a tumulus known as Monte del Grano. Inside the mound was a secret sepulchre, leading to three chambers above it. In the largest of these was a sarcophagus, carved with groups of warriors and horses, and an inscription dedicated to the memory of Emperor Alexander Severus and his mother, Julia Mamae, both of whom met their death during a revolt led by Maximinus the Thracian in AD 235. The sixteenth-century antiquary who discovered the sarcophagus prised it open and found what looked like a cinerary urn, with a decoration in relief portraying the young emperor and his mother.

This was one story in the history of the vase that ended up in the library of Cardinal Francesco Barberini, nephew of Pope Urban VIII. The vase appeared to be black, but when held up against the sun it was shown to be a translucent dark blue, leading people to believe that it was carved from onyx. It was not large, under ten inches in height and seven inches wide, but its mysterious history and qualities made the 'Barberini Vase' a much-desired object when it was put on sale by the Princess of Palestrina in 1780 when she was in need of money to pay off her gambling debts.[1]

It was purchased by James Byers, a Scottish dealer in antiquities who had been in Rome for forty years, and who knew Sir William Hamilton well. When Sir William saw the vase in Byers' collection in 1783, the inveterate collector was awestruck. 'Is it yours,' he asked, 'will you sell it?'[2] Byers agreed to do so, but would only accept the staggering sum of £1,000, which Sir William promptly paid, 'tho' God knows it was not very convenient at that Moment'.

Soon after making the brazen decision to pay out such an extravagant sum for the vase, Sir William found himself in financial difficulties and forced to send the vase to his niece, Mary Hamilton, in London, in the hope that she might sell it on his behalf. As a former lady-in-waiting to Queen Charlotte, she was well placed to find a rich buyer, and interest in the vase was virtually immediate. It started with the Queen, who desired to see the vase but made no overtures to purchase it. Another regular visitor to Court, however, the Duchess of Portland, was captivated. Through her extensive European travels she had formed her own museum of natural history specimens, rare manuscripts and medals. Looking to add some Etruscan vases, she had already bought a number of treasures from Sir William, but the Barberini vase would be the centrepiece of her cabinet. He offered it to her with two other items: 'the Vase, the Head of Jupiter & my Picture of Correggio are the cream of all the Virtu I have ever possessed in my life', asking £4,000 for the lot. At the beginning of 1784, the Duchess snapped it up.[3]

Sadly, the Duchess did not enjoy the vase for long, for she died the following year, and her estate, including her precious cabinet of curiosities, was sold at auction. Given Sir William's opinion that 'I do not believe that there are any monuments of Antiquity existing that were executed by so great an artist', it is not surprising that the vase caught the attention of London artists, such as John Flaxman, who brought it to Josiah's attention. 'I wish you may soon come down to see William Hamilton's Vase', Flaxman wrote to Josiah, for whom he had been doing some work; 'it is the finest production of Art that has been brought to England and seems to be the very apex of perfection to which you are endeavouring to bring your bisque & jasper.'

Josiah was not the only person interested in the vase. The Duchess's son, the third Duke of Portland, was determined to get hold of it and, hearing of Josiah's interest in it, devised a plan to ward off any competition from this quarter. He offered Josiah the loan of the vase for study and copying so long as he did not bid at the auction. That Josiah was wealthy enough to threaten to outbid a duke on an item of ancient antiquity is remarkable testimony to his success, but Josiah was not committed to owning the piece, and probably agreed that it was only fair that it be kept in the Duchess's family. His principal interest was to imitate it and he therefore only needed it for a relatively short period of time. Josiah was happy merely to have the vase on loan, as was agreed in June 1786.

'I begin to count how many different ways the vase itself may be copied to suit the tastes, the wants & the purses of different purchasers,' Josiah wrote to William Hamilton, wasting no time in devising a scheme for its reproduction.[4] Like other unique and challenging pieces – whether Queen's Charlotte's first order of creamware or Catherine the Great's Frog Service – he knew that reproducing what he now called the 'Portland Vase' would be time-consuming and expensive. He had already hired a modeller named Henry Webber, who according to Sir Joshua Reynolds was 'esteemed the first in his profession in England', but it would take a team of modellers, engravers, mould makers and other artists to make the fine white bas-relief figures and patterns that would decorate the vase.

He estimated a cost of no less than £5,000 for all the 'best artists capable of the work', if they cared to spend the time mastering the techniques involved. Josiah had repeatedly mentioned how difficult jasper was to work with – how delicate the wet clay was when worked thinly to imitate Chinese porcelain – but jasper had 'a property peculiar to itself', he wrote, 'which fits it perfectly for this imitation', since the dark blue, translucent effect could be attained in the same way as his popular light blue jasper ware, the tint darkened merely by the amount of cobalt used in its production.

Josiah had already tried to make an imitation of it based on an engraving, 'but now that I can indulge myself with full and repeated examinations of the original work itself, my crest is much fallen'. He confessed his initial shortcomings to Sir William, from whom he sought some 'advice & directions' on his plan. The more Josiah studied the vase, the more he found that 'the form of this vase is not so elegant as it might be made'. It seemed the primary feature of the vase was its bas-relief decoration, and he speculated that there had been two artists working on the original: a talented sculptor who carved the precious white figures, and 'another artist, of an inferior class', who seemed to have difficulty working with the material from which the vase was made, which many thought was enamel. Would it, he wondered, be appropriate to render the vase more elegant – more simple and true to the principles of ancient beauty as propagated by Sir William and other *virtuosi*. In essence, would it be acceptable to *improve* on a celebrated piece of ancient art?

Sir William thought not. 'I admire your Enthusiasm on the frequent & close examination of the Vase,' he told Josiah, '& am happy that its superior merit is felt by some few in England.'[5] However, while he conceded that there were some 'little defects' in the production of the original vase, 'it would be dangerous to touch that', he said, preferring to see an exact copy of the vase to help 'diffuse the seeds of good taste'.[6] Josiah gracefully accepted the advice, and set to work on the long process of exact reproduction.

Working on the Portland Vase gave Josiah the perfect opportunity to introduce Joss, now nineteen, to the different stages of high-end manufacturing – to teach him that innovative skills are developed slowly through trial and error. Jack meanwhile was in Europe, on a Grand Tour under the supervision of Henry Webber and John Flaxman. Josiah hoped Jack would benefit from being immersed in Italy's artistic culture, that it would polish his liberal education and give him the chance to 'fix ultimately upon some plan of life'. Josiah had sent Webber and Flaxman with him, not only to supervise his eldest son, but to explore the possibility of setting up an artists' studio there.

Fifteen-year-old Tom was now studying at Edinburgh University, long a haven for wealthy Dissenters, where Josiah wanted him to receive the best scientific education available in the country. Erasmus Darwin had sent his son, Robert, to medical school there three years earlier, before enrolling him at the more prestigious University of Leiden where he received his MD. Tom was easily distracted at Edinburgh. He was excited to join the newly founded Philological Society, 'in which I must exert all my oratory powers'. And as Josiah predicted, Tom pursued experimental science too with enthusiasm. 'I wish to have some chemical books,' Tom wrote to his father at the end of 1786, '& want only a list of what we have at home & permission to buy others. I think I shall be able with a good deal of reading improve myself greatly in this Science.'[7] But Tom did a little bit of everything. He stayed after class and discussed medicine with the popular professor Joseph Black, and learned geology from the famous natural historian James Hutton. When Tom returned to Etruria, Josiah hired the brilliant young Edinburgh mathematician John Leslie as his private tutor in natural philosophy. It was an indulgence that Josiah hoped would begin to lead Tom to productive habits.

Sukey was now twenty-one, and a woman of considerable charm and beauty. She took after her mother in her interest in politics and literature, and, like her father, had a talent for being thoughtful and provocative in her letters. By 1786, she was travelling down to London to socialise with the *ton*, at one point teasing her father about drawing-room gossip regarding her family's religious and political principles. They 'cannot be right', Sukey wrote, 'or you would not be acquainted with such a man as – as – Dr Darwin – as for her Ladyship [Lady Clive, her hostess], she would rather die than have his advice if there was no another physician in the world'.[8]

Catherine and Sarah, the two youngest daughters, were only just turning twelve and ten respectively, and were following in their older sister's footsteps, being educated at Etruria and spending all their time with Sally and a dozen servants, from butler to maids to a coachman. After building works in 1780, when symmetrical north and south wings were added, Etruria Hall was, as William Wilberforce (a visitor with whom Josiah shared a disgust for slavery) described, 'rather grand, Pictures, &c'.[9] The paintings were by Reynolds, Wright and Stubbs; an elaborate allegorical subject was painted on a salon ceiling by Flaxman, and carved chimneypieces were inset with Josiah's own fine jasper tablets. In décor alone, their home was certainly grand, with each ornamental display reflecting the attention to detail and elegance that characterised Etruria's output. The idea of moving the finest of the wares from the factory to the home was Sally's, indicative of a discerning style that had long been an influence on Josiah. As Josiah had earlier admitted to Bentley: 'I speak from experience in Female taste, without which I should have made but a poor figure amongst my Potts, not one of which, of any consequence, is finished without the approbation of my Sally.'[10]

Josiah and Joss spent much of their time throughout the next year in the workshops and the laboratory. It was the most intimately Josiah had worked with anyone since Sally took notes for him when they were first married. They were struggling to get their imitation Portland Vase just right – to get the precise shade of dark blue, to prevent the thinly thrown vase from collapsing or blistering in the intense heat of the kiln. As Josiah had anticipated, it was frustratingly difficult, and the long hours soon exhausted him.

'My great work is the Portland Vase', Josiah stubbornly insisted, wanting to put off the second stage of a prescription that the eminent London physician William Heberden gave him in answer to Josiah's complaint about a pain in his head and 'a general weakness'.[11] He had already been blistered and sent to 'rest' in London, where he and Sally managed to find some time alone in the apartment above the Greek Street showroom, now under Tom Byerley's management. But he finally conceded that he had to leave the finishing touches to Joss, who wrote regular updates on his progress and the daily management of Etruria.

Never at rest, Josiah took the opportunity while in London to contemplate the best way to publicise his vases. He thought about how he could use its fascinating history to his advantage. He decided that he should start collecting 'all the explications of this vase that have hitherto been published, which I mean to print and deliver with the copies of the vase, that the purchaser may see the whole that has been said upon it, in a small compass'.[12] Calling on all his literary and antiquarian connections to help, he began reading through all the reference works he could lay his hands on, searching for anything 'that I can find quoted or containing any mention of it', taking notes, for instance, from d'Hancarville's *Collection of Etruscan, Greek, and Roman Antiquities*, Montfaucon's, *L'Antiquité expliqueé* (which Joss transcribed for him), Caylus's *Recueil d'antiquités* and others. In a letter to Sir William Hamilton he listed twenty sources he had already consulted, hoping that Sir William might suggest some yet unknown to him, which might especially inform the debate regarding the fable represented in relief on the vase. It was ironic that Josiah was preparing a lesson in classical antiquity to be provided for the enlightenment of his aristocratic – classically Oxbridge-educated – customers.

Writing his letter to Sir William, Josiah took the opportunity to thank him for receiving Jack when he arrived in Naples. Jack had been much impressed by the Grand Tour, during which he had collected some busts from Sir William's collection which he sent home to Etruria, and in line with his father's wishes, he was beginning to 'fix upon some plan' of life, but not quite what Josiah had anticipated. In 1788, Jack wrote to his father declaring his intention to stand for Parliament, 'unconnected with any party'. Josiah found it hard to hide his disappointment. Of his three sons, he had hoped that Jack, the eldest, would 'take some time to consider your own inclination before you gave your final determination', namely, to forgo entering the family trade, but Jack's 'aversion to the business' remained.[13]

Josiah, clearly annoyed but careful not to lose his temper, hoped that Jack would return home from the Continent with a different outlook, 'as I believed the ideas upon which that aversion was founded were taken up in your travels'. That same month, Josiah reached a decision about 'the proposed scheme of Tom going to Rome'. Josiah was beginning to worry about Tom's own lack of a 'plan of life' and his restlessness. Having received Henry Webber's opinion that 'the degree of knowledge he has acquired of the arts . . . has not yet a sufficient stock to be exported to Rome', Josiah decided it was best to keep him under closer supervision, a decision which sent nineteen-year-old Tom into a petulant fit.[14] Even more worrying for Josiah was that the only son who was showing an interest in pottery, Joss junior, was changing his tune as well.

Joss was making progress on the Portland Vase and reported on each new attempt as it came out the kiln, writing critical comments about how the modellers 'undercut' the moulds for the pattern. Josiah was impressed with his son's developing skills. He had recently received a flowerpot which Joss produced entirely on his own, and which Josiah thought 'is very well executed & a very good thing'. 'These two articles do you credit as a potter, & will help you to gain our confidence on future orders.' Josiah studied the details of the piece – the application of the gilt, the shape of the handles, the form of the pot's 'feet'. 'Such little touches and finishings shew the master in works of art,' he told Joss, 'as minute attentions in behaviour shew the well bred man & polite gentleman.'[15] The problem was, Joss preferred to live the life of a polite gentleman rather than a master artist.

Like Tom, Joss wanted to travel, to be a gentleman engaged in pleasures of the imagination rather than as the agent on business Josiah hoped he would become. When Tom Byerley fell ill and

Josiah asked Joss to stand in, he agreed, then worried his father might misinterpret his commitment. 'What I mean,' Joss wrote to his father, 'is that I would live in the house and take care of the correspondence while Mr B is unfit for it, and do what other business I could, except attending in the rooms any farther than waiting upon some particular people,' adding, 'I have been too long in the habit of looking upon myself as the equal of everybody to bear the haughty manners of those who come into the shop.'[16] The last thing Joss wanted was to be seen working behind a shop counter.

Useful Tom was fifty-four years old, four years younger than Josiah, and had worked as a potter for the last thirty years. For twenty-two of these he had been in partnership with Josiah, receiving from him an eighth of the firm's profits, and during that time he proved he could solidly manage the useful works and keep the cash coming in while Josiah and Bentley dreamt up extravagantly expensive ornamental wares, for much greater public recognition. He and his wife Mary had one daughter and three sons.

In 1788, he told Josiah he was ready to retire, that he was planning on moving to the Hill Works in Burslem, owned by his father-in-law, to see out the rest of his days, looking after the future of his children. They agreed that his partnership would end eight weeks later, on 11 November 1788. But with one month to go came the shocking news that Useful Tom had been found drowned in the canal. He was buried with the other Wedgwood potters in the churchyard at St John's.

Josiah was too tired to manage the entire business of which he was now sole proprietor by himself. Therefore, 'to ease myself of increasing care in the decline of life', Josiah gave his three sons and Tom Byerley their own shares in the business. Jack, Joss and Tom were each given a quarter share, while Josiah and Byerley split the remaining quarter. The firm was now known as Josiah Wedgwood, Sons, and Byerley. 'By this division of the burden,' said Josiah, 'I hope it will become light to each of us, at least a little less to my share,' and underlining that their share of the profits required them to put in hard work.

1789 had been an eventful year. After three years' work, he and Joss had finally perfected the Portland Vase, and one of the first good copies was sent to Erasmus Darwin, with whom Josiah reflected on the latest war to threaten political stability in Europe. 'I know you will rejoice with me in the glorious revolution which has taken place in France,' he wrote to Darwin just after the fall of the Bastille. 'The politicians tell me that as a manufacturer I shall be ruined if France has her liberty, but I am willing to take my chance in that respect.'[17] Life, Josiah knew, was full of gambles. Despite the uncertainties surrounding his sons' future interest in the business, he now came to the conclusion that the time was right to find 'a little more quiet for myself'.

THIRTY-THREE

'A Giant Malady'

'A FTER AN UNREMITTING ATTENTION of nearly forty years
to a manufactory which I have had the happiness to establish, and to see flourish beyond my most sanguine expectations,'
Josiah announced to his customers in a printed handbill, he wished
'to enjoy that ease and relaxation from the severity of business,
so necessary in advanced years.'[1] He would turn sixty this year,
1790.

The Portland Vase had been another instant success, gaining
publicity of the sort that Josiah was now accustomed to each time
he 'surprised the world' with a new product. Sir Joshua Reynolds,
Sir Joseph Banks and Sir William Hamilton had all publicly praised
it, and the historical painter Benjamin West selected the vase as
one of the objects illustrating the theme 'Etruria' in his painting
*Genius calling forth the Fine Arts to adorn Manufactures and Commerce,
and recording the names of eminent men in these pursuits* (1791). The
Portland Vase would become an icon of Etruria's achievements.

After Erasmus Darwin received a Wedgwood copy of the vase
and learned of his good friend's retirement plans he wasted no time
composing his own story about the progress of the arts, writing a
poem to celebrate Josiah's successes. Josiah was touched. 'You have
been extremely happy in describing the particular excellencies of
the ancient Etruscan potters,' Josiah wrote; 'whether your prophecies
respecting the productions of modern Etruria be as true . . . it will
take some time to discover.'[2] Indeed, though content to bask in

glory for the moment, Josiah was increasingly worried about the future of 'modern Etruria'.

Jack returned to England in 1790 unchanged in his 'aversion' to taking over the business his father had spent his life creating. In fact, as Joss admitted, Jack 'disliked' the idea 'very much'.[3] Josiah was disappointed but willing to support him in his chosen career path, and helped him buy a partnership in the new London banking firm of Alexander Davidson & Co.

Tom appeared ever more disgruntled about the direction his own life was heading, and had developed a tendency to disappear into his room at Etruria Hall and write long, philosophical letters. 'I know my father is afraid of secluding myself too much from the world, & becoming too hermetical,' he wrote to his brother Joss; 'I can only say that I think it would be greatly to the advantage of most young people to pass three or four most important years of their life, in a calm retired manner.'[4] That year, nineteen-year-old Tom proposed that he move out of Etruria Hall and into one of the houses in Etruria village with his Edinburgh friend John Leslie. However Josiah was far from keen on the proposed arrangement.

Writing from London, Josiah conceded that 'an uninterrupted intercourse & conversation with a man of Mr L's extensive learning' could be useful, and he certainly supported the idea of serious study, he worried that Tom was sacrificing family life and sociability to do it. 'Even knowledge itself,' said Josiah, 'if received in exchange for the blessings of society & the family charities would be dearly bought.'

Tom did not give up. He picked up a blank invoice sheet from his father's office at Etruria when Sally and Josiah were still in London and penned an emotional note. Under the letterhead 'BOUGHT OF JOSIAH WEDGWOOD: POTTER TO HER MAJESTY', Tom scribbled:

I am well aware that the next three or four years of my life are the most important ... our passions & affections are all to be moderated & corrected, in the season of youth – whilst the wax is yet capable of receiving impressions – in this crucial moment, I shall strive hard to fashion myself so that I may best perform the grand dutys of this life – I reflect every day on the relation between the creator & creature & hope by these instructive speculations to arrive at the knowledge of the purpose of creation & hence of what these dutys consist. The Question is extremely intricate & comprehensive ... You perceive my tendency to retirement & are uneasy to trust me from under your eyes.[5]

This time, Tom's neo-Lockean, Puritan appeal persuaded Josiah. Tom and his friend were given permission to set up home, providing they do it economically 'with the plainest possible furniture'. Tom was delighted. 'I am happy that some of my arguments have had some weight.'[6] To prove that it was the right move, Tom showed unusual dedication to a particular course of study, and with John Leslie's help, engaged in detailed experiments on the chemical action of light. He wrote up the results of his experiments in two papers which he submitted to the Royal Society, which were published the next year in the Society's prestigious *Philosophical Transactions*. Tom knew this would impress his father, and Josiah could not help but be proud of his boy.

Joss remained, for the time, at Etruria, managing the factory and writing to his father with new ideas for wares they should produce. He learned quickly, and had his father's sense of timing and politics. In July the previous year, 1789, he had asked Josiah if they should start producing something 'which should relate to the late revolution in France & to the support given to public credit by the national assembly? What do you think of a figure of public faith on an altar & France embracing Liberty in the front?'[7]

Josiah again thought that Joss was adapting perfectly to the business – showing the right instinct for providing mementos of an historical moment, objects which in circulation became pieces of propaganda – and they soon started the manufacture of jasper medallions with relief emblems symbolic of the Revolution, 'a cornucopia, a bonnet of liberty on a stick and an olive branch contained within a fleur-de-lis border'.[8]

The French Revolution became a central topic of discussion in Josiah's letters to Erasmus Darwin, now his principal correspondent besides Joss. Darwin and Josiah both celebrated the French Revolution, believing it a just political expression to dispense with a tyrannical regime in favour of equality amongst human kind. In a long poem which Darwin was writing on the history of the world, he waxed lyrical about the progress made in the history of humanity in which he honoured scientific achievements such as Wedgwood's Etruria factory, the 'liberation of America', and finally the French Revolution, where the 'Giant-form of Liberty' had long

> *Inglorious slept, unconscious of his chains;*
> *Round his large limbs were wound a thousand strings*
> *By the weak hands of Confessors and Kings . . .*
> *Touch'd by the patriot-flame, he rent amazed*
> *The flimsy bonds, and round and round him gazed.*[9]

But democrats such as Josiah and Darwin found events following the Revolution disturbing, not least when a close family friend was the target of a brutal assault owing to his apparent support for the events abroad.

In 1791, what the Reverend J. Bartlam described as the 'bunting, beggarly, brass-making, brazen-faced, brazen-hearted, blackguard, bustling, booby Birmingham mob'[10] was indeed agitated. They had heard that a dinner celebrating the French Revolution was being held at a Birmingham hotel. To the mob, these royalty-hating unbelievers posed a threat to the pillars of established society. They believed the seeds of revolution were being sown in the fiery landscape around them, fuelled by the bubbling chemicals and moon-lit meetings of radical freethinkers – Dissenters with Republican principles.

'A storm is gathering, depend upon it,' the Whig curate of Hatton, Dr Samuel Parr, had written, ever vigilant of events unfolding in Birmingham. On the night of the infamous dinner, slogans were scrawled on building walls proclaiming 'destruction to the Presbyterians' and 'Church and King forever'. From inside the hotel chants of 'no Popery' were heard and a crowd, 'some hundreds' strong, gathered in the streets. The mob began marching to a nearby village, to Fair Hill, in Sparkbrook. This was no factory, Dissenting chapel, or industrial estate. In their eyes, this was a more seditious and dangerous place. They were heading for the home and laboratory of Josiah and Erasmus Darwin's friend, Dr Joseph Priestley.

Priestley's reputation as an experimental philosopher had spread internationally since his days at the Warrington Academy. For over twenty years he had buried himself in philosophical books, sur-rounded by scientific apparatus with which to conduct experiments. His laboratory instruments included an air pump, a selection of microscopes, and an 'electrical machine' ('a pretty good machine' he assured others), which he used to generate sparks, dissolve water into gases, and ponder what Newton was only able to describe as a kind of 'aether', a mysterious universal fluid, the 'electric fire' that Wedgwood, Darwin, and many others interested in the secrets of nature were experimenting with.

Priestley's experiments seemed immediately promising, and Josiah had long recognised their potential benefits to his own craft. 'I am much pleased with your disquisition upon the *Capabilities* of Electricity,' he had written.[11] If he could contribute anything 'towards rendering Doctr. Priestleys very ingenious experiments' more useful, he was always eager to do so.

Throughout the 1760s and 1770s, Priestley, Josiah and Bentley were in correspondence about a range of applications of electricity, including its use 'to decorate . . . tea boards and baubles', something useful not only to Wedgwood but to Boulton as well. Another potential area of interest was Priestley's work on adding a 'metallic tinge to glass', leading Josiah to wonder whether he could conduct 'experiments relating to gilding by Electricity'. In fact, Boulton was the one to come up with a useful technique for that some years later, but it was the endless possibilities, the wonder of the unknown, explored by Priestley's 'delightful and ingenious researches into the secrets of nature' that so appealed to Josiah.[12] His enthusiasm for Priestley's experiments turned into practical support for the chemist, something for which Priestley was decidedly grateful. 'Such is the interest in philosophical discoveries,' he wrote to Josiah, 'and such are my numerous obligations to you with respect to those that I had in this business, that I cannot help giving you an early account of everything that I do.' Priestley owed Josiah a particular debt of gratitude not merely for his close attention to his work – subscribing to his work to aid publication and making copious marginal comments – but for his consideration in supplying him with apparatus with which to conduct his experiments. 'The Dr seems much at a loss for a mortar, not metal, for pounding in,' Josiah noted in his Commonplace Book – the large bound volume in which he reserved various, miscellaneous thoughts – while reading the latest account of Priestley's experiments. 'Make him a deep one or two.' In fact, over time Josiah supplied his experimentally oriented friends with a whole range of utilities made from 'compact hard porcelain': pestles and mortars, crucibles, and other chemical wares, which, when he later began marketing them, were described as 'excellently adapted also for evaporating pans, digesting vessels, basons, filtering funnels, siphons, tubes, such as Dr Priestley uses in some of his experiments', though Priestley received them gratis.

Josiah knew that science, Royal Society-style, was governed by great patronage. Priestly confirmed this view when conducting experiments with electricity and writing the history of achievements in that science: 'Natural philosophy is a science which more especially requires the aid of wealth.' Scientific progress 'provincial-style' was based on collaboration, trust, mutual solidarity, the exchange of apparatus and, most controversially, ideas. Priestley's experiments seemed to give birth to *dangerous* ideas, which made him the immediate object of the Birmingham mob's attack.

For years, Priestley had been feverishly analysing the properties of isolated gases and investigating their role in respiration. In gruesome detail, Priestley described his experiments on animals that were forced to breathe 'fixed air' (carbon dioxide), noting the different times it took for the life to expire in mice, frogs, and even flowers. Finally, after a decade of laboratory work, Priestley announced that he was now able to convert *'pure water* into *permanent air'* and that this new air could be purified in such a way so as to 'prepare it for respiration' by measuring the 'goodness' (capacity for respiration) of air.[13] Priestley was suggesting a way to manufacture a new atmosphere – a step closer to revitalising the stagnant or noxious air in schools and factories.

When the conservative MP Edmund Burke read about Priestley's experiments in 1790, while taking a break from writing his anti-Jacobin tract, *Reflections on the Revolution in France*, he was alarmed by what Priestley announced were the implications of his researches. Enlightened, experimental inquiry, said Priestley, was 'putting an end to all undue and usurped authority in the business of religion . . . and all the efforts of the interested friends of corrupt establishments of all kinds'. Lest anyone miss the point, Priestley spelled it out: 'the English hierarchy, if there be anything unsound in its constitution, has equal reason to tremble before an air pump, or an electrical machine' – the most familiar instruments found in a chemist's laboratory. For anyone who knew Priestley – the Unitarian champion of both the American and French Revolutions – there was little doubt that he already detected something constitutionally 'unsound' in the English hierarchy.

An agitated Burke quickly returned to writing and launched his *Reflections* with allusions to Priestley, where the aerated 'spirit of liberty' was likened to 'the wild *gas*, the fixed air [that] is plainly broke loose'. Who else, he wondered, was culpable of spreading such seditious, revolutionary ideas in society?

Suspicious eyes turned towards the Midlands. London prejudices had long catalogued the ways that provincial communities were inherently different from the metropolitan elite. Satirists mocked the Staffordshire dialect, suggesting locals did not know 'ow ter toke raight'. But throughout the century, they had watched as obscure manufacturers emerged from the rugged fields, were entertained at Court, bought political patronage, built walls to hide their scientific secrets, and propagated their radical philosophy of equality and freedom of thought.

Since the American Revolution, such mutterings had begun to sound all the more alarming, foreign and unpatriotic. Such were the perceived democratising effects of scientific practices that, especially after 1789, conservative critics were prompted to accuse French 'natural philosophers' – philosophers of nature – as being the culprits of the French Revolution, particularly chemists, who believed in gases rather than holy spirits, 'the *wrongs* of Providence, and the *rights* of man', as Erasmus Darwin boldly stated. Such expressions agitated the likes of Edmund Burke. 'The revolution in France is the grand ingredient in the cauldron,' he warned. If the chemists who in Britain were actively organising themselves into satellite scientific societies and labouring in their seditious laboratories had their way, they would disintegrate society, like the polluted air we breathe, into a 'chaos of elementary principles'.

Like the collapsed, convulsing cockatoo suffocating in a vacuum at the hands of the experimental scientist in Joseph Wright's *Bird in the Air Pump*, these philosophers – these 'fanatics' as Burke called them – 'would sacrifice the whole human race to the slightest of their experiments'.

Priestley was warned that a torch-waving mob, inflamed by

Anglican preachers and free drink, was descending on his house, and he fled with his family, having no time to gather any personal belongings. His home and laboratory were ransacked and razed to the ground, along with his manuscripts, library and scientific instruments. Everything, save his and his family's lives, was lost.[14]

'The Birmingham riots are a disgrace to mankind,' Darwin wrote to Josiah, but he was careful not to say more. He knew that Priestley's own words had incited the attack against him, and from then on Darwin and his friends were guarded in their opinions about France, science, and the Revolution. Who knew how much each of them had agreed with their friend Priestley. Josiah himself, when applauding Priestley's electrical experiments, had playfully declared 'But what daring mortals you are! To rob the Thunderer of his Bolts – & for what? – no doubt to blast the oppressors of the poor.'[15] Priestley's sentiment exactly. Who was to say that Etruria, or Darwin's Derby home, was not next on their list?

Wedgwood warned Joss to be vigilant at Etruria and Boulton and Watt armed their men at the Soho works. But the 'Church and King' riots snuffed out much of their enthusiasm for the latest act of 'liberation'.

Concerned for his family's safety, Priestley sent them off to America. With some financial help from Josiah and his other friends to help rebuild his life, Priestley soon followed his family, taking a job as Professor of Chemistry at 'a liberal college in the back settle-ments of America'.[16] Shortly before he set sail in April 1794, he wrote a note for the friends he was leaving behind. 'When the time for reflection shall come,' he said, 'my countrymen, I am confident, will do me justice.' Erasmus and Josiah wished they had as much confidence as Priestley. In fact, just as Priestley left, Josiah had heard that 'every name supposed to think different' from the government was put into a doomsday book, 'and that if the French land, these recorded gentlemen are to be all imprison'd'. Josiah had heard that his name was 'high on the list'.[17]

In 1794, twenty-nine-year-old Sukey and Erasmus Darwin's twenty-eight-year-old son, Robert, announced their engagement.

Sukey had been in and out of the Darwins' household since childhood, even giving Robert's older brother, Erasmus, music lessons. Erasmus junior was also infatuated with her. She was 'an accomplished lady', he wrote, congratulating his younger brother; she is someone 'I always much esteemed'.[18]

Their fathers were jubilant. Josiah and Erasmus's long friendship had grown stronger in the years after Bentley's death. Erasmus, once merely described as Sally's 'favorite Esculapius', had become Josiah's closest friend. The marriage would not be immediate, but knowing that one day their families would be united through their children gave Josiah a pleasure that could only have been surpassed if Bentley had had children whose names could have been added to the Wedgwood family tree.

Unfortunately Josiah's other children were not giving him as much pleasure. In 1792, eager to see the Bastille Day celebrations first-hand, Tom joined James Watt's son in Paris. James Watt junior was, according to Tom, 'a furious democrat – detests the king'. Tom's description of the events in France added no relief to their worry about their son's travels or the state of affairs in Europe. 'French politics are as mutable as the wind,' he said. 'Watt says that a new revolution must inevitably take place, & that it will in all probability be fatal to the King, Fayette, and some hundred others.'[19] This trip ignited a new passion for travel in Tom, and the next year he followed his older brother Jack's lead and formally resigned his partnership in the 'Wedgwood & Sons' firm.

Josiah worried about the future of the business. The only hope of keeping it in the family now rested solely with Joss, to whom the factory and all its contents were left in the will that Josiah drew up late in 1793.

Erasmus and Josiah agreed these were depressing times. As the 'liberation' of France turned into a regime of horror in 1794, their thoughts turned to the 'giant malady' that plagued their own lives.

As students of the Enlightenment holding Rousseau and Voltaire to be their heroes, Dissenters including Josiah and Darwin had long believed that by studying Nature they would effect a revolution in society not only empowering people to think and speak freely and allow humanity to prosper, but which would lead to a *healthier* world. Priestley's experiments on air gave them hopes for that, and Darwin himself pursued the medical benefits of administering pure oxygen to patients. Disappointingly, it was precisely where wealth was being created based on scientific innovation that the scourge of environmental disease persisted. It appeared that the ability to manufacture a physically healthier environment still eluded them. 'Nothing now remains' in the desire for money, lamented James Watt, 'as I find it can neither bring health nor happiness.'[20]

In the growing manufacturing regions across the world, consumption, the disease of the lungs that 'like war, cuts off the young in their prime of life', was rife. Josiah and Darwin's own friends and family were affected by it. Richard Lovell Edgeworth had just lost two children to consumption; Joseph Priestley's daughter was suffering from it, as was James Watt's daughter. Erasmus Darwin's daughter, Emma, had developed a 'nervous cough', and Tom, Josiah's own son, was suspected by Darwin of languishing from the disease. Josiah and Erasmus financially supported the research on the treatment of consumption by one Thomas Beddoes, a bright young doctor who had been thrown out of Oxford for his outspoken support of the French Revolution. 'In a future letter,' Beddoes wrote to Darwin, 'I hope to present you with a catalogue of diseases in which I have effected a cure.' But all such confidence evaporated for Darwin when he was summoned to Josiah's own sickbed.

THIRTY-FOUR

'Mix Again
with their Original Clay'

SHORTLY AFTER Sally and Josiah returned to Etruria from London in November 1794, Josiah complained of heart palpitations and general fatigue. Darwin prescribed a mixture of alum and nutmeg with ground rhubarb, along with water treatment at the spas in Buxton. He hoped 'taking the waters' would also help relieve pains he had in his joints which had been irritating him for some time. At first, it seemed to help.

'Your letter gives me great pleasure in assuring me, what your son Josiah had before mention'd, that you have become free from your complaint – the ceasing of the palpitation of your heart and of the intermission of your pulse is another proof of your increase in strength.' Josiah, however, was less sure about the progress of his convalescence, complaining to Darwin about shortness of breath as he climbed hills or stairs, fearing it was asthma. Darwin assured him it was merely his sixty-four years that was slowing him down. 'You know how unwilling we all are to grow old,' said the doctor, who recommended that Josiah leave off taking his medicine.[1] But his confidence was misjudged.

Days later Josiah was bed-bound. His face was swollen and he complained of acute pain in his jaw, which was attributed to a decayed tooth. When his trusted surgeon, James Bent, arrived to extract it, he found something much worse. He immediately sent for Darwin, saying that Josiah was showing signs of 'mortification', and needed urgent treatment.

Darwin rushed to Etruria Hall from Derby. There was nothing that he could do. He remained at Josiah's bedside with Sally. Jack and Tom returned to be with the family as did Tom Byerley, who arrived from London. Joss was joined by his wife and their eighteen-month-old daughter Sarah, Sally and Josiah's first grandchild. Sukey comforted her younger sisters and showed her strength of character. She had 'a distinct understanding and an excellent heart during her father's illness', Erasmus Darwin the younger wrote, who was there with his brother, Sukey's fiancé Robert.[2]

Josiah's health steadily deteriorated. 'For several days,' Tom Byerley told an old family friend, 'the physicians had declared he could not live two hours – such was the state of his pulse.'[3] His throat swelled and he developed an intermittent high fever. He could not talk – Darwin said it was because his jaw had rotted – but he was comforted by the presence of his friends and family. While not able to converse, he had a lifetime to reflect on: falling in love with Sally; plucking up the courage to approach Long John and Cousin Thomas to help him go into business on his own; the adrenalin and excitement he felt at being given the chance to produce a 'Sett of tea things' for the Queen; the sorrow of his brother John's drowning in the Thames; the thousands of dear and cherished letters he received from Bentley, and the care and smiles of his children as they now surrounded him.

On New Year's Day, 1795, he slipped into unconsciousness. Two days later, on Sukey's thirtieth birthday, Josiah Wedgwood died.

THIRTY-FIVE

Unremitting Fires

'THE DEATH OF Mr Wedgwood grieves me very much,' Darwin wrote to a friend. 'He is a public as well as private loss.'[1]

As such a well-known public figure, newspaper reports across Britain were quick to announce his passing – from the local *Aris's Birmingham Gazette* and *Derby Mercury* to the national *Times*. The eulogies praised both his professional career and his personal benevolence. He was 'possessed of great public spirit, and unremitting perseverance, with a mind fraught with general intelligence', said the *Staffordshire Advertiser*, while the *Gentleman's Magazine* commended his promotion of public utilities, such as the canal and turnpikes, and his employment of the 'deserving poor'.[2] He was ranked amongst the finest chemists by his contemporaries for his untiring and innovative scientific experiments which yielded such extraordinarily diverse results.[3]

When tourists floated down the Trent and Mersey Canal and passed by Etruria they were impressed at the sight of the modern factory built along its banks but knew more its special place in history. The buildings, noted John Aikin, in his travel guide to the area, 'constitute nearly the whole of the present fine English earthen wares and porcelain, which are now become the source of a very extensive trade, and which, considered as an object of national art, industry, and commerce, may be ranked amongst the most important manufactures of the kingdom'. Others agreed. The 'ingenious and industrious Wedgwood', wrote Samuel Parkes, a prominent nineteenth-century chemist, created a manufactory that became 'a national source of wealth'.[4]

Josiah's fame and reputation, as other commentators observed, was international. The Swiss traveller Faujas de St Fond remarked in 1797 that Wedgwood had created 'a commerce so active and universal, that in Travelling from Paris to St Petersberg, from Amsterdam to the farthest point of Sweden, from Dunkirk to the southern extremity of France, one is served at every inn from English earthenware. The same fine article adorns the tables of Spain, Portugal & Italy, and it provides the cargoes of ships to the East Indies, the West Indies and America.'[5] During his life, Josiah had dreamt of conquering the farthest shores. Once, he contemplated whether his wares could be taken by British diplomats and introduced to the market in China. He saw it happen before he died, when in 1793 Lord Macartney presented examples of Wedgwood's vases to the Emperor Qian Long.

Josiah was even more amazed, however, when Sir William Hamilton told him his Etruscan wares and other ornamental pieces were 'much admired' and were fetching high prices in Italy. Drawing inspiration from ancient Tuscany and selling his imitation pots back to the Italian marketplace was the ultimate coup.[6] In the eyes of some (though not Josiah's), it was even more flattering to see Wedgwood ware being imitated in Italy. As Arthur Young said when he spotted this during his travels: 'It is surely a triumph of the arts in England to see in Italy Etruscan forms copied from English models.'[7] That he sold his 'china' in China and his Italian vases in Italy was the most ironic expression of his marketing genius. That his wares eliminated much of the competition in Europe was more proof. By the time of his death, most of the Delft factories were closed – a fate attributed to the introduction of Wedgwood's creamware which replaced the older-style imitations of oriental porcelain. Josiah's trade had endured wars, revolutions, privateering and espionage to become a global success. But the difficult times that the company soon faced, at the beginning of the Napoleonic Wars, once again threatened everything. Josiah's son Joss did not think he had it in him to pull the company through.

Josiah died a very rich man. His estimated wealth was £600,000. Sally was left £10,000 and Etruria Hall where she remained until 1802, when she and her youngest two daughters, Catherine and Sarah, who never married, moved to a comfortable country cottage nearby. Josiah left each of his daughters £25,000 inheritance. Tom and Jack were each left £30,000.[8]

Joss inherited the majority share of the factory, where he worked for another five years. By 1800, however, with continental trade devastated from continuing war, he lost his nerve. He saw other European factories on the verge of bankruptcy, including Meissen, which had recently introduced its own imitation *Wedgwoodarbeit* ('Wedgwood work') in an effort to revitalise their trade.[9]

Byerley, who was bequeathed another eighth of the business, giving him a full quarter share, held out. After treating his clerkship cavalierly for so many years in his youth, repeatedly abandoning it with the hopes of succeeding in a more 'entertaining' life, he was now the only one left who retained any faith in Etruria. As good as his intentions were, however, he was not able to successfully manage the entire business on his own. Discipline in the factory became slack and the standard of production dropped. Less than five years after Josiah's death, the future of Etruria looked bleak.

In 1800, however, Jack purchased back his share of the partnership in Etruria and in 1804 took a leading role in restoring its fortunes. In 1806, Joss returned to work, and 'Josiah Wedgwood Sons & Byerley' regained considerable lost ground, proving that the Wedgwood touch was still alive.[10] But concerns for the health of the youngest brother soon dampened their spirits.

Addicted to opium, Tom often silently contemplated philosophical questions, writing notes in his diary: What limit was there to the perfectibility of man or society? What are the true laws of nature? What is the essence of human consciousness? What is the most effective way to relieve human suffering?

These were the ponderings of the man that the poet Thomas Campbell described as 'full of goodness, benevolence, with a mind stored with ideas, with metaphysics the most exquisitely fine I ever heard delivered, a man of wonderful talents, a tact of taste acute beyond description'. But by 1803, thirty-two-year-old Tom had become chronically ill.

One of his closest friends was Samuel Taylor Coleridge, another chronic sufferer with a passionate philosophical bent. The two men would spend immeasurable hours discussing their dreams and visions, and experimenting with a cornucopia of drugs hoping to relieve their pathological misery. 'We will have a fair trial of *Bang*,' wrote Coleridge in anticipation of an imminent visit from Tom in 1803, referring to some recently arrived Indian hemp. 'Do bring down some of the Hyoscyamine Pills – & I will give a fair Trial of opium, Hensbane, & Nepenthe.'[11]

Coleridge, referred to by Wordsworth as 'The most intense of Nature's worshippers', in turn referred to Tom as 'the benefactor of my intellect', eternally grateful for the annuities he received from Tom and which brought him 'tranquillity & leisure of independence' and the ability to 'inspire and purify' his poetry.

It was a mission in life that Tom had also settled on. Once, he had been the little boy idolised by his father, 'jumping up & clapping his hands in joy' as his elder brother performed chemical experiments. And, indeed, like Josiah, Tom proved to be quite an experimentalist. In a scientific paper he had published just the previous year, in a journal edited by the promising young chemist Humphry Davy, he described how an image could be obtained on a piece of paper if a source of light is projected on a sheet moistened with nitrate of silver. Despite the fact that he knew of no way to 'fix' the images, his discovery was later hailed as the invention of photography. But after this, ill health forced him to quit the laboratory.[12]

Joss agonised over his brother's ailing condition. While Joss managed Etruria, Tom searched for his health at home and abroad. His efforts were supported by the companionship of his growing circle of artistic friends, including John Leslie, Coleridge, and a new friend, William Godwin, all of whom Tom supported, as he was, he confessed, 'possessed of a considerable superfluity of fortune'.

The group, along with others including the engineer James Watt's son, Gregory, formed a social club in London, which one member immodestly described as a 'gathering place of brilliant talkers, dedicated to meetings of the reigning wits of London'. Among the topics debated by the group was something which Tom and Coleridge had mused on for some time: social progress. William Godwin was particularly outspoken on this subject. He was a radical thinker and author, a Dissenting minister turned atheist and utopian philosopher. He argued that the abolition of rank and riches would promote the happiness, welfare and perfectibility of mankind. His was a doctrine of extreme individualism, arguing that small self-sustaining groups should replace government and social institutions to ensure the future improvement of society. Large forms of social organisation – judicial, religious, educational, and so on – were oppressive, he argued, and after their removal humankind would be liberated from misery, ignorance and poverty to live in a world of morality, virtue and happiness.

Godwin found many disciples in the society of London poets and philosophers, and the Wedgwoods' philanthropy fitted well with his Rousseauvian optimism about the benevolence of human nature. So enthused were his friends by this new utopian philosophy that a number of them, especially the poet Robert Southey, Coleridge and Tom, drew up plans to emigrate to America to start a utopian community free from the prejudices of British society. Why not? They even had a role model – Tom's scientific mentor Joseph

Priestley, whose new life in the Susquehanna Valley in Pennsylvania they found adventurous and exciting.

But another of Godwin's readers was fiercely sceptical about his philosophy. This was the Reverend Thomas Robert Malthus, who published a response to 'the general question of the future improvement of society', titled *An Essay on the Principle of Population* (1798). In this polemical tract, Malthus mused on the fate of humanity, declaring that 'those whose minds are not suited to a purer and happier state of existence, shall perish, and be condemned to mix again with their original clay'. To expose the problems that humanity faced in attempting to avoid a fate akin to a rejected piece of Wedgwood's pottery, Malthus controversially pointed to the misguided drive to industrialise Britain.

Look around, Malthus demanded, was it right that manufacturers were producing 'trinkets and baubles' when disease, warfare and death still haunted the world?[13] It was a particularly cutting criticism, written in the wake of the 'great hunger' that had preceded the French Revolution and amid anxieties caused by the scarcity of 1795 in England. There was not enough food to go round, Malthus warned, so why waste effort producing dinnerware! The 'best stimulus to industry', he wrote, was 'the hope of bettering our condition, and the fear of want, rather than want itself'. As Josiah and Erasmus Darwin had earlier feared, people believed that manufacturers and industrialists were, ultimately, manufacturing dearth and disease; the best way to secure a healthy future, Malthus said, was to encourage agricultural production.

This was not the line of reasoning that the sons (whether Wedgwoods, Darwins, or Watts) of major industrialists and enlightened entrepreneurs were keen to embrace, and neither were their friends. Godwin, who corresponded with Malthus about this, stuck by his original argument politely. Behind the scenes, however, the group mocked Malthus's 'exceedingly illogical' (in Coleridge's words) argument.[14]

Malthus's critique of manufacturers and utopian philosophy

exposed the social tensions emerging in what the previous generation considered industrial triumphs. Before his death in 1803, Erasmus Darwin senior wrote paeans to industrial progress in his poem, *The Botanic Garden*, applauding the work at Etruria and working in allusions to divine creation and ancient ideals of perfection:

> *And pleased on WEDGWOOD ray your partial smile,*
> *A new Etruria decks Britannia's isle.*
> *Charmed by your touch, the kneaded clay refines,*
> *The biscuit hardens, the enamel shines;*
> *Each nicer mould a softer feature drinks,*
> *The bold Cameo speaks, the soft Intaglio thinks.*
>
> *Whether, O Friend of Art! Your gems derive*
> *Fine forms from Greece, and fabled Gods revive;*
> *Or bid from modern life the Portrait breathe,*
> *And bind round Honour's brow the laurel wreath;*
> *Buoyant shall sail, with Fame's historic page,*
> *Each fair medallion o'er the wrecks of age.*

However not all their offspring inherited the optimism of Erasmus's generation. Erasmus's own son, Erasmus, appeared to be a successful solicitor (he acted on behalf of the Wedgwood firm), but inwardly deep neuroses were festering. He proved a poor businessman, badly mismanaging his finances while overextending his financial security in buying a beautiful but extravagant home, Breadsall Priory, just north of Derby. This is where the forty-year-old hoped to relax in early retirement, or where he would 'sleep away the remainder of his life', as his father disapprovingly put it, maybe thinking of the example of the listless Tom Wedgwood. But it was worse than that.

One month after moving into Breadsall Priory, on 29 December 1799, the young Erasmus fled his house in a frantic state, ran the mile through the grounds of his house to the River Derwent, threw himself in and was drowned. On that same day, an uninformed Erasmus senior wrote a letter to Dr Thomas Beddoes in Bristol,

saying he was 'truly sorry to hear Mr T Wedgwood is in so indifferent a stage of health'. But Tom managed to hang on a bit longer.
He died, emaciated and intoxicated, on 10 July 1805, age thirty-four.

Tom's tragic life had made his friend William Wordsworth ponder.
Among the schemes and visions for the 'progress of human improvement' that Tom had discussed with him had been an 'academy for
genius', in which certain children would be reared in laboratory
conditions, with 'plain grey walls with one or two vivid objects for
sight & touch . . . the child must never go out of doors or leave his
own apartment'. Eventually, Wordsworth grew sceptical of the plan.
He was, after all, as Tom later observed, a man who enjoyed medit-
ating on nature, 'with no other companions, than the flowers, the
grass, the cattle, the sheep that scamper away from him when he
makes a vain unexpecting chase after them'.

Wordsworth also grew sceptical about the benefits to nature that
industry could bring. He shared his ideas with Coleridge, who had
earlier listened to Wordsworth reading the first part of his poem,
The Excursion, in 1797. It was a simple story in which a man contem-
plates the difference between the ruined cottage as it appears before
him and as he used to know it, before he was forced to leave in search
of work, for war had blighted the rural economy. The transition of
the landscape around him he finds breathtaking:

> *At social Industry's command,*
> *How quick, how vast an increase'.*
> *I grieve, when on the darker side*
> *Of this great change I look; and there behold*
> *Such outrage done to nature as compels*
> *The indignant power to justify herself;*
> *Yea, to avenge her violated rights,*
> *For England's bane. – When soothing darkness spreads*
> *O'er hill and vale, the Wanderer thus expressed*
> *His recollections . . .*[15]

'One of the most beautiful poems in the language,' thought Coleridge.[16] How different this reaction to that of Tom's father, Josiah Wedgwood, when he first wandered a few miles from his birthplace and cast his eyes over the vast vales. He did not see an area 'O'er which the smoke of unremitting fires/Hangs permanent.'[17] Nor did he foresee 'outrage done to nature'. Rather, he saw a promising future and a new way of life.

Tom's death and his friends' Romantic struggles with the transformation of nature and society were harsh reminders of the problems faced by the next generation, but the spirit of scientific progress that Josiah senior so passionately believed in remained alive. Sally lived until 1815, to the age of eighty-one, long enough to see all of her nineteen grandchildren begin to grow. Joss's youngest daughter, Emma, was born in 1808. Sukey and Robert's youngest son was born in 1809. He was Sally's last grandchild, who would eventually marry his cousin Emma. They named him Charles Darwin.

Epilogue[1]

JOSIAH WEDGWOOD possessed a number of special qualities that enabled him to succeed beyond all expectations, barring his own. He clearly could not have accomplished what he did without the support of his family and friends – Sally's dowry and lifelong guidance and assistance was essential, Bentley's advice and experience was invaluable – but without Josiah's own traits, he would have been as lost to history as the imperfect pieces of his pottery that were smashed into piles of shards.

It is ironic that Josiah's own abilities as a master craftsman were not enough to elevate his pottery to international admiration. Struggling with physical disability throughout most of his life, it is almost certain that if he had had to rely on his own labour – performing all the traditional aspects of the potter's craft in the way his brother was forced to – he would not have survived in business at all. Rather, his crucial skill was getting those he employed to improve the quality of their work to meet his standards. While he could be demanding and stern, Josiah was in many ways a model employer. Through confidence most likely gained from the encouraging education he received from his brother-in-law Reverend Willets, his intelligent and compassionate mother, and his dedicated friends, Josiah developed an ability to inspire people to rally round his cause. His acute political sense of enticing action through rewards was vital. His own workers enjoyed unprecedented guarantees of family housing, health insurance and retirement benefits in return for dedication and loyalty to the Wedgwood business.

Timing, of course, was essential. It was the moment to be a manufacturer in an age when Adam Smith elaborated the principles of the division of labour, when chemists such as Joseph Priestley were finding new ways to standardise products for consistency, and, in the broader social context, when a wealthier consumer class was eager to spend money on home décor. Wedgwood's was the first pottery in England to be bought for display purposes, as ornaments. But capitalising on opportunities works especially effectively when risks are taken, and Josiah was prepared to take risks, both with his materials and with money.

Whenever the economy was threatened by another war, or sales were dropping off due to a waning fashion, Josiah put his faith in his experimental trials, spending long hours in his laboratory working to invent a new glaze or unique characteristic within the clay. Science, he firmly believed, would provide the solution to consumer lethargy. Few of Josiah's contemporaries grasped as quickly as he did the practical implications for business that the 'chemical revolution' would offer.

While late in life Josiah despaired about the problems that existed in the world – war, despotism, disease – things which his youthful ideology believed would be eliminated by science and Enlightened thought, he could rest proud that his own example of success, created from practically nothing, could inspire others with few prospects before them. Being seen as possessing wealth was always far less important to Josiah than knowing that through determined inquiry and tenacity he could succeed without aristocratic advantage. Indeed, Josiah was proud to have his name symbolise the creation of something desirable from raw, unrefined materials. Though, after his death, the future of the Wedgwood name and firm looked as uncertain as ever.

The promising recovery of Josiah Wedgwood Sons & Byerley following Jack and Joss's return to the firm did not last long. The last years of the eighteenth century saw respectable sales – profits in 1800 are estimated at nearly £8,000 – and Byerley, keeping with Josiah's spirit of improvement, purchased a steam engine from Boulton & Watt to power some of the factory machinery, which was installed in 1802. They employed a workforce of about 300 people most of whom lived in Etruria village (though a few workers preferred living in boats on the canal). But, as had so often plagued Josiah throughout his career, politics and war once again interfered with business.

War with France was disastrous for continental trade. During the Napoleonic wars exports of Staffordshire pottery fell by half. Thirty local potteries went bankrupt. Worse, between 1815 and 1820, sales to the United States of America, the largest market, plummeted by 75 per cent. 'Trade is very bad,' reported a worried Josiah Bateman, the firm's senior salesman, 'and people everywhere are very low-spirited.'

At such a moment Josiah would have been straight in the laboratory toiling for hours on a new scheme, writing cryptic letters to Bentley about a modified design and new kind of material with which he planned to 'surprise the world'. But none of the present partners – his two sons, or the dutiful nephew Thomas Byerley – had the creative vision or indefatigable commitment to keep Wedgwood pottery one step ahead of its competitors. While they enjoyed a brief revival of the so-called 'Egyptian' ware, in the *rosso antico* body (the red paint on black basaltes first introduced twenty years earlier), the taste for other styles of pottery had changed. The neo-classical vases that had captured public attention years before were no longer in vogue. More detrimental to the account books was that sales of jasperware had substantially fallen off too.

Rather than working collaboratively to introduce an improvement that might recapture their customers' imaginations, the three partners concentrated on their own personal interests and left the pottery in relative neglect. Both Jack and Joss continued to live their lives as country gentlemen. Jack, who before returning to work at the firm had run up a staggering debt by employing a retinue of servants and gardeners to assist him in his hobby of studying botany and horticulture – building greenhouses for cultivating exotic plants and growing tropical fruit – drew far more money from the business than his share of the partnership provided. The same was true of Joss and Tom Byerley. Joss also had an interest in horticulture, planting 65,000 trees of rare species on his property in one year alone, and travelling around the country *en prince*. Byerley, meanwhile, drew phenomenal sums from the firm to provide for the education of his thirteen children. While none wanted to acknowledge it, the largest problem they had to tackle in their ailing business was the debt they were principally responsible for incurring.

The brothers were forced to confront the unpleasant state of their finances in 1810 when Byerley died and they examined the accounts to pay Byerley's widow her share of the partnership. It was disappointing to say the least. His share was assessed at just over £6,300, to be set against his debt to the firm of £8,600. Jack owed the firm just above £11,000, but more alarming still was the discovery that the firm was owed £48,000 in unpaid bills, a figure nearly double the estimated value of the entire business. Never before had the firm fallen so fast toward bankruptcy.

When Joss sent letters to customers announcing Byerley's death and giving notice that business would be continued under the name 'Josiah Wedgwood', he devised a plan which he hoped would rescue the firm. However, it required that his partnership with Jack also be dissolved. Jack did not take it well, and wrote a self-deprecating letter to Joss, complaining that 'all my endeavours to render myself useful to society are vain', adding that he hoped 'the dissolution of the partnership should not be put in the Gazette'. Agreeing to bow out, Jack, with his wife Jane and their children, thereafter relied on a series of family trusts established by other members of the family. None of Jack's children or descendants ever became involved with the family trade. From the beginning of 1812 until his retirement in 1841, the Wedgwood business was under the primary management of Joss.

In the 1810s, the principal new type of ware that Joss introduced to the market was bone china, a translucent porcelain that other Staffordshire potters had made, but which had never before been manufactured by Wedgwood. It was an unsuccessful venture. Instead, the business was kept alive by the production of common wares – a nineteenth-century variation on the stock-in-trade wares that provided the reliable sales in difficult times for their father. They produced large quantities of toilet ware – closet pans, urinals, washbasins and stands.

Joss and his wife, Bessie, had eight children, four daughters and four sons. It was their youngest daughter, Emma, who went on to marry her cousin, Charles Darwin. The boys were all well educated, two being sent to Eton and two to Rugby. The three younger boys were then educated at Cambridge, where they planned to study for the bar. The eldest, Josiah (the Third), was sent to Edinburgh where he studied chemistry and natural history. Perhaps worried that his son might fall into the desultory habits that afflicted his own generation, Joss wrote to remind him that 'You are in a house with tried young men whose fathers are much richer than I am. Do not attempt to vie with them in expense.'

While Josiah III managed to stay sober and received an education that would have provided a sound basis for the technical aspects of the potter's craft, his father was as uncertain about who would take over the family business as his own father had been, writing 'I am very doubtful if any one of my sons will succeed me in my business.' However, in 1823, Josiah III did join his father in a partnership, mainly because, in the words of one historian, the boy 'showed no particular enthusiasm or aptitude for anything else'. In fact, there was little to suggest that Josiah III would offer any useful improvements to the firm's performance. This condition was only moderately improved when Josiah III's younger brother, Francis – known as Frank – determined that his chances at the bar were less than favourable and accepted an offer to enter into partnership with his brother and father. From 1827, the firm was once again called 'Josiah Wedgwood & Sons'.

While business did show signs of picking up in the 1820s – certainly relative to the slump a decade earlier – it was necessary for Joss to devise new ways of raising money to keep the ailing business afloat. One possible solution was to sell the London show-rooms, which he opted for in 1828. Unfortunately, the £16,000 he raised from that sale amounted to a loss when the cost of all the alterations and renovations to the building was included as part of the original investment. Over the next ten months they auctioned off the general stock of all useful and ornamental ware, including enamelled Queen's Ware, stone china, and blue-printed patterns, as well as irreplaceable models, moulds and experimental pieces. With the added money this raised, and without the expense of London staff, the three partners of Josiah Wedgwood & Sons managed to concentrate their resources on the Etruria factory.

In 1841, Joss turned seventy-two-years old and his health was deteriorating. Over the past decade he had withdrawn from the business and left the minutiae of managing the firm to his two sons. Like his father before him, Joss was stimulated by parliamentary debates, especially the arguments surrounding the passing of the great reform bills, and he became active in politics. He saw the practical impact of the reforms around him. The organisation of trade unions was made legal by the repeal of the Combination Acts in 1824, and the period 1831–50 has been described as 'the heroic age of trade unionism in the Potteries'. The Factory Act of 1833 forbade the employment of children under the age of nine and limited children under thirteen to a thirty-eight-hour working week. The simple 'rules of conduct' that his father had pinned to the factory door no longer acted as the foundation for terms of employ-ment. Etruria, like all other factories that emerged during the age of industrialisation, was now regulated by the state.

By the beginning of the 1840s, the firm was making gross profits in the region of £5,000 a year, enough to allow Joss to retire in peace in 1841, and enough for Josiah III to sell his share of the partnership the next year and retire to his four-hundred acre estate in Surrey. Joss died two years later.

In 1859, the year Charles Darwin published the *Origin of Species*, his cousin, Frank Wedgwood, accepted his son, Godfrey, into a partnership, thus beginning the fourth generation of Wedgwoods at Etruria. The factory employed 445 people and began what has been described as 'a new era of endeavour and development'. Besides a number of mechanical modernisations, Godfrey brought new vigour to the production line, and was more committed to design standards and innovation than anyone since Josiah Wedgwood himself. He hired distinguished artists as decorators and raised the popularity and commercial value of Wedgwood pottery to a nineteenth-century peak. Their new products received critical acclaim at the 1862 International Exhibition in London, a vast improvement on the 1851 Great Exhibition where their display had been ignored during Queen Victoria's visit to see the best examples of the 'industry of all nations'. The firm's performance continued to improve.

Part of the growing success of the firm in the latter half of the nineteenth century was due to the new fashion in Victorian high society for rediscovering early Wedgwood, a revitalised taste for jasperware, as well as heavy investment in hiring the best artists to decorate the new wares. So improved were the accounts of the business that in 1875 the firm was able to reopen showrooms in London. By 1882 – twelve years after Frank retired and the business was placed in the partnership of Godfrey and his two younger brothers, Clement and Laurence – the firm recorded profits of £13,600.

In 1884, the fifth generation of Wedgwoods took over Josiah Wedgwood & Sons. However, this was the last generation that would manage the firm as a family partnership that had existed since its foundation 136 years earlier. In 1895, company law reforms required the firm change from a partnership to a limited liability company. In a personal way, this marked the end of a family saga.

It did not, of course, mark the end of the production of Wedgwood pottery. Indeed, in 1920 Wedgwood expanded to America while in Britain, the firm continued to modernise. In 1936 the directors decided to build a new factory in Barlaston, some six miles south of Etruria, where a village for its workers was also built. Boasting an improvement that would have made Josiah proud, it was the first pottery to power their kilns by electricity, thus creating a healthier environment for the workers. It is still the main factory for the production of Wedgwood pottery today.

On 15 June 1950, 181 years to the day after Josiah and Bentley ceremoniously opened Etruria by throwing the 'First Day's Vases', Etruria was officially closed. To commemorate the event, six 'Last Day's Vases' – replicas of the early pieces – were thrown. In the 1960s the original factory was bulldozed to the ground, save one round room that stood at the south-east corner of the building, and in its place is now a car park next to the Trent and Mersey Canal. If one pulls back the branches of an overgrown shrub on the east side of the canal, a bent, rusted metal sign can be found which states that that was once the spot of the famous Etruria factory.

Look elsewhere, however, and the Wedgwood name is not hard to find. The well-known pale blue jasper vases, saucers, and bowls, offset by the white classical figures, have remained in continuous production since Josiah first introduced jasperware in 1774 and are on prominent display in shops across the world. The name – and the range of products the company offers – endures through a combination of its historical status and a commitment to innovative, quality design.

Reaffirming their commitment to the principles that Josiah adhered to – the highest standard of production and unceasing search for new designs – the company now, as in the eighteenth century, recruits renowned artists and uses the latest technologies for guaranteeing accuracy and efficiency. Academics from Harvard Business School use Wedgwood as an example of the first manufacturer 'to command widespread consumer recognition and loyalty'; his was the first 'brand name', and it became synonymous with fine taste.[2] One of Josiah's main competitors, Matthew Boulton – at the height of their rivalry in 1771 – learned the lesson. 'Our pottery does very well,' commented James Watt, 'tho' we make damned bad ware.' Soon after this Josiah received the largest and most prestigious commission of his life, Catherine the Great's Frog Service, and thereby announced his victory over Boulton and Watt's outfit.[3]

Consistency and quality have been two key characteristics of Wedgwood's success. In October 1863, William Gladstone, then Chancellor of the Exchequer, gave a speech at the opening of the Wedgwood Institute in Burslem, remarking that Josiah 'was the greatest man who ever, in any age or country, applied himself to the important work of uniting art with industry'. Gladstone was not only recalling the sophisticated manufacturing techniques that allowed Wedgwood to combine artistic craftsmanship with mass production, but he was also establishing Wedgwood's place in history. Like the industrial scenes portrayed on the items of Catherine the Great's Frog Service, Wedgwood became both a symbol and a product of Britain's innovation and expanding economy. 'No one better than Gladstone could have made us understand the true genius of a Wedgwood,' remarked Louis Solon, himself a renowned potter of the late nineteenth century. After Gladstone's speech, buying Wedgwood pottery became a matter of national pride. It meant literally possessing a piece of British soil, which through revolutionary innovations had been transformed into elegant and functional pieces of art.

It is the history and symbolism that Wedgwood pottery embodies that has made it sought-after as collectables and memorabilia. In 1903 President Theodore Roosevelt commissioned a 1,300-piece dinner service for the White House, with the United States Great

Seal hand-enamelled on each piece of the service in silver and gold. Since then, prestigious orders have continued to attract attention. In 1995, a new Russian service was commissioned which rivalled Catherine the Great's in size and magnitude. It was for 47,000 pieces – the largest commission for Wedgwood ever – and is now in the Kremlin.

But as always, Wedgwood also represents elite taste without social prejudice. The name carries the status of an Old Master, but is accessible to those without aristocratic wealth. Never one to ignore the interests of the 'middling sorts' in favour of the rich, Josiah would be gratified to learn of the favourable impression his wares continue to make on customers, whether royalty, presidents, or the everyday tourist.

NOTES
BIBLIOGRAPHY
INDEX

NOTES

While there are two sources in which a portion of Josiah Wedgwood's correspondence is published, the letters – particularly the Lady Farrer (ed.), *Letters of Josiah Wedgwood*, 3 volumes (1904–6) – are poorly edited and abridged, arbitrarily eliding much that any biographer would find illuminating on Josiah's thoughts and character. Therefore I have mainly used, and refer readers to, the original documents, citing the archive in which they are housed and their reference number. Many of these have not been previously consulted.

One collection of primary source material relating to Wedgwood's extended family (particularly the Wedgwoods of Bignall End and Big House) which is very useful and surprisingly underused is the Potteries Museum Collection at Stoke-on-Trent City Archives, Hanley Library, Stoke-on-Trent. The catalogue to the collection alone is telling of the kinds of activities the family engaged in, especially as small landowners. Recently this catalogue has begun to be placed on-line by the Staffordshire and Stoke-on-Trent Archive Service (*www.archives.staffordshire.gov.uk*), which will prove invaluable to future researchers.

Archives referred to in Notes:

BL   *British Library*
CUL   *Cambridge University Library*
Keele *Wedgwood Etruria and Liverpool Collections at Keele University*
PM   *Potteries Museum, Hanley, Stoke-on-Trent*
RSL   *Royal Society London*
SOT   *Stoke-on-Trent City Archives, Hanley Library*
SRO   *Stafford Record Office*
WSL   *William Salt Library, Stafford*

ONE *A Place for Thomas*

1 'calling himself Thomas of
Burslem': Fred Hughes, *Mother
Town: Episodes in the History of
Burslem,*(Staffordshire: Burslem
Community Development Trust,
2000), p. 13; 'The place name
"Burslem"', M. W. Greenslade,
'A History of Burslem' in *The
Victoria County History of
Staffordshire*, Vol. 8, 1963,
p. 121.

2 'He was born in 1588': see Josiah
C. Wedgwood, *A History of the
Wedgwood Family* (London:
St Catherine Press, 1908),
pp. 50–55 for Gilbert's
background; the next eldest
brother married a woman with
family wealth.

3 'round oven, eight feet high':
Simeon Shaw, *History of the
Staffordshire Potteries, and the Rise
and Progress of the Manufacture of
Pottery and Porcelain* (Hanley,
1829; reprinted David & Charles,
Ltd., 1970), p. 101.

4 'interests in coal mining': Hughes,
Mother Town, pp. 13–14.

5 'over a hundred acres of land': see
note 18 below on the family wills
for a breakdown of the lots of
property that ended up in the
Wedgwood family in 1670.
Another 400 acres which
Margaret's sister Katherine owned
were sold and divided up amongst
other children of Gilbert and
Margaret. The 150 acres or so
which Thomas Wedgwood would
soon own would make him the
largest single landowner at the
time.

6 'suddenly, at fifty-two years of
age': Margaret's sister was
Katherine Colclough; her son,
John, had died in 1666. Upon
Katherine's death in 1669, most
of the property in question was
bequeathed to Burslem
Wedgwood II (1649–1696), the
son of Thomas's older brother,
Burslem Wedgwood. But it was a
heavily encumbered estate,
requiring a massive £950 be raised
through sale or rent for future
legacies. To meet this, he sold
much of the property to Thomas
in 1670 and settled for the
remainder of his life at Dale Hall.
(Source: property deed, Keele
E21–17776 and E21–17798; also see
comments in John Ward, *The
Borough of Stoke-upon-Trent*,
London, 1843, p. 196.) The
Overhouse estate itself was around
100 acres of property.

7 'barns, stables, outhouses . . .': in
the will of Thomas Wedgwood
(1617–1679), reprinted in
Wedgwood, *History*, p. 111.

8 'the greater the scope for further
expansion': compare to the
analysis of land labour in the early
stages of industrialisation in E. A.
Wrigley, *Continuity, Chance &
Change:The Character of the
Industrial Revolution in England*
(Cambridge: Cambridge
University Press, 1988).

9 'he added a third pottery later':
see property deed, Keele
E21–17798; and will of great-
grandfather Thomas Wedgwood
(1617–1679).

10 'Crown and Mitre': Hughes,
Mother Town, p. 15.

11 'workhouses and pot ovens', from
the will of Thomas Wedgwood.

12 'he was apparently content': Josiah
C. Wedgwood, *A History of the*

Wedgwood Family (London: St. Catherine Press, 1908), p. 130. This assessment of father Thomas's talents is widely supported, but more recent scholars have challenged the idea that Burslem at the time was merely 'peasant pottery'; see Lorna Weatherill, *The Pottery Trade and North Staffordshire 1660–1760* (Manchester: Manchester University Press, 1971), chapter 4. For the purposes of this book, it is relevant that Josiah himself was critical of his father's achievements.

13 'Men necessary to make . . .': from 'Memorandums relative to the pottery', Keele, L96–17695; Josiah calculated annual profits at forty-six weeks to the year.

14 'The wear and tear', JW's 'Memorandums', Keele, L96–17695.

15 'typical income': see Elizabeth Waterman, *Wages in Eighteenth-Century England* (Cambridge, Mass: Harvard University Press, 1934).

16 'workhouses', 'shops', 'plank boards . . .': described in the will of Thomas Wedgwood (1617–1679).

17 'an insatiable maw': the mill is mentioned in Thomas's will, and the process is described in these terms in Malcolm Graham, *Cup and Saucer Land* (1908; reprinted by the Staffordshire and Stoke on Trent Archive Service, 2000), p. 16.

18 Much of the information regarding the content and distribution of real and personal property amongst Josiah Wedgwood's family draws from their wills and probate records, including inventories. The wills of Josiah's great-grandfather, Thomas (1687–1739), grandmother Mary Leigh (? – 1719), father Thomas (1687–1739), and brother Thomas (1716–1773) are preserved in the Lichfield Record Office. Portions, in full or extract, were first printed in 1908 by Josiah C Wedgwood, *Story of the Wedgwood Family*, and some of the documents (in full or abridged) have since been put on-line as part of the 'Wedgwood Family History' site (www.geocities.com/heartland/3230/alt.html), along with miscellaneous other documents relating to the transfer or lease of property by the Wedgwoods of Burslem. Where certain details have been given inaccurately (i.e. some wrong names, variously incorrect birth and death dates) in the on-line versions, I refer specifically to the manuscript sources.

TWO *A Will and a Prayer*

1 'the freezing temperatures': Meteorological Office statistics for winter 1739/40 at http://www.meto.go.uk/climate/uk/extremes/index.html.

2 'twenty-year-old trade agreement': this was the Treaty of Utrecht (1713) that ended Queen Anne's war and permitted Britain to participate in slave traffic in the Spanish colonies.

3 'great yearly value': see the bill of complaint lodged by the rector of Stoke challenging the ownership of Churchyard House, which was eventually resolved in the

Wedgwoods' favour, reprinted in Wedgwood, *Family*, pp. 255–68.

4 'Convenient': see the discussion by John E. Crowley, 'The Sensibility of Comfort', in *American Historical Review* 104 (1999), pp. 749–82. For a general sense of the average size of houses in the region at this time, see the discussion in D. G. Vaisey (ed.), *Probate Inventories of Lichfield and District 1568–1680* (Staffordshire: Staffordshire Record Society, 1969), pp. 23–7.

5 'Mary and six of her children': in ascending order, the children were Josiah (aged nine), Catherine (thirteen), Richard (fourteen), Aaron (seventeen), John (eighteen), Margaret (nineteen), Thomas (twenty-three) and Anne (twenty-seven). Anne was already married and living with her husband; Margaret seems not to have been married yet (unlike Anne, whose dowry probably acted as her share of the inheritance, Margaret was still included in her father's will). John had probably already gone to make his living as a merchant in London, and Aaron probably secured his living in Burslem.

6 'intolerable smoke and stink': a complaint from the Norfolk parson, Reverend James Woodforde, quoted in Crowley, 'Sensibility of Comfort', who examines common living conditions as recorded in contemporary diaries.

7 'Downstairs . . . was the kitchen': Meteyard, Eliza, *The Life of Josiah Wedgwood from his Private Correspondence and Family Papers*, 2 vols (London: Hurst and Blackett, 1865; reprint 1980), I, pp. 200–01, provides a physical description of the house; she saw the buildings around one hundred years later when they were extended, but she also relies on an oral history from talking to grandchildren of locals.

8 'china': as a general point, here and below the description of any household item is drawn from the probate inventories of Josiah's brother, Thomas: Keele, L96–17800-45, 'Accounts, receipts, inventories, letters, abstract of will, relating mainly to Thomas, brother of Josiah Wedgwood'. The kitchen contents are specifically described in Keele, L96–17808.

9 'iron boylers . . .': Keele, L96–17811.

10 'They bake 'em in kilns': see Barrie Trinder, *The Making of the Industrial Landscape* (London: J. M. Dent & Sons, 1982; reprinted 1997), p. 36.

11 'water from the spring well': E. J. D. Warrillow, *History of Etruria: Staffordshire, England 1760–1951* (Stoke-on-Trent: Etruscan Publications, 1953), p. 177.

12 'evaporating finances': the probate records for Josiah's father begin the story of Thomas's financial struggles: Keele, E22–17930, 'Letters of Administration, granted in the consistory court of Coventry and Lichfield, to Mary, widow of Thomas Wedgwood'.

13 'forty newborns baptised': *Burslem Parish Registers*, see Hughes, *Mother Town*, p. 26.

14 'bakehouses' and 'nineteen ale houses': description in Greenslade, *Burslem*, p. 130.

15 'right' to dig: H. J. Steele ('Glimpses into the Social Conditions in Burslem during the 17th and 18th Centuries', *North Staffordshire Field Club Transactions* 78, 1943–44, pp. 16–39) cites references in the Tunstall Manor Court Rolls of annual fees of 4 shillings paid for the right to dig, and penalties for failing to fill up the pits.

16 'The greatest pottery they have': Robert Plot, *The Natural History of Staffordshire* (Oxford, 1686), p. 422.

17 'seven shillings a week': wages information from Weatherill, *Pottery Trade*, chapter 7.

18 'poor *Crate men*': Plot, *Natural History*, p. 124; Meteyard, *Life*, I, p. 146.

19 'only one horse and one mule': Josiah's 'Memorandums relative to the pottery', Keele, L96–17695.

20 'mean and poor': Ward, *Stoke-upon-Trent*, p. 31.

21 'Jolly Potters': map of Burslem c1750; 'Dredge Malt', see Plot, *Natural History*, p. 127.

22 'Up the Potter!': Hughes, *Mother Town*, p. xviii.

23 'the manners of the inhabitants': Ward, *Stoke-upon-Trent*, p. 31.

24 'bull and bear-baiting': Meteyard, *Life*, I, p. 106.

25 'coom, sup it Rafy . . .': this remarkable conversation about Burslem in the 1750s took place in 1810 and was transcribed by the local historian John Ward and printed in his *History of the Borough of Stoke-upon-Trent*.

26 'teazed of my life': Josiah to Bentley, 7 August 1765, Keele, E25–18089.

27 'behave and demean himself' and 'at Cards, Dice . . .': indentures reprinted in Llewellynn Jewitt, *The Wedgwoods: Being a Life of Josiah Wedgwood* (London, 1865), p. 66, p. 93.

28 'responsible for supplying bread . . .': from 'Churchwarden's Accounts of Stoke on Trent', Keele, E49–32807.

29 'one of the gentry': Meteyard, *Life*, I, p. 193; Robin Reilly, *Josiah Wedgwood 1730–1795* (London: Macmillan, 1992), p. 2.

30 'Throughout January and February': Weatherill, *Pottery Trade*, p. 94.

31 'The village had in the past relieved': Greenslade, *Burslem*, p. 129, who analysed the Burslem parish register and Churchwarden's and Overseers' Accounts.

32 'first parish poorhouse': opened in 1741; it is also referred to as a 'workhouse', but I will persist with the former to avoid confusion with the potters' workhouses; see Greenslade, *Burslem*, p. 129; Sidney and Beatrice Webb, *English Local Government: English Poor Law History*, Part 1 (London: Longmans, Green and Co., 1927); M. A. Crowther, *The Workhouse System 1834–1929: The History of an English Institution* (Athens, GA: University of Georgia Press, 1982), chapter 1.

33 'a croft or two': Meteyard, *Life*, I, p. 193; the price of food from a household account book kept between 1738–41 mentioned in Pitt's *Topographical History* is also quoted by Meteyard.

34 'employing class': although probably not used at the time, a

more appropriate term than 'middle-class' which is analysed with relation to income earned from rents and property in Leonore Davidoff and Catherine Hall, *Family Fortunes: Men and Women of the English Middle Class, 1780–1850* (Chicago: University of Chicago Press, 1987), pp. 205–7.

35 'they rendered no account': Shaw, *History of Staffordshire Potteries*, p. 155. Sometimes the problems were compounded when the customer was given leave to pay on credit, but did not pay: Weatherill, *Pottery Trade*, p. 54.

36 'Money': these tokens had no legal value, but where the issuer (the potter's customer) was well known and trusted, his tokens would be accepted. Different people had distinctive tokens – 130 different kinds of tokens have been found by archaeologists in Staffordshire. When merchants would accumulate enough, they would take them to the issuer and exchange them for silver. See E. A. Watkin, 'Staffordshire Tokens and their Place in the Coinage of England', *North Staffordshire Journal of Field Studies* 1 (1961), pp. 1–25; Peter Mathias, *English Trade Tokens: The Industrial Revolution Illustrated* (London, 1962).

37 'in the bringing up . . .': Will of Thomas Wedgwood.

38 'bound himself for £50' and 'mortgaged': Wedgwood, *Family*, p. 130; Greenslade, *Burslem*, p. 133. Father Thomas refers to the mortgage in his will as part of his debts.

THREE *'Creators of Fortune and Fame'*

1 'interest therein determined': Thomas Wedgwood (1617–1679) will, Lichfield; Margaret (Shaw) Wedgwood, will, Lichfield; Wedgwood, *Family*, p. 115.

2 'lessons in Newcastle-under-Lyme': Josiah's contemporary cousins attended this school, as discussed below; evidence that Josiah might have attended this school is the statement by his great-granddaughter Julia Wedgwood in her *Personal Life*, p. 10.

3 'English Charity Schoole': history discussed in Steele, 'Glimpses into Social Conditions', p. 28.

4 'a fair arithmetician': Meteyard, *Life*, I, p. 208.

5 'Blunging': these early stages of the preparation of clay are discussed in Weatherill, *Pottery Trade*, pp. 19–22; 'beat it till it be well mixed': description of process by the contemporary Plot, *Staffordshire*, p. 123. Neither of these specifically refer to Josiah, but children of Josiah's age, nine or ten, usually performed these necessary activities.

6 'twelve-hour days': average working hours nationally amongst manufactory labourers in this period (generally 6a.m.-6p.m.); Saturdays were often 'half-days', ending at 3p.m; from the 'spring of the day . . . till night of the same day': see M. A. Bienefeld, *Working Hours in British Industry: An Economic History* (London: Weidenfeld and Nicolson, 1972) pp. 22–23, 228. In later chapters I mention slightly reformed

working hours set by
Josiah.

7 'real food prices . . . demanded
more intense work': there has
been much debate about the
agricultural production and the
working conditions of labourers
moving into the manufactories in
the 'early' industrial revolution.
Josiah's circumstance is a good
example of the difficult transition
faced by families. See the
discussion in Jan de Vries,
'Between Purchasing Power and
the World of Goods:
Understanding the Household
Economy in Early Modern
Europe', in Brewer and Porter
(eds), *Consumption and the World
of Goods* (London: Routledge,
1993), pp. 107, 114–15; see also
Herman Freudenberger and
Gaylord Cummins, 'Health,
Work, and Leisure before the
Industrial Revolution', in
Explorations in Economic History
13 (1976), pp. 1–12.

8 'administer all the goods': Keele,
E22–17930, 'Letters of
Administration'.

9 'judiciously renounced their right':
Keele, E22–17930.

10 'a bankrupt estate': Wedgwood,
Family, p. 132.

11 'left their father's service': Shaw,
History of Staffordshire Potteries,
p. 157.

12 'premises they paid £280 for': John
Wedgwood's Rent Book, Hanley
archives, D4842/14/1/62–75, John
Wedgwood property title deeds.

13 'There was no ware made . . .':
Wedgwood, Commonplace Book,
Wedgwood Museum, E39–28408.

14 'East Indian rareities': reference to
his trade in a letter from J. B.

Crafft to Leibniz, 1672, quoted in
Gordon Elliott, *John and David
Elers and their Contemporaries*
(London: Jonathan Horne, 1998),
p. 9; Elliott's study is the best
source of information on the Elers
brothers. For reference to their
uncle, see Rhoda Edwards,
'London Potteries circa 1570–1710',
Journal of Ceramics History 6
(1974), p. 18.

15 'tay, alias tee': advertisement
in the *Mercurius Politicus*,
30 September 1658, advertising a
new drink at the 'sultaness Head,
a Cophee-house in Sweetings
Rents, by the Royal Exchange,
London'.

16 'Home – for there I find':
Pepys's 'Potticary' refers to an
apothecary.

17 'The drink is declared to be . . .':
Excerpt from 'An Exact
Description of the Growth,
Quality, and Virtues of the Tea
Leaf, by Thomas Garway, in
Exchange Alley, near the Royal
Exchange, in London,
Tobacconist, and Seller and
Retailer of Tea and Coffee',
reprinted in Francis Leggett &
Co., *Tea Leaves* (New York, 1900)
and reproduced in the website:
http://www.ibiblio.org/herbmed/
eclectic/tea/chapter-ii.html.

18 'nearly 5,000 pounds of the leaf':
John E. Wills Jr, 'European
Consumption and Asian
Production in the Seventeenth
and Eighteenth Centuries', in
Brewer and Porter (eds),
*Consumption and the World of
Goods*, p. 141; K. N. Chaudhuri,
*The Trading World of Asia and the
English East India Company
1660–1760* (Cambridge:

Cambridge University Press, 1978), chapter II.

19 'for health' (Cornelis Bontekoe): Simon Schama, *The Embarrassment of Riches: An Interpretation of Dutch Culture in the Golden Age* (London: Fontana, 1991), p. 172.

20 'fifty cups of tea a day': statistic from Philip Lawson, *The East India Company: A History* (London and New York: Longman, 1993) p. 60; Twining's was established in 1734.

21 'base, black, thick': from *The Women's Petition against Coffee, Representing to Publick Consideration the Grand Inconveniences accruing to their Sex from the Excessive Use of that Drying, Enfeebling Liquor* (1678), quoted in Charles Wilson, *England's Apprenticeship 1603–1763* (2nd edition, London: Longman, 1984), p. 307; coffee houses were made rowdier at about that time when they began selling alcohol as well, see Wills, 'European Consumption', pp. 141–2.

22 'Holland more "modern"': Wrigley, *Continuity, Chance, Change*, p. 103.

23 'The potters made dishes': 'Mr Sadler' to the committee on manufactures, quoted in Edwards, 'London Potteries', p. 22.

24 'to bring a person well skilled': Thomas Oade, *The Unnatural Parent* (London, 1718), p. 47.

25 'society of Experimenters': Joseph Glanvill's 'Address to the Royal Society' quoted in Peter Dear, '*Totius in Verba*: Rhetoric and Authority in the Early Royal Society', *Isis* 76 (1985), p. 148.

26 'the misterie of the stone ware':

Dwight's patents (1672 and 1684) quoted in Dennis Haselgrove and John Murray, 'John Dwight's Fulham Pottery 1672–1978: A Collection of Documentary Sources', *Journal of Ceramics History* 11 (1979).

27 'experimentally minded Dutch entrepreneurs': a sketch of their educational background, including the claim that links them to Becher, is from an account written by David Philip Elers's grandson, reprinted in Elliott, *Elers*, p. 8.

28 'Etruria Formation': for this information I am grateful to Bernard Besley from the Earth Sciences department at Keele University.

29 'Their extreme precaution': Stebbing Shaw, *History and Antiquities of Staffordshire* (London: J. Robson, 1798–1801) p. 18.

30 'to intimate the approach': Shaw, *History and Antiquities*, p. 197; the story of the clay 'speaking tubes' resurfaced in the twentieth century with alleged proof of their existence: 'It is a curious tribute to the value of such legends,' wrote Josiah C. Wedgwood in his *Staffordshire Pottery and its History* (London: Sampson Low, Marston & Co., 1913), p. 35, 'that, within the last few years, white earthenware voice-pipes have actually been dug up on the site of the Bradwell factory. They did not of course really extend from Bradwell to Dimsdale, but they went from one part of the factory to another, and were probably devised to secure secrecy rather than modern economy. These

pipes are now to be seen at the Hanley Museum'; this material was reproduced in Josiah C. Wedgwood and Thomas Ormsbee, *Staffordshire Pottery* (London: Putnam & Co., 1947), p. 19, but modern analysis shows that the material composition of these pipes dates them to the later nineteenth century.

31 'The people of Burslem': Wedgwood, *Family*, appendix XII.

32 'soft oar like clay': Martin Lister to Royal Society, 1693, in *Philosophical Transactions of the Royal Society of London*; their activities were also announced in an advert in the *Husbandry and Trades Improv'd*, 13 October 1693.

33 'hinder and restrayne': suit filed 10 August 1693, quoted in Haselgrove and Murray, 'John Dwight's Fulham Pottery', p. 95. For a later case where Staffordshire potters interact with the Royal Society and patents result in competitive means, see Arnold Mountford, 'Thomas Briand – Stranger', *Transactions of the English Ceramic Circle* 7 (1969), pp. 87–99.

34 'idiot': from later in the eighteenth century the story went that 'Astbury' , presumed by many to be the Shelton potter Robert Astbury, pretended to be the 'idiot' (see Wedgwood, *Staffordshire Pottery*, p. 37 fn). Occasionally writers have wrongly assumed it was John Astbury, who would have been too young. Josiah only writes – in his notes on the Elers brothers – that 'Astbury of Shelton made white ware with the addition of flint the

first in Shelton', but this qualifies him as an 'idiot'. Weatherill, *Pottery Trade*, p. 32, concedes the possibility that such a type of person might have been employed in an effort to protect trade secrets, but who exactly this was and whether this allowed the Elers' business to be penetrated remains an historical enigma. What is important for the purposes of considering Josiah's life is the fact that much contemporary emphasis was put on the possibility of such radical measures of espionage, which was a lesson Josiah never forgot.

35 'unjust and injurious': 15 December 1693, quoted in Haselgrove and Murray, 'John Dwight's Fulham Pottery', p. 97.

36 'The Fulhamites can come and go': quote from the *Stoke-on-Trent Historical Pageant and the Josiah Wedgwood Bicentenary Celebrations* (Anon., May 19–24, 1930) p. 52.

37 'Where they went': Keele, Josiah's commonplace book, E39–28408, f. 212. They had, in fact, returned to London where they declared bankruptcy.

38 'concealing pieces in the garret': Josiah C. Wedgwood and G. E. Wedgwood, *Wedgwood Pedigrees: Being an Account of the Complete Family Reconstructed from Contemporary Records* (Kendal: Titus Wilson & Son, 1925), p. 173.

39 'pyrometrical beads': Meteyard, *Life*, I, p. 159.

40 'the one an excellent thrower': Shaw, *History of Staffordshire Potteries*, p. 157.

41 'a most pertinent illustration':

Shaw, *History of Staffordshire Potteries*, p. 183.

FOUR *Acts of Toleration*

1 'It was a sign of prosperity': Joan Lane, *Apprenticeship in England, 1600–1914* (London: UCL Press, 1996), p. 13.
2 'to learn his Art': 1744 indenture, Keele, L134–26845; reprinted in Jewitt, *Wedgwoods*, pp. 92–3.
3 'Josiah's brother Richard ... became a soldier': Wedgwood and Wedgwood, *Pedigrees*, p. 100.
4 'run one of the most profitable potteries': Josiah estimated that his weekly turnover was £6, the most of any potter in Burslem around 1715; Keele, L96–17695.
5 'Oldfields ... Oxley Croft': a list of approximately twenty-one properties that she leased, with notes on the annual value of each, can be found in Wedgwood, *Family*, p. 135.
6 Katherine Wedgwood Egerton's will, copy in Keele, W/M 21–17778.
7 'earnest money': see appendix to Arnold Mountford, 'Thomas Wedgwood, John Wedgwood and Jonah Malkin: Potters of Burslem' (unpublished MA thesis, Keele University 1972); for examples of wages for apprentices, also, Wedgwood, *Staffordshire Pottery*, p. 76, for earnest money.
8 'borrow £100': Wedgwood, *Family*, p. 135.
9 'Unitarians': see Earl Morse Wilbur, *A History of Unitarianism in Transylvania, England and America* (Cambridge, MA: Harvard University Press, 1952), volume II.
10 'two corruptions of Scripture': Newton's *Historical Account of Two Corruptions of Scripture*, published posthumously in 1754.
11 'God that made the world': John Bellers, *Essays about the Poor, Manufactures, Trade, Plantations, & Immorality* (London, 1699), reprinted in George Clarke (ed.), *George Bellers: His Life, Times and Writings* (London: Routledge, 1987), p. 105; for the relations between Quakerism and Unitarianism, see also the debate expressed in William Penn's *The Spirit of the Quakers Tried* (London, 1672).
12 'Thankfully, it was the last ...': the student, Thomas Aikenhead, was hanged in 1697; Wilbur, *History of Unitarianism*, pp. 231–2.
13 'full "toleration"': came in 1813 with the passing of the so-called 'Trinity Act'.
14 'febrile state': Theophilus Lobb, *A Treatise on the Small Pox* (London, 1741), p. vii.
15 'we dare not eat milk': comment from Horace Walpole in 1745 referring to the gloom of the period, quoted in Wilson, *England's Apprenticeship*, p. 243; for discussion of the relationship between smallpox, hunger, and death see J. Landers, *Birth and Death in the Metropolis: Studies in the Demographic History of London 1670–1830* (Cambridge: Cambridge University Press, 1992).
16 'it turns many into frightful spectacles': David Some, *The Case of Receiving the Small-Pox by Inoculation, Impartially considered, and especially in a Religious View*, published from the original

manuscript by Philip Doddridge (London, 1750), published posthumously, p. 12.

17 'never intend that': Crowther, *The Workhouse*, p. 207.

18 'the small-pox in him': Meteyard's description, in *Life*, I, p. 220; compare, however, with Robin Reilly's more cautious account: *Josiah Wedgwood*, p. 4.

19 'a season of severe bodily affliction': Tom Byerley, manuscript 'Life of Josiah Wedgwood', Keele, W/M 1131.

20 'However ill the practice': from an anonymous tract titled 'The origin, object, and operation of the apprentice laws' (1814), quoted in Lane, *Apprenticeship*, p. 1.

21 'Booth had been experimenting': Donald Towner, *Creamware* (London: Faber, 1978), p. 23 notes that Booth is usually attributed with having introduced liquid lead glazes but it is more likely he was one of the first to use the method. See also Hilary Young (ed.), *The Genius of Wedgwood* (London: Victoria & Albert Museum, 1995), p. 22 and A. Meiklejohn, 'The Successful Prevention of Lead Poisoning in the Glazing of Earthenware in the North Staffordshire Potteries', *British Journal for Industrial Medicine* 20 (1963), p. 169.

22 'flint stones shipped in from the English coast': see analysis in Weatherill, *Pottery Trade*, pp. 25–7.

23 'Any person ever so healthful': quoted in A. Meiklejohn, 'The Successful Prevention of Silicosis among China Biscuit Workers in the North Staffordshire Pottery Industry', *British Journal for Industrial Medicine* 20 (1963), p. 255.

24 'potter's rot': A. Meiklejohn, 'Successful Prevention of Silicosis'; Benson took out two patents for the construction of flint mills, the first on 5 November 1726, the second on 14 January 1732 which improved on the first by substituting iron balls with granite used for crushing and grinding the flint stones. See Weatherill, *Pottery Trade*, pp. 24, 65.

25 'To take, farme & Rent': quoted in Mountford, 'Thomas Wedgwood', p. 23.

26 'Fortunately for the Staffordshire potters': Young, *Genius*, p. 10.

27 'mottled . . . combed': mottled ware was produced through the application of metal oxides to the ware before glazing, while 'agate' ware was formed either by wedging different coloured clays together (known as solid agate) or by using stained surface slip (known as marbled ware). See the description by Plot, *Natural History*, reprinted in Jewitt, *Wedgwoods*, pp. 30–31. Weatherill, *Pottery Trade*, p. 28, points out that, although Plot identifies 'magnus' as manganese, it is 'more likely to have been the workman's term for iron-ore, for the glaze of black wares contains iron but not manganese'.

28 'seated at two corners': comment by John Fletcher, who was paid four pence weekly to prepare the clay for Josiah and Richard; from Shaw, *History of Staffordshire Potteries*, p. 180.

29 'considered a ridiculous expense': Enoch Wood reporting the

sentiment, quoted in Wedgwood and Wedgwood, *Pedigrees*, p. 173.

30 'endless illusive projects': a sentiment suggested by Meteyard, *Life*, I, 233, but see Reilly's scepticism of the oft-cited allegation of excessive 'bitterness' between Josiah and his brother, *Josiah Wedgwood*, p. 8.

31 'As if the frailties of life': Wedgwood and Wedgwood, *Pedigrees*, p. 101.

32 'No single-handed man': quoted in de Vries, 'Purchasing Power', p. 116.

FIVE *Discipline & Dissent*

1 'Tailor, Draper, Man's Mercer': Shaw, *History of Staffordshire Potteries*, p. 182.

2 'Family apartments': brief description offered by Meteyard, *Life*, I, p. 235.

3 'Flowerers': Shaw, *History of Staffordshire Potteries*, 177; Meteyard, *Life*, I, p. 232.

4 'It was the perceived subversive threat': see John Gascoigne, *Cambridge in the Age of Enlightenment: Science, Religion and Politics from the Restoration to the French Revolution* (Cambridge: Cambridge University Press, 1989) for a discussion of the ways that dissenting beliefs are aligned with the pursuit of experimental natural philosophy and the associated political prejudices at this time, a general argument that I have adapted to analyse the commitments of provincial dissenting tradesmen.

5 'In the 1750s, Staffordshire might not . . .': see Eric Hobsbawm, 'Methodism and the Threat of Revolution in Britain' in *Labouring Men: Studies in the History of Labour* (London: Weidenfeld & Nicolson, 1964) for related discussion of nineteenth-century sentiments and demography in Staffordshire.

6 'Everyone in his family was indoctrinated': in 1747, for instance, Josiah's brother Thomas had voted Whig, and the Whig politics of Josiah himself become increasingly clear as he gets older; Wedgwood and Wedgwood, *Pedigrees*, p. 101; for the Whig party suspicions about Church authority, see Alan Gilbert, *Religion and Society in Industrial England: Church, Chapel, and Social Change 1740–1914* (London and New York: Longman, 1976), p. 4, though it is worth qualifying that there was also growing awareness of the gradual secularisation of social institutions in the beginning of the eighteenth century.

7 'the aim of business': Courtauld quoted in Davidoff and Hall, *Family Fortunes*, p. 207.

8 'free enquiry': for a catalogue of 'social improvers' that shared the Unitarian faith – which addresses not only religious but political views – see Raymond Holt, *The Unitarian Contribution to Social Progress in England* (London: George Allen & Unwin, 1938).

9 'potmaking chiefly depends': Long John's essay published as an appendix to Mountford, 'Thomas Briand', pp. 96–9. I have altered a sentence to make grammatical sense of it (the original sentence reads 'Earth according to ye Chymist principles for in the

potters Art it is to be considered in yt [that] light because it undergoes ye operation of fire . . .').

10 'one clear Annuity': Long John's will quoted in Mountford, 'Thomas Wedgwood', p. 28; Long John also supported dissenting congregations in other nearby areas, giving, for instance, £5 in cash to the Congleton Dissenting Society in 1758.

11 'good will to Philosophy': Willets to C. Mortimer, secretary to the Royal Society, 20 January 1737/8, BL Add MS 4434, f. 213r.

12 'assured by a stranger': Willets to Mortimer, 10 October 1738, BL Add MS 4434, f. 211.

13 'truly good man': Keele, E25–18837.

14 'great philosophic fact': Meteyard's comment, in *Life*, I, pp. 246–7; she and Josiah's great granddaughter, Julia Wedgwood, both state that Josiah borrowed books from Willets's personal library, and Meteyard adds a note that the books Josiah personally copied 'are now in the possession of Mr Dingwell, of Edinburgh': Meteyard, *ibid*; Julia Wedgwood, *The Personal Life of Josiah Wedgwood*, revised and edited by C. H. Herford (London: Macmillan, 1915), p. 17, cites a later letter where Wedgwood mentions Willets' library. Reilly, *Josiah Wedgwood*, p. 23, questions the way the story was embellished to put Wedgwood on a sickbed and being visited by Erasmus Darwin at the same time;.Willets' intellectual influence, however, seems convincing. 'Service to Philosophy' is what Willets

declared he was committed to: BL Add MS 4434, f. 213.

15 '"secrets" that he knew Josiah alone possessed': point raised by Wolf Mankowitz in his *Wedgwood*, 3rd edition (London: Barrie and Jenkins, 1980), p. 24.

16 'Pot ovens, houses, Buildings': indenture reprinted in Arnold Mountford, 'Thomas Whieldon's Manufactory at Fenton Vivian', *Transactions of the English Ceramic Circle* 8 (1972), pp. 175–81; the article gives an interesting account of the archaeological digs carried out in 1968 under the aegis of the City Museum, Stoke-on-Trent.

17 'shawd tips': otherwise referred to as 'shard' or 'sherd' piles.

18 'he was shrewd enough': Mankowitz, *Wedgwood*, p. 24.

19 'from whom he exacted': these were the traits he passed on to his best apprentice, Josiah Spode: Leonard Whiter, *Spode: A History of the Family, Factory and Wares from 1733 to 1833* (London: Barries & Jenkins, 1970; reprinted 1989), p. 17.

20 '£106 annual supplement': Weatherill, *Pottery Trade*, p. 55.

21 'The Grove': Mountford, 'Thomas Whieldon's Manufactory', p. 171; additional biographical information provided in A. T. Morley-Hewitt, 'Early Whieldon of the Fenton Low Works', *Transactions of the English Ceramic Circle* 3 (1954), pp. 142–54.

22 'not a very likeable character': Morley-Hewitt, 'Early Whieldon', p. 142.

23 '8 shillings a week': Whieldon's wages from his account book, see Whiter, *Spode*, p. 5.

24 '6 tenements or dwghouses': from

the indentures reprinted in
Mountford, 'Thomas Whieldon's
manufactory', p. 173; point about
his workers' housing on p. 171,
where it is also noted that
Wedgwood is often attributed
with doing this for the first time;
for his London aristocratic clients,
see Mountford, *ibid*, and p. 173
for Lady Leicester's order.

25 'Visitation returns': Gilbert,
Religion and Society,
p. 12.

26 'delicacy of taste': the quotations
in this and the next paragraph are
from Doddridge, *Free thoughts on
the most probable means of reviving
the dissenting interest* (London,
1730), pp. 7–20.

27 'the Neglect of the Poor': Sir
Francis Brewster, *New Essays on
Trade* (London, 1702), pp. 52, 122;
Wilson, *England's Apprenticeship*,
p. 350 for point about 'secret
weapon'. Brewster was arguing
that better trade would help
secure the nation against growing
concern about the commercial
power of the French.

28 'parish manufactories':
Mackworth's proposals are from
the printed *Bill for the Better
Relief, Imployment, and Settlement
of the Poor, as the same was
Reported from the Committee to the
Honourable House of Commons*
(London, 1704), pp. 3–7; bill read
4 January 1704.

29 Daniel Defoe, *Giving Alms no
Charity, and Employing the Poor:
A Grievance to the Nation, Being
an essay upon this Great Question*
(London, 1704), reprinted in
W. R. Owens (ed.), *Political and
Economic Writings of Daniel Defoe*,
volume VIII: Social Reform

(London: Pickering & Chatto,
2000) pp. 171–5.

30 'House of Industry': from Webb
and Webb, *English Local
Government*, pp. 127–8.

31 'the highest wages': Whiter, *Spode*,
p. 4.

32 'man of Energy': Whiter, *Spode*,
p. 17.

33 'I had already made': this, and the
following comments are from
Josiah's famous 'Experiment
Book': Keele, E26–19115, f. 71.

34 'block maker': William
Greatbatch: it has been generally
assumed that an entry in
Whieldon's account book referring
to 'Daniel Greatbachs son' is a
reference to William Greatbatch
(see Donald Towner, 'William
Greatbatch and the Early
Wedgwood Wares', *Transactions
of the English Ceramic Circle* 5
(1963), pp. 180–93, for instance;
but recently David Barker, in his
*William Greatbatch: A Staffordshire
Potter* (London: Jonathan Horne,
1991), p. 29, casts doubt on this.
While the evidence is
inconclusive, is seems likely that
Greatbatch was employed by
Whieldon at some point, and it is
certain that Josiah had great
respect for his talents and they
remained close throughout
Josiah's life.

35 'ingenious young man': opinion of
Thomas Byerley, Josiah's nephew:
Keele, W/M 1131.

36 'STILE ornament': Keele, W/M
1131 ('e'ware' in the original altered
to 'earthenware' here).

37 'solid-agate teapot lids . . .': this
list covers some of the items that
were excavated during an
archaeological dig on the

Whieldon site, discussed in Mountford, 'Thomas Whieldon's Manufactory', p. 174.

38 'the age is running mad': Johnson quoted in Wilson, *England's Apprenticeship*, p. 311.

39 'few countries are equal': Josiah Tucker, *Instructions to Travellers* (London, 1757), p. 20.

40 'religion of trade and manufacturers': Tucker's sentiments are expressed in his *A Treatise concerning Civil Government* (London, 1781), p. 33; the quotation about dissent is from Wilson, *England's Apprenticeship*, p. 342, in discussing the evolution of Matthew Arnold's onslaught in his *Culture and Anarchy*.

41 'for the improvement of our manufacture': Keele, E26–19115.

42 'should cover the piece': Keele, E26–19115; 'JW': an extant example of a green tea canister from about this period with his initials on its base is at the Victoria & Albert Museum, Arthur Hurst Bequest, C.16–1940; see also Young, *Genius*, p. 26, illustration B10.

43 'Willy': Keele, E26–18862.

SIX *Dues & Demands*

1 'few could afford so many mirrors': and for social function of mirrors see Clive Edwards, *Eighteenth-Century Furniture* (Manchester: Manchester University Press, 1996), p. 113; for rise of popularity of mirrors see Lorna Weatherill, *Consumer Behaviour and Material Culture in Britain, 1660–1760* (London: Routledge, 1988); the Big House

still stands in the centre of Burslem, but some of the contemporary designs have been removed – see Greenslade, *Burslem*, p. 110.

2 'stillborn girl': Mountford, 'Thomas Wedgwood', p. 29.

3 'there may not be above Sixty': Katherine Wedgwood Egerton's will, 9 January 1756: Keele, W/M 21–17778.

4 'gambling, duelling, sporting': see discussion of 'middle-class' management of landed property in Davidoff and Hall, *Family Fortunes*, p. 205, and the uniqueness of a woman in the first half of the eighteenth century performing these sorts of duties.

5 'tread the wheel': Weatherill, *Pottery Trade*, p. 32.

6 'flint supplier that Whieldon used': Weatherill, *Pottery Trade*, p. 65.

7 'all the appearances of a Laboratory': Shaw, *History of Staffordshire Potteries*, p. 30, describing the slightly later potworks of Enoch Wood; the description of the skills involved is nicely summarised by J. G. Crowther in *Social Relations of Science* (New York, 1941), p. 19, quoted in Archibald and Nan Clow, *The Chemical Revolution: A Contribution to Social Technology* (London: Batchworth Press, 1952), p. 296.

8 'manifestly ineligible': discussion from George Rae, *The Country Banker* (London: John Murray, 1886; reprinted London: Routledge, 1999), see also Davidoff and Hall, *Family Fortunes*, p. 211.

9 'yeoman' Jonah Malkin: for the story of Malkin's crisis, I have

relied on the information provided
in the late Arnold Mountford's
unpublished MA thesis from
Keele University, 'Thomas
Wedgwood, John Wedgwood,
and Jonah Malkin', to which I
would like to register my debt of
thanks.

10 'His father lent him . . .':
Mountford, 'Thomas Wedgwood',
p. 39.

11 'J. W. has taken to his Account':
Mountford, 'Thomas Wedgwood',
p. 39.

12 'It is more money': Mountford,
'Thomas Wedgwood', p. 40.

13 'I saw the field was spacious':
quoted in Robin Reilly,
Wedgwood, I (New York: Stockton
Press, 1989) p. 32.

SEVEN *'A Good White Glaze!'*

1 'Ruffley's': the situation is gleaned
from Enoch Wood's map of
'Burslem in 1750'; also Josiah's list
of potters from his
'Memorandum': Keele, L96–17695,
reprinted in Meteyard, *Life*, I,
pp. 190–91.

2 'first town hall': Ward, *Stoke-on-
Trent*, p. 206.

3 'first year's bill £17': Long John's
account books reprinted in
Mountford, 'Thomas Wedgwood',
p. 52.

4 'a potter ambitious to improve':
comment from Reilly, *Wedgwood*,
p. 28, where the family
relationship is also stated; see
Mankowitz, *Wedgwood*, p. 25 for
the 'memorandum of agreement'.

5 'idle, slovenly, irregular':
Meteyard's summary, *Life*, I, 260;
'Useful Tom's' salary is from the
'Memorandum of an Agreement',

Keele, WMS 27–19281,
30 December 1758; Spode's
equivalent salary is from Whiter,
Spode, p. 4; see also Kathy
Niblett, 'A Useful Partner –
Thomas Wedgwood 1734–1788',
*Journal of the Northern Ceramic
Society* 5 (1984).

6 'a scattered town': Wesley's
account of Burslem from
Nehemiah Curnock (ed.), *The
Journal of the Rev. John Wesley,
A. M.* (New York: Eaton &
Mains, 1913), IV, pp. 370–72.

7 'full of fierce Ephesian beasts':
Charles Wesley's experience
quoted by Meteyard, *Life*, I,
p. 265.

8 'preaching publicly in the streets':
the account of the Wesleys' visit
and the subsequent riots they
caused is from [anon], *Some
Papers Giving an Account of the
Rise and Progress of Methodism in
Wednesbury in Staffordshire and
other Parishes adjacent, as likewise
of the Late Riot in these parts*
(1744).

9 'Milton for the masses': Roy
Porter's phrase to describe
Wesley's literary commodities, in
his *Enlightenment: Britain and the
Creation of the Modern World*
(London: Penguin, 2000), p. 85;
for *Primitive Physick* see Roy
Porter and Dorothy Porter,
*Patient's Progress: Doctors and
Doctoring in Eighteenth-Century
England* (Stanford: Stanford
University Press, 1989),
p. 198.

10 'Electricity made plain': for
discussion of Wesley's approach to
'popular science' see John Hedley
Brooke, *Science and Religion: Some
Historical Perspectives* (Cambridge:

Cambridge University Press, 1991), p. 191.

11 'lathes, whirlers': see Meteyard, *Life*, I, p. 2617; Jewitt, *Wedgwoods*, pp. 130–31.

12 'greengrocery': Reilly, *Wedgwood*, I, p. 44.

13 'pineapple wares': colour illustrations of the pineapple wares can be seen in Young (ed.), *Genius*, p. 26, plates B5/B6; Reilly, *Wedgwood*, I, plate C16, opposite p. 169.

14 'had other difficulties': Josiah's nephew Thomas Byerley's biographical notes: Keele, W/M 1131.

15 'biscuit ware only': account of Josiah's Ivy House business from Byerley: Keele, 121–23528; Reilly, *Wedgwood*, I, p. 44.

16 'It was necessary for Josiah to strike an agreement': see Barker, *Greatbatch*, for more on this.

17 'Sarah Meir': an interesting example of a domestic manufacturer's division of labour that includes well-placed positions for women; see Percy Adams, *Notes on some North Staffordshire Families, Including those of Adams, Astbury, Breeze, Challinor, Heath, Warburton* (Tunstall: Edwin Eardley, 1930), p. 20.

18 'dealing with customers': this new interpretation of Greatbatch's early career and relationship with Josiah in Barker, *Greatbatch*, p. 46.

19 'without aid or assistance': Cyril Williams-Wood, *English Transfer-Printed Pottery and Porcelain: A History of Over-Glaze Printing* (London: Faber, 1981), p. 102.

20 'India porcelain': see Young (ed.), *Genius*, p. 27.

21 '406 . . .': Experimental page from Keele, E26–19115, a photograph of this page is reproduced in Reilly, *Wedgwood*, I, p. 183 (illustration 159).

22 '5 doz 18s': Price, *John Sadler*, (not in bibliog. needed in full here too) p. 34; Keele, W/M 1431.

23 'Law, Physick, and Divinity': verse from 'The Triple Plea', a picture of Josiah's mug is reproduced in Reilly, *Wedgwood*, I, p. 212, illustration 219.

24 'Plates & Drawings!': Sadler to Josiah, 23 February 1764: Keele, W/M 1431.

25 'blind simpleton': this and Wesley's quote from Linda Colley, *Britons: Forging the Nation, 1707–1837* (New Haven and London: Yale University Press, 1992), pp. 208–9.

26 'very bad things': (25 September 1766): Keele, E25–18129.

27 'the trade of the West Indies': quoted in Patrick Crowhurst, *The Defence of British Trade 1689–1815* (Folkestone: Dawson, 1977), p. 60.

28 'were more English': James Deetz, *In Small Things Forgotten: the Archaeology of Early American Life* (New York: Anchor Press, 1977), p. 38.

29 'two penny earthen porringer': Franklin quoted in Richard Bushman, 'American High-Style and Vernacular Cultures', in Jack Greene and J. R. Pole (eds), *Colonial British America: Essays in the New History of the Early Modern Era* (Baltimore and London: Johns Hopkins University Press, 1984), p. 374; see also the article Franklin wrote addressing gentile accoutrements

in *Philadelphia Gazette* 10 July
1732.

30 'Our importation of dry goods':
William Smith writing in 1762,
*History of the Late Province of
New York*, quoted in T. H. Breen,
'An Empire of Goods: The
Anglicanisation of Colonial
America, 1690–1776', *Journal of
British Studies* 25 (1986), p. 487,
who surveys the literature on
colonial consumption.

31 'Our people . . .': Breen, 'Empire
of Goods', p. 478.

32 'sought English manufactured
goods': James Lemon, 'Spatial
Order: Households in Local
Communities and Regions', in
Greene and Pole (eds), *Colonial
British America: Essays in the New
History of the Early Modern Era*,
p. 102.

33 'Not until after the Revolution':
this comment from Rodris Roth,
'Tea Drinking in Eighteenth-
Century America: Its Etiquette
and Equipage', in *Contributions for
the Museum of History and
Technology*, US National Museum
Bulletin, p. 225 (1961), cited in
Breen, 'Empire of Goods',
p. 488.

34 'the colonists set their tables':
John J. McCusker and Russell R.
Menard, *The Economy of British
America, 1607–1789* (Chapel Hill
and London: University of North
Carolina Press, 1985), p. 287; see
also C. Malcolm Watkins and
Ivor Noël Hume, *The 'Poor Potter'
of Yorktown* (Washington, D.C.,
1967).

35 'Already it is possible': Gottlieb
Mittelberger, German minister,
quoted in Breen, 'Empire of
Goods', p. 489. In the two

decades after 1750, England's
exports rose 120 per cent
(McCuster and Menard, *Economy
of British America*, p. 277), and
pottery, along with other 'luxury'
items such as silk, brass and
furniture, accounted for nearly 40
per cent of goods legally exported
from Britain to the American
colonies in the 1760s, or just
under £900,000 of merchandise:
James F. Shepherd and Gary M.
Walton, *Shipping, Maritime
Trade, and the Economic
Development of Colonial North
America* (Cambridge: Cambridge
University Press, 1972),
pp. 180–86.

36 '*Boston Gazette* was advertising':
Mankowitz, *Wedgwood*, p. 22.

37 '*Boston News Letter*': Jean Gorley,
Wedgwood (New York: Gramercy
Publishing Company, 1950),
p. 27.

38 '£13 million': Fred Anderson,
*Crucible of War: The Seven Years
War and the Fate of Empire in
British North America 1754–1766*
(London: Faber and Faber, 2000),
pp. 308–9.

EIGHT *By the Docks*

1 'Convenient for Lancashire textile
industry': see Neil Ewins,
'"Supplying the Present Wants of
Our Yankee Cousins":
Staffordshire Ceramics and the
American Market 1775–1880',
Journal of Ceramic History 15
(1997),p. 11; Josiah's interests in
Liverpool discussed in Gaye Blake
Roberts, 'Josiah Wedgwood and
his Trade Connections with
Liverpool', *Proceedings of the
Wedgwood Society* 11 (1982).

2 'for 10 pence': observation of
Samuel Derrick, a traveller to
Liverpool who left a detailed
contemporary account of the
community, cited in W. J.
Roberts and H. C. Pigeon,
'Biographical Sketch of Mr John
Wyke, with some remarks on the
Arts and Manufactures of
Liverpool from 1760–1780',
*Historic Society of Lancashire and
Cheshire Proceedings and Papers*, vi
(1854), p. 68.

3 'The dwelling house': Roberts
and Pigeon, 'Biographical Sketch',
70.

4 'Old Dock': general description in
Smith, 'The Past', in J. F. Smith,
Gordon Hemm, and A. Ernst
Shennan, *Liverpool: Past, Present,
Future* (Liverpool: Northern
Publishing, 1948).

5 'You may rest assured': Sadler to
Josiah, 11 October 1763: Keele, W/
M 1431; Reilly, *Wedgwood*, I,
p. 209.

6 'I have a good deal of talk': this
is the report of a later
conversation with Sadler but
typical of the level of supervision
Josiah had exercised over their
professional relationship for the
last decade; 12 May 1770: Keele,
E25–18299. Reilly and others
agree that, contrary to
Mankowitz's suggestion that
Sadler & Green would send the
printed wares back to Josiah for a
final firing, for practical reasons
they would have finished the job
themselves, which would also
expedite their export. This latter
point further stresses the
importance of feeding the foreign
market which has consistently
been downplayed in the histories
of Wedgwood's pottery.

7 'two glass factories': Roberts and
Pigeon, 'Biographical Sketch',
p. 69; 'Earthenware manufacture':
statement in connection with
Sadler's affidavit, 1756; 'all of
whom were connected': both
quotes from Knowles Boney,
*Liverpool Porcelain of the
Eighteenth Century and its Makers*
(London: Portman Press, 1989;
reprint of 1957 edition),
p. 4.

8 '700 annual tons': Boney,
Liverpool Porcelain, p. 4.

9 'Liverpool China Manufactory':
unless otherwise stated, all the
information cited about William
Reid's Liverpool pottery comes
from Boney, *Liverpool Porcelain*,
pp. 127–8 – a useful but
lamentably short work.

10 'any young persons': *Liverpool
Advertiser*, 19 November 1756; for
information about the locale of
Reid's establishments, see Charles
T Gatty, *Liverpool Potteries*
(Liverpool: T. Brakewell, 1882),
and Sir James Picton's map he
discusses on p. 13.

11 'rising to anywhere between six
and ten per cent': an average,
from Crowhurst, *Defence of British
Trade*, pp. 94–5.

12 'All perils of the seas': Nicolas
Magens, *Essay on Insurances* (1755),
I, p. 50.

13 'however unable he might be':
from Park, *System of Law of
Marine Insurance*, reproduced in
George Atkinson, *The Shipping
Laws of the British Empire;
consisting of Park on Marine
Insurance and Abbott on Shipping*
(London: Longman, Brown,
Green, & Longmans, 1854), p. 3.

14 'In a market that could yield':
Harold Raynes, *A History of
British Insurance* (2nd ed.,
London: Pitman, 1964), p. 71.

15 'provide a vessel': Atkinson,
Shipping Laws, p. 179.

16 'merchants are hospitable': quoted
by Dorothy Wane, *A History of
Liverpool* (1910), on-line at
www.fortunecity.com/meltingpot/
park/346/history4.html; Daniel
Defoe, *A Tour through the Whole
Island of Great Britain* (1724),
p. 88.

17 'over £3 per capita annually':
statistic from Carole Shammas,
'How Self-Sufficient Was Early
America?', *Journal of
Interdisciplinary History* 13 (1982),
pp. 247–72.

18 'The territory of Great Britain':
quoted in F. Crouzet, 'The
Sources of England's Wealth:
Some French Views in the
Eighteenth Century', in P. L.
Cottrell and D. H. Aldcroft (eds),
*Shipping, Trade and Commerce:
Essays in Memory of Ralph Davis*
(Leicester: Leicester University
Press, 1981), p. 61.

19 'France would become dependent':
Marquis de Torcy quoted in
Crouzet, 'Sources of England's
Wealth', p. 62.

20 'trade, which has made richer':
these and the following quotations
from French critics from Crouzet,
'Sources of England's Wealth',
pp. 69, 64.

21 'prize was usually taken':
information from Crowhurst,
Defence of British Trade, pp. 16,
34, 37.

22 'most ships that sailed out of
Liverpool': Crowhurst, *Defence of
British Trade*, p. 63. In 1720,
Nicholas Magens, an insurance
broker who wrote the well-known
treatise on British insurance law
Essay on Insurances, commented
that 'it is notorious to all the
mercantile world that as the
English insurers pay more readily
and generously than any others,
most insurances are done in
England'. Crowhurst points out
that because 'London dominated
the European market for marine
insurance . . . many French
merchants insured their ventures
in London during Anglo-French
wars, a practice that was not
considered unpatriotic to begin
with, for it brought considerable
business to London underwriters.
When they were forced to pay
heavy compensation to French
merchants for losses inflicted by
British warships public opinion
changed' (p. 89). It should also be
noted that the French were not
the only privateers – the British
and Americans were, for instance,
notable for privateering during the
American Revolutionary war (see
David Starkey, *British Privateering
Enterprize in the Eighteenth
Century*, Exeter: University of
Exeter Press, 1990).

23 'refuse to pay their said
subscriptions': this fascinating case
has never – to the best of my
knowledge – been linked to
Josiah's own export activities, and
yet, I believe, it is crucial to
explaining his financial difficulties
at the time, which has been seen
as a puzzling historical incidence.
This case not only helps to
illustrate some of the challenges
Josiah faced in the first years of
his own business, but it

illuminates some of the practices involved with arranging foreign exports. (I therefore would disagree with Neil McKendrick, 'Josiah Wedgwood and the Commercialization of the Potteries' in McKendrick, Neil, John Brewer and J. H. Plumb, *The Birth of a Consumer Society: The Commercialisation of Eighteenth-Century England* (London: Hutchison, 1983), pp. 134–5, and Reilly, *Wedgwood*, I, p. 94, that Josiah's own claim that trade with America was the most important market for him should be treated with 'scepticism'.) The case I refer to is 'petition of Josiah Wedgwood and John Dobson Assignor': British Library ADD Mss 36191, f. 361–364.

24 'an order be had for the creditors': 'Petition', in British Library, ADD Mss 36191, f. 364, and the above quotation.

25 'To be sold': advertisement quoted in Boney, *Liverpool Porcelain*, p. 128.

26 'He was only able to stay afloat': Josiah needed to hand over goods valued at £5 which was deducted from his rent in 1760; Mountford, 'John Wedgwood', p. 52.

27 'am come to the resolution': Greatbatch's letter to Josiah, 31 January 1762, quoted in Barker, *Greatbatch*, p. 42.

28 'I have four men': Greatbatch to Josiah, end of January 1762, Barker, *Greatbatch*, p. 42.

29 '. . . 3d ½ and selling them': see Reilly, *Wedgwood*, I, p. 188 for account.

30 'consider the discount': Sadler quoted in Reilly, *Wedgwood*, I, p. 212.

NINE *Paradise Street*

1 'large oblong dishes': example of content of crates in invoices from Greatbatch to Josiah; see Barker, *Greatbatch*, p. 44.

2 'the ware getting wet': Reilly, *Wedgwood*, I, p. 214; Sadler to Josiah, 11 October 1763 and Josiah to Bentley, 10 December 1774, Keele, W/M 1431.

3 'I know not . . .': Arthur Young's travelling difficulties are recorded in his *A Six Months Tour through the North of England* (London, 1770), IV, pp. 580–85.

4 'Burslem remained the most difficult town': a startling fact, gleaned from the survey 'The Turnpike Network', in Nigel J. Tringham, A. G. Rosser and R. N. Swanson (eds), 'The Turnpike Network of Staffordshire, 1700–1840. An Introduction & Handlist of Turnpike Acts', *Collections for a History of Staffordshire* 13 (1988), p. 90; J. Ogilby, *The Traveller's Guide, or Most Exact Description of Roads in England* (London, 1711). 'rugged Pot-making spot': Josiah to Bentley, 16 June 1763, Keele E25–18054.

5 'Since 1755 preparatory surveys': Mountford, 'Thomas Wedgwood', pp. 33–4; John Phillips, *General History of Inland Navigation* (1792), discusses the 1755 survey; *Derby Mercury*, 7 December 1758 announced Brindley's 1758 survey.

6 'Here let me pause': Young, *Six Months Tour*, IV, pp. 584, 580.

7 'Josiah crashed to the ground': for lack of other evidence, I have followed here Meteyard's (*Life*, I, pp. 299–300) description –

essentially followed in many subsequent biographical accounts – though Reilly (*Wedgwood*, p. 354, n 12) points out that no documentary evidence of this precise accident has been located.

8 'Great conflagration': Bentley, *Thomas Bentley, 1730–1780: Of Liverpool, Etruria, and London* (Guilford: Billing & Sons, 1927; reprinted by the Wedgwood Society of New York, 1975), p. 17; 'Dale Street' in Liverpool, see J. Chadwick's 1725 'Mapp of all the Streets, Lanes, & Alleys within the Town of Liverpool'.

9 'a good surgeon': assessment of his talents by Meteyard, *Life*, I, p. 300; 'very clever indeed': *Historic Society of Lancashire and Cheshire Proceedings and Papers*, V (1853), p. 147.

10 'young laymen': James Kendrick, 'A Morning's Ramble in "Old Warrington"', *Transactions of the Historic Society of Lancashire and Cheshire* 7 (1855), p. 83; F. W. Gibbs, *Joseph Priestley: Adventurer in Science and Champion of Truth* (London: Nelson, 1965), pp. 22–3; 'anatomy and the theory of forms': his lectures are referred to in Roberts and Pigeon, 'Biographical Sketch', p. 72.

11 'varnishes, fumigations': summary in entry for Matthew Turner in *Dictionary of National Biography*; 'some of the principal Experiments': from course syllabus quoted in H. McLachlan, *Warrington Academy: Its History and Influence* (Manchester: Chetham Society, 1943), p. 40.

12 'As near as I can guess': 16 March 1762, Matthew Turner to John Seddon, the chief dissenting minister at Warrington, explaining his interests in lecturing, quoted in Robert E. Schofield (ed.), *A Scientific Autobiography of Joseph Priestley (1733–1804): Selected Scientific Correspondence* (Cambridge, MA: MIT Press, 1966), p. 8.

13 'arrangements for obtaining': description by Dr William Turner, a former student of Warrington, whose history of the academy has been reprinted in McLachlen, *Warrington Academy*; see also Derek Orange, 'Rational Dissent and Provincial Science: William Turner and the Newcastle Literary and Philosophical Society', in Ian Inkster and Jack Morrell (eds), *Metropolis and Province: Science in British Culture, 1780–1850* (Philadelphia: University of Pennsylvania Press, 1983), pp. 205–30.

14 'a room was properly fitted up': Warrington Academy's trustees' report for 1763, quoted in Gibbs, *Joseph Priestley*, p. 23; 'instruments alone costing £100' information from McLachlan, *Warrington Academy*, p. 26.

15 'dear girl': Meteyard, *Life*, I, p. 300.

16 'courtly': Blake Roberts, 'Josiah Wedgwood and his Trade Connections with Liverpool'.

17 'His father was . . .': biographical information on Bentley from Bentley, *Thomas Bentley*, passim.

18 'James Boardman': Bentley, *Thomas Bentley*, p. 257; also *Historic Society of Lancashire and Cheshire Proceedings and Papers*, VI (1854), p. 42.

19 'persuade the merchants and masters': James Boardman, *Bentleyana; or, A Memoir of Thomas Bentley, Sometime of Liverpool, with Extracts from his Correspondence* (Liverpool: Wareing Webb, 1851), p. 10.

20 'to take charge': Bentley, *Thomas Bentley*, pp. 15, 10.

21 'mechanist': Roberts and Pigeon, 'Biographical Sketch'.

22 'The tutors at Warrington': Priestley quoted in Meteyard, *Life*, I, p. 309.

23 'the serious pursuit of truth': Priestley quoted in McLachlan, *Warrington Academy*, p. 23.

24 'intended for a life of Business': McLachlan, *Warrington Academy*, p. 39.

25 'an engraver for the potters': *Historic Society of Lancashire and Cheshire Proceedings and Papers*, V (1853), p. 148.

26 'without missing a word': Robert E. Schofield, *The Enlightenment of Joseph Priestley: A Study of his Life and Work from 1733 to 1773* (University Park, PA: Pennsylvania University Press, 1997), p. 7.

27 'furious freethinker' and 'not a single pupil': Gibbs, *Priestley*, pp. 10–12.

28 'I greatly admire Mr. Priestley': Turner to Seddon, 16 March 1762, quoted in Schofield, *Enlightenment of Joseph Priestley*, p. 137.

TEN *'Improveable Subjects'*

1 'much esteemed Friend': Josiah to Bentley, 15 May 1762, Keele E25–18408. A large percentage of the letters from Josiah to Bentley are published in Lady Farrer (Katherine Euphemia), *Letters of Josiah Wedgwood*, 3 vols (1903–6; reprint Manchester: E. J. Morten and The Wedgwood Museum, 1973), though more complete copies can be found in the John Rylands Library, Manchester. I cite the original manuscript reference for each letter, particularly since I have tried to draw out comments and sentiments not included in the published versions.

2 'crucible making': from copy of letter from Turner to Josiah, 11 December 1762, commonplace book, Wedgwood Museum, E39–28408, f. 33.

3 'I have told you what a troublesome': Josiah to Bentley, 26 October 1762, Keele, E-25-18049.

4 'I have lately purchased': Josiah and Catherine Willets to a 'close friend', 8 February 1762, printed transcription in Keele, E25-18051.

5 'Critical and curious': a category of readers used, for example, by the editors of the *Critical Review*, as opposed to 'vulgar' readers; blurred boundaries of knowledge and reading habits discussed in Richard Yeo, *Encyclopaedic Visions: Scientific Dictionaries and Enlightenment Culture* (Cambridge: Cambridge University Press, 2001).

6 'more numerous': Frank Donoghue, 'Colonizing Readers: Review Criticism and the

Formation of a Reading Public', in Ann Bermingham and John Brewer (eds), *The Consumption of Culture, 1600–1800* (London and New York: Routledge, 1995), p. 68.

7 'those pimps of literature': *Critical Review*, 1763, quoted in Donoghue, 'Review Criticism', p. 69.

8 'excellent piece upon *female education*': Josiah to Bentley, 15 May 1762, Keele, E25–18048; 'Octagon chapel': see Ruth Watts, *Gender, Power and the Unitarians, 1760–1860* (London: Longman, 1998), for further discussion of dissenting religious and educational theory linked to Bentley's context.

9 'instinctive goodness'; 'the finest feelings': Josiah to Bentley, 26 October 1762, Keele, E25–18049.

10 'It is perfect enough': Josiah to Bentley, 26 October 1762, Keele, E25–18049.

11 'I am about to furnish a shelf': Josiah to Bentley, 26 October 1762, Keele, E25–18049.

12 'younger part of our species', 'instinct' and 'charity' are all used as part of the same discussion which conveys these points in Josiah's letter to Bentley, 26 October 1762, Keele, E25–18049; I, not Josiah, use the term 'self-improvement' to summarise all that Josiah grapples with that is involved with encouraging an 'improved human mind' (Josiah's phrase).

13 'Mr Locke's excellent Treatise': from Chambers' *Cyclopaedia* (1728), quoted in Porter, *Enlightenment*, p. 342.

14 'You cannot think how happy':

Josiah to Bentley, 16 September 1769, Keele E25–18256; see also Uglow, *Lunar Men*, p. 56.

15 'my Magazines, Reviews . . .': quoted in Reilly, *Josiah Wedgwood*, p. 33.

16 'instruct the ignorant': Josiah to Bentley, discussing the futile attempts of a local dissenting chaplain to get the blessing of the Bishop to educate the locals from his newly built chapel using his own prayer books which he 'altered to his own liking'; 26 October 1762, Keele, E25–18049.

17 'O lord, our heavenly Father': 'A Prayer for the King's Majesty', from the 'Accession Service' in the Book of Common Prayer, read each anniversary of the day of the accession of the reigning sovereign after the Restoration. The Dissenters' objections to the reaffirmation of a fundamental right to rule based on the teachings of this and other services will be further explored below; see also J. A. W. Gunn, *Beyond Liberty and Property: The Process of Self-Recognition in Eighteenth-Century Political Thought* (Kingston and Montreal: McGill-Queen's University Press, 1983).

18 'Submit yourself to every ordinance': first general epistle of St Peter, 2:13–16, a text which provides the 'crucial foundation' to the tenets of the Church of England in the eighteenth century; see Robert Hole, *Pulpits, Politics and Public Order in England, 1760–1832* (Cambridge: Cambridge University Press, 1989), part 1.

19 'excellent little essay': Josiah's description of Willets' piece on 'prayers for public worship' in 'The Library'; his sarcastic comment which I quote was a lament that there were not more authors like Willets who expressed the 'true' Christian spirit. Josiah to Bentley, 26 October 1762, Keele, E25–18049.

20 'There is a clear demonstration': Brady, *Complete History of England* (1685), quoted in H. T. Dickinson, *Liberty and Property: Political Ideology in Eighteenth Century Britain* (London: Weidenfeld and Nicolson, 1977), pp. 24–5.

21 'Goddess of Liberty': James Thomson, *The Works of Mr Thomson* (London, 1738) I, p. 105.

22 'formed a strong desire to educate': Josiah's soon-to-be friend, Richard Lovell Edgeworth, writing about his son's education in 1765: Desmond Clarke, *Memoirs of Richard Lovell Edgeworth: Begun by Himself and Concluded by His Daughter Maria Edgeworth* (Dublin: Shannon, 1969), I, p. 173.

23 'good or evil': Locke, *Some Thoughts Concerning Education*, in Porter, *Enlightenment*, p. 340; 'we make scientific instruments of ourselves' is my paraphrase of Rousseau's proposal, in *Emile*, that 'I want us to make all our machines ourselves', by which he not only meant that 'we' should make (rather than obtain) machines or instruments for investigation, but that our natural enquiries undertaken without manufactured instruments will allow people to develop precision faculties within themselves. 'By dint of gathering machines around us,' he wrote, 'we no longer find any in ourselves.' Jean-Jacques Rousseau, *Emile; or, On Education*, introduced, translated and notes by Allan Bloom (New York: Basic Books, 1979), p. 176.

ELEVEN *'Grief of Griefs'*

1 'pretty but not expensive': the words of one Dutch retailer in 1763, in Mankowitz, *Wedgwood*, p. 31.

2 'one hundred pieces of pottery per crate': a local average calculated by Lorna Weatherill, cited in her 'The Growth of the Pottery Industry in England, 1660–1815', *Post-Medieval Archaeology* 17 (1983), p. 16.

3 'the trade flourishes': from the printed proposal to Parliament for a turnpike, drafted by Burslem potters in 1762, reproduced by the 'history of the borough of Stoke-on-Trent' website, http://www.netcentral.co.uk/steveb/borough/008_turnpike.htm.

4 'North Staffordshire [potteries] were the largest in the country': see Weatherill, 'Growth of the Pottery Industry', p. 22, where she qualifies the statistic with the note that there were a 'few exceptions, such as Leeds'.

5 'it might be asked': Josiah's speech was copied into his Commonplace Book, Wedgwood Museum, E39–28408, ff. 193–4.

6 'the ware in these potteries': see the 1762 petition as referred to above.

7 'pot-*wabblers*': see Roy Porter, *London: A Social History* (London: Hamish Hamilton, 1994), p. 151.

8 'prototype teapot or china plate':

Reilly, Josiah *Wedgwood*, p. 33 refers to Josiah's expenditure on such items for this trip.

9 'sister Willet's little lasses': Josiah to John Wedgwood, 11 November 1763, quoted in Barbara Wedgwood and Hensleigh Wedgwood, *The Wedgwood Circle 1730–1897* (New Jersey: Eastview, 1980), p. 18.

10 'Josiah shopped for shirts': see reference in Reilly, *Josiah Wedgwood*, p. 33; 'an ordinance was passed' and 'faggots had to be laid': from André Parreaux, *Daily Life in England in the Reign of George III*, translated by Carola Congreve (London: George Allen & Unwin, 1969), pp. 79, 80.

11 'This day I had the mortification': Josiah to Bentley, 31 March 1763, Keele, E25–18052.

12 'with candour equal' and 'lofty strain': Josiah to Bentley, 31 March 1763, Keele, E25–18052.

13 'excise officers who collected excise': see for instance J. Steven Watson, *The Reign of George III 1760–1815* (Oxford: Clarendon Press, 1960), p. 91.

14 'The extension of the excise laws': Josiah to Bentley, 12 April 1763, Keele, E25–18053; later, Josiah conducted his own investigation into how customs officers define 'earthen ware' in their records, which he believed was unclear and affected how their foreign trade was evaluated: Josiah to his brother John Wedgwood, 19 February 1765, Keele, E25–18064.

15 'Brick House': information on the rent and family from Percy Adams, *A History of the Adams Family of North Staffordshire & of their Connection with the Development of the Potteries* (London: St Catherine Press, 1914), pp. 125–6; see also William Turner, *William Adams, an Old English Potter* (London: Chapman, 1904).

16 'Byerley was one of three children': Reilly, *Josiah Wedgwood*, p. 38.

17 'trunk came down with all his papers': Josiah to Bentley, 16 June 1763, Keele, E25–18054.

18 'a very good boy': Josiah to Bentley, 28 May 1764, Keele, E25–18057; Josiah to Bentley, 28 May 1764, Keele, E25–18057, for Byerley's attempts to learn French; E25–18063, Josiah to John Wedgwood, 16 February 1765, for allusion to Byerley's important work on the accounts.

19 'lascivious erudition': I refer to the survey by Théodore Tarczylo, 'From lascivious erudition to the history of mentalities', in G. S. Rousseau and Roy Porter (eds), *Sexual Underworlds of the Enlightenment* (Manchester: Manchester University Press, 1987), pp. 26–45, for the eighteenth-century context.

20 'if their imaginations were charmed': *Aristotle's Master-Piece* (1710), p. 76, quoted in Roy Porter and Lesley Hall, *The Facts of Life: The Creation of Sexual Knowledge in Britain 1650–1950* (New Haven and London: Yale University Press, 1995), p. 42, which also surveys the popularity and uses of such literature in the period.

21 'His head is turned': Josiah quoting Bentley back to himself in reference to an acquaintance's

marriage in 1766, in Josiah to Bentley, 11 April 1766, Keele, E25–18143.

22 'Being single was good for business': these points are discussed in Lawrence Stone's classic *The Family, Sex and Marriage in England, 1500–1800* (Harmondsworth: Penguin, 1979), pp. 44–6.

23 'In 1763 his income . . .': Keele, WMS 32–24293, for his accounts; 'Squire Western', from Fielding's *Tom Jones*, the archetypical Old English gentleman, concerned to marry his daughter off to a wealthy man.

24 'marry a woman who lived over twenty miles away': results of a study discussed in Stone, *Family, Sex and Marriage*, p. 51.

25 'exchanging numerous orders a year with them': Josiah's dealings with his cousins is documented in his account books, namely Keele, 6–30442 and 6–30443 for these dates.

26 'in the region of £20,000': Jewitt, *Life of Wedgwood*, p. 157.

27 'every other Sunday Josiah rode': Wedgwood and Wedgwood, *Wedgwood Circle*, p. 13.

28 '£4,000 of jointure money': this figure comes from Jewitt, cited with scepticism by Reilly, *Josiah Wedgwood*, pp. 34, 354n.

29 'Reid the bankrupt': for Josiah's management of the accounts here, see Keele, E54–30700.

30 'consider my case': Reid to Dobson (who forwarded it to Josiah), 19 April 1763, Keele, E55–30959.

31 'Desire you'l Remit . . .': Greatbatch to Josiah, 30 May 1763, and the two following letters

quoted in Barker, *Greatbatch*, p. 35.

32 'glazing', 'Love': Keele, 11–9272, verso; his debts also named in Keele, 49–29894.

33 'I would have acknowledged': this and the rest of the letter quoted, Josiah to Bentley, 9 January 1764, Keele, E25–18055.

34 'All things being amicably settled': this and the rest of the letter in Josiah to Bentley, 23 January 1764, Keele, E25–18057.

TWELVE *Recipe for Success*

1 'solemnised their marriage': Astbury Parish Registers, microfilm at Cheshire County Council for which I would like to thank the curator Paul Newman.

2 'to hear, see, feel' and 'Gossiping friends' : Josiah's recollections to Ralph Griffiths, 21 December 1767, Keele, E25–18180.

3 'bundle': Stone, *Family, Sex and Marriage*, p. 384.

4 'two married lovers . . .': Josiah to Bentley, 28 May 1764, Keele, E25–18057.

5 'spending £200 on a new house for the rector': Greenslade, *Burslem*, p. 123.

6 'the Birmingham iron master Matthew Boulton': his marriage tactics discussed in Uglow, *Lunar Men*, p. 25.

7 'they made up 20 per cent': Davidoff and Hall, *Family Fortunes*, p. 211, their only comment on this issue. Indeed, to the best of my knowledge there do not appear to be any studies that look directly at this issue, the majority of historians tending to concentrate on women as

labourers during this time; the same is true of studies of women and capitalism such as Pamela Sharpe's *Adapting to Capitalism: Working Women in the English Economy, 1700–1850* (Basingstoke: Macmillan, 1996), Roberta Hamilton's *The Liberation of Women: A Study of Patriarchy and Capitalism* (London: George Allen & Unwin, 1978) and Mary Murray's *The Law of the Father? Patriarchy in the Transition from Feudalism to Capitalism* (London and New York: Routledge, 1995). Even Neil McKendrick's 'Home Demand and Economic Growth' subtitled 'A New View of the Role of Women and Children in the Industrial Revolution', in N. McKendrick (ed.), *Historical Perspectives: Studies in English Thought and Society, in Honour of J. H. Plumb* (London: Europa, 1974), which includes information from the Wedgwood archive, says nothing about how women's wealth contributed to the industrialising process.

8 'What forlorn Animals': Josiah to Bentley, 4 November 1766, Keele, E25–18131.

9 'Sally is my chief helpmate': Josiah to his brother John Wedgwood, 6 March 1765, Keele, E25–18070.

10 'I often think . . .': Josiah to his brother John Wedgwood, 6 March 1765, Keele, E25–18070.

11 'Richard Wedgwood began giving Josiah hundreds of pounds': account book of Richard Wedgwood, Keele, 32–24293, e.g., f. 183 verso (July 1764), £200; f. 145 verso (1765), £150. Other writers, such as Wedgwood and Wedgwood, *Wedgwood Pedigrees*,

p. 174, followed by Reilly, *Josiah Wedgwood*, p. 36, refer to a gift of £500 from Josiah's new brother-in-law John which he used to improve the pot-works. Reilly points out that no documentary source was given for this, but no one refers to the money transferred from Richard, which seems to offer a better explanation of where the money came from.

12 'discipline amongst his workers': though it mainly deals with a later period of Wedgwood's career, Neil McKendrick's 'Josiah Wedgwood and Factory Discipline' (*Historical Journal* 4, 1961, pp. 30–55) is a useful source for this issue.

13 'Time wasted is existence': Boney, *Liverpool Porcelain*, p. 69; Meteyard, *Life*, I, p. 308.

14 'an excellent book': Josiah to Bentley, 28 May 1764, Keele, E25–18057; 'Art of the Turner': Charles Plumier, *L'art de tourner* (Paris, nouvelle édition, 1749); Meteyard, *Life*, I, pp. 338–9.

15 'parallel lathes': for Josiah's thoughts about the Elers brothers' role in this see Josiah to Bentley, 19 July 1777, Keele, E25–18772; for an account of engine turning as it affected Wedgwood pottery, see Appendix C to Reilly's, *Wedgwood*, I, pp. 691–3; see Meteyard, *Life*, I, p. 339, for Taylor and Cox.

16 'forming a big hoop': bills for work on his lathe at Keele, E49–29829.

17 'This branch hath cost me much': Josiah to Bentley, 28 May 1764, Keele, E25–18057.

18 'just begun a course of experiments': Josiah to his brother

John Wedgwood, 6 March 1765, Keele, E25–18070.

19 'Meredith was elected MP': information on his position and glimpses of London life can be gleaned from his correspondence in the British Library, Add 38201 and Add 38204, letters to the 1st Earl of Liverpool.

20 'in sorting out my 2nd ware': Josiah to Tom Byerley, 1 February 1765, Keele, E25–18060 – a letter which puts to bed any doubt that Josiah was engaged in this very low-end market, which has been reluctantly supposed by a number of scholars. The prices for the goods varied, with the full crates which he sent to London, packed with up to ten-dozen teapots of varying sizes, were valued between £5 and £7 each.

21 'If you can spare Tom': Josiah to John Wedgwood, 13 February 1765, Keele, E25–18062.

22 '£13,000 on acquiring property' and '£800 sales in 1765': see Mounteford, 'John and Thomas Wedgwood', Appendix III for their accounts.

23 'with my humble thanks': Josiah to Sir William Meredith, 2 March 1765, Keele, E25–18067.

24 'I wish Sir William would give me . . .': Josiah to John Wedgwood, 13 February 1765, Keele, E25–18062.

25 'Cream Colour teapots' for Enoch Booth: Booth to Josiah, 1764, Keele, E11–9280; for accounts of the orders of Enoch and George Booth, see Keele, E11–9272 — E11–9280 (1762–65).

26 'trying a trick upon us?': Josiah to John Wedgwood, 13 February 1765, Keele, E25–18062.

27 'small service of printed dishes': Josiah to John Wedgwood, 19 February 1765, Keele, E25–18064.

28 'You have heaped your favours on me': Josiah to Sir William Meredith, 2 March 1765, Keele, E25–18067.

THIRTEEN *Fit for a Queen*

1 'Sukey is a fine sprightly lass': Josiah to John Wedgwood, 1 February 1765, Keele, E25–18059; Susanna, always called Sukey, was baptised 17 January.

2 'The finest Girl!': Josiah to John Wedgwood, 11 March 1765, Keele, E25–18071.

3 'Tell John Wedgwood': Josiah reporting to John Wedgwood, 1 February 1765, Keele, E25–18059.

4 'I shall hardly find time': Josiah to John Wedgwood, 1 February 1765, Keele, E25–18059.

5 'about eight tons of pot ware': Sir Richard Whitworth quoted in Peter Lead, *The Trent and Mersey Canal* (Wiltshire: Cromwell Press, 1980; reprint 1993), p. 6. General accounts of the canal movement which are drawn on here include Charles Hadfield, *Canals of the West Midlands* (Newton Abbot: David & Charles, 1974); J. Lindsay, *The Trent and Mersey Canal* (Newton Abbot: David & Charles, 1979) and S. H. Beaver, 'The Potteries: A Study in the Evolution of a Cultural Landscape', *Transactions of the Institute of British Geographers* 34 (1964). For the particular context of industrialists' activities in building canals, see the discussion in Uglow, *Lunar Men*, chapter 10.

6 'the Uniting of Seas': Josiah to Bentley, 15 October 1765, Keele, E25–18095.

7 'Our Gentlemen seem very warm': Josiah to John Wedgwood, 11 March 1765, Keele, E25–18071; information about the Leopold Hotel from Hughes, *Mother Town*, p. xxv.

8 'is undoubtedly the best thing': Josiah to John Wedgwood, 11 March 1765, Keele, E25–18071.

9 'with one Mr Loyd': Josiah to John Wedgwood, 11 March 1765, Keele, E25–18071.

10 'freeholders, tradesmen . . .': his letter of introduction is copied in the commonplace book, Wedgwood Museum, E39–28408, f. 195; 'I had the honour': Josiah to Bentley, 20 April 1765, Keele, E25–10875.

11 '*Countenance* is of extreme consequence': Samuel Garbett to Josiah, 18 April 1765, Keele, E25–10875.

12 'I have been waiting upon his grace': Josiah to John Wedgwood, 6 July 1765, Keele, E25–18080.

13 'that close, smoaky place': Josiah to John Wedgwood, 16 February 1765, Keele, E25–18063; 'you have not set the finishing hand': Josiah to John Wedgwood, 25 February 1765, Keele, E25–18066.

14 'Dear Brother': this to the series of questions for Chetwynd in Josiah to John Wedgwood, no date, early July 1765, Keele, E25–18073.

15 'You may be sure my best endeavours': Josiah to John Wedgwood, 6 July 1765, Keele, E25–18080.

16 'the pleasure of your letter': Josiah to John Wedgwood, 24 July 1765, Keele, E25–18079.

17 'appear to be made for each other': Josiah to John Wedgwood, 6 July 1765, Keele, E25–18080.

18 'night & day': Josiah to John Wedgwood, 22 July 1765, Keele, E25–18082; 'preparing sprigs, handles, spouts . . .' Josiah to John Wedgwood, no date, July 1765, Keele, E25–18083.

19 'but suppose we fail': Josiah to John Wedgwood, 6 July 1765, Keele, E25–18080.

20 'the foolish wakes': Josiah to John Wedgwood, 6 July 1765, Keele, E25–18080.

21 ' 2 Millions of Working People': Henry Pollexfen, *A Discourse on Trade and Coyne* (London, 1697), p. 50; see related discussion in E. P. Thompson, 'Time, Work-Discipline and Industrial Capitalism', reprinted in his *Customs in Common* (London: Penguin Books, 1993), pp. 352–403.

22 'I am teased of my life': Josiah to John Wedgwood, 7 August 1765, Keele, E25–18089.

23 'You cannot think how busy' and 'the Queen is impatient': Josiah to John Wedgwood, 24 July 1765, Keele, E25–18100.

24 'take any quantity of gold leaf': Robert Dossie, *The Handmaid to the Arts*, 2 vols (London, 1758), pp. 385–6.

25 'From experience I can tell you': this and the following quotes in the paragraph: Josiah to John Wedgwood, no date, July 1765, Keele, E25–18083.

26 'helped to double the income of Staffordshire potters': McKendrick, 'Home Demand and

Economic Growth'; see also
Maxine Berg, *The Age of
Manufactures: Industry, Innovation
and Work in Britain 1700–1820*
(Oxford: Basil Blackwell, 1985),
chapter six for elaboration of
women's work in early
industrialisation.

27 'I cannot find any French book':
Josiah to Bentley, 2 November
1765, Keele, E25–18096.

28 'For some tryals I made today':
Josiah to John Wedgwood, 29 July
1765, Keele, E25–18085.

29 'I will forward the Creamcolour':
Josiah to John Wedgwood, 29 July
1765, Keele, E25–18087.

30 'I sent a crate of patterns': Josiah
to Bentley, 26 August 1765, Keele,
E25–18080.

FOURTEEN *The Vexed & the
Virtuosi*

1 'even the King had expressed
admiration for': for King George's
'influence on the design of the
famous green and gold service',
see Stanley Edward Ayling,
George the Third (London:
Collins, 1972), pp. 204–5.

2 'Dr Swan dined with Ld Gower':
Josiah to John Wedgwood, no
date, July 1765, Keele, E25–18083.

3 'His Ld Ship said that . . .': Josiah
to John Wedgwood, 29 July 1765,
Keele, E25–18085.

4 '100,000 acres of land stretching
across twenty-seven counties':
Amanda Foreman, *Georgiana,
Duchess of Devonshire* (London:
HarperCollins, 1998),
p. 4.

5 'a madness to gaze': Adrian
Tinniswood, *The Polite Tourist: A
History of Country House Visiting*

(London: The National Trust,
1998), p. 104.

6 'they have bought some things':
Josiah to John Wedgwood,
7 August 1765, Keele, E25–18089.

7 'I sent a parcel': this and the
following quotes about executing
orders: Josiah to John Wedgwood,
25 November 1765, Keele,
E25–18101.

8 'to distribute as occasion serves':
an early example is Keele,
E25–17831.

9 'trade tokens': see E. A. Watkin,
'Staffordshire Tokens and their
Place in the Coinage of England',
*North Staffordshire Journal of Field
Studies* 1 (1961), pp. 1–25, for
discussion.

10 'I have this year sent goods':
Josiah to John Wedgwood,
2 August 1765, Keele,
E25–18087.

11 'for ready money': information on
the payment structure for Josiah's
orders explained in Josiah to
Bentley, 26 June 1766, Keele,
E25–18120 and 18 July 1766, Keele,
E25–18123.

12 'astonish'd, Confounded & vexed':
this and the following quotations
relating to the canal debate in the
company of Gower are from
Josiah to Bentley, 2 January 1765,
Keele, E25–18058.

13 'new wig. . . expensive shave':
details from his account book,
Keele, L47–8673; 'Queen's House':
see Wedgwood and Wedgwood,
Wedgwood Circle, p. 20; for
encounter with Queen Charlotte;
see also the portrait medallion of
Josiah in court dress, illustrated in
Reilly, *Wedgwood*, I, 327, plate
416A.

14 'already introduced several

improvements': Josiah quoted in Barker, *Greatbatch*, p. 21.

15 'if a Royal or Noble introduction': Josiah to Bentley, no date, Keele, E25–18167.

16 'Mr Josiah Wedgwood, of Burslem': *Aris's Birmingham Gazette*, 9 June 1766.

17 'Potter to King Charles': referred to in Edwards, 'London Potteries', p. 16.

18 'to have the success of all our manufactures': Bentley writing in his journal, following a visit to meet the King and Queen with Josiah, 15 December 1770, quoted in Boardman, *Bentleyana*, p. 17.

19 'Vase maker General': Josiah to Bentley, February 1769, Keele, E25–18232. This famous phrase was also in fact used by Josiah to describe Bentley on the eve of the opening of Etruria.

20 'I have not a Warehouse in London': Josiah to John Wedgwood, 7 August 1765, Keele, E25–18089.

21 'I have often mentioned': Josiah to John Wedgwood, 2 August 1765, Keele, E25–18087.

22 'The demand for this said *Creamcolour*': Josiah to Bentley, no date, Keele, E25–18167.

23 'In 1765, over 7 million kilograms': Wills, 'European Consumption', p. 144.

24 'I am quite clearing my Wareho.': Josiah to Bentley, 18 July 1766, Keele, E25–18123.

FIFTEEN *Exquisite Models*

1 'fearful ordeal': Pliny's account quoted from C. F. C. Letts, *The Eruption of Vesuvius. Adapted from the Letters of Pliny with notes* (Cambridge: Cambridge University Press, 1937); for a contemporary account of the story see W. Fordyce, *Memoirs concerning Herculaneum, the subterranean city, lately discovered at the foot of Mount Vesuvius, giving a particular account of the ... buildings, statues, paintings, medals, and other curiosities found there* (London: 1750).

2 'cities of the dead': for accounts of the activities of agents, see Julia Williams, *Gavin Hamilton: 1723–1798* (Edinburgh: National Galleries of Scotland, 1994); Lord Edmond Fitzmaurice, *Letters of Gavin Hamilton* (London, 1879); for excavation activities, see Rodolfo Lanciani, *New Tales of Old Rome, Profusely Illustrated* (London: Macmillan, 1901).

3 'It is the custom': John Moore, *A View of the Society and Manners in Italy* (London, 1781).

4 'who play very well': Charles Burney's account from his *Music, Men and Manners in France and Italy, 1770, Being the Journal Written during a Tour through Those Countries Undertaken to collect Material for a General History of Music* (London: Eulenburg Books, 1969).

5 'who had travelled in Italy': Lionel Cust, *History of the Society of Dilettanti* (London, 1898).

SIXTEEN *Creators of Beauty*

1 'I have now bought': Josiah to Bentley, 18 July 1766, Keele, E25–18123.

2 'dirty spot of Earth': Josiah to Bentley, 19 September 1766, Keele, E25–18128.

3 'be a Pot merchant': Josiah to Bentley, 26 June 1766, Keele, E25–18120.

4 'My Sally says': Josiah to Bentley, 15 September 1766, Keele, E25–18127.

5 'Cargoes of Creamcolour': Josiah to Bentley, 26 June 1766, Keele, E25–18120; 'green and gold for Pensacola': Pensacola was the capital of 'British West Florida' between 1763 and 1781, Josiah to Bentley, Keele, E25–18123.

6 'sent Mr Pitt over in shoals': Josiah to Bentley, 18 July 1766, Keele, E25–18123.

7 'The American business': Josiah to Bentley, early [February] 1767, Keele, E25–18186.

8 'Townshend Act': the bill can be read in full on-line at www.ahp.gatech.edu/ townshend_act_1767.html; Townshend proposed this despite the fact that he had previously supported Pitt's attack on the Stamp Act. For the dynamics of party politics in this period, see John Brewer's excellent *Party Ideology and Popular Politics at the Accession of George III* (Cambridge: Cambridge University Press, 1976). For the politics of British customs and excise, see W. J. Ashworth, *Customs and Excise: Trade, Production and Consumption in England, 1640–1845* (Oxford: Oxford University Press, 2003).

9 'Tho the subject of commerce': Bentley writing in the *Monthly Review*, 35 (December 1766), pp. 439–46.

10 'the amusement of Deary': Josiah to Bentley, 14 February 1767, Keele, E25–18135.

11 'The bulk of our particular manufacture': Josiah to Sir William Meredith, 2 March 1765, Keele, E25–18067; more information on Bartham in Keele, E14–13490.

12 'Mr Grenville & his party': Josiah to Bentley, 20 May 1767, Keele, E25–18146.

13 'would you think it': Josiah to Bentley, 23 May 1767, Keele, E25–18147.

14 'which surprised me a good deal': Josiah to Bentley, July 1766, Keele, E25–18119.

15 'kaolin will come out of the fire': see Watt to Josiah, Wedgwood Museum, Keele, E39–28408.

16 'must be got as clean from soil': Josiah to Bentley, 17 November 1766, Keele, E25–18133.

17 'kept incognito': Josiah to Bentley, 27 May 1767, Keele, E25–18148.

18 'The Chancellor of the Exchequer might be applyd to': Josiah to Bentley, 23 May 1767, Keele, E-25–18147; Josiah's reference to Samuel Garbett is identified by Meteyard, *Life*, II, p. 4.

19 'hath resided many years in N. A.': Josiah to Bentley, 20 May 1767, Keele, E25–18146.

20 'downright serious business': this and the following exchange between Bentley and Josiah, from Josiah to Bentley, 8 November 1766, Keele, E25–18132, where Josiah quotes Bentley's own words. For stylistic purposes, I have altered Josiah's quotations to put Bentley's words in the first person. The original text of the letter is reprinted (in abridged form) in Farrer (ed.), *Letters*, vol. 1, pp. 183–88 (where it is incorrectly dated as 1767).

21 'Sally & I pronounced its doom':

Josiah to Bentley, February 1767, Keele, E25–18186.

22 'Etruria': at this point Josiah spelled it 'Hetruria', but soon changed the spelling to Etruria.

23 'This building of houses': Josiah to Bentley, 3 March 1768, Keele, E25–18191. '£9000': the exact estimate was £10,053, discussed further in next chapter; Keele, E43–28632, 'first cost of buildings at Etruria'.

24 'Indeed I am not in possession': Josiah to Bentley, 20 May 1767, Keele, E25–18146.

25 'I have some thoughts': Josiah to Bentley, 3 March 1768, Keele, E25–18191; 'antiquities': topic of conversation inaugurated in Josiah to Bentley, February 1767, Keele, E25–18137.

SEVENTEEN *An Afflicted Heart*

1 'Your friend & my poor brother': Josiah to Bentley, 14 June 1767, Keele, E25–18151.

2 'It is indeed too much for me': these and the following quotations in Josiah to Hodgson, 13 June 1767, Keele, E25–18153 and 14 June 1767, Keele, E25–18154.

3 'Monday evening a man . . .': *Lloyd's Evening Post*, Wednesday, 10 June 1767, p. 551.

4 'I know you will sympathise': Josiah to Bentley, 14 June 1767, Keele, E25–18152.

5 'Valley of Tears': Josiah to Ralph Griffiths, 4 July 1767, Keele, E25–18157; the printed version in Lady Farrer (ed.), *Letters*, volume 1, p. 161. misprints 'Vale' for 'Valley'.

6 'Besides all pecuniary considerations': Josiah to Bentley, late July 1767, Keele, E25–18159; since the information on Bentley's business affairs is sketchy I have inferred from information in Josiah's letters and from activities described in Bentley, *Thomas Bentley*, p. 33.

7 'Mrs Wedgwood & her Wedgwoodikin': Josiah to Bentley, late July 1767, Keele, E25–18159.

8 'I am now sunk over head': Josiah to Bentley, 24 August 1767, Keele, E25–18164.

9 'Why you never knew': Josiah to Bentley, 8 September 1767, Keele, E25–18166.

10 'every rarity soon grows stale': Josiah to Bentley, 31 May 1767, Keele, E25–18149.

11 'Many of my experiments': Josiah to Bentley, 5 August 1767, Keele, E25–18161.

12 'a mode of introducing': Josiah to Bentley, no date, Keele, E25–18132.

13 'COMMAND SUCCESS': Josiah to Bentley, 27 September 1767, Keele, E25–18168; 'if you can make this branch': to Bentley, no date, Keele, E25–18132.

14 'what may be of use to me': Josiah to Bentley, no date, Keele, E25–18183.

15 '*Written instructions*': Josiah to Bentley, 3 March 1768, Keele, E25–18191.

16 'wanting nothing but arrangement': Josiah to Bentley, 31 May 1767, Keele, E25–18149; see Una des Fontaines, 'Portland House: Wedgwood's London Showrooms', *Proceedings of the Wedgwood Society* 11 (1982), for an excellent survey of his different showrooms.

17 'One of the objects': Josiah to Bentley, 24 March 1768, Keele, E25–18196.

18 'work'd several years': Josiah to Bentley, 21 March 1768, Keele, E25–18197.

19 'several hours': Josiah to Bentley, 24 March 1768, Keele, E25–18196.

20 'surprise *the World*': Josiah to Bentley, 31 October 1768, Keele, E25–18212.

21 'overwhelm my patience': Josiah to Bentley, 28 April 1767, Keele, E25–18178.

22 'leaving home in a great hurry': Sally to Bentley, 30 November 1767, Keele, microfilm reel ii, p. 85.

23 'about 50 people': Josiah to Bentley, 12 October 1767, Keele, E25–18169.

24 'We are making sagars': Josiah to Bentley, 3 January 1768, Keele, E25–18222.

25 'has good fingers': Josiah to Bentley, 31 December 1767, Keele, E25–18182; 'to know when they must begin': Josiah to Bentley, 8 September 1767, Keele, E25–18166.

26 'Root flowerpots . . .': planned products from Josiah to Bentley, 8 November 1767, Keele, E25–18132; 'my hands are so cold': Josiah to Bentley, 31 December 1767, Keele, E25–18182.

27 'the hazardous state of my health': Josiah to Bentley, 3 July 1767, Keele, E25–18160; *cf.* earlier complaints, Josiah to Bentley, July 1767, Keele, E25–18159. The inclement weather is complained about continuously.

28 'over-walk'd & over-work'd': Josiah to W. Cox, 30 April 1768, Keele, E96–17660; various modern interpretations of the medical condition that led to Josiah's amputation have been proffered. Leonard and Juliette Rakow in 'Wedgwood's Peg Leg Portraits', *Ars Ceramica* 1 (1984), pp. 10–13, summarise it thus: 'Small pox produces multiple skin vesicles which become secondarily infected. The bacteria from the resultant abscesses frequently enter the blood stream and lodge in the end of long bones where they cause osteomyelitis . . . The bacteria growing in the ends of the long bones produce bone abscesses [and in certain circumstances] drainage does not occur . . . The body's immune processes wage a constant war with the infecting bacteria which nest in the ends of the long bones . . . Unfortunately small injuries to the infected area, excessive use of the extremity and reduction of immune activity for other reasons, all result in moderate or severe flare-up of the symptoms.' See also Andrew Meiklejohn, 'English Domestic Medicine in the Eighteenth Century from the Letters of Josiah Wedgwood', *Post-Graduate Medical Journal* 26 (1950), pp. 541–2.

29 'the pain had no soon left my knee': quoted in Meiklejohn, 'English Domestic Medicine', p. 541.

30 'I am in no fear': Josiah to Bentley, 10 April 1768, Keele, E25–18198.

31 'brotherly love & affection': Josiah to Bentley, June 1768, Keele, E25–18199; various accounts of the amputation stem from Meteyard, *Life*, II, pp. 40–41.

32 'Your favor of the 26th': invoice

dated 28 May 1768; Reilly, *Josiah Wedgwood*, p. 707; 'I think Mrs. Wedgwood': Swift to Cox, Keele, E96–17666.

33 'one grain of variolous matter': Erasmus Darwin, *Temple of Nature*, quoted in Desmond King-Hele (ed.), *The Essential Writings of Erasmus Darwin* (London: MacGibbon & Kee, 1968), p. 291.

34 'that it is bringing a Distemper': Doddridge, *Case of Receiving the Small-Pox*, quotes from pp. 9, 18, 25.

35 'Convulsions at the first appearance': information on Josiah's children in letters of 2 March 1767, Keele, E25–18139 and 31 December 1767, Keele, E25–18182.

EIGHTEEN *The Arts Reborn*

1 'left off my laudanum': Josiah to Bentley, June 1768, Keele, E25–18199.

2 'a wooden leg maker': Josiah to Bentley, 14 July 1768, Keele, E25–18205; for portraits of Josiah with a straight wooden prosthesis, see Rakow, 'Wedgwood's Peg Leg Portraits'.

3 'a long time ago' and 'mouth a watering': Josiah to William Cox, 13 July 1768, Keele, E96–17665.

4 'there are some statues': Montesquieu quoted in Francis Haskell and Nicholas Penny, *Taste and the Antique: The Lure of Classical Sculpture 1500–1900* (New Haven and London: Yale University Press, 1981), p. 73, a book which provides an excellent account of the spread and lure of classicism throughout this period.

5 'as a Society of Artists': Josiah to Bentley, [February 1769], Keele, E25–18232.

6 'prevail upon any artist': Josiah to Bentley, 1767, Keele, E25–18167.

7 'figurines modelled after *Spinario*': Haskell and Penny, *Taste and the Antique*, p. 96, who point to examples in the Victoria and Albert Museum. I am also grateful to Hilary Young at the V&A for discussing the collections there with me.

8 'in making ornamental earthenware': partnership agreement between Josiah and Bentley signed 15 November 1767, Keele, W/M 1826; see Blake Roberts, 'Wedgwood and His Partners'; McKendrick, 'Josiah Wedgwood and Thomas Bentley'; 'in the original works of the ancients': Bentley reviewing Hamilton's volumes upon their publication in the *Monthly Review* 42 (1770), p. 514; see also the useful guide to Josiah's and Bentley's book collection, Harwood A. Johnson, 'Books Belonging to Wedgwood and Bentley the 10th of August 1770', *Ars Ceramica* 7 (1990), pp. 13–23.

9 'I apprehend the Etruscan body': notes in Josiah's commonplace book, Wedgwood Museum, Keele, E39–28408, f. 153.

10 'all my patterns as they arrive': Josiah to William Cox, 31 August 1768, Keele, E96–17667.

11 'Sèvres' and 'Capodimonte': Haskell and Penny, *Taste and the Antique*, p. 96.

12 'plinth height': Josiah to Bentley, 25 July 1768, Keele, E25–18205.

13 'does not seem to consider . . .':
Josiah to Bentley, 30 August 1768,
Keele, E25–18208.

14 'some 600 men were busy':
Meteyard, *Life*, I, p. 497.

15 'Some of my good Neighbours':
Josiah to Bentley, 10 April 1768,
Keele, E25–18198.

16 'I believe you will think me . . .':
Josiah to Bentley, 24 December
1767, Keele, E25–18181.

17 'to ship himself in the cheapest
way': Josiah to Bentley, 6 July
1768, Keele, E25–18204; E25–18199
for advance of £70.

18 'Mr Cox is as mad': Josiah to
Bentley, 21 November 1768, Keele,
E25–18215.

19 'serpent handled antique vases':
Peter Swift (with post-script by
Josiah) to William Cox on an
invoice, 3 September 1768, quoted
in Meteyard, *Life*, II, p. 69.

20 'I am collecting some figures':
Josiah to Bentley, [February 1769],
Keele, E25–18232.

21 'new cabinets are opening': Josiah
to Sally, 7 March 1769, Keele,
E25–18235; for Lady Bessborough
and a glimpse of the activities on
the Grand Tour of some of Josiah's
best customers, see my *Ladies of the
Grand Tour* (London and New
York: HarperCollins, 2001).

22 'so they will be looked over':
Josiah to Bentley, [February 1769],
Keele, E25–18232.

23 'Etruscan Vases are the run at
present': Josiah to Bentley,
6 February 1769, Keele,
E25–18227; in order to encourage
further patronage he sent free
examples of the new wares to Mrs
Chetwynd and the Prince of
Wales, see letter to Cox with
instructions, Keele, L96–17672.

24 'fine old Gentleman': Josiah to
Bentley, 7 February 1769,
amended to Keele, E25–18227.

25 'The great demand . . .': Josiah to
Bentley, 14 February 1769, Keele,
E25–18229.

26 'works are cover'd in': Josiah to
Bentley, 6 November 1768, Keele,
E25–18213.

27 'Etruria Village': the cost of the
various buildings was: Etruria
Hall and offices, £2660; 'the
house and offices of Mr JW',
£633; the barn, £240; the house
Swift lives in, £82; the Inn, £681;
the useful works, £2646; the
ornamental works, £1041; dwelling
houses, in no. 42 including the 6
houses at the works, £1880; the
Mill, £190: Keele, E43–28632.

28 'The slip kiln is nearly finish'd':
Josiah to Bentley, 9 April 1769,
Keele, E25–18237.

29 'dare not acquaint her': Josiah to
Bentley, 18 June 1769, Keele,
E25–18243.

30 'slops': see, for instance,
Wedgwood and Wedgwood,
Wedgwood Circle, p. 42.

NINETEEN *Ingenious People
& Formidable Opponents*

1 'Amid the hoary Ruins':
Thomson, *Liberty* from *Works of
Mr Thomson*, I, p. 103.

2 'Wedgwood & Bentley': the most
comprehensive study to date of
Bentley's influence on Josiah is
McKendrick, 'Josiah Wedgwood
and Thomas Bentley'.

3 'In general we owe the
possession': Young, *Six Months
Tour*, III, p. 309.

4 '300 houses': Young, *Six Months
Tour*, III, p. 306.

5 'narrow selfish views': Josiah to
  Bentley, 22 February 1768, Keele,
  E25–18187.

6 'doctrines of *money getting*':
  Bentley quoted by Josiah in
  12 March 1767, Keele, E25–18140.

7 'Society for the Encouragement of
  Arts, Manufactures and
  Commerce': my discussion of this
  draws from Allan and Abbott,
  The Virtuoso Tribe of Arts &
  Sciences.

8 'against foreign despotism' and
  'No truly benevolent': from
  D. G. C. Allan and John L.
  Abbott (eds), *The Virtuoso Tribe of*
  Arts & Sciences: Studies in the
  Eighteenth-Century Work &
  membership of the London Society of
  Arts (Athens and London: The
  University of Georgia Press, 1992),
  pp. xvi-xvii.

9 'That the national improvement
  of skill': Dossie, *Handmaid*, I,
  p. v.

10 'there is a rivalship': Dossie,
   Handmaid, II, p. 407.

11 '£11 million . . .': these figures from
   Peter Mathias, *The Transformation*
   of England: Essays in the Economic
   and Social History of England in
   the Eighteenth Century (London:
   Methuen, 1979), p. 125; for a
   discussion of the differences
   between customs and excise
   revenue and land assessments see
   Peter Mathias and Patrick
   O'Brien, 'Taxation in England
   and France 1715–1810: A
   comparison of the Social and
   Economic Incidence of Taxes
   Collected for the Central
   Governments', *Journal of European*
   Economic History 5 (1976); John
   Brewer, *The Sinews of Power:*
   War, Money and the English State

   1688–1783 (London: Routledge,
   1989), p. 100; Ashworth, *Customs*
   and Excise.

12 'mechanic invention, toys and
   utensils': Robert Schofield, *The*
   Lunar Society of Birmingham: A
   Social History of Provincial Science
   and Industry in Eighteenth-Century
   England (Oxford: Clarendon
   Press, 1963), p. 24; Eric Roll, *An*
   Early Experiment in Industrial
   Organisation: Being a History of
   the Firm of Boulton and Watt,
   1775–1805 (London: Frank Cass &
   Co., 1968), p. 8; for a recent
   account of the relationship
   between Boulton, Erasmus
   Darwin and others discussed in
   this chapter, see Uglow, *Lunar*
   Men.

13 'industrious, ingenious working
   people': Franklin quoted in
   Uglow, *Lunar Men*, p. 58.

14 'to shew the Difference of
   Workmanship': Franklin quoted
   in Ronald Clark, *Benjamin*
   Franklin: A Biography (London:
   Weidenfeld and Nicolson, 1983),
   p. 147.

15 'two successive marriages': the first
   was to Mary Robinson, and upon
   her death to her younger sister,
   Anne, who were worth £14,000
   each.

16 'I intend to ask him' and 'He is I
   believe the first': Josiah to
   Bentley, 23 May 1767, Keele,
   E25–18147.

17 'you have public spirit enough':
   Josiah to Darwin, 3 April 1765, in
   King-Hele, *Erasmus Darwin*,
   p. 55.

18 'formal and parsonic': Darwin's
   comments in King-Hele (ed.),
   Letters of Erasmus Darwin, I,
   p. 33.

19 'there are no wheels or Cogs': Darwin's comments quoted in Josiah to Bentley, 3 March 1768, Keele, E25–18191.

20 '68,000 bricks . . .': see King-Hele (ed.), *Letters of Erasmus Darwin*, I, p. 50.

21 'we settled many important matters': Josiah to Bentley, 15 March 1768, Keele, E25–18193.

22 'The Artists have even come': Josiah to Bentley, 15 March 1768, Keele, E25–18193.

23 'Mr Boulton is picking up Vases': Josiah to Bentley, 21 November 1768, Keele, E25–18215; Boulton tried to forge a union again at the beginning of January, but Josiah was still uncertain how Bentley would react: Josiah to Bentley, 3 January 1769, Keele, E25–18222.

24 'I have got the start of my Brethren': Josiah to Bentley, 9 April 1769, Keele, E25–18237.

25 'No getting to the door': Josiah to Bentley, 1 May 1769, Keele, E25–18240.

TWENTY *French Frippery &
Russian Husks*

1 'I have waited upon Lord Cathcart': Josiah to Boulton, January 1768, 'Lunar Society Correspondence', Adam Matthew microfilm.

2 'an East Indian Captain': Josiah to Bentley, April 1767, Keele, E25–18167.

3 'I cannot raise the prices': Josiah to Bentley, April 1767, Keele, E25–18191.

4 'If the Bills are sent': Lady Cathcart to Josiah, quoted by him in letter to Bentley, 4 September 1769, Keele, E25–18250.

5 'We have a large order': Josiah to Bentley, 4 September 1769, Keele, E25–18250.

6 'Ld Barrington is angry': Josiah to Bentley, 12 or 13 September 1769, Keele, E25–18253.

7 'take a little weight': Josiah to Bentley, 13 September 1769, Keele, E25–18252.

8 'I shall hire all the Men': Josiah to Bentley, 12 or 13 September 1769, Keele, E25–18253.

9 'several others would fain to hire': Josiah to Bentley, 20 September 1769, Keele, E25–18258.

10 'A Porter has offer'd': Josiah to Bentley, 13 September 1769, Keele, E25–18252.

11 'making habitations for a colony': Josiah to Bentley, 24 march 1768, Keele, E25–18196.

12 'A full-blown retirement scheme': see Priestley's plan, *Lectures on History and General Policy* (Birmingham: 1788).

13 'Lazy & fickle': Josiah to Bentley, 9 April 1769, Keele, E25–18237.

14 'They must not be presented': Josiah to Bentley, 20 September 1769, Keele, E25–18258.

15 'I am on the spot to be of service': Lady Cathcart to Josiah, 19 March 1771, W/M 1442.

16 'I was not order'd to insure': Josiah to Bentley, 25 September 1769, Keele, E25–18260.

17 'Saturday is the busiest': this and the following quotations relating to Boulton from Josiah to Bentley, 27 September 1769, Keele, E25–18261.

18 'Conquer France in Burslem?': Josiah to Bentley, 13 September 1769, Keele, E25–18252.

19 'for the *Virtuosi* of France': Josiah (repeating Bentley's words) to

Bentley, 17 September 1769, Keele, E25–18255; Reilly, *Wedgwood*, I, p. 98.

20 'The field is vast indeed': Josiah to Bentley, 1 October 1769, Keele, E25–18264.

21 'Avenue to the Russian Empire': Josiah to Bentley, 2 July 1770, Keele, E25–18312.

22 'Orders from Russia': Josiah to Bentley, 16 February 1771 in Farrer (ed.), *Letters*, II, p. 13.

23 'What is good will sell here': Lady Cathcart to Josiah, 17 April 1771, W/M 1442.

24 'The Russian trade comes': Josiah to Bentley, 21 April 1771, in Farrer (ed.), *Letters*, II, p. 24.

25 'How many Lords': Josiah to Bentley, January 1771, in Farrer (ed.), *Letters*, II, p. 1.

26 '£650 a month': Reilly, *Wedgwood*, p. 31.

27 'Generalissimo': Josiah to Bentley, 23 January 1771 in Farrer (ed.), *Letters*, II, p. 6.

TWENTY-ONE *Wanting Air for Sally*

1 'Sukey & Jack at my elbows': Josiah to Bentley, 22 December 1770, Keele, E25–18333; E25–18329.

2 'we have all things in common': Sally to Bentley, 29 November 1769, Keele, microfilm reel ii, f. 162.

3 'New grates are put up': from Meteyard, *Life*, II, p. 95; the household inventory by Cox is at Keele, W/M 1360.

4 'Wet mornings and fine afternoons': this, and the following quotations (until otherwise noted) from Sally to Bentley, 29 November 1769,

5 'If ministers can once usurp': Wilkes quoted in H. T. Dickinson, 'Radicals and Reformers in the Age of Wilkes and Wyvill', in Jeremy Black (ed.), *British Politics and Society from Walpole to Pitt 1742–1789* (Basingstoke: Macmillan, 1990), p. 126.

6 'As I am deeply enter'd': and following quotations until otherwise referenced, Sally to Bentley, 8 December 1768, Keele, microfilm, ii, ff. 185–6.

7 'such fine things of my Lad' and 'Jacks smile Pleased': Sally and Catherine to Bentley, 29 November 1768, Keele, microfilm, ii, f. 162.

8 'I will not trust to writing': Josiah to Bentley, [December] 1768, Keele, E25–18216.

9 'My good man is upon the ramble': Sally to Bentley, December 1768, Keele, microfilm, ii, ff. 178–9.

10 'just arriv'd': Sally to Bentley, December 1768, Keele, microfilm, ii, f. 188.

11 'We met with several accidents': Josiah to Bentley, 11 November 1769, Keele, E25–18268.

12 'They are near': Josiah to Bentley, 1 January 1770, Keele, E25–18280.

13 'My *life*': Josiah to Bentley, 24 January 1770, Keele, E25–18286.

14 'I am often practicing': Josiah to Bentley, 15 January 1770, Keele, E25–18284.

15 'little Tom': Josiah to Bentley, 15 May 1771, in Farrer (ed.), *Letters*, II, p. 29.

16 'nail'd down here': Josiah to

Bentley, 30 March 1772, Keele, E25–18360; '*hard weather*': Josiah to Bentley, 22 March 1772, Keele, E25–18358; 'removing our Wheels': Josiah to Bentley, 23 April 1772, Keele, E25–18369.

17 'My landlord is married': Adams, *North Staffordshire Families*, p. 125.

18 'The sun shines': Josiah to Bentley, 22 March 1772, Keele, E25–18358.

19 'Mrs Wedgwood is Ill': Josiah to Bentley, 22 March 1772, Keele, microfilm, iii, f. 14.

20 'Carried to & from': Josiah to Bentley, 30 March 1772, Keele, microfilm, iii, f. 17.

21 'Take an airing on Horseback': Josiah to Bentley, 11 April 1772, Keele, E25–18365.

22 'He says he is afraid': Josiah to Bentley, 30 March 1772, Keele, E25–18360.

23 'central fires': Darwin's interest in Buxton discussed in King-Hele, *Erasmus Darwin*, p. 245.

24 'Patients would have no confidence' and 'is not to be trifled with': both physicians' opinions quoted in David Harley, 'A Sword in a Madman's Hand: Professional Opposition to Popular Consumption in the Waters Literature of Southern England and the Midlands, 1570–1870', in R. Porter (ed.), *The Medical History of Waters and Spas, Medical History* supplement, 10 (1990), p. 52.

25 'I believe London': Josiah to Bentley, July 1769, Keele, E25–18247.

26 'to prepare a sortment': Josiah to Bentley, 22 March 1772, Keele, E25–18358.

27 'mention'd going to Bath': Josiah to Bentley, April 1772, Keele, microfilm, iii, f. 30.

28 'Mrs Wedgwood is again confined': Josiah to Bentley, 20 April 1772, Keele, E25–18368.

29 'half remov'd': Josiah to Bentley, 12 May 1772, Keele, E25–18373.

30 'I have left them': Josiah to Bentley, 9 May 1772, Keele, E25–18372.

31 'Coal Carts': Josiah to Bentley, 6 June 1772, Keele, E25–18376.

32 'a very rich shop': this and the following quotes relating to this story from Josiah to Bentley, 6 June 1772, Keele, E25–18376.

33 'especially her knees': Josiah to Bentley, 14 June 1772, Keele, E25–18378.

34 'Mr Willets has just been': Catherine to Sally, 20 May 1772; 'Tom grows every way': Catherine to Sally, 6 June 1772; 'Tommy has four teeth': William Willets to Josiah and Sally, 12 June 1772; all from Keele, W/M 5.

35 'almost a skeleton': Josiah to Bentley, August 1772 (they returned to Etruria 13 July), Keele, microfilm, iii, 106.

36 'Breeding disease': Josiah to Bentley, 23 August 1772, Keele, E25–18392.

37 '& nothing but the greatest': Josiah to Bentley, 7 September 1772, Keele, E25–18399.

38 'a course of steel': King-Hele, *Erasmus Darwin*, p. 110, where he refers to a three-page letter of advice from Darwin to the Wedgwoods written on 30 September 1772, but this is not printed in King-Hele (ed.), *Letters of Erasmus Darwin*.

39 'the dear partner': King-Hele, *Erasmus Darwin*, p. 91.

40 'to fortify her': Josiah to Bentley, 13 September 1772, Keele, E25–18403.

41 'I have lost': Josiah to Bentley, 12 October 1772, Keele, E25–18412.

42 'in a very dangerous': Josiah to Bentley, 2 November 1772, E25–18415.

43 'revolution in our household': Josiah to Bentley, 9 November 1772, E25–18418.

44 'if we can preserve her': Josiah to Bentley, 26 December 1772, Keele, E25–18430.

TWENTY-TWO *All the Gardens in England*

1 'sortables': Thomas Wedgwood's inventory of earthenware from Keele, L96–17804.

2 'a mere £130': 'Inventory of workhouse equipment and values': Keele, L96–17807.

3 'Ailments of Various Kinds': Josiah to Bentley, 3 February 1773, Keele, E25–18442.

4 'ill treated & almost ruined' and 'her daily study': from Josiah to Bentley, 30 May 1773, Keele, E25–18465.

5 'the foolish talk': Josiah to Bentley, 15 March 1773, Keele, E25–18449.

6 '£50 worth of furniture': 'An account of the household goods Mrs Wedgwood hath . . .', Keele, L96–17808.

7 'borrow money from Josiah': promissory notes, Keele, L96–17819.

8 'Mrs W has had a good night': Josiah to Bentley, 2 March 1773, Keele, E25–18446.

9 'upon the verge of the Holy Estate': Josiah to Bentley, 23 April 1772, Keele, E25–18369.

10 'dessert Table': description of the Adelphi showroom in Josiah to Bentley, 4 April 1772, Keele, microfilm, iii, ff. 23–26; and 11 April 1772, Keele, E25–18365.

11 '£400 annually': see Una des Fontaines, 'Wedgwood's London Showrooms', *Proceedings of the Wedgwood Society* 8 (1970), p. 221, for further discussion.

12 'I like the idea': see Fontaines's 'Portland House', for full story.

13 'simple, beautiful and varied': *Acts of Parliament* (1772), British Library 215.i.2 (f. 132).

14 'chemical concoction': see Josiah's patent reprinted in Jewitt, *The Wedgwoods*, p. 201.

15 'The *selling*': Josiah to Bentley, 25 October 1770, Keele, E25–18328.

16 'clever': Josiah to Bentley, November 1770, Keele, E25–18346.

17 'a sharer in the patent': see Reilly, *Wedgwood*, p. 81, for this point.

18 'there is nothing relating to business': this and the following quotations relating to 'surprising the world' are from a long letter to Bentley, 27 September 1769, Keele, E25–18261.

19 'in order of time': Josiah to Bentley, 1 October 1769, Keele, E25–18264.

20 'Variations': Josiah to Bentley, 27 September 1769, Keele, E25–18261.

21 'I am not without': Josiah to Bentley, 11 April 1772, Keele, E25–18365.

22 'my Great Patroness': Josiah to Bentley, 23 March 1773, Keele, E25–18450; much has been written about this commission, for

instance see George Charles Williamson, *The Imperial Russian Dinner Service* (London: George Bell, 1909); a useful article which summarises the story is Alison Kelly, 'Wedgwood's Catherine Services', *Ars Ceramica* 8 (1991), pp. 6–13.

23 '*every piece*': Josiah to Bentley, 23 March 1773, Keele, E25–18450.

24 'Do you think the subjects . . .': Josiah to Bentley, 29 March, 1773, Keele, E25–18452.

25 'rap his knuckles': Josiah to Bentley, 30 July 1773, Keele, E25–18484.

26 'not be *fit*': Josiah to Bentley, 5 April 1773, Keele, E25–18454.

27 '*the publish'd views*': Josiah to Bentley, 30 July 1773, Keele, E25–18484; 'published views', as Kelly, 'Wedgwood's Catherine Services' notes included well-illustrated volumes such as Bickham's *Beauties of Stow*, Chambers' *Description of Kew*, and so on.

28 'first Empress': Josiah to Bentley, 9 April 1773, Keele, E25–18455.

29 'all the centuries and styles': from Bentley's catalogue of the service, written in French. The British Library copy of Williamson's book, *Imperial Russian Dinner Service*, contains a full translation of Bentley's original catalogue, BL K.T.C.36.b.9.

30 'it would bring an immense': Josiah to Bentley, 14 November 1773, Keele, E25–18498.

31 'It consists I believe': from Delany's autobiography, quoted in Jo Dahn, 'Mrs Delany and Ceramics in the Objectscape', in the on-line journal *Interpreting Ceramics*, http://www.uwic.ac.uk/ICRC/issue001/delany/delany.htm.

32 'her approbation': quoted in Kelly, 'Wedgwood's Catherine Services', p. 12.

33 '16,000 roubles': this is the figure stated by L. N. Voronikhina, in her Russian monograph *The Service with Green Frog*, cited by Kelly in 'Wedgwood's Catherine Services', p. 12. James Harris, an English traveller to Russia in 1779, was shown the 'very remarkable service . . . and this led us to a conversation on English gardening, in which the Empress is a great adept': Malmesbury, The Third Earl, *Diaries and Correspondence of James Harris, First Earl of Malmesbury*, 4 vols (London: Richard Bentley, 1844), I, p. 231.

TWENTY-THREE *Deep in the Cherokee Backcountry*

1 'a miserable hot': this and all the following quotes relating to Griffiths' journey, unless otherwise noted, from his 'Journal of the Voyage to South Carolina, 1767', a transcript of which is in the Wedgwood Museum, Barlaston to whom I am grateful for providing a copy and permission to quote from it. It is interesting to compare Griffiths' journey to that of William Bartram in 1775, described in his published *Travels through North and South Carolina* (Philadelphia, 1791); see also the account by the North Carolina Bartram Trail Society (http://www.ncbartramtrail.org/index.htm). Griffiths' journey is discussed by Bill Anderson in his

'Cherokee Clay, from Duché to Wedgwood: The Journal of Thomas Griffiths, 1767–1768', *North Carolina Historical Review* (1976), and in an article by George Ellison in *Mountain Voices*, 7 March 2001 (www.smokeymountainnews.com).

2 'an Englishman named Mr Downy': this, I believe, is the same couple who later extended hospitality to William Bartram during his travels.

TWENTY-FOUR *Poison & Porcelain*

1 'Cookworthy discovered deposits': this, of course, is a much simplified version of what happened; see Selleck, *Cookworthy*, for more comprehensive analysis of unfolding series of events that led to Cookworthy's discovery. Also, Anderson, 'Cherokee Clay, from Duché to Wedgwood'.

2 'enhanced the cream colour': Gaye Blake Roberts, 'Josiah Wedgwood and Richard Champion, Adversaries and Friends', *Ars Ceramica* 17 (2001), p. 45.

3 'I apprehend our customers': Josiah to Bentley, 12 December 1774, Keele, E25–18572.

4 'the Great People have had their Vases': Josiah to Bentley, 23 August 1772, Keele, E25–18392.

5 'Few Ladies, you know': Josiah to Bentley, 21 June 1777, Keele, E25–18766.

6 'present vogue for imitating': *Monthly Magazine* (1763), quoted in Bushman, 'American High Style'.

7 'never his primary market': in another instance, when Josiah was considering resurrecting the agate and green ware that he stopped producing a decade earlier when they became unfashionable, he reasoned that 'there are, and ever will be a numerous class of People, to purchase *shewy* & *cheap* things. The Creamcolour is of a superior class, & I trust has not yet run its race by many degrees', 7 March 1774, Keele, E25–18521. A number of recent studies have looked at Wedgwood as a pioneer in marketing and branding, see for instance Nancy Koehn, *Brand New: How Entrepreneurs Earned Consumers' Trust from Wedgwood to Dell* (Boston, MA: Harvard Business School Press, 2001) and Regina Lee Blaszczyk, *Imagining Consumers: Design and Innovation from Wedgwood to Corning* (Baltimore and London: Johns Hopkins University Press, 2000).

8 'we have hitherto appeared': Josiah to Bentley, 7 December 1772, Keele, E25–18427.

9 'receive, by the Mouth': Bernardino Ramazini, *A Dissertation on endemial Diseases . . . Together with a treatise on the diseases of Tradesmen, by B. Ramazini*, translated by Friedrich Hoffmann (London, 1745), p. 62. My thanks to Paul Blanc for allowing me to use his library of eighteenth-century medical tracts relating to occupational health, and for his input.

10 'First of all': Ramazini, *Diseases of Tradesmen*, p. 62; Edward Strother, *An Essay on Sickness and Health . . . in which Dr. Cheyne's mistaken opinions in his late essay are occasionally taken notice of*

(London, 1725), p. 447, where he essentially repeats the symptoms and recommends 'chalybeates and mercurial purges as Remedies'.

11 'May it not reasonably': George Baker, 'An Examination of Several Means, by which the Poison of Lead may be supposed frequently to gain admittance into the Human Body, unobserved, and unsuspected', *Medical Transactions of the College of Physicians, London* (1768), p. 300.

12 'That part of the old earthenware': Baker, 'An Examination of Several Means', pp. 359–60.

13 '& I told him it was': Josiah to Bentley, 21 July 1773, Keele, E25–18481.

14 'I do not dispute': Josiah to Bentley, 17 August 1773, Keele, E25–18488.

15 'to shew how pernicious': Josiah to Bentley, 22 August 1773, Keele, E25–18490.

16 'it is now very difficult': Benson's patent, quoted in Harold Owen, *The Staffordshire Potter* (London: Grant Richards, 1901), p. 276.

17 'I will try in earnest': Josiah to Bentley, 22 August 1773, Keele, E25–18490; for more on the issue of lead poisoning, see Meiklejohn, 'The Successful Prevention of Lead Poisoning', p. 169.

18 'stop the Rascals career': Josiah to Bentley, 4 December 1774, Keele, E25–18571. A year earlier, Josiah hoped that by publishing a descriptive catalogue of their wares they would not only gain an advertising tool, but perhaps it would also help to distinguish their brand of wares from anyone else's. Their first catalogue was published in 1774, but it does not seem to have worked as a deterrent to forgers. Part of the difficulty, as Josiah explained to Bentley, was that some pieces, such as seals or cameos, were so small that there was not space enough to add more distinguishing marks and numbers. See Josiah to Bentley, 7 June 1773, Keele, E25–18469.

19 'Man of Science, who loves everything English': Erasmus Darwin to Josiah, 27 April 1766, in King-Hele (ed.), *Letters of Erasmus Darwin*, I, p. 40.

20 'I do not wish to purchase': Josiah to Bentley, 6 February 1774, quoted in Blake Roberts, 'Wedgwood and Champion', p. 45.

21 'some very promising experiments': Josiah to Bentley, 6 February 1773, Keele, E25–18443.

22 'I am fairly enter'd into' and 'bad policy': Josiah to Bentley (and Josiah therein quoting Bentley), 7 March 1774, Keele, E25–18521.

23 'Moorstone & Spaith fusible': Josiah to Bentley, 21 July 1774, Keele, E25–18548. For a further discussion of these experiments, which relate to the creation of jasper, see Reilly, *Wedgwood Jasper* (London: Thames and Hudson, 1994), particularly pp. 70–71 where he discusses the work of William Burton and Sir Arthur Church, who worked out, in modern terms, the chemical properties of jasper.

24 'If I had more *time*': these and quotations to 'crazy' from Josiah to Bentley, 30 August 1774, Keele, E25–18555.

25 'Aged & affectionate father':

Josiah to Bentley, 19 November 1774, Keele, E25–18565.

26 'the place & the scenes': Josiah to Bentley, 26 November 1774, Keele, E25–18569.

27 'my dear Girl': Josiah to Bentley, 30 November 1774, Keele, E25–18570.

28 'impenetrable veil': Josiah to Bentley, 12 December 1774, Keele, E25–18573.

29 'it is too precious to reveal': Josiah to Bentley, 3 February 1776, Keele, E25–18650.

30 '4 black & Blue onyx Intaglios': see Reilly, *Wedgwood Jasper*, p. 76.

31 'crucifixes, Saints': Josiah to Bentley, 5 November 1774, Keele, E25–18561.

32 'so you see a spirit': Josiah to Bentley, 23 July 1775, Keele, E25–18612.

33 'the Manufactures of Dresden' and 'ASTONISH': Josiah to Bentley, 6 August 1775, Keele, E25–18614.

34 'nobody but W & B': Josiah to Bentley, 5 July 1776, Keele, E25–18680.

35 'very civil': Josiah to Bentley, 5 July 1776, Keele, E25–18680.

36 'suitable for setting in boxes': it seems the earliest this was proposed was 7 June 1773, Keele, E25–18469.

37 'the Art of *Jasper making*': Josiah to Bentley, 14 January 1776, Keele, E25–18642. For Josiah's account of the production of jasper, written in a memorandum on 23 November 1777, see Reilly, *Wedgwood Jasper*, pp. 87–8.

38 'I have often thought': Josiah to Bentley, 15 December 1777, Keele, E25–18802. 'A Portion of

Cherokee clay is *really used*', emphasis mine.

39 ''23, the secret code': Reilly, *Wedgwood Jasper*, p. 90.

TWENTY-FIVE *Mad Ministers*

1 'I am no polititian': Josiah to Bentley, 8 January 1775, Keele, E25–18582.

2 'cruel and oppressive': 'Resolves of the First Continental Congress', 14 October 1774.

3 'empire of goods': see Breen 'Empire of Goods', p. 498; Franklin cited in Jack P. Greene (ed.), 'The Examination of Benjamin Franklin in the House of Commons, February 13, 1766' in *Colonies to Nation: 1763–1789* (New York, 1979), p. 73.

4 'around half of all English exports': McCusker and Menard, *Economy of British America*, p. 286; also see Blake-Roberts, 'Wedgwood to America'.

5 'necessaries, mere conveniences, or superfluities': Greene, 'Examination of Benjamin Franklin', p. 73.

6 'To impose servitude': Lord Chatham in House of Lords, 20 January 1775, see Young, *Genius*, p. 88.

7 'froth'd at the mouth': Josiah's observations from Josiah to Bentley, 6 February 1775, Keele, E25–18590.

8 'to my astonishment': Josiah to Bentley, 5 November 1775, Keele, E25–18623.

9 'Those who are neither converted': Josiah to Bentley, 24 February 1776, Keele, E25–18657; Richard Price, *Observations on the Nature*

of Civil Liberty, the Principles of Government, and the Juſtice and Policy of the War with America (London, 1776), which went through five editions in under two months of its first publication and sold over 60,000 copies.

10 'without a sacrifice of principle': Josiah to Bentley, 27 November 1775, Keele, E25–18626.

11 'There is no doubt': Josiah to Sir John Wrottesley, 29 November 1775, Keele, E25–18627; for wars and the state of the British economy, see Brewer, *Sinews of Power*, pp. 178–9.

12 'In 1775, under 139,000': Ewins, 'Supplying the Present Wants', Table 1; Elizabeth Boody Schumpeter, *English Overseas Trade Statistics, 1697–1808* (Oxford: Clarendon Press, 1960).

13 'absurdity, folly': Josiah to Bentley, 3 March 1778, Keele, E25–18815.

14 'the Gentlemen who repose': Josiah to Byerley, April 1774, Keele, E25–18529.

15 'She had much rather': Josiah to Bentley, 23 June 1775, Keele, E25–18603.

16 'I should be asham'd': Josiah to Bentley, 3 February 1776, Keele, E25–18650; 'Asiatic Porcelains': Josiah discussing Byerley's letter on behalf of the committee, 7 February 1776, Keele, E25–18652.

17 'very good things *for England*': Josiah to Bentley, 2 July 1776, Keele, E25–18679.

TWENTY-SIX *The Philosophes & Plaster Shops of Paris*

1 'to the Duke or Count': quoted in Harwood Johnson, 'Thomas Bentley's Journal of his Visit to Paris in 1776', *Ars Ceramica* 9 (1992), p. 8.

2 'professedly a journey': Bentley to Samuel Boardman, 3 October 1776, quoted in Johnson, *Thomas Bentley's Journal*, pp. 9–10.

3 'Many of the buildings': Bentley to Samuel Boardman, 3 October 1776, quoted in Johnson, *Thomas Bentley's Journal*, pp. 9–10; the journal has been published as Thomas Bentley, *A Journal of a Visit to Paris 1776*, edited by Peter France (University of Sussex Library, 1977), and is cited here as Bentley, *Journal*.

4 'tell me': Montagu in Bentley, *Journal*, p. 29; Dolan, *Ladies of the Grand Tour*, pp. 131–2; 'your remark': Josiah to Bentley, 8 August 1776, Keele, E25–18687.

5 'the causes': Bentley, *Journal*, p. 30.

6 'my heart expanded': this and the following account of his meeting with Rousseau in Bentley, *Journal*, pp. 59–61.

7 'Lunar Society': see Uglow, *The Lunar Men* and Schofield, *Lunar Society of Birmingham*, for comprehensive discussions of this.

8 'a form of social worship': David Williams, 'A Liturgy on the Universal Principles of Religion and Morality' (1776), preface; for more, see David Williams, 'Incidents in my Life', Cardiff Central Library, MS 2.191–2.

9 'ah yes': the Rousseau–Bentley dialogue recorded in Bentley, *Journal*, p. 60.

10 'prefers exile': Thomas Day, *The Dying Negro: A Poem* (London, 1773; third edition, 1775), preface.

11 'upon examination': Bentley, *Journal*, p. 42.

12 '*à l'anglaise*': Bentley in Johnson, 'Thomas Bentley's Journal', p. 11; see also J. R. Harris, *Industrial Espionage and Technology Transfer: Britain and France in the Eighteenth Century* (Aldershot: Ashgate, 1998), p. 328.

TWENTY-SEVEN *A Poor Regiment*

1 'before our people are up': Josiah to Bentley (on a Saturday morning), 7 March 1774, Keele, E25–18521.

2 'Nay, you need not': Josiah to Bentley, 15 May 1776, Keele, E25–18669.

3 'a healing Balsam': this and the following account of the dispute with the workers from Josiah to Bentley, 22 July 1776, Farrer (ed.), *Letters*, II, pp. 299–301.

4 'This will not do': Meteyard, *Life*, I, p. 219.

5 'It is *hard*': Josiah to Bentley, 23 December 1770, Keele, E25–18310.

6 'industrial paternalism': see David Roberts, *Paternalism in Early Victorian England* (London: Croom Helm, 1979), for the development of this role. For a view of paternalism in apprenticeships, where the role of the Master replaces the 'negligence' of local government supervision and care for children, see Pinchbeck and Hewitt, *Children in English Society* (details in bibliog. and in full here).

7 'taking & keeping him out': Josiah to Bentley, 1 September 1772, Keele, E25–18397.

8 'charity may incline us': Josiah to Bentley, 4 October 1772, Keele, E25–18411.

9 'They seem to have got the notion': Roberts, *Paternalism*, p. 173.

10 'A *waking notion*': Josiah to Bentley, 23 May 1770, Keele, E25–18302.

11 'scheme for taking Girls': Josiah to Bentley, 19 May 1770, Keele, E25–18301; 'I am more & more in Love': Josiah to Bentley, 25 July 1772, Keele, E25–18382.

12 'improved in their *wages*': Josiah to Bentley, 10 January 1770, Keele, E25–18283.

13 'everyone but an idiot': Young quoted in Mathias, *Transformation*, p. 148; numerous similar comments can be found in Brian Inglis, *Poverty and the Industrial Revolution* (London: Hodder and Stoughton, 1971).

14 'Expenses move on like clockwork': Josiah to Bentley, 23 August 1772, Keele, E25–18392.

15 'who can subsist on three days': quoted in de Vries, 'Purchasing Power', p. 112.

16 'all the Men at the Ornamental': Josiah to Bentley, 22 July 1776, Farrer (ed.), *Letters*, II, pp. 299–300.

TWENTY-EIGHT Arrivistes

1 'In May the following year, 1777': Lead, *Trent & Mersey Canal*, p. 9; cost of canal in Josiah to Richard Lovell Edgeworth, 13 February 1786, Keele, E3–2488.

2 'a very pleasant expedition': Josiah to Bentley, 19 September 1774, Keele, E25–18559.

3 'The whole face of this country':
Wesley in 1781, quoted in Hughes,
Mother Town, p. 12. An excellent
overview of the transformation of
the industrial landscape is Barrie
Trinder, *The Making of the
Industrial Landscape* (London:
J. M. Dent & Sons, 1982;
reprinted 1997).

4 'Blacklands': Josiah to Bentley,
4 May 1776, Keele,
E25–18666.

5 'Poor Crisp': Josiah to Bentley,
6 August 1775, Keele, E25–18614.
See also J. V. G. Mallet,
'Nicholas Crisp, Founding
Member of the Society of Arts',
in Allan and Abbott (eds),
Virtuoso Tribe, pp. 56–74.

6 'Poor Champion': Josiah to
Bentley, 24 August 1778, Keele,
E25–18846.

7 'I have often wish'd': Josiah to
Bentley, 3 September 1774, Keele,
E25–18556.

8 'Illustrious Moderns': Reilly,
Wedgwood, I, p. 553.

9 '*begs without ceasing*': Josiah to
Bentley, 19 July 1777, Keele,
E25–18772 for this and the
following account of Elers's ideas,
unless otherwise noted.

10 'Bomb proof fortifications': Josiah
to Bentley, 1 August 1777, Keele,
E25–18775; Reilly, *Wedgwood*, I,
p. 553.

11 'to mark her father's profession':
for a succinct account of Wright
see Stephen Daniels, *Joseph
Wright* (London: Tate Gallery,
2000); Josiah to Bentley, 5 May
1778, Keele, E25–18834; quote
from Joseph Wright to Josiah,
11 February 1782 (Josiah's initial
idea to commission a painting did
not further develop until this

time), Keele, WMS 1–670; see
Reilly, *Wedgwood*, pp. 304–7.

12 'I can be instructing them': Josiah
to Bentley, 23 November 1779,
E26–18939.

13 'mixing fixible air': Josiah to
Bentley, 30 May 1779, Keele,
E25–18894.

14 'Jack is to be settled': Josiah to
Bentley, 19 December 1779, Keele,
E26–18946.

15 'full of pouks': Josiah to Bentley,
12 June 1773, Keele,
E25–18472.

16 'We know our dear Sukey': Josiah
to Bentley, 26 October 1775,
Keele, E25–18620.

17 'language & manners': Josiah to
Bentley, 11 July 1779, Keele,
E25–18909.

18 'slipt upstairs': Josiah to Bentley,
19 August 1778, Keele, E25–18845;
though Josiah's attitude about
childbirth had some way to go to
be enlightened. When Sally
wanted to stay in bed the next
night and skip the afternoon meal,
he put it down to 'a sort of
decorum establish'd amongst the
sex, originally intended, no doubt,
to impose upon us poor men, &
make us believe what sufferings
they underwent for us & our
bantlings'.

19 'My dear boy': Josiah to his son
John Wedgwood, 1774,
Wedgwood Museum, E39–28408,
f. 292.

20 'I am convinc'd': Josiah to
Bentley, 9 October 1779, Keele,
E26–18929.

21 'give them some lessons in latin':
Josiah to Bentley, 24 October
1779, Keele, E26–18934.

22 'very idle waste of time': Josiah
relaying what Darwin said to

Bentley, 8 November 1779, Keele,
E26–19836.

23 'Before breakfast': Josiah to
Bentley, 23 November 1779, Keele,
E26–18939.

24 'Your little boys': Erasmus Darwin
to Josiah, December 1779, in
King-Hele (ed.), *Letters*, p. 99.

25 'a long course of drinking': Josiah
to Bentley, 7 May 1777, Keele,
E25–18755.

26 'In turning my back': Josiah to
Bentley, 15 September 1778, Keele,
E25–18851.

27 'retir'd from this bustling World':
Josiah to Bentley, 23 July 1775,
Keele, E25–18612.

TWENTY-NINE *Renewed
Grief*

1 'My dear affectionate father':
Wedgwood and Wedgwood,
Wedgwood Circle, p. 79.

2 'Dr Darwin has bin here':
Catherine Wedgwood to Josiah
and Sally, February 1780: this and
the following quotations from
Catherine from a series of letters,
all in February 1780, at Keele,
W/M 5.

3 'All the boasted nostrums':
Darwin quoted by Wedgwood,
12 December 1779, Keele,
E26–18943.

4 'I have this morning': Josiah to
Bentley, 19 February 1780, *Letters*,
II, p. 560.

5 'brought on convulsions': Josiah to
Bentley, 8 November 1779, Keele,
E26–18936.

6 'drawing lightening': for electrical
machines, see Maurice Daumas,
*Scientific Instruments of the
Seventeenth and Eighteenth
Centuries and their Makers*

(London: Portman Books, 1989);
for uses in medicine, see Margaret
Rowbottom and Charles
Susskind, *Electricity and Medicine:
A History of their Interaction*
(London: Macmillan, 1984).

7 'I am in great pain': Josiah to
Bentley, 17 November 1779, Keele,
E26–18937.

8 'As soon as I think': Josiah to
Bentley, 28 October 1780, *Letters*,
II, p. 603.

THIRTY *'Half myself'*

1 'Our friend yet breathes': Ralph
Griffiths to Josiah, 25 November
1780, quoted in Bentley, *Bentley*,
p. 77.

2 'apoplectic seizure': according to
one account – other circumstances
have been posited, including
pleurisy and gout. There are no
extant sources to throw any
more light on the cause of his
death.

3 'I have not any friend': Bentley to
Josiah, 18 December 1778, quoted
in Blake Roberts, 'Josiah
Wedgwood and his Partners',
p. 18.

4 'Our esteemed friend': Samuel
Boardman writing on
31 December 1780, quoted in
Bentley, *Bentley*, p. 83.

5 'Your letter communicating to
me': Erasmus Darwin to Josiah,
29 November 1780, in King-Hele
(ed.), *Letters*, pp. 102–3.

6 'I was indeed as much grieved':
Sulpicius to Cicero, from *Cicero's
Letters*, Harvard Classics, edited
by Charles Eliot (New York:
Bartleby, Conn, 2001) volume 9,
part 3, letter 13.

7 'for his uncommon ingenuity':

quoted in Boardman, *Bentleyana*, p. 12.

8 'Mr Wedgwood was the intelligent man': quoted by Peter France in his edition of Bentley, *Journal*, p. 12; McKendrick, 'Josiah Wedgwood and Thomas Bentley', analyses in further detail the dynamics of their partnership.

9 'preserved from considerable': Wedgwood quoted in Reilly, *Josiah Wedgwood*, p. 251.

10 'a great many discriminating': Byerley quoted in Reilly, *Josiah Wedgwood*, p. 252.

THIRTY-ONE *'A Most Riotous and Outrageous Mob'*

1 'twenty-two separate work stations': inventory and description of factory at Keele, W/M 1578; also William Heath's notebooks on the maintenance of Etruria, 1782, Keele, W/M 1818.

2 'colour thermoscope': the best account of the development of what becomes known as Wedgwood's pyrometer is in Reilly, *Wedgwood*, I, pp. 130–5. For this and other aspects of Josiah's experiments in chemistry see Schofield, 'Josiah Wedgwood, Industrial Chemist'.

3 'turned the art of Pottery': Banks to Josiah, 6 February 1792, quoted in John Gascoigne, *Joseph Banks and the English Enlightenment: Useful Knowledge and Polite Culture* (Cambridge: Cambridge University Press, 1994), p. 180.

4 'a most riotous and outrageous mob': Josiah to Bentley, 9 October 1779, Keele, E26–18929.

5 'We have had several foreigners':

Josiah to Bentley, 1 August 1779, Keele, E26–18912.

6 'prepare it for respiration': for an elaboration on the concerns over industrial disease and the chemical researches on air, see Brian Dolan, 'Conservative Politicians, Radical Philosophers, and the Aerial Remedy for the Diseases of Civilization', *History of the Human Sciences* 15 (2002), pp. 35–54.

7 'May not Dr Priestley's': Commonplace Book, Wedgwood Museum, WMS 39–28408.

8 'fixed air': carbonated water: Gibbs, *Priestley*, pp. 57–9; Jan Golinski, *Science as Public Culture: Chemistry and Enlightenment in Britain, 1760–1820* (Cambridge: Cambridge University Press, 1992), p. 115.

9 'lay by a little money': Josiah's observations of the 'Female Club', recorded in his travelogue of his Cornish tour, reprinted in the *Proceedings of the Wedgwood Society* 2 (1957); see also E. Posner, 'Eighteenth-Century Health and Social Service in the Pottery Industry of North Staffordshire', *Medical History* 18 (1974), pp. 138–47, and Denis Stuart, 'Service of Truth: Early Quaker Poor Relief in Staffordshire to the Mid-Eighteenth Century', in Philip Morgan and A. Phillips (eds), *Staffordshire Histories: Essays in Honour of M. Greenslade* (Keele: Staffordshire Record Society & Centre for Local History, University of Keele, 1999).

10 'If the ague does not weaken': Erasmus Darwin to Josiah, 4 April 1786, in King-Hele (ed.), *Letters*, pp. 149–50.

THIRTY-TWO *'Some plan of life'*

1 'Barberini Vase': the early history of the vase is still a matter of controversy, but, according to Robin Reilly and George Savage, *The Dictionary of Wedgwood* (Woodbridge, Suffolk: Antique Collectors' Club, 1980), p. 276, it is more likely an ancient Roman vase representing the marriage of Peleus and Thetis. The history of the vase is summarised in Dwight Beeson, 'Reproductions of Documents concerning the Slate Blue Wedgwood Copy of the Portland Vase', privately printed in Birmingham, Alabama, 1964; see also Charlotte Wilcoxen, 'Peregrinations of a Letter from Sir William Hamilton to Josiah Wedgwood', *Ars Ceramica* 17 (2001), pp. 36–45.

2 'Is it yours?': Sir William Hamilton relaying the story to Josiah in a letter of 24 July 1786, reprinted in Wilcoxen, 'Peregrinations'.

3 'the Vase, the Head of Jupiter': in Dolan, *Ladies of the Grand Tour*, p. 196.

4 'I begin to count': this and the following quotes until otherwise indicated from Josiah to Sir William Hamilton, 24 June 1786, Keele, E26–18976.

5 'I admire your enthusiasm': Sir William Hamilton to Josiah, 24 July 1786, reprinted in Wilcoxen, 'Peregrinations', pp. 36–7.

6 'diffuse the seeds': expression is Josiah's in his previously cited letter to Sir William (24 June 1786).

7 'I wish to have some': Tom Wedgwood to Josiah, 30 December 1786, Keele, W/M 12.

8 'cannot be right': Sukey to Josiah, in Wedgwood, *Personal Life*, p. 360.

9 'rather grand': Wilberforce quoted in Reilly, *Josiah Wedgwood*, p. 289, and p. 333 for the information on the contents of the house.

10 'I speak from experience': Josiah to Bentley, January 1768, Keele, E25–18183.

11 'My great work': Josiah to Heberdeen, 25 April 1788, Keele, uncatalogued letter.

12 'all the explications': Josiah to William Hamilton, 1787, British Library MSS ADD 40717, f. 230.

13 'fix upon some plan': for Josiah's sons' attitudes toward the family business I am indebted to Reilly's account in *Josiah Wedgwood*, pp. 335–40.

14 'as I believed the ideas'; 'the proposed scheme of Tom', and 'a degree of knowledge', all Josiah to Joss, 16 April 1788, Keele, E26–18979.

15 'is very well executed': Josiah to Joss junior, 16 April 1788, Keele, E26–18979, appendix.

16 'What I mean' and 'I have been too long in the habit': Reilly, *Josiah Wedgwood*, pp. 338–40.

17 'I know you will rejoice', and 'The politicians tell me': Josiah to Erasmus Darwin, July 1789, Farrer (ed.), *Letters*, III, p. 90.

THIRTY-THREE *A Giant Malady*

1 'AFTER an unremitting': notice dated 18 January 1790, reproduced in Reilly, *Josiah Wedgwood*, p. 332.

2 'You have been extremely': Josiah to Erasmus Darwin, July 1789,

Keele, E26–19002; Darwin's interpretation of the scene is discussed in Wolf Mankowitz, *The Portland Vase and the Wedgwood Copies* (London: Andre Deutsch, 1952), pp. 58–9; Desmond King-Hele, *Doctor of Revolution: The Life and Genius of Erasmus Darwin* (London: Faber & Faber, 1977), pp. 244 and 391n, notes that there were forty-four interpretations of the depiction.

3 'disliked it very much': Joss to Josiah, 16 April 1793, in Reilly, *Josiah Wedgwood*, p. 339.

4 'I know my father is afraid': Tom Wedgwood to Joss, 27 April 1790, Keele, W/M 12.

5 'I am well aware': Tom Wedgwood to Josiah, 8 May 1790, Keele, W/M 12.

6 'I am happy my arguments': Tom Wedgwood to Josiah, [*ca*, 11] May 1790, Keele, W/M 12.

7 'which should relate to the late revolution': Joss to Josiah, 28 July 1789, Keele, LHP; *Letters*, III, p. 95.

8 'a cornucopia, a bonnet': Dawson, *Masterpieces of Wedgwood*, p. 63.

9 'Inglorious slept': Darwin, *The Economy of Vegetation* (1792), Canto II, lines 378–80; 385–6, cited in King-Hele, *Life and Genius of Erasmus Darwin*, p. 261.

10 'bunting, beggarly, brass-making . . .': quoted in R. B. Rose, 'The Priestley Riots of 1791,' *Past and Present* 8 (1960): p. 857.

11 'I am much pleased': Josiah commenting on the early results of Priestley's experiments to Bentley, 9 October 1766, Keele, E25–18130. Priestley had received an honorary doctorate from Edinburgh for his well-received *Chart of Biography*.

12 'delightful and ingenious experiments': quoted in Gibbs, *Joseph Priestley*, p. 34.

13 'prepare it for respiration': Priestley writing in 1782 while preparing his *Experiments and Observations on Air*, for an elaboration of the following few paragraphs, see Dolan, 'Conservative Politicians, Radical Philosophers'.

14 'Priestley was warned': the best study concerning Priestley and the 'Church and King' riots of 1791 is Kramnick, 'Eighteenth-Century Science and Radical Social Theory'.

15 'But what daring mortals': Josiah to Bentley, 9 October 1766, Keele, E25–18130.

16 'a liberal college': Priestley, letter dated 16 May 1793, printed in J. F. Marsh, 'On Some Correspondence of Dr Priestley Preserved in the Warrington Museum and Library', *Transactions of the Historic Society of Lancashire and Cheshire* 7 (1855), p. 71.

17 'every name supposed to think different': Erasmus Darwin quoting Josiah, in King-Hele, *Life and Genius of Erasmus Darwin*, p. 295.

18 'An accomplished lady': Erasmus Darwin junior quoted in King-Hele, *Life and Genius of Erasmus Darwin*, p. 303.

19 'a furious democrat': Tom Wedgwood to Sally and Josiah, 7 July 1792, Keele, W/M 12.

20 'Nothing now remains': quoted in King-Hele, *Life and Genius of Erasmus Darwin*, p. 248.

THIRTY-FOUR *Mix Again with their Original Clay*

1 'Your letter gives me': Erasmus Darwin to Josiah, 9 December 1794, in King-Hele (ed.), *Letters of Erasmus Darwin*, p. 269.

2 'a distinct understanding': quoted in King-Hele, *Life and Genius of Erasmus Darwin*, p. 303.

3 'For several days': Tom Byerley to Samuel Boardman, 18 January 1795, the only contemporary account of Josiah's last days, printed at length in Reilly, *Wedgwood*, I, p. 142.

THIRTY-FIVE *Unremitting Fires*

1 'The death of Mr Wedgwood': Erasmus Darwin to William Hayley, 21 January 1795, in King-Hele (ed.), *Letters of Erasmus Darwin*, p. 274.

2 'possessed of great public spirit': more obituary reports were collected by Rodney Hampson in 'Josiah Wedgwood: 1795 Obituaries', *Northern Ceramics Society* 96 (1994), pp. 8–9.

3 'ranked among the finest chemists': see Samuel Parkes's encomium in his *Chemical Essays*, (London, 1815), I, p. 47; also, Robert Schofield, 'Josiah Wedgwood, Industrial Chemist', *Chymia* 5 (1959), pp. 180–92, assesses his scientific achievements.

4 'ingenious and industrious Wedgwood': Parkes, *Chemical Essays*, p. 47.

5 'a commerce so active': quoted in Reilly, *Wedgwood*, I, p. 143.

6 'are much admired': Hamilton in Wilcoxen, 'Peregrinations', p. 37.

7 'It is surely a triumph': quoted in Roger Hudson (ed.), *The Grand Tour 1592–1796* (London: Folio Society, 1993), p. 25.

8 '£600,000': 'Examination of the Estate of Josiah Wedgwood', Keele, W/M 989; probate copy of the will of Josiah Wedgwood, E26–19108; according to 'assets of Josiah Wedgwood', he left £153,800 cash in legacies; much of his money was in stock (India Bonds) and real estate.

9 '*Wedgwoodarheit*': Reilly & Savage, *Dictionary*, p. 236.

10 'the Wedgwood touch was still alive': Production at Etruria remained active until 1949, when the new works at Barlaston, Staffordshire, were completed. The original buildings of Etruria were demolished in 1965, and sadly only one small round original brick building survives today.

11 'We will have a fair trial': Coleridge quoted in Rosemary Aston, *The Life of Samuel Taylor Coleridge: A Critical Biography* (Oxford: Blackwell, 1996), p. 215.

12 'silver nitrate': R. B. Litchfield, *Tom Wedgwood: The First Photographer* (London: Duckworth, 1903), p. 1.

13 'trinkets and baubles': for Malthus's attack on manufactures, see Brian Dolan (ed.), *Malthus, Medicine, and Morality: 'Malthusianism' after 1798* (Atlanta and Amsterdam: Rodopi, 2000), chapter one.

14 'exceedingly illogical': Patricia James, *Population Malthus: His*

Life and Times (London: Routledge, 1979), p. 103.

15 'at social Industry's command': William Wordsworth, *The Excursion* (1814), penned in 1797 and then tentatively titled *The Ruined Cottage*, II. 1–2, 27–31.

16 'One of the most beautiful poems': Stephen Gill, *William Wordsworth: A Life* (Oxford: Oxford University Press, 1989), p. 133.

17 'O'er which the smoke': Wordsworth, *The Excursion*, ll. 9–10.

Epilogue

1 For the most thorough account of the history of the Wedgwood firm since Josiah Wedgwood's death see Reilly, *Wedgwood*, volume II, which covers in some detail the developments in the business right up to 1986. I am indebted to Reilly's study from which this summary is largely drawn.

2 'to command widespread': Nancy Koehn, *Brand New: How Entrepreneurs Earned Consumers' Trust from Wedgwood to Dell* (Boston, MA: Harvard Business School Press, 2001)

3 'Our pottery does very well': Watt quoted in 'Capital and Labor – The Invention of the Steam Engine: Roebuck', at www.history.rochester.edu/steam/lord/4–2.htm.

BIBLIOGRAPHY

Adams, Percy, *A History of the Adams Family of North Staffordshire & of their Connection with the Development of the Potteries* (London: St Catherine Press, 1914)

——*Notes on some North Staffordshire Families, Including those of Adams, Astbury, Breeze, Challinor, Heath, Warburton* (Tunstall: Edwin Eardley, 1930)

Aikin, John, *A Description of the Country from Thirty to Forty Miles Round Manchester* (London, 1795)

Allan, D. G. C., '"The Present Unhappy Disputes": The Society and the Loss of the American Colonies, 1774–1783', in Allan and John L. Abbott (eds), *The Virtuoso Tribe of Arts & Sciences* (Athens and London: University of Georgia Press, 1992), pp. 214–36

Allan, D. G. C. and John L. Abbott (eds), *The Virtuoso Tribe of Arts & Sciences: Studies in the Eighteenth-Century Work & membership of the London Society of Arts* (Athens and London: University of Georgia Press, 1992)

Anderson, Fred, *Crucible of War: The Seven Years War and the Fate of Empire in British North America 1754–1766* (London: Faber and Faber, 2000)

Anderson, William L., 'Cherokee Clay, from Duché to Wedgwood: The Journal of Thomas Griffiths, 1767–1768', *The North Carolina Historical Review* 63 (1986), pp. 477–510

Anon., *Stoke-on-Trent Historical Pageant and the Josiah Wedgwood Bicentenary Celebrations* (May 19–24, 1930)

Ashton, Rosemary, *The Life of Samuel Taylor Coleridge: A Critical Biography* (London: Blackwell, 1996)

Ashworth, W. J., *Customs and Excise: Trade, Production and*

Consumption in England, 1640–1845 (Oxford: Oxford University Press, 2003)

Atkinson, George, *The Shipping Laws of the British Empire; consisting of Park on Marine Insurance and Abbott on Shipping* (London: Longman, Brown, Green, & Longmans, 1854)

Ayling, Stanley Edward, *George the Third* (London: Collins, 1972)

Baker, George, 'An Examination of Several Means, by which the Poison of Lead may be supposed frequently to gain admittance into the Human Body, unobserved, and unsuspected', *Medical Transactions of the College of Physicians, London* (1768)

Barker, David, *William Greatbatch: A Staffordshire Potter* (London: Jonathan Horne, 1991)

Beaver, S. H., 'The Potteries: A Study in the Evolution of a Cultural Landscape', *Transactions of the Institute of British Geographers* 34 (1964)

Beeson, Dwight, 'Reproductions of Documents concerning the Slate Blue Wedgwood Copy of the Portland Vase', privately printed in Birmingham, Alabama, 1964

Bellers, John, *Essays about the Poor, Manufactures, Trade, Plantations, & Immorality* (London, 1699), reprinted in George Clarke (ed.), *George Bellers: His Life, Times and Writings* (London: Routledge, 1987), pp. 80–112.

Bentley, Richard ['R.B.'], *Thomas Bentley, 1730–1780: Of Liverpool, Etruria, and London* (Guilford: Billing & Sons, 1927; reprinted by the Wedgwood Society of New York, 1975)

Bentley, Thomas, *Journal of a Visit to Paris 1776*, edited by Peter France (Brighton: University of Sussex Library, 1977)

Berg, Maxine, *The Age of Manufactures: Industry, Innovation and Work in Britain 1700–1820* (Oxford: Basil Blackwell, 1985)

Berg, Maxine, Pat Hudson and Michael Sonenscher (eds), *Manufacture in Town and Country before the Factory* (Cambridge: Cambridge University Press, 1983)

Bienefeld, M. A., *Working Hours in British Industry: An Economic History* (London: Weidenfeld and Nicolson, 1972)

Blake Roberts, Gaye, 'Josiah Wedgwood and his Trade Connections with Liverpool', *Proceedings of the Wedgwood Society* 11 (1982)

——'Wedgwood Showrooms in London During the Eighteenth Century', *Ars Ceramica* 2 (1985), pp. 3–6

——'Wedgwood to America: Trading Concerns During the Eighteenth Century', *Ars Ceramica* 4 (1987), pp. 4–8

——'Josiah Wedgwood and His Partners', *Ars Ceramica* 13 (1996), pp. 14–23

——'Josiah Wedgwood and Richard Champion, Adversaries and Friends', *Ars Ceramica* 17 (2001), pp. 43–53

Blaszczyk, Regina Lee, *Imagining Consumers: Design and Innovation from Wedgwood to Corning* (Baltimore and London: Johns Hopkins University Press, 2000)

Bloch, Raymond, *The Etruscans* (New York: Frederick and Praeger, 1958)

Boardman, James, *Bentleyana; or, A Memoir of Thomas Bentley, Sometime of Liverpool, with Extracts from his Correspondence* (Liverpool: Wareing Webb, 1851)

Boney, Knowles, *Liverpool Porcelain of the Eighteenth Century and its Makers* (London: Portman Press, 1989; reprint of 1957 edition)

Breen, T. H., '"Baubles of Britain": The American and Consumer Revolutions of the Eighteenth Century', in Cary Carson, Ronald Hoffman, and Peter Albert (eds), *Of Consuming Interests: The Style of Life in the Eighteenth Century* (Charlottesville and London: United States Capitol Historical Society and the University Press of Virginia, 1994), pp. 444–82

——'An Empire of Goods: The Anglicanisation of Colonial America, 1690–1776', *Journal of British Studies* 25 (1986), pp. 467–99

Brewer, John, *Party Ideology and Popular Politics at the Accession of George III* (Cambridge: Cambridge University Press, 1976)

——*The Sinews of Power: War, Money and the English State 1688–1783* (London: Routledge, 1989)

Brewer, John and Roy Porter (eds), *Consumption and the World of Goods* (London: Routledge, 1993)

Brooke, John Hedley, *Science and Religion: Some Historical Perspectives* (Cambridge: Cambridge University Press, 1991)

Burney, Charles, *Music, Men and Manners in France and Italy, 1770,*

Being the Journal Written during a Tour through Those Countries Undertaken to collect Material for a General History of Music (London: Eulenburg Books, 1969)

——*Music, Men and Manners in Italy, 1770 (The Present State of Music in France and Italy)*, with an introduction by E. Edmund Poole (London: Folio Society, 1969)

Bushman, Richard, 'American High Style and Vernacular Cultures', in Jack Greene and J. R. Pole (eds), *Colonial British America: Essays in the New History of the Early Modern Era* (Baltimore and London: Johns Hopkins University Press, 1984), pp. 345–83

Chaldecott, J. A., 'Josiah Wedgwood (1730–95): Scientist', *British Journal for the History of Science* 8 (1975), pp. 1–16

Champion, Richard, *Considerations on the Present Situation of Great Britain and the United States of America, with a View to their Future Commercial Connexions*, 2nd ed. (London, 1784)

Chaudhuri, K. N., *The Trading World of Asia and the English East India Company 1660–1760* (Cambridge: Cambridge University Press, 1978)

Cheyne, George, *An Essay on Health and Long Life* (Bath, 1725)

Christie, Ian, 'A Vision of Empire: Thomas Whately and The Regulations Lately made Concerning the Colonies', *English Historical Review* April (1998)

Clark, George N., *Guide to English Commercial Statistics, 1696–1782* (London: Royal Historical Society, 1938)

Clark, Ronald, *Benjamin Franklin: A Biography* (London: Weidenfeld and Nicolson, 1983)

Clarke, Desmond, *Memoirs of Richard Lovell Edgeworth: Begun by Himself and Concluded by His Daughter Maria Edgeworth* (Dublin: Shannon, 1969)

Clow, Archibald and Nan Clow, *The Chemical Revolution: A Contribution to Social Technology* (London: Batchworth Press, 1952)

Colley, Linda, *Britons: Forging the Nation, 1707–1837* (New Haven and London: Yale University Press, 1992)

Cookson, J. E., *The Friends of Peace: Anti-War Liberalism in England 1793–1815* (Cambridge: Cambridge University Press, 1982)

Crouzet, F., 'The Sources of England's Wealth: Some French Views in the Eighteenth Century', in P. L. Cottrell and D. H. Aldcroft (eds), *Shipping, Trade and Commerce: Essays in Memory of Ralph Davis* (Leicester: Leicester University Press, 1981), pp. 61–79

Crowhurst, Patrick, *The Defence of British Trade 1689–1815* (Folkestone: Dawson, 1977)

Crowley, John E., 'The Sensibility of Comfort', *American Historical Review* 104 (1999), pp. 749–82

Crowther, M. A., *The Workhouse System 1834–1929: The History of an English Institution* (Athens, GA: University of Georgia Press, 1982)

Curnock, Nehemiah, (ed.), *The Journal of the Rev. John Wesley, A. M.*, 8 vols (New York: Eaton & Mains, 1913)

Cust, Lionel, *History of the Society of Dilettanti* (London, 1898)

Daniels, Stephen, *Joseph Wright* (London: Tate Gallery, 2000)

Daumas, Maurice, *Scientific Instruments of the Seventeenth and Eighteenth Centuries and their Makers* (London: Portman Books, 1989)

Davidoff, Leonore and Catherine Hall, *Family Fortunes: Men and Women of the English Middle Class, 1780–1850* (Chicago: University of Chicago Press, 1987)

Dawson, Eileen, *Masterpieces of Wedgwood* (London: British Museum, 1995)

de Vries, Jan, 'Between Purchasing Power and the World of Goods: Understanding the Household Economy in Early Modern Europe', in Brewer and Porter (eds), *Consumption and the World of Goods* (London: Routledge, 1993), pp. 85–132

Dear, Peter, '*Totius in Verba*: Rhetoric and Authority in the Early Royal Society', *Isis* 76 (1985), pp. 145–61

Deetz, James, *In Small Things Forgotten: the Archaeology of Early American Life* (New York: Anchor Press, 1977)

Defoe, Daniel, *Giving Alms no Charity* (1704), in W. R. Owens (ed.), *Political and Economic Writings of Daniel Defoe* (London: Pickering & Chatto, 2000), pp. 167–91

Dickinson, H. T., *Liberty and Property: Political Ideology in Eighteenth Century Britain* (London: Weidenfeld and Nicolson, 1977)

——'Radicals and Reformers in the Age of Wilkes and Wyvill', in Jeremy Black (ed.), *British Politics and Society from Walpole to Pitt 1742–1789* (Basingstoke: Macmillan, 1990), pp. 123–46

Dolan, Brian, '"Representing Novelty": Charles Babbage, Charles Lyell and Experiments in Early Victorian Geology', *History of Science* 36 (1998), pp. 299–327

——*Exploring European Frontiers: British Travellers in the Age of Enlightenment* (Basingstoke: Macmillan, 2000)

——*Ladies of the Grand Tour* (London and New York: HarperCollins, 2001)

——'Conservative Politicians, Radical Philosophers, and the Aerial Remedy for the Diseases of Civilization', *History of the Human Sciences* 15 (2002), pp. 35–54

Dolan, Brian (ed.), *Malthus, Medicine, and Morality: 'Malthusianism' after 1798* (Atlanta and Amsterdam: Rodopi, 2000)

Donoghue, Frank, 'Colonizing Readers: Review Criticism and the Formation of a Reading Public', in Ann Bermingham and John Brewer (eds), *The Consumption of Culture, 1600–1800* (London and New York: Routledge, 1995), pp. 54–74

Dossie, Robert, *The Handmaid to the Arts*, 2 vols (London, 1758)

Edwards, Clive, *Eighteenth-Century Furniture* (Manchester: Manchester University Press, 1996)

Edwards, Rhoda, 'London Potteries circa 1570–1710', *Journal of Ceramics History* 6 (1974), pp. 1–30

Elliott, Gordon, *John and David Elers and their Contemporaries* (London: Jonathan Horne, 1998)

Erdman, David, 'Coleridge, Wordsworth and the Wedgwood Fund', *Bulletin of the New York Public Library* 60 (1956), pp. 425–43, 487–507

Ewins, Neil, '"Supplying the Present Wants of Our Yankee Cousins": Staffordshire Ceramics and the American Market 1775–1880', *Journal of Ceramic History* 15 (1997)

Farrer, Lady Katherine Euphemia (ed.), *Letters of Josiah Wedgwood*, 3 vols (1903–6; reprinted Manchester: E. J. Morten & The Wedgwood Museum, 1973)

Fontaines, Una des, 'Portland House: Wedgwood's London Showrooms', *Proceedings of the Wedgwood Society* 11 (1982)

——'Wedgwood's London Showrooms', *Proceedings of the Wedgwood Society* 8 (1970), pp. 193–221

Fordyce, W., *Memoirs concerning Herculaneum, the subterranean city, lately discovered at the foot of Mount Vesuvius, giving a particular account of the . . . buildings, statues, paintings, medals, and other curiosities found there* (London: 1750)

Foreman, Amanda, *Georgiana, Duchess of Devonshire* (London: HarperCollins, 1998)

Freudenberger, Herman and Gaylord Cummins, 'Health, Work, and Leisure before the Industrial Revolution', *Explorations in Economic History* 13 (1976), pp. 1–12

Gascoigne, John, *Cambridge in the Age of Enlightenment: Science, Religion and Politics from the Restoration to the French Revolution* (Cambridge: Cambridge University Press, 1989)

——*Joseph Banks and the English Enlightenment: Useful Knowledge and Polite Culture* (Cambridge: Cambridge University Press, 1994)

Gatty, Charles T, *Liverpool Potteries* (Liverpool: T. Brakewell, 1882)

Gibbs, F. W., *Joseph Priestley: Adventurer in Science and Champion of Truth* (London: Nelson, 1965)

Gilbert, Alan, *Religion and Society in Industrial England: Church, Chapel, and Social Change 1740–1914* (London and New York: Longman, 1976)

Golinski, Jan, *Science as Public Culture: Chemistry and Enlightenment in Britain, 1760–1820* (Cambridge: Cambridge University Press, 1992)

Gorley, Jean, *Wedgwood* (New York: Gramercy Publishing Company, 1950)

Graham, Malcolm, *Cup and Saucer Land* (1908; reprinted by the Staffordshire and Stoke on Trent Archive Service, 2000)

Greene, Jack P. (ed.), The Examination of Benjamin Franklin in the House of Commons, February 13, 1766, *Colonies to Nation: 1763–1789* (New York, 1979), pp. 72–7

Greene, John, *American Science in the Age of Jefferson* (Ames, IW: Iowa State University Press, 1984)

Greenslade, M. and G. C. Baugh, 'Stebbing Shaw and the History of Staffordshire', in M. W. Greenslade (ed.), *Essays in Staffordshire History* (Staffordshire: Staffordshire Record Society, 1979), pp. 224–54

Greenslade, M. W. 'A History of Burslem', *The Victoria County History of Staffordshire*, Vol. 8 (1963; reprinted in extract by the Staffordshire and Stoke on Trent Archive Service, 2000).

Gunn, J. A. W., *Beyond Liberty and Property: The Process of Self-Recognition in Eighteenth-Century Political Thought* (Kingston and Montreal: McGill-Queen's University Press, 1983)

Hadfield, Charles, *Canals of the West Midlands* (Newton Abbot: David & Charles, 1974)

Hamilton, Roberta, *The Liberation of Women: A Study of Patriarchy and Capitalism* (London: George Allen & Unwin, 1978)

Hampden, John, *An Eighteenth-Century Journal, Being a Record of the Years 1774–1776* (London: Macmillan, 1940)

Harley, David, 'A Sword in a Madman's Hand: Professional Opposition to Popular Consumption in the Waters Literature of Southern England and the Midlands, 1570–1870', in R. Porter (ed.), *The Medical History of Waters and Spas, Medical History* supplement, 10 (1990), pp. 48–55

Harris, J. R., *Industrial Espionage and Technology Transfer: Britain and France in the Eighteenth Century* (Aldershot: Ashgate, 1998)

Haselgrove, Dennis and John Murray, 'John Dwight's Fulham Pottery 1672–1978: A Collection of Documentary Sources', *Journal of Ceramics History* 11 (1979)

Haskell, Francis and Nicholas Penny, *Taste and the Antique: The Lure of Classical Sculpture 1500–1900* (New Haven and London: Yale University Press, 1981)

Hobsbawm, Eric, 'Methodism and the Threat of Revolution in Britain', in Eric Hobsbawm (ed.), *Labouring Men: Studies in the History of Labour* (London: Weidenfeld & Nicolson, 1964)

Hole, Robert, *Pulpits, Politics and Public Order in England, 1760–1832* (Cambridge: Cambridge University Press, 1989)

Holt, Raymond, *The Unitarian Contribution to Social Progress in England* (London: George Allen & Unwin, 1938)

Hudson, Pat, 'Financing Firms, 1700–1850', in *Business Enterprise in Modern Britain From the Eighteenth to the Twentieth Century*, edited by Maurice Kirby and Mary Rose (London and New York: Routledge, 1994)

Hudson, Roger (ed.), *The Grand Tour 1592–1796* (London: Folio Society, 1993)

Hughes, Fred, *Mother Town: Episodes in the History of Burslem* (Staffordshire: Burslem Community Development Trust, 2000)

Hutchison, Sidney, *A History of the Royal Academy 1768–1968* (London: Chapman & Hall, 1968)

Huxham, John, *An Essay on Fevers, and their Various Kinds* (London, 1750)

Inglis, Brian, *Poverty and the Industrial Revolution* (London: Hodder and Stoughton, 1971)

James, Patricia, *Population Malthus: His Life and Times* (London: Routledge, 1979)

Jewitt, Llewellynn, *The Wedgwoods: Being a Life of Josiah Wedgwood* (London, 1865)

Johnson, Harwood A., 'Books Belonging to Wedgwood and Bentley the 10th of August 1770', *Ars Ceramica* 7 (1990), pp. 13–23

Johnson, Harwood, 'Thomas Bentley's Journal of his Visit to Paris in 1776', *Ars Ceramica* 9 (1992), pp. 8–13

Jones, S. R. H. 'The Origins of the Factory System in Great Britain: Technology, Transaction Costs, or Exploitation?', in *Business Enterprise in Modern Britain From the Eighteenth to the Twentieth Century*, edited by Maurice Kirby and Mary Rose (London and New York: Routledge, 1994)

Kasson, John, *Civilizing the Machine: Technology and Republican Values in America, 1776–1900* (New York: Hill and Wang, 1976; 1999)

Kelly, Alison, 'Wedgwood's Catherine Services', *Ars Ceramica* 8 (1991), pp. 6–13

Kendrick, James, 'A Morning's Ramble in "Old Warrington"', *Transactions of the Historic Society of Lancashire and Cheshire* 7 (1855), pp. 82–96

King-Hele, Desmond (ed.), *The Essential Writings of Erasmus Darwin* (London: MacGibbon & Kee, 1968)

——(ed.), *The Letters of Erasmus Darwin* (Cambridge: Cambridge University Press, 1981)

——*Doctor of Revolution: The Life and Genius of Erasmus Darwin* (London: Faber & Faber, 1977)

Klingender, F. D., 'The Industrial Revolution and the Birth of Romanticism', *Apropos* 4 (1945), pp. 20–24

Klingender, Francis, *Art and the Industrial Revolution*, edited and revised by Arthur Elton (London: Paladin, 1973)

Koehn, Nancy, *Brand New: How Entrepreneurs Earned Consumers' Trust from Wedgwood to Dell* (Boston, MA: Harvard Business School Press, 2001)

Kramnick, Isaac, 'Eighteenth-Century Science and Radical Social Theory: The Case of Joseph Priestley's Scientific Liberalism', *Journal of British Studies* 25 (1986), pp. 1–30

Landers, J., *Birth and Death in the Metropolis: Studies in the Demographic History of London 1670–1830* (Cambridge: Cambridge University Press, 1992)

Lane, Joan, *Apprenticeship in England, 1600–1914* (London: UCL Press, 1996)

Lawson, Philip, *The East India Company: A History* (London and New York: Longman, 1993)

Lead, Peter, *The Trent and Mersey Canal* (Wiltshire: Cromwell Press, 1980; reprint 1993)

Lemon, James, 'Spatial Order: Households in Local Communities and Regions', in Jack Greene and J. R. Pole (eds), *Colonial British America: Essays in the New History of the Early Modern Era* (Baltimore and London: Johns Hopkins University Press, 1984), pp. 86–122

Letts, C. F. C., *The Eruption of Vesuvius. Adapted from the Letters of Pliny with notes* (Cambridge: Cambridge University Press, 1937)

Levere, Trevor, *Poetry Realised in Nature: Samuel Taylor Coleridge and Early Nineteenth-Century Science* (Cambridge: Cambridge University Press, 1981)

Lewis, Lesley, *Connoisseurs and Secret Agents in Eighteenth Century Rome* (London: Chatto & Windus, 1961)

Lincoln, Anthony, *Some Political and Social Ideas of English Dissent 1763–1800* (Cambridge: Cambridge University Press, 1938)

Lindsay, J., *The Trent and Mersey Canal* (Newton Abbot: David & Charles, 1979)

Litchfield, R. B., *Tom Wedgwood: The First Photographer* (London: Duckworth, 1903)

Lobb, Theophilus, *A Treatise on the Small Pox* (London, 1741)

Mankowitz, Wolf, *Wedgwood*, 3rd edition (London: Barrie and Jenkins, 1980)

Marsh, J. F., 'On Some Correspondence of Dr Priestley, preserved in the Warrington Museum and Library', *Transactions of the Historic Society of Lancashire and Cheshire* 7 (1855), pp. 65–81

Marshall, Dorothy, *Industrial England, 1776–1851* (New York: Charles Scribner's Sons, 1973)

——*The English Poor in the Eighteenth Century* (London: Routledge, 1926)

Mathias, Peter, *The Transformation of England: Essays in the Economic and Social History of England in the Eighteenth Century* (London: Methuen, 1979)

Mathias, Peter and Patrick O'Brien, 'Taxation in England and France 1715–1810: A Comparison of the Social and Economic Incidence of Taxes Collected for the Central Governments', *Journal of European Economic History* 5 (1976)

——*English Trade Tokens: The Industrial Revolution Illustrated* (London, 1962).

Matthew, Adam (Publications), *Industrial Revolution: A Documentary History: Series One: The Boulton & Watt Archive and the Matthew Boulton Papers*, Part I: Lunar Society Correspondence

Mayer, Joseph, 'On Liverpool Pottery', *Transactions of the Historic Society of Lancashire and Cheshire* 7 (1855), pp. 178–210

McCusker, John J. and Russell R. Menard, *The Economy of British America, 1607–1789* (Chapel Hill and London: University of North Carolina Press, 1985)

McKendrick, Neil, 'Josiah Wedgwood: An Eighteenth Century

Entrepreneur in Salesmanship and Marketing Techniques',
Economic History Review 2nd series, 12 (1960), pp. 408–33

——'Josiah Wedgwood and Factory Discipline', *Historical Journal* 4
(1961), pp. 30–55

——'Josiah Wedgwood and Thomas Bentley: An Inventor-
Entrepreneur Partnership in the Industrial Revolution',
Transactions of the Royal Historical Society 14 (1964), pp. 1–33

——'The role of science in the industrial revolution', in M. Teich
and R. Young (eds), *Changing Perspectives in the History of Science*
(London: Heinemann, 1973), pp. 274–319

——'Home Demand and Economic Growth: A New View of the
Role of Women and Children in the Industrial Revolution', in N.
McKendrick (ed.), *Historical Perspectives: Studies in English
Thought and Society, in Honour of J. H. Plumb* (London: Europa,
1974), pp. 152–210

——'Josiah Wedgwood and the Commercialization of the Potteries',
in McKendrick, Neil, John Brewer and J. H. Plumb, *The Birth of
a Consumer Society: The Commercialisation of Eighteenth-Century
England* (London: Hutchison, 1983)

McKendrick, Neil, John Brewer and J. H. Plumb, *The Birth of a
Consumer Society: The Commercialisation of Eighteenth-Century
England* (London: Hutchison, 1983)

McLachlan, H., *Warrington Academy: Its History and Influence*
(Manchester: Chetham Society, 1943)

Meiklejohn, A., 'The History of Occupational Respiratory Disease
in the North Staffordshire Pottery Industry', in C. David (ed.),
Health Conditions in the Ceramic Industry (Oxford: Pergamon,
1969)

——'The Successful Prevention of Lead Poisoning in the Glazing of
Earthenware in the North Staffordshire Potteries', *British Journal
for Industrial Medicine* 20 (1963), p. 1697

——'The Successful Prevention of Silicosis among China Biscuit
Workers in the North Staffordshire Pottery Industry', *British
Journal for Industrial Medicine* 20 (1963), p. 2557

Meiklejohn, Andrew, 'English Domestic Medicine in the
Eighteenth Century from the Letters of Josiah Wedgwood', *Post-*

Graduate Medical Journal 26 (1950), pp. 541–543; 598–602; 663–664

Meteyard, Eliza, *The Life of Josiah Wedgwood from his Private Correspondence and Family Papers*, 2 vols (London: Hurst and Blackett, 1865; reprint 1980)

Mingay, G. E. (ed.), *Arthur Young and His Times* (London: Macmillan, 1975)

Moore, John, *A View of the Society and Manners in Italy* (London, 1781)

Morley-Hewitt, A. T., 'Early Whieldon of the Fenton Low Works', *Transactions of the English Ceramic Circle* 3 (1954), pp. 142–54

Mountford, Arnold, 'Thomas Briand – Stranger', *Transactions of the English Ceramic Circle* 7 (1969), pp. 87–99

——'Thomas Whieldon's Manufactory at Fenton Vivian', *Transactions of the English Ceramic Circle* 8 (1972), pp. 164–82

——'Thomas Wedgwood, John Wedgwood and Jonah Malkin: Potters of Burslem', (unpublished MA thesis, Keele University 1972)

Murray, Mary, *The Law of the Father? Patriarchy in the Transition from Feudalism to Capitalism* (London and New York: Routledge, 1995)

Niblett, Kathy, 'A Useful Partner – Thomas Wedgwood 1734–1788', *Journal of the Northern Ceramic Society* 5 (1984)

Oade, Thomas, *The Unnatural Parent* (London, 1718)

Orange, Derek, 'Rational Dissent and Provincial Science: William Turner and the Newcastle Literary and Philosophical Society', in Ian Inkster and Jack Morrell (eds), *Metropolis and Province: Science in British Culture, 1780–1850* (Philadelphia: University of Pennsylvania Press, 1983), pp. 205–30

Owen, Harold, *The Staffordshire Potter* (London: Grant Richards, 1901)

Owens, W. R. (ed.), *Political and Economic Writings of Daniel Defoe*, Volume 8: Social Reform (London: Pickering & Chatto, 2000)

Parkes, Samuel, *Chemical Essays* (London, 1815)

Parreaux, André, *Daily Life in England in the Reign of George III*, translated by Carola Congreve (London: George Allen & Unwin, 1969)

Peck, T. Whitmore and K. Douglas Wilkinson, *William Withering of Birmingham* (Bristol: John Wright & Sons, 1950)

Peel, Derek, *A Pride of the Potters* (London: Arthur Barker Ltd, 1957)

Percival, Thomas, *Observations and Experiments on the Poison of Lead* (London, 1774)

Plot, Robert, *The Natural History of Staffordshire* (Oxford, 1686)

Porter, Dorothy and Roy Porter, *Patient's Progress: Doctors and Doctoring in Eighteenth-Century England* (Stanford: Stanford University Press, 1989)

Porter, Roy, *English Society in the Eighteenth Century* (London: Penguin, 1982; 1990)

——*London: A Social History* (London: Hamish Hamilton, 1994)

——*Enlightenment: Britain and the Creation of the Modern World* (London: Penguin, 2000)

Porter, Roy and Hall, Lesley, *The Facts of Life: The Creation of Sexual Knowledge in Britain 1650–1950* (New Haven and London: Yale University Press, 1995)

Posner, E., 'Eighteenth-Century Health and Social Service in the Pottery Industry of North Staffordshire', *Medical History* 18 (1974), pp. 138–47

Price, E. Stanley, *John Sadler: A Liverpool Pottery Painter* (Gould's: West Kirby, 1949)

Price, Jacob M., 'The Transatlantic Economy', in Jack Greene and J. R. Pole (eds), *Colonial British America: Essays in the New History of the Early Modern Era* (Baltimore and London: Johns Hopkins University Press, 1984), pp. 18–42

Priestley, Joseph, *Autobiography*, edited by Jack Lindsay (Bath: Adams and Dart, 1970)

Rakow, Leonard and Juliette Rakow, 'Wedgwood's Peg Leg Portraits', *Ars Ceramica* 1 (1984), pp. 10–13

Ramage, Nancy H., 'Owed to a Grecian Urn: The Debt of Flaxman and Wedgwood to Hamilton', *Ars Ceramica* 6 (1989), pp. 8–12

——'Publication Dates of Sir William Hamilton's Four Volumes', *Ars Ceramica* 8 (1991), p. 357

——'Restorer and Collector: Notes on Eighteenth-Century

Recreations of Roman Statues', in Elaine K. Gazda (ed.), *The Ancient Art of Emulation: Studies in Artistic Originality and Tradition from the Present to Classical Antiquity* (Ann Arbor: University of Michigan Press, 2002), pp. 61–77

Ramazini, Bernardino, *A Dissertation on endemial Diseases . . . Together with a treatise on the diseases of Tradesmen, by B. Ramazini*, translated by Friedrich Hoffmann (London, 1745)

Raynes, Harold, *A History of British Insurance* (2nd ed., London: Pitman, 1964)

Reilly, Robin, *Wedgwood*, 2 vols (New York: Stockton Press, 1989)

——*Josiah Wedgwood 1730–1795* (London: Macmillan, 1992)

——*Wedgwood Jasper: With Over 600 Illustrations* (London: Thames and Hudson, 1994)

Reilly, Robin and George Savage, *The Dictionary of Wedgwood* (Woodbridge, Suffolk: Antique Collectors' Club, 1980)

Roberts, David, *Paternalism in Early Victorian England* (London: Croom Helm, 1979)

Roberts, W. J. and H. C. Pigeon, 'Biographical Sketch of Mr John Wyke, with some remarks on the Arts and Manufactures of Liverpool from 1760–1780', *Historic Society of Lancashire and Cheshire Proceedings and Papers*, vi (1854), pp. 66–76

Roll, Eric, *An Early Experiment in Industrial Organisation: Being a History of the Firm of Boulton and Watt, 1775–1805* (London: Frank Cass & Co., 1968)

Rose, Mary, 'The Family Firm in British Business, 1780–1914', in *Business Enterprise in Modern Britain From the Eighteenth to the Twentieth Century*, edited by Maurice Kirby and Mary Rose (London and New York: Routledge, 1994)

Rose, R. B., 'The Priestley Riots of 1791', *Past and Present* 8 (1960): pp. 68–88.

Rosenblum, Robert, 'The Origin of Painting: A Problem in the Iconography of Romantic Classicism', *The Art Bulletin* December 1957, pp. 279–90

Rousseau, Jean-Jacques, *Emile; or, On Education*, introduction, translation and notes by Allan Bloom (New York: Basic Books, 1979)

Rowbottom, Margaret and Charles Susskind, *Electricity and Medicine: A History of their Interaction* (London: Macmillan, 1984)

Scarratt, William, *Old Times in the Potteries* (1906; East Ardsley, Yorks: S.R. Publishers, 1969)

Schaffer, Simon, 'Natural Philosophy and Public Spectacle in the Eighteenth Century', *History of Science* 21 (1983), pp. 1–43

Schama, Simon, *The Embarrassment of Riches: An Interpretation of Dutch Culture in the Golden Age* (London: Fontana, 1991)

Schofield, Robert E., *The Enlightenment of Joseph Priestley: A Study of his Life and Work from 1733 to 1773* (University Park, PA: Pennsylvania University Press, 1997)

——'Josiah Wedgwood, Industrial Chemist', *Chymia* 5 (1959), pp. 180–92

——*The Lunar Society of Birmingham: A Social History of Provincial Science and Industry in Eighteenth-Century England* (Oxford: Clarendon Press, 1963)

——(ed.), *A Scientific Autobiography of Joseph Priestley (1733–1804): Selected Scientific Correspondence* (Cambridge, MA: MIT Press, 1966)

Schumpeter, Elizabeth Boody, *English Overseas Trade Statistics, 1697–1808* (Oxford: Clarendon Press, 1960)

Selleck, A. Douglas, *Cookworthy 1705–80 and His Circle* (Plymouth, 1978)

Shammas, Carole, 'How Self-Sufficient Was Early America?', *Journal of Interdisciplinary History* 13 (1982), pp. 247–72

Sharpe, Pamela, *Adopting to Capitalism: Working Women in the English Economy, 1700–1850* (Basingstoke: Macmillan, 1996)

Shaw, Simeon, *History of the Staffordshire Potteries; and the Rise and Progress of the Manufacture of Pottery and Porcelain* (Hanley, by the author, 1829; reprinted David & Charles, Ltd., 1970)

Shaw, Stebbing, *History and Antiquities of Staffordshire* (London: J. Robson, 1798–1801)

Shepherd, James F. and Gary M. Walton, *Shipping, Maritime Trade, and the Economic Development of Colonial North America* (Cambridge: Cambridge University Press, 1972)

Smith, D. M., 'Industrial Architecture in the Potteries', *North Staffordshire Journal of Field Studies* 5 (1965), pp. 81–94

Some, David, *The Case of Receiving the Small-Pox by Inoculation, Impartially considered, and especially in a Religious View*, published from the original manuscript by Philip Doddridge (London, 1750) published posthumously

Steele, H. J., 'Glimpses into the Social Conditions in Burslem during the 17th and 18th Centuries', *North Staffordshire Field Club Transactions* 78 (1943–44), pp. 16–39

Stone, Lawrence, *The Family, Sex and Marriage in England, 1500–1800* (Harmondsworth: Penguin, 1979)

Strother, Edward, *An Essay on Sickness and Health . . . in which Dr. Cheyne's mistaken opinions in his late essay are occasionally taken notice of* (London, 1725)

Stuart, Denis, 'Service of Truth: Early Quaker Poor Relief in Staffordshire to the Mid-Eighteenth Century', in Philip Morgan and A. Phillips (eds), *Staffordshire Histories: Essays in Honour of M. Greenslade* (Keele: Staffordshire Record Society & Centre for Local History, University of Keele, 1999)

Tait, Hugh, 'The "Etruscan Service" of King Ferdinand IV and Josiah Wedgwood', *Ars Ceramica* 3 (1986), pp. 31–4

Tarczylo, Théodore, 'From lascivious erudition to the history of mentalities', in G. S. Rousseau and Roy Porter (eds), *Sexual Underworlds of the Enlightenment* (Manchester: Manchester University Press, 1987), pp. 26–45

Thomas, John, *The Rise of the Staffordshire Potteries* (Bath: Adams & Dart, 1971)

Thompson, E. P., 'Time, Work-Discipline and Industrial Capitalism', reprinted in his *Customs in Common* (London: Penguin Books, 1993), pp. 352–403

Thomson, James, *The Works of Mr Thomson*, 2 vols (London, 1738)

Tinniswood, Adrian, *The Polite Tourist: A History of Country House Visiting* (London: The National Trust, 1998)

Towner, Donald, 'William Greatbatch and the Early Wedgwood Wares', *Transactions of the English Ceramic Circle* 5 (1963), pp. 180–93

——*Creamware* (London: Faber, 1978)

Trinder, Barrie, *The Making of the Industrial Landscape* (London: J. M. Dent & Sons, 1982; reprinted 1997)

Tringham, Nigel J., A. G. Rosser and R. N. Swanson (eds), 'The Turnpike Network of Staffordshire, 1700–1840. An Introduction & Handlist of Turnpike Acts', *Collections for a History of Staffordshire* 13 (1988), pp. 122–53

Turner, William, *William Adams, an Old English Potter* (London: Chapman, 1904)

Uglow, Jenny, *The Lunar Men: The Friends Who Made the Future* (London: Faber and Faber, 2002)

Vaisey, D. G. (ed.), *Probate Inventories of Lichfield and District 1568–1680* (Staffordshire: Staffordshire Record Society, 1969)

Walvin, James, *The Quakers: Money and Morals* (London: John Murray, 1997)

Ward, John, *The Borough of Stoke-upon-Trent* (London, 1843)

Warrillow, E. J. D., *History of Etruria: Staffordshire, England 1760–1951* (Stoke-on-Trent: Etruscan Publications, 1953)

Warrillow, Ernest, *A Sociological History of the City of Stoke-on-Trent* (Newcastle: Ironmarket, 1977)

Waterman, Elizabeth, *Wages in Eighteenth-Century England* (Cambridge, Mass.: Harvard University Press, 1934)

Watkin, E. A., 'Staffordshire Tokens and their Place in the Coinage of England', *North Staffordshire Journal of Field Studies* 1 (1961), pp. 1–25

Watson, J. Steven, *The Reign of George III 1760–1815* (Oxford: Clarendon Press, 1960)

Watts, Ruth, *Gender, Power and the Unitarians, 1760–1860* (London: Longman, 1998)

Weatherill, Lorna, 'The Growth of the Pottery Industry in England, 1660–1815', *Post-Medieval Archaeology* 17 (1983), pp. 15–46

——*Consumer Behaviour and Material Culture in Britain, 1660–1760* (London: Routledge, 1988)

——*The Pottery Trade and North Staffordshire 1660–1760* (Manchester: Manchester University Press, 1971)

Webb, Sidney and Beatrice Webb, *English Local Government:*

English Poor Law History, Part 1 (London: Longmans, Green and Co., 1927)

Wedgwood, Barbara and Hensleigh Wedgwood, *The Wedgwood Circle 1730–1897* (New Jersey: Eastview, 1980)

Wedgwood, Josiah C., *A History of the Wedgwood Family* (London: St Catherine Press, 1908)

——*Staffordshire Pottery and its History* (London: Sampson Low, Marston & Co., 1913)

Wedgwood, Josiah C. and Thomas Ormsbee, *Staffordshire Pottery* (London: Putnam & Co., 1947)

Wedgwood, Josiah C. and Joshua G. E. Wedgwood, *Wedgwood Pedigrees: Being an Account of the Complete Family Reconstructed from Contemporary Records* (Kendal: Titus Wilson & Son, 1925)

Wedgwood, Julia, *The Personal Life of Josiah Wedgwood*, revised and edited by C. H. Herford (London: Macmillan, 1915)

Whiter, Leonard, *Spode: A History of the Family, Factory and Wares from 1733 to 1833* (London: Barries & Jenkins, 1970; reprinted 1989)

Wilbur, Earl Morse, *A History of Unitarianism in Transylvania, England and America*, 2 vols (Cambridge, MA: Harvard University Press, 1952)

Wilcoxen, Charlotte, 'The Peregrinations of a Letter from Sir William Hamilton to Josiah Wedgwood', *Ars Ceramica* 17 (2001), pp. 36–45

Williamson, George Charles, *The Imperial Russian Dinner Service* (London: George Bell, 1909)

Williams-Wood, Cyril, *English Transfer-Printed Pottery and Porcelain: A History of Over-Glaze Printing* (London: Faber, 1981)

Wills, John E., Jr, 'European Consumption and Asian Production in the Seventeenth and Eighteenth Centuries', in Brewer and Porter (eds), *Consumption and the World of Goods* (London: Routledge, 1993), pp. 133–47

Wilson, Charles, *England's Apprenticeship 1603–1763* (2nd edition, London: Longman, 1984)

Wrigley, E. A., *Continuity, Chance and Change: The Character of the Industrial Revolution in England* (Cambridge: Cambridge University Press, 1988).

Wylie, Ian, *Young Coleridge and the Philosophers of Nature* (Oxford: Clarendon Press, 1989)

Yeo, Richard, *Encyclopaedic Visions: Scientific Dictionaries and Enlightenment Culture* (Cambridge: Cambridge University Press, 2001)

Young, Arthur, *A Six Months Tour through the North of England*, 4 vols (London, 1770)

Young, Hilary (ed.), *The Genius of Wedgwood* (London: Victoria & Albert Museum, 1995)

INDEX

Observations on the Nature of Civil Liberty (Price) 292
Octagon Chapel 120
Overhouse estate 4–5, 16, 23, 24, 38–39, 70, 259

Paine, Thomas 293
Palmer, Humphrey 210, 263–264, 283–284
Paradise Lost 80
Parkes, Samuel 373
Parr, Dr Samuel 363
Pars, Miss (artist) 267
Pepys, Samuel 25
Percival, Thomas 280–282
Philological Society 353
Pickford, Joseph 189–190, 200, 212, 215, 218
Pigalle (sculptor) 301, 306
Pitt the Elder, William 91, 182–184, 291
Plot, Robert 12–13
Plumier, Charles 147–148
Pollexfen, Sir Henry 161
Poor Law 58
Poor Richard's Almanack (Franklin) 1
Pope, Alexander 25, 134
Porcelain 46, 64, 77, 132, 186, 273, 275–276
  Asiatic 297
  bone china 387
  jasperware 287–289, 297, 299, 307, 311, 318, 338, 344, 350, 361, 385, 389
  kaolin 186–187, 273, 276, 284, 317
Portland, Duchess of 350
Portland (Barberini) Vase 349–352, 354–356, 358–359
Portland, Duke of 351
Portobello Victory 59–60
Potters, Committee of 297
Pottery
  origins of 320–323
  styles
    agate ware 50, 61, 63, 81, 90, 126
    biscuit ware 82–83, 103
    black ware 63

blue ware 49–50
China ware 27, 30, 31, 320, 374
creamware 44–45, 50, 77, 84–85, 90, 93, 150, 157, 163, 168, 196, 208, 240, 278, 374
Delft ware 64, 374
Dutch jugs 27
earthen ware 94
Egyptian ware 385
Queen's Ware 168–169, 172, 196, 240, 276, 278, 282, 351, 388
red ware 30, 32, 33, 63, 126, 320
Royal Pattern 163
Russian Service 240, 265–269, 351, 391, 392
slipware 46–47, 129
stoneware 27, 28, 62
tiles 27, 102
Tortoiseshell ware 50, 55, 62, 90
White House service 391–392
techniques
  Essay on 52–53
  green glaze 66, 81, 145
  lathes 147
  lead glaze 81, 278–279
  salt glaze 33, 44, 51, 63, 126, 208
  transfer printing 83–86, 93, 148
  white glaze 24, 82, 145–146
  yellow glaze 82, 145
Powell, Charles 222
Price, Richard 292–293
Priestley, Joseph 112–113, 116, 125, 186, 210, 227, 237, 244, 246, 281, 295, 324, 333, 338, 341, 346–347, 363–369, 378, 384
Primitive Physick 80
Proclamation of Rebellion 292
Protestantism 80
Prussia, King of 266

Qian Long, Emperor 374

Racehorse incident 89, 91, 95–101, 138
Radcliffe, Anne 337
Ramazini, Bernardino 278–279
Raphael 265